ALCOHOL IN LATIN AMERICA

Alcohol in Latin America

A Social and
Cultural History

Edited by
GRETCHEN PIERCE AND ÁUREA TOXQUI

THE UNIVERSITY OF
ARIZONA PRESS

TUCSON

The University of Arizona Press
© 2014 The Arizona Board of Regents
All rights reserved

www.uapress.arizona.edu

Library of Congress Cataloging-in-Publication Data
  Alcohol in Latin America : a social and cultural history / edited by Gretchen Pierce and
Áurea Toxqui.
    pages cm
  Includes bibliographical references and index.
  ISBN 978-0-8165-3076-2 (cloth : alk. paper)
  1. Drinking of alcoholic beverages—Latin America—History. 2. Alcoholic
beverages—Social aspects—Latin America—History. 3. Alcoholic beverage industry—
Social aspects—Latin America—History. 4. Alcoholism—Social aspects—Latin
America—History. 5. Temperance—Latin America—History. I. Pierce, Gretchen,
1978– II. Toxqui, Áurea, 1970–
  GT2883.L29A53 2014
  394.1'3098—dc23
        2013034784

Cover image: *Interior of a Pulquería*, José Agustín Arrieta, ca. 1850, one of the earliest depictions of *pulquerías*, which shows the active presence of women as bartenders and cooks.
(Museo Nacional de Historia, Mexico City. CONACULTA-INAH-MEX [Consejo Nacional para la Cultura y las Artes-Instituto Nacional de Antropología e Historia]. Authorized
reproduction by Instituto Nacional de Antropología e Historia.)

Publication of this book is made possible in part by the proceeds of a permanent endowment created with the assistance of a Challenge Grant from the National Endowment for
the Humanities, a federal agency.

Manufactured in the United States of America on acid-free, archival-quality paper contain-
ing a minimum of 30% post-consumer waste and processed chlorine free.

19 18 17 16 15 14   6 5 4 3 2 1

Contents

Illustrations

Figures

Tables

Maps

Acknowledgments

We would like to thank the many people who have helped this book to become a reality. Thanks to the contributors for writing such insightful pieces and for working with two junior scholars who had to balance editing with teaching responsibilities. Elena Jackson Albarrán, Jonathyne Briggs, and María Muñoz read and commented on the initial book proposal. Bill Beezley, Jeff Pilcher, Stephanie Mitchell, Steve Lewis, and David Fahey served as mentors, reading drafts and providing overall insight into the process of writing an edited collection. Several students helped with editing and standardizing format, including David Humphrey, Amanda Clark, and Tommy Carroll. Kristen Buckles has been an incredibly supportive editor, patiently answering our many questions. Finally, we would both like to thank our very supportive spouses, Jerry Pierce and Greg Newcomb.

ALCOHOL IN LATIN AMERICA

Map I.1. Latin America

Introduction

Gretchen Pierce and Áurea Toxqui

A soldier, a priest, a girl, an old woman, a vagrant, a few country dwellers, and cattle bosses of different ethnicities seemingly have nothing in common that could encourage them to fraternize. But a deeper reading of the painting *Interior of a Pulquería* (ca. 1850) sheds light on multiple aspects surrounding the presence of alcohol in the history of Latin America (see book cover). The painting shows a scene from a *pulquería*, a tavern that sells the traditional beverage pulque, fermented sap of the maguey plant. A young woman acts as a bartender while an older one prepares the meals for the male customers at the bottom of the scene. Among the patrons are representatives of different ethnicities, institutions, and locations, such as *castas* (the racially mixed), the clergy, the army, the countryside, and the city. In depicting a common scene of a tavern, the Mexican artist José Agustín Arrieta (1803–1874) left a testimony of the several ways in which alcohol touched the everyday life of his contemporaries—community bonding, drunkenness, and the reinforcement of socioeconomic and gender hierarchies, among many others—which represent some of the topics of this book. The chapters of this anthology explore how alcohol production, consumption, and regulation have been intertwined with the social and cultural history of Latin America from the pre-Columbian era through the present.

Alcohol in Latin American Historiography

Research that focuses on the cultural history of alcohol as its central component is fairly new, appearing within the last decade. Some of the first

3

historical studies that considered intoxicating beverages, beginning in the 1970s, did so less explicitly, usually in connection with the social history of crime and rebellion. For instance, William Taylor examined peasant villages in New Spain and found that after native peoples were conquered by Spain, intoxicants shifted from controlled substances used in pre-Columbian religious rituals to commercial goods associated with secular socializing and occasional solitary inebriation. He further argued that although the Crown and the Church blamed drunkenness for homicides and rebellions, these were frequently not associated with alcohol, but rather were reactions to perceived threats, such as an adulterous wife or a male who had used "fighting words."[1] In contrast, Lyman Johnson asserted that in late-colonial Buenos Aires, intoxication frequently preceded assaults and homicides, as drunkenness aggravated already tense situations and caused them to escalate to the point of violence.[2] Pablo Piccato discovered that Mexican elites during the late nineteenth and early twentieth centuries insisted that the lower classes and the indigenous imbibed more than other people and fomented crime, while their supposed sloth impeded modernization.[3]

Around the same time that Taylor published his seminal study, economic historians largely explored alcohol's profitable aspect by looking at production, sales, and taxation.[4] Since then, social historians have drawn on the same sources but have come to different conclusions.[5] In his studies on entrepreneurs, John Kicza found that some of the most prestigious families in late colonial Mexico traded pulque because of its steady profitability. They dominated production and retail distribution through their ownership of pulquerías in the large market of Mexico City. To avoid dishonor by running these taverns, to minimize risks, and to maximize profits, these entrepreneurs rented out their pulquerías. However, the government could not impose order in these places of social interaction and crime, because many officials were heavily involved in the trade, which provided considerable tax revenues and personal income.[6] Mercedes García Rodríguez, in her studies on sugarcane production in Cuba, explores the participation of African slaves in the distillation of *aguardiente*, or rum. The profitability of the beverage mainly consumed by the poor and slaves encouraged some members of the elite and even royal officials who were owners of sugarcane plantations to participate in the trade. Although aguardiente became associated with slave identity, in the late eighteenth century *criollos* (people of European descent born in the Americas) adopted it as their beverage to flaunt their patriotism.[7]

Since the 1990s, authors influenced by cultural as well as social history have shown how concerns about crime, laziness, and disease, especially among the indigenous, African, and racially mixed masses, led to attempts to reduce alcohol consumption and other vices like gambling, drug abuse, and prostitution.[8] As Susan Deans-Smith, Thomas Miller Klubock, and Michael Snodgrass revealed, some businesses, like New Spain's royal tobacco manufactory, Braden Copper Company (a North American firm located in Chile), and, ironically, the Mexican Cuauhtémoc Brewery, were concerned that drunken workers would be less efficient and docile and thus forbade intoxicants in their domains.[9] Research by scholars such as Erin O'Connor, Cristina Teresa de Novaes Marques, Alan Knight, Óscar Ivan Calvo Isaza, and Marta Saade Granados demonstrated that government officials in late nineteenth- and early twentieth-century Ecuador, Brazil, Mexico, and Colombia also strove to limit the production and consumption of alcohol through heavy taxation or restrictive legislation. Presidents, governors, and other leaders were often assisted by teachers, public health bureaucrats, scientists, and middle-class reformers. These officials and temperance advocates were inspired by some of the same motivations of business people—to encourage worker productivity—but they also hoped to create healthy, engaged, and modern citizens.[10] Finally, Jocelyn Olcott, Stephanie Mitchell, and Gretchen Pierce, as well as Calvo Isaza and Saade Granados, argued that regular citizens in Mexico and Colombia also worked with authority figures to promote temperance, claiming that excess bars led to moral decay and noise in their neighborhoods and that drunken husbands kept food from their children.[11]

Since the 1980s, works that examine the physical space of social interactions have viewed taverns not only as sites of drunkenness and loitering but also of conviviality among the masses, and therefore as targets of government reforms. Jane Mangan, Juan Pedro Viqueira Albán, Charles Walker, and Alvis Dunn studied different drinking places in colonial Potosí, Mexico City, Lima, and Santiago, Guatemala, and found widespread consumption of intoxicating beverages among the poor, which included native and African-descent peoples. In spite of the government's intention of reforming these places, there was an ambiguous attitude about implementing the law because of the economic benefits that alcohol production and sales represented for royal and municipal treasuries.[12] Áurea Toxqui analyzed Mexico City's taverns as spaces where the urban masses socially interacted and developed their culture. Since the late eighteenth century, their lives were affected by regulations banning food, music, and walls that obstructed police surveillance. They also dealt with restrictive hours of operation and the imposition of tavern-free zones in the city. These people defended their customary practices against these policies through the emergence of illegal drinking establishments, the consumption of stronger intoxicating beverages, and the constant trespassing of the law.[13]

Since the 1980s, scholars studying women's lives, their active participation in the economy, and their use of the law and custom to defend their rights and property have explored some aspects of female involvement in alcohol production and trade throughout Latin America.[14] In doing so, they have revealed that women of a variety of class and ethnic backgrounds have participated in the process. João Azevedo Fernandes demonstrated that in precolonial and colonial Brazil, indigenous women made the fermented manioc beverage, *cauim*, as well as the ceramic vessels it was stored in. As the drink was used in important social and political rituals, like those marking marriage, death, war, and cannibalism, women's involvement in its production reflected the fairly egalitarian nature of gender relations in the area.[15] Edith Couturier, Pablo Lacoste, Jane Mangan, and René Reeves showed that elite women, many of them widows or single, in Mexico, Argentina, Bolivia, and Guatemala often owned rural, alcohol-producing estates or establishments that sold intoxicating beverages. These businesses granted them a degree of autonomy that their married peers lacked. Some poorer and nonwhite females demonstrated their independence by brewing or selling drinks in small shops in spite of regulations designed to prevent them from doing so.[16] Gina Hames analyzed the integration of *cholas* (mixed-race women) into urban life, producing and selling maize beer in Sucre, Bolivia, from 1870 to 1930. During this period of modernization and formation of national identity, these women, through their trade, managed to move from being just disdained poor migrants to more powerful entrepreneurs who were able to negotiate with politicians and the rich.[17]

Since the 1990s, a few authors have begun problematizing masculinity, recognizing that it is as much a socially constructed category as is femininity. In many Latin American communities, alcohol consumption has been considered largely a male activity, making drinking part of the very definition of manhood. In fact, in larger studies about gender, power, and violence, Taylor, Johnson, and Steve Stern found that in colonial New Spain and Buenos Aires, imbibing was a vital part of lower-class, racially nonwhite, male sociability. However, not only could it strengthen camaraderie, it could just as frequently erupt into male-on-male violence. Alcohol often exacerbated jealousies and domestic disputes, which contributed to violence between men and women as well.[18] The perception that men used and abused alcohol more than women continued into the nineteenth and twentieth centuries. Therefore, employers, political leaders, and temperance reformers especially promoted the message of sobriety among men, as William French, as well as Pierce, O'Connor, and Klubock, demonstrated for Mexico, Ecuador, and Chile. In doing so, these authors showed that sobriety advocates were not just trying to keep men from drinking—they were attempting to transform poor, indigenous, and African-descent men into peaceful and sober patriarchs, traits largely based on middle-class values. In other words, they were trying to redefine lower-class masculinity.[19]

In the last decade, historical and anthropological studies on the formation of national, regional, or local identities demonstrated the pivotal role of alcohol consumption among different ethnic and social groups. Fernandes studied intoxicating beverages among the Brazilian natives before and after Portuguese colonization. Alcohol was a nutritional complement to their diet, a status and gender marker, and a mediator in the interaction among unequal groups. It also served as a metaphor for nature. Natives formulated metaphysical explanations of the world based on the physical changes of beverages during fermentation. The importance of these beverages to indigenous culture in part led European colonizers to perceive of drunkenness as innate to natives' identity.[20] Christine Eber, Tim Mitchell, Stephen Lewis, and Toxqui found alcohol to be a defining element among Mexicans of diverse regional, racial, and social backgrounds.[21] Consumption of intoxicating beverages implies more than a habit or a vice. Alcohol is used in a variety of rituals during holidays or in everyday life, such as to seal a deal, to promote healing or a good harvest, or to reinforce communal bonding. This explains why individuals have so strongly defended their right to drink, despite government efforts in eradicating alcohol consumption: changing drinking practices also transforms people's culture and identity.

As the previous paragraphs have indicated, scholars' interest in the history of alcohol is not new but has grown out of the rise of studies in social and cultural history over the last several decades. Often, as explained above, alcohol was not the main focus of these works, but within the last ten years or so, more theses and dissertations are being written with a primary focus on alcohol.[22] Additionally, an increasing number of recent books have examined alcohol or drugs from a national, regional, or global perspective. For instance, Renato Pinto Venâncio, Henrique Carneiro, Steve Stein, Ana María Mateu, and David Carey Jr. have edited collections on the role of intoxicants in Brazil, Argentina, and Guatemala.[23] Ernest Sánchez Santiró's multiauthor volume looks at alcohol across Latin America, although nine of the twelve chapters focus on Mexico.[24] José C. Curto studies the importance of Portuguese and Brazilian wines in Africa, while William Jankowiak, Daniel Bradburd, and Gina Hames situate intoxicants in Latin America as part of larger global histories.[25]

Outcomes in the emerging field of the history of drugs in the region demonstrate that both substances share connections with religion, medicine, economics, gender, and racial stereotypes, among others. Vicki Cassman, Larry Carmell, and Eliana Belmonte analyzed the multiple functions of *coca* (the plant from which Coca-Cola and cocaine are made) in the Andes.[26] Before the arrival of the Europeans, different ethnic groups used it as religious offerings, medicine, and currency. Colonizers later found coca to be an important labor enhancer and encouraged its consumption among indigenous groups and African slaves. Similarly, as Isaac Campos demonstrated, the Spanish Crown introduced hemp production to New Spain due to its salt-resistant qualities that made it suitable for maritime trade.[27] Soon, native healers discovered the pharmacological properties of this newly introduced plant and adopted it as part of their medicinal repertoire. By the late nineteenth century, however, drugs had come to be valued by North Americans and Europeans for their profitable medicinal properties, as Paul Gootenberg showed for coca and its cocaine alkaloid.[28] Meanwhile, in Mexico, marijuana use became perceived as a vice associated with prisoners and soldiers. Elites related its use with the acts of violence supposedly characteristic of the lower classes to justify issuing different policies intending to stop racial and cultural degeneration. The rise of marijuana and cocaine for recreational purposes in the early twentieth century led to the development of transnational drug chains, as Campos's and Gootenberg's works reveal. Particularly, the latter explored the ways producers and retailers have employed global networks to their advantage.[29] Other authors, such as Elaine Carey, focused on the gendered dynamic of transnational drug smuggling. She looked at activities in the United States of leading twentieth-century Mexican and Colombian female drug traffickers who were perceived as international threats. She argued that their involvement in this illicit traffic not only brought them wealth and access to power but also challenged gender and racial stereotypes.[30] These contributions of social and cultural history demonstrate the similar ways in which alcohol and drugs have taken part in larger historical processes in the region.

Contributions to the History of Alcohol in Latin America

In spite of the multitude of studies that focus on alcohol, not a single text looks at alcohol across all of Latin America or a broad span of time. This book intends to fill that gap with ten chapters, ranging from the pre-Columbian period through the present, covering six locations—the Andean region, Argentina, Brazil, Chile, Guatemala, and Mexico. The book is also interdisciplinary: contributors have a diverse background, with training in anthropology, archaeology, art history, ethnohistory, history, and literature and thus make use of a variety of sources. Visual evidence includes archaeological remains, paintings, *ex-votos* (popular religious offerings), advertisements, and participant observation. These sources are further enriched by firsthand interviews. Written sources include novels, criminal and official records, newspaper articles, and letters to presidents. The wide time span, geographic focus, and interdisciplinary style allow the book to demonstrate both the singularities and commonalities among Latin American societies and their intoxicating beverages. Furthermore, the variety of types of alcohols analyzed in this book—from ones that are fermented or native to the Americas, such as pulque, *chicha*, or *frucanga*, to ones that are distilled or relatively recent arrivals to the continent, like *aguardente*, beer, or wine—mirror the diversity of Latin American societies, artisanal and industrialized, traditional and modern.[31]

Although *Alcohol in Latin America* was intended to be comprehensive, as the title implies, unfortunately it was unable to include information on every Latin American country, type of alcohol, or potential historical topic. A few of the original chapters never made it to the final version for one reason or another. Additionally, many important issues and countries simply have yet to be analyzed through the lens of alcohol history. Therefore, this work is meant to inspire future research.

Each of the contributors uses alcohol as a way to understand bigger topics within Latin American history, such as identity, ethnic and communal bonding, race, class, gender, power relations, state-building, and resistance. In doing so, the volume argues that the production, commercialization, and consumption of intoxicating beverages were not separate from the region's larger history but, rather, were an integral part of it. For instance, various authors show that alcohol consumption has solidified communal ties for Latin Americans for centuries. As Justin Jennings and José Orozco demonstrate in chapters 1 and 8, in the ancient Andes and

Mesoamerica chicha and pulque reinforced kinship bonds as people shared these drinks with one another. Because ordinary men and women had access to them only through their social superiors, the beverages also solidified ruling hierarchies. They further played a role in religious rituals and thus brought the community together to worship the gods. In chapter 3, Aaron Althouse examines rural colonial Michoacán, an area far from the center of power in Mexico City. He finds that although drink had lost its religious significance, it remained an important tool in forging social ties—in this case, a strong regional identity. Typically, individuals exerted their autonomy by reacting violently to perceived insults, such as not removing one's hat when greeting another. Adding alcohol to these situations made it all the more likely that the reaction also became a political statement against the imposition of outside authority. In chapter 10, Anton Daughters reveals that the production and consumption of *chicha de manzana*, a hard apple cider, has stayed at the center of local identity in contemporary rural Chile. It is produced communally through a reciprocal labor project, and sharing it further enhances community solidarity threatened by globalization.

Especially in the nineteenth and twentieth centuries, various types of alcohol came to be linked to national identity and patriotism. For instance, João Azevedo Fernandes shows in chapter 2 that in Brazil, *cachaça*, a distilled drink produced from sugarcane, evolved from being perceived as the beverage of the natives and African slaves at the beginning of the colonial period to the drink of creole patriots at the end of this era. They saw the drink, made locally in spite of imperial prohibitions, as emblematic of their *patria*, or fatherland. Nancy Hanway (chapter 4), Orozco (chapter 8), and Steve Stein (chapter 9) examine how wine, pulque, and tequila have participated in state-building and the advent of nationalist policies in Argentina and Mexico. Nineteenth-century Argentine statesmen felt that French grapes and production techniques would help their country to separate itself from, in their mind, inferior Spanish grapes and practices and, at the same time, symbolically reinforce their independence. In the 1920s and 1930s, bourgeois Mexican revolutionaries embraced pulque as an avant-garde way to demonstrate their nationalistic pride in their indigenous heritage. Two decades later, Argentine leaders were asserting wine to be their national beverage and demanding that the beverage remain cheap enough for the *descamisados* (the poor, "shirtless" supporters of populist leaders Juan and Eva Perón) to purchase. Finally, by the end of the twentieth century, Mexican elites had rejected pulque in favor of tequila, which to them represented their "true" nation—romantically rural, Catholic, and of Spanish descent.

As Latin America has become increasingly integrated into a global economy since the nineteenth century, alcohol has also come to promote a broader, international identity based around notions of modernity and progress. Hanway demonstrates that Argentine leaders thought that transforming vineyards in the manner described above would create a modern, Western European–style nation. Stein and Orozco show that Argentine wine producers and the Mexican tequila barons, the Sauzas, used the language of progress to advertise in the late nineteenth and early twentieth centuries. These beverages were "clean," industrial, and thus modern. Stein also claims that Argentine wine producers have been sensitive to the changing, and increasingly global, needs of twenty-first-century consumers. They cater to a savvy, international public that wants a high-quality beverage associated with luxury and status.

Certain types of alcohol have long been linked with particular racial and class groups in Latin America and have helped to cement the identities of these groups as either socially dominant or marginalized. In chapter 5, Áurea Toxqui reveals that in Mexico pulque was perceived as the beverage of the poor, the natives, and castas after independence, while the white elite chose wine and other European drinks to demonstrate their prominence. In chapter 6, David Carey Jr. finds that, in late nineteenth- and early twentieth-century Guatemala, alcohol consumption and abuse came to be erroneously associated with the Maya, so sobriety was seen as a way of creating a *ladino* (or nonnative) nation. Finally, Orozco proves how the taste, smell, and consistency of pulque became connected with Mexican indigenous heritage. In both the late nineteenth and late twentieth centuries, marketers promoted tequila's clear, nonviscous nature and tried to identify it with an idyllic, mestizo (a racial mixture combining European and native heritage) past.

Several chapters demonstrate the important contributions that women have made to their societies as producers, vendors, and consumers of alcohol. Jennings reveals that many ancient Andean females brewed chicha, including the Incas' *mamakona* ("chosen" women who labored for the state) and the women of the Xauxa (an Andean people defeated by the Inca). This work was essential to the maintenance of the empire as the Inca used this beverage to establish a relationship of political dependency with both their allies and those they conquered. Toxqui finds that women also played a key role in the retail distribution of pulque at the beginning of the

colonial period, as well as in the state-building and economic development of nineteenth-century Mexico. The taxes collected from the pulque
they produced and the pulquerías they owned helped the government to
maintain solvency. Likewise, women selling food outside these taverns
also contributed to their household income. In chapter 7, Gretchen Pierce
shows that, a few decades later, Mexican women who worked in the alcohol industry continued participating in the process of nation-forging.
When bureaucrats and reformers tried to limit their ability to support their
families by placing restrictions on alcohol sales, they not only protested but
also questioned the supposed revolutionary nature of their leaders. Carey
finds agency in women's carousing in late nineteenth- and early twentieth-
century Guatemala. By getting drunk, venturing out without male oversight, and otherwise "misbehaving," they were flouting social norms.

At the same time, examining women's roles as both alcohol producers
and consumers demonstrates that their lives still faced patriarchal constraints. Jennings points out that although Xauxa women's work was pivotal, it was nevertheless devalued. Isotope data suggests that as women's
labor increased, their consumption of maize remained constant and men's
consumption of both chicha and meat went up. Similarly, Toxqui finds
that as pulque producers and vendors, women played an essential role in
the economy, but they were still criticized as indecent individuals who
ventured outside of the domestic sphere. Carey notes that while some
women exhibited their independence, many more looked upon aguardiente with distrust, because when their husbands, lovers, or fathers imbibed it, they often turned violent. Finally, Pierce shows that even as female alcohol producers and vendors raised their voices in protest, they
seemed to feel that they would be most likely to receive help from the paternalistic Mexican state by emphasizing their frailty and their attempts to
live up to more traditional gender roles as mothers.

Several authors discuss how alcohol has long been linked to patriarchy
and masculinity. In some cultures, like the patriarchal Xauxa and Inca, as
Jennings reveals, alcohol was dominated by, if not reserved for, male consumers. Other communities in theory may not have prevented women
from drinking but still discouraged it, and therefore, men ended up imbibing more. Carey and, to a lesser extent, Althouse find this to be the case in
late nineteenth- through mid-twentieth-century Guatemala and colonial
Michoacán. Examples like these have encouraged people to believe that
men, by their very nature, are just more inclined to drink alcohol than are
women. Playing on these stereotypes of masculinity, then, producers in

twentieth- and twenty-first-century Mexico and Argentina, as Orozco and Stein note, marketed their products to male consumers. Sauza Añejo Tequila advertisements claimed to refine "men's good taste," and in ones for Argentine wine, some of the figures depicted included male immigrants, the iconic *gaucho*, or cowboy, and an elegantly dressed man about to meet a beautiful young woman. Finally, as Pierce claims, small alcohol producers and vendors in revolutionary Mexico relied on different conceptions of masculinity to argue that they ought to be able to make or sell a product that was potentially harmful to society. These men asserted that they were involved in the alcohol business purely for economic reasons, as they needed to support their families. For them, "real" men were not necessarily drinkers—they were caring husbands and fathers who provided a stable income for their wives and children.

Numerous authors in this collection demonstrate that officials' control of the production, distribution, and consumption of intoxicating substances can be linked to larger state-building projects. Jennings finds that many leaders from across the pre-Columbian Andes oversaw the distribution of chicha to their subjects. By providing beverages at important feasts, Inca officials could emphasize their magnanimity and then demand labor in return. Other political authorities, such as those in nineteenth- and twentieth-century Argentina and Mexico, according to Hanway and Orozco, promoted various types of alcohols, such as Malbec wine and tequila, as tools in their drive to modernize and Europeanize their nations. Even more frequently, though, leaders, assisted by moral reformers, attempted to limit alcohol production or consumption, also for political purposes. Jennings argues that Wari elites restricted commoners' access to intoxicants, which the former would consume publicly as a way of highlighting their own status. Fernandes reveals that authorities in Portugal unsuccessfully tried to curtail the production of local drinks in colonial Brazil because they competed with the Crown's monopolies on peninsular wines and liquor. Leaders in mid-nineteenth- through early twentieth-century Mexico and Guatemala wanted to inculcate a sober workforce and peaceful populace, but Toxqui and Carey demonstrate that these officials did not want to eliminate the tax revenue they received from alcohol sales, so they regulated sales, targeted clandestine beverages, and policed unruly public displays of intoxication. Pierce explores the difficulties Mexicans faced in their attempt to create a temperate nation. Federal authorities sponsored anti-alcohol campaigns, but some regional leaders sabotaged these efforts because they threatened their supplemental, illegal sources of income, which came in the form of bribes from local producers or from their own clandestine sales. The resulting reduction in revenue, to the Portuguese monopoly, Mexican and Guatemalan national treasuries, or corrupt figures' personal accounts, would have reduced these leaders' abilities to achieve their political goals, honest or otherwise, and thus can explain in part why the restriction of alcoholic beverages often fails.

Small-scale, impoverished alcohol consumers, producers, and vendors questioned stereotypes that labeled them as immoral and fought back against attempts to limit their livelihood or control their lives. In doing so, they also contributed to the state-building project, demonstrating that it was not just a top-down process. Althouse shows that poor *indios* and mixed-race individuals living in colonial Michoacán were fierce individualists who did not like the imposition of outside rule. Alcohol often loosened their tongues and allowed them to critique authority figures, whether from the area or farther away. Toxqui reveals that poor women in late nineteenth-century Mexico City resisted government regulations that affected their trade as food sellers outside pulque taverns. They perceived these regulations as detrimental to their source of income and an imposition on their right to free trade. In fact, she argues that their sales (as well as the revenue generated from taxing elites' pulque haciendas and pulquerías) added to national coffers, and thus to the act of nation-forging. Carey suggests that in judicial testimonies, Maya and other poor Guatemalans often blamed their inebriation on their poverty and complained that the government had not adequately provided for their well-being. Similarly, in 1920s- and 1930s-era Mexico, small alcohol producers attempted to defend themselves from the attacks of temperance reformers and revolutionary politicians who sought to restrict their sales. As Pierce finds, they claimed that they were not trying to peddle poison but, rather, to take care of their families in the only way they could. In each of these examples, the makers, sellers, and drinkers of alcohol played a role in the process of state-building by demanding that the government benefit *them* as subjects and citizens.

Conclusion

The painting on the cover of this book, *Interior of a Pulquería*, depicts a typical Mexican tavern, with its vat of pulque, a barmaid, tortilla server, and a group of racially mixed, poor men waiting expectantly for the beverage. Examining it allows one to draw a number of conclusions about alcohol's relationship to the larger social and cultural history of Latin America that this book will expand upon in greater detail. One can see the enduring importance of certain types of intoxicating beverages, including pulque (analyzed in chapters 5, 7, and 8), chicha (chapters 1 and 10), and wine (chapters 4 and 9). The painting depicts the stereotype that linked drunkenness and cheap, locally produced drinks, like pulque, *teshuino*, *charape*, *k'uxa*, mezcal, and aguardiente, with people on the lower end of the socioeconomic scale, as well as those with little to no European heritage (chapters 2, 3, 5–8, and 10).[32] This work of art further reveals the perception that women should be domestic and docile while men can lead a more public and adventurous lifestyle—it is only the men who appear to be drinkers. It shows, as well, lived realities—women did, in fact, work in public and helped to make important contributions to their communities' political and economic structures (chapters 1, 5, 6, and 7). Many religious and secular leaders might have looked at this painting as representing some of the sad consequences of alcohol consumption—they might assume that the patrons would go outside and commit crimes or otherwise be too inebriated to contribute to the modernization of their nations. Chapters 3, 5, 6, and 7 look at these so-called problems and authorities' attempts to ameliorate them. Above all, the image expresses the idea that alcohol can bring people together. We hope that just as these patrons are about to enjoy themselves, you will also enjoy *Alcohol in Latin America*. ¡*Salud y saúde!*[33]

Notes

1. William B. Taylor, *Drinking, Homicide, and Rebellion in Colonial Mexican Villages* (Stanford, CA: Stanford University Press, 1979).

2. Lyman L. Johnson, "Dangerous Words, Provocative Gestures, and Violent Acts: The Disputed Hierarchies of Plebian Life in Colonial Buenos Aires," in *The Faces of Honor: Sex, Shame, and Violence in Colonial Latin America*, ed. Lyman Johnson and Sonya Lipsett-Rivera (Albuquerque: University of New Mexico Press, 1998), 127–51.

3. Pablo Piccato, "'El Paso de Venus por el disco del Sol': Criminality and Alcoholism in the Late Porfiriato," *Mexican Studies/Estudios Mexicanos* 11, no. 2 (1995), 203–41.

4. Marco Bellingeri, *Las haciendas en México. El caso de San Antonio Tochatlaco* (Mexico City: Secretaría de Educación Pública [hereafter SEP], Instituto Nacional de Antropología e Historia [hereafter INAH], 1980); José Jesús Hernández Palomo, *La renta del pulque en Nueva España, 1663–1810* (Seville: Escuela de Estudios Hispano-Americanos de Sevilla, 1979); Ricardo Rendón Garcini, *Dos haciendas pulqueras en*

Tlaxcala, 1857–1884 (Mexico City: Gobierno del Estado de Tlaxcala-Universidad Iberoamericana, 1990).

5. Mario Ramírez Rancaño, *Ignacio Torres Adalid y la industria pulquera* (Mexico City: Plaza y Valdés-Instituto de Investigaciones Sociales, Universidad Nacional Autónoma de México [hereafter UNAM], 2000); José C. Curto, *Enslaving Spirits: The Portuguese-Brazilian Alcohol Trade at Luanda and Its Hinterland, c. 1550–1830* (Leiden: Brill, 2004); Ernest Sánchez Santiró, ed., *Cruda realidad. Producción, consumo y fiscalidad de las bebidas alcohólicas en México y América Latina, siglos XVII–XX* (Mexico City: Instituto Mora, 2007).

6. John Kicza, "The Pulque Trade of Late Colonial Mexico City," *The Americas* 37, no. 2 (1980), 193–221; Kicza, *Colonial Entrepreneurs, Families and Business in Bourbon Mexico City* (Albuquerque: University of New Mexico Press, 1983).

7. Mercedes García Rodríguez, "El aguardiente de caña y otras bebidas en la Cuba Colonial," unpublished manuscript [2010]; García Rodríguez, *Entre haciendas y plantaciones. Los orígenes azucareros de La Habana* (Havana: Ciencias Sociales, 2007).

8. Robert Buffington, "Prohibition in the Borderlands: National Government Border Community Relations," *Pacific Historical Review* 63, no. 1 (1994), 19–38; Katherine Elaine Bliss, *Compromised Positions: Prostitution, Public Health, and Gender Politics in Revolutionary Mexico City* (University Park: Pennsylvania State University Press, 2001); Elaine Carey and Andrae M. Marak, eds., *Smugglers, Brothels, and Twine: Historical Perspectives on Contraband and Vice in North America's Borderlands* (Tucson: University of Arizona Press, 2011); Alan McPherson, "More Notes from a Cockfight: Resistance Through Gambling in *La Española* during US Occupations," paper presented at the annual meeting of the Rocky Mountain Council on Latin American Studies (Santa Fe, NM, 2011); Isaac Campos, *Home Grown: Marijuana and the Origin of Mexico's War on Drugs* (Chapel Hill: University of North Carolina Press, 2012).

9. Susan Deans-Smith, "The Working Poor and the Eighteenth-Century Colonial State," in *Rituals of Rule, Rituals of Resistance: Public Celebrations and Popular Culture in Mexico*, ed. William H. Beezley, Cheryl English Martin, and William E. French (Wilmington, DE: SR Books, 1994), 47–75; Thomas Miller Klubock, "Working-Class Masculinity, Middle-Class Morality, and Labor Politics in the Chilean Mines," *Journal of Social History* 30, no. 2 (1996), 435–63; Marcos Fernández Labbé, "Las comunidades de la sobriedad: la instalación de zonas secas como método de control del beber inmoderado en Chile, 1910–1930," *Scripta Nova: Revista Electrónica de Geografía y Ciencias Sociales* 9, no. 194 (August 2005), 59, http://www.ub.es/geocrit/sn/sn-194-59.htm; Michael Snodgrass, "'We Are All Mexicans Here': Workers, Patriotism, and Union Struggles in Monterrey," in *The Eagle and the Virgin: Nation and Cultural Revolution in Mexico, 1920–1940*, ed. Mary Kay Vaughan and Stephen E. Lewis (Durham, NC: Duke University Press, 2006), 314–35.

10. Virginia Guedea, "México en 1812: Control político y bebidas prohibidas," *Estudios de historia moderna y contemporánea de México* 8 (1980), 23–64; Michael C. Scardaville, "Alcohol Abuse and Tavern Reform in Late Colonial Mexico City," *Hispanic American Historical Review* 60, no. 4 (1980), 643–71; Pamela Voekel, "Peeing on the Palace: Bodily Resistance to Bourbon Reforms in Mexico City," *Journal of Historical Sociology* 5, no. 2 (1992), 183–208; Alan Knight, "Popular Culture and the Revolutionary State in Mexico, 1910–1940," *Hispanic American Historical Review* 74, no. 3

(1994), 393–444; Anne Staples, *"Policía y Buen Gobierno*: Municipal Efforts to Regulate Public Behavior, 1821–1857," in *Rituals of Rule, Rituals of Resistance,* 115–26; Mary Kay Vaughan, *Cultural Politics in Revolution: Teachers, Peasants, and Schools in Mexico, 1930–1940* (Tucson: University of Arizona Press, 1997); Guillermo Palacios, *La pluma y el arado: Los intelectuales pedagogos y la construcción sociocultural del "problema campesino" en México, 1932–1934* (Mexico City: Colegio de México, 1999); Juan Pedro Viqueira Albán, *Propriety and Permissiveness in Bourbon Mexico* (Wilmington, DE: SR Books, 1999); Ben Fallaw, "Dry Law, Wet Politics: Drinking and Prohibition in Post-Revolutionary Yucatán, 1915–1935," *Latin American Research Review* 37, no. 2 (2001), 37–64; Óscar Iván Calvo Isaza and Marta Saade Granados, *La ciudad en cuarentena: Chicha, patología social y profilaxis* (Bogotá: Ministerio de Cultura, 2002); Christopher R. Boyer, *Becoming Campesinos: Politics, Identity, and Agrarian Struggle in Postrevolutionary Michoacán, 1920–1935* (Stanford, CA: Stanford University Press, 2003); Patience A. Schell, *Church and State Education in Revolutionary Mexico City* (Tucson: University of Arizona Press, 2003); Alexander S. Dawson, *Indian and Nation in Revolutionary Mexico* (Tucson: University of Arizona Press, 2004); Stephen E. Lewis, *The Ambivalent Revolution: Forging State and Nation in Chiapas, 1910–1945* (Albuquerque: University of New Mexico Press, 2005); Teresita Martínez-Vergne, *Nation and Citizen in the Dominican Republic, 1880–1916* (Chapel Hill: University of North Carolina Press, 2005); Derek Williams, "The Making of Ecuador's *Pueblo Católico,*" in *Political Culture in the Andes, 1750–1950,* ed. Nils Jacobsen and Cristóbal Aljovín de Losada (Durham, NC: Duke University Press, 2005), 207–29; Katherine E. Bliss, "For the Health of the Nation: Gender and the Cultural Politics of Social Hygiene in Revolutionary Mexico," in *The Eagle and the Virgin,* 196–218; Teresa Cristina de Novaes Marques, "Beer and Sugar-Cane Spirit Under Temperance in Brazil, in the Beginning of the 20th Century," paper presented at the Alcohol in the Making of the Atlantic World: Historical and Contemporary Perspectives international workshop (York University, Toronto, 2007); Erin O'Connor, "Helpless Children or Undeserving Patriarchs? Gender Ideologies, the State, and Indian Men in Late Nineteenth Century Ecuador," in *Highland Indians and the State in Modern Ecuador,* ed. A. Kim Clark and Marc Becker (Pittsburgh, PA: University of Pittsburgh Press, 2007), 56–72; Gretchen Kristine Pierce, "Sobering the Revolution: Mexico's Anti-Alcohol Campaigns and the Process of State-Building, 1910–1940" (PhD diss., University of Arizona, 2008); Pierce, "Parades, Epistles and Prohibitive Legislation: Mexico's National Anti-Alcohol Campaign and the Process of State-Building, 1934–1940," *Social History of Alcohol and Drugs* 23, no. 2 (2009), 151–80; Daniela Bouret, "El consumo de vinos en el Uruguay del novecientos. El desarrollo de la industria vitivinícola vrs. campañas antialcoholistas," *Boletín Americanista* 59 (2009), 155–76.

11. Calvo Isaza and Saade Granados, *La ciudad en cuarentena*; Jocelyn Olcott, *Revolutionary Women in Postrevolutionary Mexico* (Durham, NC: Duke University Press, 2005); Stephanie Mitchell, "Por la liberación de la mujer: Women and the Anti-Alcohol Campaign," in *The Women's Revolution in Mexico, 1910–1953,* ed. Stephanie Mitchell and Patience A. Schell (Wilmington, DE: Rowman and Littlefield, 2007), 165–85; Pierce, "Sobering the Revolution."

12. Scardaville, "Alcohol Abuse and Tavern Reform"; Voekel, "Peeing on the Palace"; Viqueira, *Propriety and Permissiveness in Bourbon Mexico*; Jane E. Mangan, *Trading Roles: Gender, Ethnicity, and the Urban Economy in Colonial Potosí* (Durham,

NC: Duke University Press, 2005); Charles F. Walker, "Civilize or Control?: The Lingering Impact of the Bourbon Urban Reforms," in *Political Culture in the Andes*, 74–95; Alvis E. Dunn, "'A Sponge Soaking Up All the Money': Alcohol, Taverns, *Vinaterías*, and the Bourbon Reforms in Mid-Eighteenth Century Santiago de los Caballeros," in *Distilling the Influence of Alcohol: Aguardiente in Guatemalan History*, ed. David Carey Jr. (Gainesville: University Press of Florida, 2012), 71–95. For a discussion of both colonial and nineteenth-century Mexican pulquerías, *vinaterías* (wine shops), and cafés, see Deborah Toner, "Everything in Its Right Place? Drinking Places and Social Spaces in Mexico City, c. 1780–1900," *Social History of Alcohol and Drugs* 25 (2011), 26–48.

13. María Áurea Toxqui Garay, "'El Recreo de los Amigos': Mexico City's Pulquerías During the Liberal Republic (1856–1911)" (PhD diss., University of Arizona, 2008); Áurea Toxqui, "Taverns and Their Influence on the Suburban Culture of Late Nineteenth Century Mexico City," in *The Growth of Non-Western Cities: Primary and Secondary Urban Networking, c. 900–1900*, ed. Kenneth R. Hall (Lanham, MD: Lexington Books, 2011), 241–69.

14. Silvia Marina Arrom, *The Women of Mexico City, 1790–1850* (Stanford, CA: Stanford University Press, 1985); Kimberly Gauderman, *Women's Lives in Colonial Quito. Gender, Law, and Economy in Spanish America* (Austin: University of Texas Press, 2003).

15. João Azevedo Fernandes, *Selvagens Bebedeiras: Álcool, Embriaguez e Contatos Culturais no Brasil Colonial (Séculos XVI–XVII)* (São Paulo: Alameda, 2011).

16. Edith Couturier, "Women in a Noble Family: The Mexican Counts of Regla, 1750–1830," in *Latin American Women: Historical Perspectives*, ed. Asunción Lavrín (Westport, CT: Greenwood Press, 1978), 129–49; Couturier, "Micaela Angela Carrillo: Widow and Pulque Dealer," in *Struggle and Survival in Colonial America*, ed. Gary B. Nash and David G. Sweet (Berkeley: University of California Press, 1980), 362–75; Mangan, *Trading Roles*; Pablo Lacoste, "Wine and Women: Grape Growers and *Pulperas* in Mendoza, 1561–1852," *Hispanic American Historical Review* 88, no. 3 (2008), 361–91; René Reeves, "From Household to Nation: The Economic and Political Impact of Women and Alcohol in Nineteenth-Century Guatemala," in *Distilling the Influence of Alcohol*, 42–70.

17. Gina Hames, "Maize-Beer, Gossip, and Slander: Female Tavern Proprietors and Urban, Ethnic Cultural Elaboration in Bolivia, 1870–1930," *Journal of Social History* 37, no. 2 (2003), 351–64.

18. Taylor, *Drinking, Homicide, and Rebellion*; Steve J. Stern, *The Secret History of Gender: Women, Men, and Power in Late Colonial Mexico* (Chapel Hill: University of North Carolina Press, 1995); Johnson, "Dangerous Words." For a discussion of alcohol's influence on male behavior, whether involving camaraderie and duty to the nation or violence, irresponsibility, and betrayal, in nineteenth-century Mexican literature, see Deborah Toner, "Drinking to Fraternity: Alcohol, Masculinity, and National Identity in the Novels of Manuel Payno and Heriberto Frías," *Bulletin of Hispanic Studies* 89, no. 4 (2012), 397–412.

19. William E. French, *A Peaceful and Working People: Manners, Morals, and Class Formation in Northern Mexico* (Albuquerque: University of New Mexico Press, 1996); Klubock, "Working-Class Masculinity"; O'Connor, "Helpless Children or

Undeserving Patriarchs?"; Pierce, "Sobering the Revolution"; Gretchen Pierce, "Fighting Bacteria, the Bible, and the Bottle: Projects to Create New Men, Women, and Children, 1910–1940," in *A Companion to Mexican History and Culture*, ed. William H. Beezley (London: Wiley-Blackwell, 2011), 505–17.

20. João Azevedo Fernandes, "Feast and Sin: Catholic Missionaries and Native Celebrations in Early Colonial Brazil," *Social History of Alcohol and Drugs* 23, no. 2 (2009), 111–27; Renato Pinto Venâncio and Henrique Carneiro, eds., *Álcool e drogas na história do Brasil* (São Paulo/Belo Horizonte: Alameda/Editora Pontifícia Universidade Católica de Minas Gerais, 2005).

21. Christine Eber, *Women and Alcohol in a Highland Maya Town: Water of Hope, Water of Sorrow* (Austin: University of Texas Press, 1995); Eber, "'Take My Water': Liberation Through Prohibition in San Pedro Chenalhó, Chiapas, Mexico," *Social Science and Medicine* 53 (2001), 251–62; Tim Mitchell, *Intoxicated Identities: Alcohol's Power in Mexican History and Culture* (New York: Routledge, 2004); Toxqui Garay, "'El Recreo de los Amigos'"; Toxqui, "Taverns and Their Influence."

22. See, e.g., José C. Curto, "Alcohol and Slaves: The Luso-Brazilian Alcohol Commerce at Mpinda, Luanda, and Benguela During the Atlantic Slave Trade c. 1480–1830 and Its Impact" (PhD diss., University of California at Los Angeles, 1996); Gina Hames, "Honor, Alcohol, and Sexuality: Women and the Creation of Ethnic Identity in Bolivia, 1870–1930" (PhD diss., Carnegie Mellon University, 1996); Alvis E. Dunn, "Aguardiente and Identity: The Holy Week Riot of 1786 in Quetzaltenango, Guatemala" (PhD diss., University of North Carolina at Chapel Hill, 1999); Deborah Toner, "Maize, Alcohol, and Cultural Identity in Colonial Mexico" (MA thesis, University of Warwick, 2006); Pierce, "Sobering the Revolution"; Toxqui Garay, "'El Recreo de los Amigos'"; and Uttam Bajwa, "Immigrant Family Firms in the Mendoza Wine Industry, 1884–1914" (PhD diss., Johns Hopkins University, 2012).

23. Pinto Venâncio and Carneiro, *Álcool e drogas na história do Brasil*; Carey, *Distilling the Influence of Alcohol*; Ana María Mateu and Steve Stein, eds., *El vino y sus revoluciones: Una antología histórica sobre el desarrollo de la industria vitivinícola argentina* (Mendoza, Argentina: Editorial de la Universidad Nacional de Cuyo, 2008).

24. Sánchez Santiró, *Cruda Realidad*.

25. William Jankowiak and Daniel Bradburd, eds., *Drugs, Labor, and Colonial Expansion* (Tucson: University of Arizona Press, 2003); Curto, *Enslaving Spirits*; Gina Hames, *Alcohol in World History* (New York: Routledge, 2012).

26. Vicki Cassman, Larry Carmell, and Eliana Belmonte, "Coca as Symbol and Labor Enhancer in the Andes. A Historical Overview," in Jankowiak and Bradburd, *Drugs, Labor, and Colonial Expansion*, 150–52.

27. Campos, *Home Grown*.

28. Paul Gootenberg, *Andean Cocaine. The Making of a Global Drug* (Chapel Hill: University of North Carolina Press, 2008).

29. Peter Andreas and Brazilian scholars such as Renato Pinto Venâncio, Henrique Carneiro, and Ricardo Ferreira Ribeiro have explored the close connections between stimulants and global economy influencing how some intoxicants became illegal while others such as tobacco, coffee, sugar, and alcohol did not. Peter Andreas, *Smuggler Nation: How Illicit Trade Made America* (New York: Oxford University Press, 2013); Pinto Venâncio and Carneiro, *Álcool e drogas na história do Brasil*; Ricardo

Ferreira Ribeiro, "Tortuosas raízes medicinais: as mágicas origens da farmacopéia popular brasileira e sua trajetória pelo mundo" in Venâncio and Carneiro, *Álcool e drogas na história do Brasil,* 155–84.

30. Elaine Carey, "'Selling Is More of a Habit Than Using.' Narcotraficante Lola la Chata and Her Threat to Civilization, 1930–1960," *Journal of Women's History* 21, no. 2 (2009), 62–89; Carey, "A Colombian Queen's Tale: The End and Beginning of Griselda Blanco," *Points: Blog of the Alcohol and Drugs History Society,* September 26, 2012, http://pointsadhsblog.wordpress.com/2012/09/26/a-colombian-queens-tale-the-end-and-beginning-of-griselda-blanco/.

31. Chicha is maize beer. Frucanga, or *hidromiel,* is the fermented mix of water and honey with some kind of fruit such as pineapple, orange, or lime. Aguardente, the Portuguese spelling of aguardiente, is rum.

32. Teshuino is a fermented beverage made from corn in the Sierra Madre region of Mexico. It is sacred to the Tarahumara people. Charape is a Mexican fermented beverage, often associated with indigenous peoples, made from barley or pineapple and sugarcane molasses. K'uxa is a Maya Guatemalan homemade brew derived from sugarcane. Mezcal is a distilled Mexican drink with a chemical composition similar to tequila. All were cheap beverages with high intoxicating powers.

33. Cheers, in Spanish and Portuguese.

PART ONE

The Prehispanic and Colonial Periods

The societies living in the Americas before the arrival of the Europeans were characterized by a strong sense of community reinforced through religious practices, rituals, and daily life patterns. Although societies developed along with the beginnings of agriculture as a regular activity (ca. 5000 BCE), the first major civilizations—the Olmecs in Mesoamerica and the Chavín in the Andes—did not flourish until between 1500 and 200 BCE. Mesoamerica encompassed what nowadays is Mexico and Central America, while the Andean region covered current Ecuador, Peru, Bolivia, and part of Chile. The reliance on agriculture of these early civilizations encouraged them to build the first sites of worship to the gods of nature. Shamans, a small elite emerging in this time, legitimized their power by claiming a divine connection. They used stimulating substances as part of their rituals.

Powerful priests replaced these shamans in subsequent theocratic states flourishing between 200 BCE and 1000 CE. These states included the Maya and the Toltec in Mesoamerica and the Wari, the Tiwanaku, the Recuay, and the Moche in the Andes. Urban growth encouraged a careful consideration of planting cycles, labor assignment, and tribute collection over rural peoples. Fermented beverages became important elements in the elaborate rituals, enhancing status and identity, recruiting labor, promoting community bonding, delineating gender roles, and forging reciprocity. Social discontent, environmental problems, corruption, and political rivalries eventually led to the collapse of these theocratic states, and some of their scientific and artistic achievements were lost.

By the 1300s an excessive reliance on luxury items and products from client states forced empires, such as the Aztec in Mesoamerica and the Inca in the Andes, to depend largely on war. In these militaristic states, rulers relied highly on rituals that sometimes included human sacrifices to justify their power. These cultures made alcohol an essential element of their politics. The Inca used *chicha* in several feasts to maintain the loyalty of their subjects to the state, as they did with the Xauxa living in the central highlands of Peru. In contrast, the Aztecs strictly limited *pulque* consumption to specific groups and circumstances. They highly penalized drunkenness to avoid social disorder.

At the same time that empires were flourishing in Central America and the Andes, there were also a number of smaller states in the Amazon and the Caribbean regions. The Muiscas in current-day Colombia were highly organized regional confederations with a powerful economy resulting from the mining of emeralds, gold, copper, and coal, as well as agriculture. In contrast, the Carib in the Lesser Antilles and the Orinoco Delta and the Tupi in coastal Brazil were local self-governed tribes with different development levels. The Carib manufactured silver artifacts and boats, besides fishing and farming, whereas the Tupi relied exclusively on agriculture. In these cultures, women had the important task of making alcohol. Among the Tupinambá, chaste and pretty young women mostly ground manioc roots, but also corn and cashews, by chewing them. Their saliva contributed to the fermentation of the grains and roots. In the eyes of their fellow men, their virtues gave the beverage mystic qualities and facilitated interaction with the spiritual world. Among the Potiguara, Caeté, and Tabajaras living in the current states of Maranhão, Paraíba, and Ceará in Brazil, acai was the fruit employed to make fermented beverages.

In this section, Justin Jennings (chapter 1) provides an overview of the role of chicha throughout the centuries in the Andes. This beer serves as a window to look at how alcoholic beverages were closely connected to the development of prehispanic Andean cultures. In parts 2 and 3, Áurea Toxqui and José Orozco explore the similar role that pulque played among the civilizations developing in Mesoamerica.

The arrival of the Europeans in the 1490s led to the fall of these militaristic empires and the beginning of the colonial period (1500s to 1820s). Spain, and then Portugal, established viceroyalties, but they faced several challenges, such as keeping power in distant, vast, and diverse societies; ambitious conquerors and royal officials; and other European rivals hoping to seize the continent for their own. The encounter of the Old and New World brought the emergence of lively societies developing a unique character, a consequence of the contact among Europeans, Native Americans, Africans, and, later on, some Southeast Asians.

Colonial societies were characterized by the emergence of mixed ethnic groups or *castas*, as well as new economic systems, political structures, and cultural practices. In the realm of alcohol, chicha and pulque transitioned from being sacred beverages to commodities, Europeans introduced distilled beverages, and drunkenness spread among natives, African slaves, and the poor. The Catholic Church became more powerful in the Americas than in Europe as a consequence of its participation in the conquest and colonization of the new territories. The fact that three devout cultures, the Iberians, the Americans, and the Africans, encountered one another also allowed Catholicism to influence every aspect of colonial life from rural production and moneylending to the formation of gender roles and societal values. Slavery, tributary work drafts, and free wage labor, performed by a combination of native peoples, those of African descent, and the castas, provided the products demanded overseas and in local mining and urban areas. These workers patronized *pulquerías, chicherías,* and *frucanguerías* (taverns that sold pulque, chicha, and *frucanga* or *hidromiel*). Free and enslaved Africans and their descendants living in plantations, mills, and the poorest urban neighborhoods produced *zambumbía* in their homes, with fermented molasses and sugarcane juice.

In the 1700s, influenced by the ideas of liberalism, Spain and Portugal promoted diverse reforms, intending to modernize their empires, maximize profits, and create productive citizens through laws to eradicate drunkenness and loitering. Spanish and Portuguese American colonists challenged many of those reforms and in some cases revolted against them. Patriotic feelings also had started developing as a consequence of the influence of the Enlightenment, the independence of the United States and Haiti, the French Revolution, and the Napoleonic invasion of the Iberian Peninsula. All of these circumstances provided room for the wars of independence in the early 1800s. The patriotic feelings characterizing late-colonial societies led *criollos* to adopt sugarcane distilled beverages. Thus, *aguardiente*, as rum was called in places such as Cuba or Colombia; *guaro*, as it was named in Guatemala; and *aguardente* or *cachaça*, as it was referred to in Brazil—all drinks previously identified with natives or slaves—became criollos' beverages of choice because of their local ties.

In this section, João Azevedo Fernandes (chapter 2) and Aaron Althouse (chapter 3) provide examples of the role of alcohol in colonial societies. They discuss the rupture of daily life in rural areas of Brazil and Mexico as a consequence of the spread of new intoxicating beverages and colonial rule. Fernandes analyzes the European introduction of distilled alcohol among natives to promote colonization in Brazil. This was so successful that later on the Crown had to restrict aguardente production because its profitability challenged the royal monopoly on wines and other liquors. Althouse explores the role of alcohol in facilitating individuals' willingness to express their true feelings and exacerbate tensions already within the community. Drunken speech illuminates not only everyday interaction among individuals and their personal grievances but also rural perception of the colonial order.

CHAPTER ONE

A Glass for the Gods and a Gift to My Neighbor

The Importance of Alcohol in the Pre-Columbian Andes

Justin Jennings

When the Spanish conquered Peru in 1532, they were both fascinated and repulsed by alcohol consumption in the Andes. Excessive drinking seemed to be encouraged, and, as the sixteenth-century chronicler Bernabé Cobo suggested, people often drank until they could not stand up.[1] In the decades that followed the conquest, many Spaniards took the ubiquity of native alcoholic beverages as a sign of the devil's work, and the curtailment of excessive drinking became a key part of campaigns to stamp out heresy in the fifteenth and sixteenth centuries.[2] These campaigns revealed the important role of alcohol in ritual activities, just as Spaniards were also coming to grips with the centrality of alcohol in the political, social, and economic realms of the region's indigenous cultures, as the following two chapters in this volume demonstrate.

Colonial records, of course, cannot be read as pre-Columbian realities—so much was changing in the wake of conquest[3]—yet these records, when combined with archaeological data, give us a glimpse into the past that reveals the staggering importance of fermented beverages in the ancient Andes. For hundreds of years before the Spanish, the majority of a household's pots were dedicated to alcohol, and drinking was a critical part of the relationships within and between communities.[4] To distill ancient Andean life to a relationship with alcohol is gross hyperbole. Yet, without understanding the role of beer, one cannot understand the pre-Columbian world.

This chapter discusses the pivotal role played by alcohol in the Andes from the beginning of the first millennium CE until the Spanish conquest in the early sixteenth century. Daily and at special events, people consumed a wide variety of fermented beverages made from corn, *molle* (a fruit native to the Andes), peanuts, and other plants.[5] Although the term *chicha* is often used today as an umbrella term for Andean fermented beverages, this term was introduced to the region only after the conquest, when it was used to refer to both fermented and unfermented indigenous drinks. In the pre-Columbian world, many different terms, such as *kusa*, *guiñapo*, and *tekti*, were used for alcoholic beverages.[6] The drinks were consumed in a wide variety of settings and were essential in maintaining and transforming the gender roles, kinship bonds, status hierarchies, ethnic identities, exchange relationships, and production regimes that structured Andean communities.

Like in other regions of the world, it is difficult to pinpoint when people starting making fermented beverages in the Andes.[7] There are no written records before the Spanish conquest, and work on identifying chemical residues for beverages in the Andes is only now beginning. Without these direct methods, archaeologists have depended on three different indirect methods to trace alcohol's history. First, archaeological correlates from historical records have been developed that use modern practices to identify possible alcohol production and consumption in the prehistoric Andes.[8] Through these methods, archaeologists can identify artifacts that were likely associated with such brewing activities as drying, grinding, cooking, straining, and fermentation. The second way that fermented beverage consumption has been studied is through depictions of drinking. These representations can sometimes lend credence to the archaeological correlates, but often little in the images allows archaeologists to identify the type of beverage being consumed. Finally, isotopic analysis of human bone has been used to trace alcohol consumption. This method, applied thus far only for corn beer, is based on how the various photosynthetic pathways used by plants take in different amounts of carbon-12 and carbon-13. The only major subsistence crop in the Andes with a C_4 carbon fixation pathway is maize, and thus one can get an idea of the amount of corn consumed by an individual by measuring the isotopic ratio of carbon.[9] Corn, of course, can be consumed in other forms beyond beer, so heightened maize consumption is not direct evidence for alcohol consumption.

By combining these indirect measures, archaeologists have built a strong case for the wide use of fermented beverages in the pre-Columbian Andes by the Early Intermediate Period (200 BCE–600 CE).[10] Consumption likely increased during the subsequent Middle Horizon Period (600–1000 CE), and the central role of beer in Andean culture continued through the Spanish conquest. Alcoholic drinks were likely consumed prior to the Early Intermediate Period, but the evidence for fermented beverages before the first millennium CE is far more equivocal.[11] Hallucinogens and other nonalcoholic drugs would have been far more important in Andean life during earlier epochs.[12]

This brief chapter is not an exhaustive description of alcohol in the pre-Columbian Andes. It neither attempts to describe the wide variety of beverages consumed in the region nor takes the reader through a detailed description of two thousand years of history.[13] Instead, this chapter seeks to illustrate the centrality of alcohol to ancient Andean life through five case studies that give the reader a sense of how the production, exchange, and consumption of beer were woven into the fabric of the pre-Columbian Andes. Our discussion begins in 1532 CE, when the *conquistadores* (the Spanish conquerors) refuse the offer of a drink from the Inca ruler. We then move backward in time to the beginning of the first millennium CE to explore the different ways in which alcohol was entangled in the development of Andean complex societies.

A Gift Refused in Cajamarca, Peru

According to almost all eyewitness accounts, the story of the Spanish conquest of Peru begins when the Inca emperor Atahualpa refuses a gift. These accounts focus on the afternoon of November 16, 1532 CE, when the emperor entered the town of Cajamarca to talk with the Spanish conquistador Francisco Pizarro. Surrounded by several thousand attendants, the emperor's litter was met in the plaza by Friar Vicente de Valverde and his translator. The Spaniards were laying a trap for Atahualpa, and they hoped that Valverde could coax the emperor inside one of the buildings that surrounded the plaza. The emperor, however, stood his ground, and the friar instead began lecturing Atahualpa on God. After his speech, the priest presented the emperor with a Catholic breviary that Atahualpa examined briefly before throwing to the ground in a mixture of frustration and disdain. Valverde fled from this sacrilege while calling his companions to battle. Pizarro ordered the cannons to fire—the conquest had begun.[14]

In Spanish eyes, the desecration of the breviary marked the beginning of the conquest and was fueled by Atahualpa's incomprehension of how to open and read a book (his action was thus a manifestation of his ignorance of the Word of God). Yet, Thomas Cummins argues in *Toasts with the Inca* that Atahualpa may have thrown down the book in retaliation for an insult that he had endured the day before, when Pizarro had sent his deputy Hernando de Soto and brother Hernando Pizarro with a group of horsemen to visit the emperor at his encampment.[15] The Spanish accounts paint a general picture of a meeting of little consequence, focusing mostly on the reaction of Atahualpa and his entourage to their horses.[16]

In contrast, the description of this meeting by the emperor's nephew, Diego de Castro Titu Cusi Yupanqui, emphasizes the importance of the encounter and stresses how an offered drink of corn beer was refused. According to Titu Cusi, the emperor cordially received de Soto and Pizarro and "gave them each to drink, a drink that we drink, from a golden cup. The Spaniard, upon receiving the drink in his hand, spilled it which greatly angered my uncle."[17] For Titu Cusi, the refused beer was the definitive moment of the encounter and a brazen insult to his uncle. He then goes on to suggest that Friar Valverde added further offense when he poured out an offered glass of beer the next day in Cajamarca.[18] In retaliation for these refused drinks, Atahualpa would throw down Valverde's offered breviary.

Titu Cusi might have lied—the eyewitness Diego de Trujillo, for example, suggests that the Spaniards drank the beer that was given to them when they visited the emperor in his camp,[19] and no other account describes an exchange of cups in Cajamarca's plaza the following day. What really happened in 1532, however, is less important than the choice that Titu Cusi Yupanqui made in emphasizing the offering of drinks in his tale of the conquest. While the Spaniards focus on a breviary, he focuses on a beer. His focus on a refused drink is not surprising when seen within the long tradition of Andean reciprocal gift exchange.[20] Drinking cups, called *keros*, had been used to cement relationships for hundreds of years, and a pair of golden keros, the *tupa cusi*, were among the sacred objects given to an Inca emperor when he took office.[21] By refusing the beer offered to them, the Spaniards had rejected "a sign of Inca rule and all that it implied."[22]

Inca rule was premised on chiefly generosity.[23] Beer was offered to gods, ancestors, peers, rivals, and subjects. Just as it occurs today,[24] the social order was expressed through drinking. The Inca emperor expressed solidarity with his guests by offering them a drink, and the order in which the drinks were given, the phrase that he or his representative used in offering the drink, the quantity of drink, and many other factors could be used to signal social ranking. To refuse a drink was unthinkable; it was an act of war that refused to recognize Inca rule. Those that denied the Inca emperor were sometimes turned into keros themselves—their heads severed and transformed into goblets for drinking.[25]

One of the keys to Inca rule was the ability to overwhelm its subjects with the empire's largess. Building on traditions of reciprocity, the empire hosted feasts to recompense people for their service to the state. Yet, the feast went far beyond the means of local leaders. Excessive drinking was encouraged at these events, and the millions of liters of beer brewed under the auspices of the Inca put his subjects in his debt by the sheer quantity of chicha provided.[26] As Marcel Mauss famously noted for the Kwakiutl of the Northwest Coast, "To accept without giving in return, or without giving more back, is to become client and servant, to become small, to fall lower."[27] Inca subjects could not reciprocate by having the emperor over for a drink. The only way to begin to repay his generosity was to provide more service to the state.

Local Female Brewers in the Mantaro Valley, Peru

The Inca feasting economy created a nearly insatiable demand for beer in the empire. To underwrite this generosity, the Inca emperor invested heavily in expanding maize production by opening up new areas to cultivation, improving yields in preexisting agricultural lands, and levying a labor duty on people in return for their right to work the land that had traditionally belonged to them.[28] These measures increased the amount of maize that could be turned into chicha, but the critical bottleneck in chicha manufacture was brewing labor rather than surplus maize production.[29]

To meet labor demands, the Incas centralized some chicha production by assigning brewing responsibilities to the *mamakona*, the sequestered "chosen women" who labored exclusively for the state.[30] The mamakona, however, could produce only a small fraction of the beer needed in the empire, and their sacred beer was instead used only for only the most important of state occasions.[31] Colonial records highlight the labor served to the Inca in mining, herding, and military service,[32] but one of the biggest demands by the state on local producers may have been for maize agriculture and the labor to turn much of this maize into beer.[33]

Christine Hastorf's work on the Xauxa provides us with a case study of how women's lives were reshaped by Inca demands for corn beer.[34] The Xauxa, a group living in the Upper Mantaro Valley in the central highlands of Peru, were organized at the beginning of the fifteenth century into large fortified towns that were run by leaders who vied with each other to attract followers.[35] When the Incas conquered the valley, a state-approved official was put in charge of the region, and local leaders were moved into a secondary, supporting rule.[36] The empire reorganized the local economy to more effectively extract agricultural, pastoral, and mineralogical wealth from the valley. Some of this increased production came from technological and organizational changes, but for the most part the Incas just made the Xauxa work harder.[37]

Hastorf excavated Xauxa domestic compounds used before and after the Inca conquest of the region and was able to compile a wealth of data that included botanical remains, cooking vessels, grinding tools, and human bones. These data suggest that the Xauxa changed from eating most of their corn as a boiled stew to drinking most of their corn as beer in the two centuries preceding Inca conquest. People started spending much more of their time grinding maize (a necessary task for making corn beer), and they were more often using varieties of corn that were better suited to beer production.[38] In a manner that was later co-opted and amplified by the Inca Empire, the local leaders were using the alcohol to attract and maintain followers in an incipient feasting economy. These elites concentrated brewing activities within their own households and likely bolstered their beer production relative to other households simply by increasing economies of scale.[39]

When the Incas came into the Upper Mantaro Valley, elite control over beer production waned as grinding implements, storage vessels, and maize remains became more common across households.[40] People began producing even more corn, while other food crops, such as potatoes and quinoa, became less common in household assemblages.[41] Culinary tasks were more limited—there are fewer charred crop remains, for example, after the Inca conquest—and processing activities became more confined to certain zones.[42] As Hastorf notes,[43] all of her data point to increased, streamlined maize processing for the production of corn beer. Diverse household economies were thus being transformed to meet an imperial goal of producing more and more beer.

As Irene Silverblatt noted more than thirty years ago, women fared worse than men under the Incas.[44] Women are associated in the Andes today with the domestic sphere and are responsible for much of the food preparation.[45] Beer production typically takes place behind the walls of the home, and women vigorously defend their right to independently produce beer.[46] If this was the case among the Xauxa, then most of the work of beer production was done by women, since most of the maize remains found by Hastorf were in and around Xauxa houses.[47] The burden of making more and more beer each day would have therefore fallen largely on the already tired shoulders and backs of Xauxa women. Yet, isotope data suggest that they were often not enjoying the fruits of their labor.

Isotopic signatures of human bones from Xauxa households occupied before and after the Inca conquest show that before the Incas came into the valley, men and women were consuming about the same amount of maize. This suggests that both sexes likely participated in events where corn beer was served. Under the Incas, however, women were producing more beer while consuming about the same amount that they had enjoyed earlier. Half of the men, however, were eating more meat and drinking significantly more corn beer.[48] Since alcohol was an essential element of Inca politics, the lower consumption of beer by females means that they may have been excluded from many of the feasts that the Incas employed to link their subjects to the state. While men's labor was celebrated in the Mantaro Valley, women's work for the state appears to have been separated from the labor rendered by men and then devalued.[49]

A State Brewery in Moquegua, Peru

A different kind of beer may have been important among the Wari (600–1000 CE), a culture that flourished across much of Peru almost a thousand years before the Incas. The eponymously named city of Wari (often spelled *Huari* to distinguish the site from the civilization) was both the inspiration for a far-flung culture and the seat of a powerful state that controlled much of the central highlands. Although the geographic extent of this state is debated,[50] there was a widespread diffusion of Wari ideas, artifacts, and, to a lesser extent, people during this period.[51] One of these ideas was an increased emphasis on "lavish hospitality" centered on beer consumption.[52] Wari hospitality, however, differed significantly from Inca generosity.

The beer drunk at Wari-related sites was made from a variety of plants. Large quantities of corn beer, for example, were likely consumed at the city of Wari,[53] and the hallucinogenic plant *Anadenanthera colubrina* may have been mixed into beverages on occasion.[54] One of the more popular beers during the Middle Horizon Period was made from the fruits of *Schinus molle*, the pepper tree.[55] To make the beer, the fruits were peeled and then steeped in water before being fermented. Since it may have taken as many as two hundred of the small molle fruits to make a liter of beer,[56] the archaeological sites where this beer was manufactured are littered with molle seeds.

One of the sites where molle beer was made was the Wari colony of
Cerro Baúl, a site located on a massif looming over the arid upper Moquegua Valley of the far south coast of Peru. Very few people from the local
Huaracane groups lived in this part of the valley at the time of Wari colonization in the early seventh century CE,[57] and settlers built extensive
agricultural terracing and irrigation systems to sustain the new colony.[58]
Agricultural investment in the valley seems to have included the planting
of *Schinus molle* trees, a group of which continues to grow in the region
today.[59] The colony thrived, and Huaracane from farther down the valley
moved into sites around Cerro Baúl. By the tenth century, Cerro Baúl was
a warren of structures, large plazas, and storage spaces.[60] Many of these
spaces were dedicated to the preparation and consumption of the feasts
that brought together Wari colonists and local elites.[61] Alcoholic beverages
were an important part of these celebrations.

In 2004 a team led by Ryan Williams uncovered a brewery complex at
the heart of the site. The brewery was trapezoidal in plan and contained
"separate compartments for milling, boiling, and fermentation."[62] In the
fermentation room, twelve large jars were found against the wall. Each of
the jars could hold up to 150 liters of beer for a total room capacity of
1,800 liters.[63] Although the excavators initially speculated that maize beer
was produced in the brewery,[64] maize remains made up less than 1 percent
of the archeobotanical assemblage in the structure. The starch grains
identified in the brewery's grinding stones also point away from the making of corn beer since only grains from tubers and chili peppers were
found.[65] The brewery, however, is littered with molle seeds and stems.
While the molle remains in other areas of the site seem to have been part
of a broad spectrum of daily activities, the molle in the brewery were the
result of "a series of productive steps . . . for a single purpose"[66]—the brewing of large amounts of molle beer.

The ubiquity of molle seeds across Cerro Baúl stands in stark contrast
to the dearth of molle seeds reported at other sites in the upper Moquegua
Valley that were occupied by local Huaracane groups.[67] People outside of
the colony were apparently using the molle tree for such things as construction material and fuel (molle remains are occasionally found), but
they do not seem to have used the molle fruits to brew beer for their own
consumption. It is unclear if the lack of molle beer production at local
sites was a result of state control or simply personal preference.[68] In either
case, it seems that molle beer was both closely associated with the Wari
colonists at Cerro Baúl and likely central to their identity.

We know that food and drink preferences have been used as identity markers in the Andes since at least the fifteenth century,[69] and gastronomy was likely used in a similar manner during the Middle Horizon Period as well. When Wari colonists arrived in Moquegua, they separated themselves from the local populations by building their site on top of a mountain. The artifact and architectural assemblages at Cerro Baúl is distinct from those found elsewhere in the valley, and the colonists sought to maintain this distinction throughout the life of the site.[70] These efforts extended into cuisine, where the colonists of Cerro Baúl used molle beer as "a marker of Wari ethnicity that likely served to represent their traditional and elite way of life."[71]

Although Inca rule depended on large-scale, inclusive patron-client feasts, those living at Cerro Baúl often used food and drink in a more exclusionary manner to emphasize status differences.[72] Their foothold in Moquegua was sustained by both demonstrating their Wari links and showcasing how they differed from local Huaracane groups. Those that came to Cerro Baúl entered a Wari world within which the daily consumption of molle beer was an important marker of the site's foreign identity. Feasts inside the compounds were elite affairs that reinforced social differences and likely helped to legitimize Huari's colonial extension into the region.

Changing Drinking Patterns in the Cochabamba Valley, Bolivia

Beer was equally important to the dynamics of another culture that emerged around the same time in the southern Andes, the Tiwanaku. Around 500 CE, the site of Tiahuanaco (like Huari, Tiahuanaco is the city, while Tiwanaku is the culture) in the Lake Titicaca Basin of Bolivia grew rapidly into a city covering six square kilometers.[73] An important pilgrimage center that hosted events in its massive plazas, courtyards, and pyramids, Tiahuanaco was also a bustling trading hub that enjoyed widespread influence, if not sometimes control, over affairs in the basin and beyond.[74] Tiwanaku power relied in large part on festivities where people enhanced their status, recruited labor, solicited favors, and settled disputes.[75] To a significant degree, Tiahuanaco was built through the labor generated at feasts, and a "chicha economy" exploded outward as Tiwanaku influence spread.[76]

At the center of this feasting culture were keros filled with beer. The vessels litter the surface of Tiwanaku-era sites in the basin, ranging from 7 to 35 percent of ceramics assemblages, demonstrating their significance in "Tiwanaku identity in the heartland."[77] Although beer could be made from a wide variety of other crops, the people living at Tiwanaku seem to have preferred maize beer.[78] This preference is surprising because Tiwanaku's high elevation makes growing corn extremely difficult, and thus much of the maize used at the site would have had to have been imported from lower elevations.[79] A desire for corn beer might have helped drive Tiwanaku connections outward, and one of the locations that likely supplied maize was the Cochabamba Valley in eastern Bolivia.

Tiwanaku influence was strong in Cochabamba. This influence can be seen on local ceramic styles by the end of the ninth century CE, and goods that were likely manufactured at Tiwanaku, such as feather mantles, snuff tablets, metalwork, and ceramic vessels, also began to appear in Cochabamba graves around this time.[80] These imports were likely carried into the region by llama caravans led by Tiwanaku traders, a few of whom may have settled into the region.[81] With Tiwanaku influence came its "mania for maize beer,"[82] and keros became ubiquitous at Cochabamba sites.

The kero is the most pervasive marker of Tiwanaku influence in Cochabamba during the eighth century CE. More than other vessels, keros are replete with Tiwanaku religious iconography, and the form is abundant in domestic and mortuary contexts in Cochabamba. Karen Anderson has studied how drinking patterns changed in Cochabamba as a result of Tiwanaku influence.[83] Drawing in large part from her excavations at the site of Piñami, she notes that people were likely drinking fermented beverages hundreds of years before Tiwanaku influence was felt in the valley. Kero-shaped drinking vessels are found in earlier assemblages, and there are also vessels that could have been used for the storage, transport, and fermentation of beer. Yet, drinking played a more limited role in pre-Tiwanaku Cochabamba. The kero-shaped drinking vessels were rare, special-purpose vessels, perhaps used only by certain individuals during important ceremonies. For the most part, people likely drank their beer out of bowls or other kinds of multipurpose vessels.[84]

With Tiwanaku influence came the association of drinking beer out of keros. People were commonly buried with at least one of these dedicated drinking cups regardless of their age, status, or gender. Keros were also ubiquitous among the living, making up 35–40 percent of the total assemblages from domestic units excavated from Piñami.[85] Cochabamba people adopted the kero size used in the Titicaca basin that held a generous amount of beer (each vessel could hold about 800 milliliters—there are 473 milliliters in a US pint of beer), as well as created for themselves a rarer supersize version that held 1,225 milliliters. Another uniquely Cochabamba form was a *vaso embudo*, a funnel-shaped vessel that would have been extremely difficult to put down once filled because of its tiny base.[86]

When Tiwanaku influence dissipated at the end of the tenth century CE, Tiwanaku motifs disappeared from Cochabamba pottery and were replaced by geometric patterns. Keros remained a part of ceramic assemblages but became less common in graves and domestic contexts. Their forms became more hyperboloid, and the large keros and vaso embudos were no longer used. The most striking post-Tiwanaku change in keros was their reduction in size (they now held just 315 milliliters). Pitchers, rare in early periods, became more common and were much bigger than earlier examples. While the few Tiwanaku-era pitchers produced were just slightly larger than a typical kero (the pitchers averaged 990 milliliters in volume), post-Tiwanaku pitchers ballooned to 4,300 milliliters in volume.

Like in other areas of Peru and Bolivia,[87] people drank beer in Cochabamba before the introduction of the Tiwanaku drinking culture. Yet few people owned special-purpose drinking cups, and beer drinking seems to have been reserved for special occasions. Tiwanaku influence brought radical changes in drinking patterns, as drinking became an important part of everyday life.[88] Everyone had a kero decorated with Tiwanaku icons, used them routinely in and around their households, and then took them (though perhaps not the same keros) to the grave with them. Although Cochabamba people had lifestyles that were different in many ways to those of the Titicaca Basin, they drank like people from Tiwanaku. When Tiwanaku influence declined, people not only drank less but also drank differently. Post-Tiwanaku keros were decorated with local motifs, and the emphasis seems to have moved away from individualism to communalism. The pitcher, and not the gaudily decorated kero, became the prominent drinking vessel.

Building Community in the Northern Highlands of Peru

Before the Wari and Tiwanaku cultures stretched across much of the region, the Andes was broken up into a rich mosaic of smaller groups during the Early Intermediate Period (200 BCE to 600 CE). In many of these societies, elites were only just emerging, and these leaders sought to maintain their positions through a wide variety of mechanisms from craft production to ancestor veneration.[89] One of the groups that formed during this period was the Recuay of Peru's northern highlands. Known for their distinctive art style seen on pottery, stonework, and architecture, the Recuay were organized into a number of warring chiefdoms by the time that the Early Intermediate Period ended in the 600s.[90]

By the fifth century CE, chiefly authority was likely represented as a great house that was protective and generous. The great houses were extensive compounds where feasting, ancestor veneration, and other rituals occurred. Most sites had only a single great house, but some of the larger late Recuay sites boasted multiple compounds built by competing social factions.[91] Great houses were the result of a centuries-long trend toward greater political consolidation of the more diminutive, likely kin-based, groups that made up the basic building blocks of Recuay society. Sites from earlier in the Early Intermediate Period were smaller, and these sites did not contain great houses that served as focal points for ritual affairs. Instead, public ceremonies occurred within patio enclosures on ridgetops.

Elites nonetheless still found a way to insert themselves into privileged positions at ceremonies in these earlier, smaller Recuay sites by building their homes adjacent to the ridgetop enclosures used for feasting. Their houses were therefore in sight when people ate, drank, and displayed prestige items in the grandiose ceremonies that took place in these enclosures.[92] Although it is unlikely that access to these enclosures was strictly controlled by elite households, there is some evidence to suggest that local leaders strove to sponsor events or at least play a significant role in organizing the affairs that took place on the ridges.[93]

Some of our best data on elite roles in early Recuay ceremonies come from Joan Gero's 1988 investigations of feasting patterns at the site of Queyash Alto.[94] The small site stretches across one hundred meters of an artificially flattened ridgetop flanked by stone terraces. In a section of this ridge, adjacent to what she called the West Mound, Gero found a partially enclosed plaza with "numerous overlapping ash and charcoal-laden pits" that contained fractured llama bones and broken shallow bowls, ladles, and open-necked jars.[95] Recuay vessels sometimes depicted well-dressed individuals who were drinking, toasting, and receiving beverages contained within shallow bowls.[96] These beverages, based upon the brewing equipment found at Recuay sites, were probably beer, and thus the shallow bowls found on the ridgetop at Queyash Alto likely served as beer-drinking vessels.

The Queyash Alto data suggest that feasting preparation occurred in the same location where feasts were later celebrated. Llamas were likely butchered and prepared on the ridgetop, for instance, because the chipped and ground stone knives and bifaces that would have been used for animal butchery were found only in this part of the site;[97] on-site brewing is suggested by fermenting jars, colanders, and other brewing paraphernalia that were concentrated in the West Mound plaza and in other locations across the ridgetop.[98] The clustering of evidence for brewing, butchering, and other aspects of feast preparation occurring in and around the enclosures suggests a community-wide affair wherein people came together from the various households of Queyash Alto to make and then consume a meal.

The artifacts excavated from the ridgetop by Gero and her crew give us a sense of how these kinds of events likely unfolded at Recuay sites. The shawl pins and spindle whorls found throughout the area, for example, suggest that women were active participants in feasts, and the llama figurines and snuff tubes found there argue for a strong ritual dimension to these parties.[99] Music, as represented by a "profusion of panpipe fragments," filled the air as people drank, prayed, dance, and sang during activities that took in settlements across the region.[100]

Emerging elites at Queyash Alto would have attempted to gain political advantages from these community-wide celebrations by pontificating, wearing prestige goods made of copper and shell, and claiming supernatural linkages to their lineage. By living next to feasting areas, they were able to monitor events, restrict access into the space, store food and drink, and perhaps offer other means of support to those celebrating within the enclosure. Yet, they did not control the means of production—everyone made the food and drink that would be consumed—and thus their influence over ridgetop activities was initially weak and ephemeral.

Over time, elites in the Recuay culture seem to have focused on celebratory performances as the principal means of gaining additional power and strove to formalize feasting areas into discrete ritual spaces festooned with symbols that legitimized their elite status. As George Lau notes for the nearby site of Chinchawas, "Effort was directed at elaborating ceremonial enclosures with fine masonry, drainage canals, and stone sculpture. Bearing images of felines and ancestors, the sculptures may have served as references to descent as well as aggrandizing expressions of political authority."[101] The creation of these ceremonial enclosures in connection to ancestor worship was a step toward the great houses that would be built at the end of the period. Feasting, initially public and community organized, was now coming under the control of elites who began to sponsor smaller events at sites that were increasingly divided between factions that were aligned with competing leaders.[102] "The smell of roasting llama, the giddiness produced by beer, [and] the cacophony of music" remained the same, but the feasts were slowly being co-opted by the elites.[103] Alcohol had bound people together in community-wide events; it was now being used to tear these Recuay groups apart into rival factions.

Conclusions

As one of the most ancient, widely used, and versatile drugs in the world,[104] alcohol production, exchange, and consumption have long structured individuals' relationships with society, the environment, and the cosmos.[105] Alcohol has been woven into social, economic, and political structures of the Andes for at least the last fifteen hundred years. Fermented beverages have been used to maintain gender roles, kinship bonds, status hierarchies, ethnic identities, exchange relationships, and production regimes within Andean society. At the same time, shifts in alcohol production, exchange, and consumption provide evidence of periods of great social change. By tracking the flow of alcohol through society, we can better understand the dialectics of pre-Columbian Andean society.

The origins of alcoholic beverages in the Andes still elude us. Fermentation is a natural process, and it is almost certain that people drank beer long before the first millennium CE. Yet during the Early Intermediate Period, alcohol became visible because of the social transformations that were occurring during that time. One might argue that the increased visibility of beer drinking is related to general trends in the period: sites were getting bigger, ceremonial spaces were becoming formalized, and status hierarchies were developing.[106] In such contexts, we would expect to find not only more brewing and drinking paraphernalia but also a greater concentration of this paraphernalia in specific locations, such as breweries and enclosures.

The general trends of the Early Intermediate Period, however, provide only a partial answer to the visibility of alcohol in the archaeology record. There were big ceremonial sites that predate the first millennium CE across the Andes, and there is little to no evidence from these sites for beer consumption. In the same region where the Recuay culture would flourish, for example, stood the site of Chavín de Huántar. The extensive urban center was built around a massive stone temple complex that was added to and renovated from 1200 to 500 BCE. The temple was decorated with tenon heads and other art that depicted human, animal, and plant features that were combined together into fanciful creatures.[107] Chavín art strongly suggests shamanistic practices and the use of hallucinogens,[108] and John Rick has argued that the rituals practiced at the site were used to establish the religious authority of Chavín leaders.[109] People came from locations throughout northern and central Peru to worship at the site, but it was hallucinogens, rather than alcohol, that played a central role in the rituals conducted at Chavín de Huántar.[110]

Yet, the emphasis on hallucinogens across the Andes appears to have slowly waned after the first millennium BCE, when alcohol began playing a more integral part in the feasts and rituals conducted during the Early Intermediate Period. The reasons that people began drinking more are unclear. Perhaps alcohol was a drug more conducive to communal imbibing, or it was an intoxicant that was easier for elites to manufacture, obtain, and control. Hallucinogens remained important—snuff tablets, for example, are among the most arresting examples of Tiwanaku art[111]—but alcohol had achieved at least equal footing with other drugs by the Middle Horizon Period.

When the Spaniards arrived, beer was the most important drug in the Andes and the sine qua non of Andean generosity. Wives brewed beer for husbands, farmers offered the beverage to friends, priests gave it to the gods, and leaders served the brew to their followers. Over the course of many centuries, alcohol became an essential part of life in the pre-Columbian world and, as the chapters in this volume demonstrate, remains incredibly important to people living in Latin America today. The Incas may no longer rule over the Andes, but an offered glass of beer is still fraught with meaning.

Notes

1. Bernabé Cobo, *History of the Inca Empire: An Account of the Indians' Customs and Their Origin Together with a Treatise on Inca Legends, History, and Social Institutions* (Austin: University of Texas Press, 1979 [1653]), 28.

2. Frances Hayashida, "Chicha Histories: Pre-Hispanic Brewing in the Andes and the Use of Ethnographic and Historic Analogues," in *Drink, Power, and Society in the Andes*, ed. Justin Jennings and Brenda Bowser (Gainesville: University Press of Florida, 2009), 240–44.

3. Ibid.; Peter Gose, *Invaders as Ancestors: On the Intercultural Making and Unmaking of Spanish Colonialism in the Andes* (Toronto: University of Toronto Press, 2008).

4. Justin Jennings and Melissa Chatfield, "Pots, Brewers, and Hosts: Women's Power and the Limits of Central Andean Feasting," in Jennings and Bowser, *Drink, Power, and Society in the Andes*, 200–31.

5. Hugh C. Cutler and Martín Cárdenas, "Chicha, a Native South American Beer," *Botanical Museum Leaflets* 13, no. 3 (Harvard University, 1947), 33–60; David J. Goldstein, Robin C. Coleman Goldstein, and Patrick R. Williams, "You Are What You Drink: A Sociocultural Reconstruction of Pre-Hispanic Fermented Beverage Use at Cerro Baúl, Moquegua, Peru," in Jennings and Bowser, *Drink, Power, and Society in the Andes*, 135–39.

6. Goldstein et al., "You Are What You Drink," 137–38.

7. For a general treatment on the early history of alcohol, see Patrick E. McGovern, *Uncorking the Past: The Quest for Wine, Beer, and Other Alcoholic Beverages* (Berkeley: University of California Press, 2009).

8. For examples of how archaeological correlates can be used to link present to past behaviors, see Jerry Moore, "Pre-Hispanic Beer in Coastal Peru: Technology and Social Context of Prehistoric Production," *American Anthropologist* 91 (1989), 682–95; Goldstein et al., "You Are What You Drink."

9. Clark Spencer Larsen, *Bioarchaeology* (New York: Cambridge University Press, 2000), 272.

10. See Christine A. Hastorf, "Gender, Space, and Food in Prehistory," in *Engendering Archaeology: Women and Prehistory*, ed. Joan M. Gero and Margaret W. Conkey (Cambridge: Blackwell, 1991), 132–59; Joan M. Gero, "Pottery, Power, and . . . Parties!" *Archaeology* 43 (1990), 52–56; Gero, "Feasts and Females: Gender Ideology and Political Meals in the Andes," *Norwegian Archaeological Review* 25 (1992), 15–30; Paul Goldstein, "From Stew-Eaters to Maize-Drinkers: The Chicha Economy and the Tiwanaku Expansion," in *The Archaeology and Politics of Food and Feasting in Early States and Empires*, ed. Tamara L. Bray (New York: Kluwer Academic/Plenum, 2003), 143–72; Goldstein, *Andean Diaspora: The Tiwanaku Colonies and the Origins of South American Empire* (Gainesville: University Press of Florida, 2005); Moore, "Pre-Hispanic Beer in Coastal Peru"; Izumi Shimada, *Pampa Grande and the Mochica Culture* (Austin: University of Texas Press, 1994); Rafael Segura Llanos, *Rito y economía en Cajamarquilla: Investigaciones arqueológicas en el conjunto arquitectónico Julio C. Tello* (Lima: Pontificia Universidad Católica del Perú, 2001).

11. Richard L. Burger and Nikolaas J. Van Der Merwe, "Maize and the Origins of Highland Chavín Civilization: An Isotopic Perspective," *American Anthropologist* 92 (1990), 85–95.

12. One discussion of the importance of other drugs in earlier Andean prehistory is Daniel A. Contreras, "A Mito-Style Structure at Chavín de Huántar: Dating and Implications," *Latin American Antiquity* 21 (2010), 3–21.

13. For book-length discussions of alcohol in the Andes, see Ranulfo Cavero Carrasco, *Maíz, chicha y religiosidad andina* (Ayacucho: Universidad Nacional de San Cristóbal de Huamanga, 1986); Justin Jennings and Brenda Bowser, eds., *Drink, Power, and Society in the Andes* (Gainesville: University Press of Florida, 2009); Rafo León, *Chicha peruana, una bebida, una cultura* (Lima: Universidad de San Martín de Porres, 2008); Thierry Saignes, ed., *Borrachera y memoria: La experiencia de lo sagrado en los Andes* (Lima: Instituto Francés de Estudios Andinos, 1993).

14. John Hemming, *The Conquest of the Incas* (New York: Harcourt Brace Jovanovich, 1970), 40–41.

15. Thomas Cummins, *Toasts with the Inca: Andean Abstraction and Colonial Images on Quero Vessels* (Ann Arbor: University of Michigan Press, 2002), 14–20.

16. Hemming, *Conquest of the Incas*, 34–35.

17. Diego de Castro [Titu Cusi] Yupanqui, *Titu Cusi, a 16th Century Account of the Conquest: Instrucción del Inga Don Diego de Castro Titu Cusi Yupanqui para el muy ilustre Señor el Licenciado Lope García del Castro* (Cambridge, MA: Harvard University Press, 2005 [1570]), 135.

18. Ibid., 136.

19. Diego de Trujillo, *Una relación inédita de la conquista: la Crónica de Diego de Trujillo* (Lima: Instituto de Raúl Porras Barrenecha, 1948 [1571]), 52.

20. Mary Weismantel, "Have a Drink: Chicha, Performance, and Politics," in Jennings and Bowser, *Drink, Power, and Society in the Andes*, 257–77.

21. Cummins, *Toasts with the Inca*, 76.

22. Ibid., 19.

23. John V. Murra, "Rite and Crop in the Inca State," in *Culture in History: Essays in Honor of Paul Radin*, ed. Stanley Diamon (New York: Columbia University Press, 1960), 393–407; Susan Elizabeth Ramírez, *To Feed and Be Fed: The Cosmological Bases of Authority and Identity in the Andes* (Stanford, CA: Stanford University Press, 2005).

24. Catherine J. Allen, *The Hold Life Has: Coca and Cultural Identity in an Andean Community*, 2nd ed. (Washington, DC: Smithsonian Institution Press, 2002), 119–22.

25. Cummins, *Toasts with the Inca*, 76.

26. Tamara L. Bray, "Inka Pottery as Culinary Equipment: Food, Feasting, and Gender in Imperial Design," *Latin American Antiquity* 14 (2003), 18–19; Christine A. Hastorf and Sissel Johannessen, "Pre-Hispanic Political Change and the Role of Maize in the Central Andes of Peru," *American Anthropologist* 95 (1993), 118–19; Moore, "Pre-Hispanic Beer in Coastal Peru"; Craig Morris, "Maize Beer in the Economics, Politics, and Religion of the Inca Empire," in *Fermented Food Beverages in Nutrition*, ed. Clifford F. Gastineau, William J. Darby, and Thomas B. Turner (New York: Academic Press, 1979), 32.

27. Marcel Mauss, *The Gift: The Form and Reason for Exchange in Archaic Societies* (New York: W. W. Norton, 1990), 74.

28. Terence N. D'Altroy, *The Incas* (Malden, MA: Blackwell, 2002), 265; Murra, "Rite and Crop in the Inca State."

29. Justin Jennings, "La Chichera y el Patrón: Chicha and the Energetics of Feasting in the Prehistoric Andes," in *Foundations of Power in the Prehispanic Andes*, ed. Christina A. Conlee, Dennis Ogburn, and Kevin Vaughn (Arlington, VA: American Anthropological Association, 2005), 241–59.

30. Morris, "Maize Beer."

31. Weismantel, "Have a Drink," 268–69.

32. For the goods and services obtained from one-quarter of the Inca Empire, see Catherine Julien, *Condesuyo: The Political Division of Territory Under Inka and Spanish Rule*, Bonner Amerikanistische Studien 19 (Bonn, Germany: Seminar für Völkerkunde, Universität Bonn, 1991).

33. Jennings, "Chichera y el Patrón"; Craig Morris, "The Infrastructure of Inka Control in the Peruvian Central Highlands," in *The Inca and Aztec States, 1400–1800: Anthropology and History*, ed. George A. Collier, Renato I. Rosaldo, and John D. Wirth (New York: Academic Press, 1982), 153–71; Murra, "Rite and Crop in the Inca State."

34. Christine A. Hastorf, "The Effect of the Inka State on Sausa Agricultural Production and Crop Consumption," *American Antiquity* 55 (1990), 262–90; Hastorf, "Gender, Space, and Food in Prehistory"; Hastorf, *Agriculture and the Onset of Political Inequality Before the Inka* (Cambridge: Cambridge University Press, 1993); Hastorf, "The Xauxa Andean Life," in *Empire and Domestic Economy*, ed. Terence N. D'Altroy and Christine A. Hastorf (New York: Kluwer Academic/Plenum, 2001), 315 24; Hastorf, "Agricultural Production and Consumption," in D'Altroy and Hastorf, *Empire and Domestic Economy*, 155–78; Hastorf and Johannessen, "Pre-Hispanic Political Change."

35. Hastorf, "The Xauxa Andean Life," 323–24.

36. Terence N. D'Altroy, "From Autonomous to Imperial Rule," in D'Altroy and Hastorf, *Empire and Domestic Economy*, 325.

37. Ibid., 339.

38. Hastorf and Johannessen, "Pre-Hispanic Political Change," 131.

39. Hastorf, "Agricultural Production and Consumption," 177.

40. Hastorf and Johannessen, "Pre-Hispanic Political Change," 129.

41. Hastorf, "Gender, Space, and Food in Prehistory," 143–45.

42. Ibid.; Hastorf, "Agricultural Production and Consumption," 173–75.

43. Hastorf, "Agricultural Production and Consumption," 176.

44. Irene Silverblatt, "Andean Women in the Inca Empire," *Feminist Studies* 4 (1978), 36–61; Silverblatt, *Moon, Sun and Witches. Gender Ideologies and Class in Inca and Colonial Peru* (Princeton, NJ: Princeton University Press, 1987).

45. Hastorf, "Gender, Space, and Food in Prehistory," 134.

46. Jennings and Chatfield, "Pots, Brewers, and Hosts."

47. Hastorf, "Gender, Space, and Food in Prehistory," 144–45.

48. Ibid., 149–51.

49. Ibid., 152.

50. See Justin Jennings, ed., *Beyond Wari Walls: Regional Perspectives on Middle Horizon Peru* (Albuquerque: University of New Mexico Press, 2010); Katharina J. Schreiber, "The Wari Empire of Middle Horizon Peru: The Epistemological Challenge of Documenting an Empire Without Documentary Evidence," in *Empires: Perspectives from Archaeology and History*, ed. Susan E. Alcock, Terence N. D'Altroy, Kathleen D. Morrison, and Carla M. Sinopoli (New York: Cambridge University Press, 2001), 70–92.

51. William H. Isbell, "Wari and Tiwanaku: International Identities in the Central Andean Middle Horizon," in *Handbook of South American Archaeology*, ed. Helaine Silverman and William H. Isbell (New York: Springer, 2008), 738–39.

52. Anita G. Cook and Mary Glowacki, "Pots, Politics, and Power: Huari Ceramic Assemblages and Imperial Administration," in Bray, *The Archaeology and Politics of Food and Feasting*, 197.

53. Brian C. Finucane, "Maize and Sociopolitical Complexity in the Ayacucho Valley, Peru," *Current Anthropology* 50 (2009), 535–45.

54. Patricia J. Knobloch, "Wari Ritual Power at Conchopata: An Interpretation of *Anadenanthera colubrina* Iconography," *Latin American Antiquity* 11 (2000), 387–402.

55. David J. Goldstein and Robin Christine Coleman, "*Schinus molle* L. (Anacardiaceae) Chicha Production in the Central Andes," *Economic Botany* 58 (2004), 523–29; Matthew Sayre, David Goldstein, William Whitehead, and Patrick Ryan Williams, "A Marked Preference: Chicha de Molle and Wari State Consumption Practice," *Ñawpa Pacha* 28 (2012), 231–58; Lidio M. Valdez, "Molle Beer Production in a Peruvian Highland Valley," *Journal of Anthropological Research* 68 (2012), 71–93.

56. Goldstein and Coleman, "*Schinus Molle* L."

57. Patrick Ryan Williams, "Rethinking Disaster-Induced Collapse in the Demise of the Andean Highland States: Wari and Tiwanaku," *World Archaeology* 33 (2002), 365.

58. Michael E. Moseley et al., "Burning Down the Brewery: Establishing and Evacuating an Ancient Imperial Colony at Cerro Baúl, Peru," *Proceedings of the National Academy of Sciences of the United States of America* 102 (2005), 17264–71; Donna J. Nash, "The Archaeology of Space: Places of Power in the Wari Empire" (PhD diss., University of Florida, 2002); Patrick Ryan Williams, "The Role of Disaster in the Development of Agriculture and the Evolution of Social Complexity in the South-Central Andes" (PhD diss., University of Florida, 1997); Williams, "Cerro Baúl: A Wari Center on the Tiwanaku Frontier," *Latin American Antiquity* 12 (2001), 67–83.

59. Goldstein et al., "You Are What You Drink," 143.

60. Williams, "Cerro Baúl," 79.

61. Donna J. Nash and Patrick Ryan Williams, "Architecture and Power on the Wari-Tiwanaku Frontier," in Conlee et al., *Foundations of Power*, 167.

62. Moseley et al., "Burning Down the Brewery," 17267.

63. Ibid.

64. Ibid.

65. Goldstein et al., "You Are What You Drink," 144.

66. Ibid.

67. Ibid.

68. Ibid., 157.

69. Goldstein et al., "You Are What You Drink"; Hastorf and Johannessen, "Pre-Hispanic Political Change."

70. Patrick Ryan Williams and Johny Isla, "Investigaciones arqueológicas en Cerro Baúl, un enclave Wari en el valle de Moquegua," *Gaceta Arqueológica Andina* 26 (2002), 87–120.

71. Goldstein et al., "You Are What You Drink," 160.

72. Michael Dietler, "Theorizing the Past: Rituals of Consumption, Commensal Politics, and Power in African Contexts," in *Feasts: Archaeological and Ethnographic Perspectives on Food, Politics, and Power*, ed. Michael Dietler and Brian Hayden (Washington, DC: Smithsonian Institution Press, 2001), 85.

73. John Wayne Janusek and Deborah E. Blom, "Identifying Tiwanaku Urban Populations: Style, Identity, and Ceremony in Andean Cities," in *Urbanism in the Preindustrial World: Cross-Cultural Approaches*, ed. Glen R. Storey (Tuscaloosa: University of Alabama Press, 2006), 240.

74. David Browman, "Political Institutional Factors Contributing to the Integration of the Tiwanaku State," in *Emergence and Change in Early Urban Societies*, ed. Linda

Manzanilla (New York: Plenum, 1997), 229–43; John Wayne Janusek, *Ancient Tiwanaku* (New York: Cambridge University Press, 2008).

75. Brian Hayden, "Fabulous Feasts: A Prolegomenon to the Importance of Feasting," in Dietler and Hayden, *Feasts*, 23–64.

76. Goldstein, "From Stew-Eaters to Maize-Drinkers."

77. Karen Anderson, "Tiwanaku Influence on Local Drinking Patterns in Cochabamba, Bolivia," in Jennings and Bowser, *Drink, Power, and Society in the Andes*, 172.

78. Goldstein, "From Stew-Eaters to Maize-Drinkers."

79. Melanie F. Wright, Christine A. Hastorf, and Heidi A. Lennstrom, "Pre-Hispanic Agriculture and Plant Use at Tiwanaku: Social and Political Implications," in *Tiwanaku and Its Hinterland: Archaeology and Paleoecology of an Andean Civilization*, Vol. 2, *Urban and Rural Archaeology*, ed. Alan Kolata (Washington, DC: Smithsonian Institution Press, 2003), 384–403; Christine A. Hastorf, William T. Whitehead, Maria C. Bruno, and Melanie Wright, "The Movements of Maize into Middle Horizon Tiwanaku, Bolivia," in *Histories of Maize: Multidisciplinary Approaches to the Prehistory, Linguistics, Biogeography, Domestication and Evolution of Maize*, ed. John Staller, John Tykot, and Bruce Benz (Amsterdam: Elsevier Academic Press, 2006), 429–48.

80. Browman, "Political Institutional Factors," 232; Amy S. Oakland, "Tiwanaku Textile Style from the South Central Andes, Bolivia and North Chile" (PhD diss., University of Texas, 1986), 245.

81. Janusek, *Ancient Tiwanaku*, 228.

82. Goldstein, "From Stew-Eaters to Maize-Drinkers," 144.

83. Anderson, "Tiwanaku Influence."

84. Ibid., 176.

85. Ibid., 180, 187–88.

86. Ibid., 180–83.

87. Goldstein, "From Stew-Eaters to Maize-Drinkers," 163–64.

88. Anderson, "Tiwanaku Influence," 190–91.

89. Lisa DeLeonardis and George F. Lau, "Life, Death, and Ancestors," in *Andean Archaeology*, ed. Helaine Silverman (Malden, MA: Blackwell, 2004), 77–115.

90. George F. Lau, "The Recuay Culture of Peru's North-Central Highlands: A Reappraisal of Chronology and Its Implications," *Journal of Field Archaeology* 29 (2004), 177–202.

91. George F. Lau, "House Forms and Recuay Culture: Residential Compounds at Yayno (Ancash, Peru), a Fortified Hilltop Town, AD 400–800," *Journal of Anthropological Archaeology* 29 (2010), 327–51.

92. George F. Lau, "Feasting and Ancestor Veneration at Chinchawas, North Highlands of Ancash, Peru," *Latin American Antiquity* 13 (2002), 279–304.

93. Gero, "Pottery, Power, and . . . Parties!"; Gero, "Feasts and Females"; Lau, "Feasting and Ancestor Veneration."

94. Gero, "Pottery, Power, and . . . Parties!"; Gero, "Feasts and Females."

95. Gero, "Feasts and Females," 18.

96. DeLeonardis and Lau, "Life, Death, and Ancestors," 92.

97. Gero, "Feasts and Females," 18.

98. Gero, "Pottery, Power, and . . . Parties!," 53.

99. Ibid., 20.

100. Ibid., 18.

101. Lau, "Feasting and Ancestor Veneration," 298.

102. Lau, "House Forms and Recuay Culture."

103. Gero, "Pottery, Power, and . . . Parties!," 56.

104. Robert Dudley, "Fermenting Fruit and the Historical Ecology of Ethanol Ingestion: Is Alcoholism in Modern Humans an Evolutionary Hangover?," *Addiction* 97 (2002), 318–88; Dwight B. Heath, "Anthropological Perspectives on Alcohol: An Historical Review," in *Cross-Cultural Approaches to the Study of Alcohol: An Interdisciplinary Perspective*, ed. Michael W. Everett, Jack O. Waddell, and Dwight B. Heath (The Hague: Mouton, 1976), 41.

105. Mary Douglas, *Constructive Drinking: Perspectives on Drink from Anthropology* (New York: Cambridge University Press, 1987).

106. DeLeonardis and Lau, "Life, Death, and Ancestors."

107. John W. Rick, "The Evolution of Authority and Power at Chavín de Huántar, Peru," in Conlee et al., *Foundations of Power*, 73–75.

108. Alana Cordy-Collins, "Chavín Art: Its Shamanic/Hallucinogenic Origins," in *Pre-Columbian Art History*, ed. Alana Cordy-Collins and Jean Stern (Palo Alto, CA: Peek Publications, 1977), 353–62.

109. Rick, "Evolution of Authority."

110. Isabelle C. Druc, *Ceramic Production and Distribution in the Chavín Sphere of Influence* (New York: Oxford University Press, 1998).

111. Janusek, *Ancient Tiwanaku*, 239.

CHAPTER TWO

Liquid Fire

Alcohol, Identity, and Social Hierarchy in Colonial Brazil

João Azevedo Fernandes

Translated by Gretchen Pierce and Áurea Toxqui

Brazil's sugarcane *aguardente*, better known as *cachaça*, is an integral element of Brazilian culture and national identity. From the origins of its production, probably at the start of the seventeenth century, cachaça played a crucial part in the history of the country, in part due to its decisive role in the trafficking of slaves from Africa,[1] in the relations between colonial society and the indigenous peoples,[2] and in the economics and politics of the period between the sixteenth century and 1822, when the country became independent.[3]

Cachaça became a relevant factor in the life experiences of those social groups that suffered the major impact of the colonial experience. As a popular verse recognizes, "de primeiro só bebia / *negro, caboco* e *mulato*" ("at the beginning, only the negro, caboco and mulatto drank"). In other words, this poem labels slaves, the indigenous, and their descendants, poor, free, mixed-race men, as drinkers.[4] This identification with the "inferior" social strata contributed to making cachaça, in the dominant discourse, a symbol of barbarism and a marker of differentiation between those who drank it (the *cachaceiros*) and the higher classes in both colonial and post-Independence Brazil. Throughout much of the colonial period, the latter group valued European wine and despised local distilled beverages. In spite of this rejection, or perhaps because of it, cachaça came to represent a symbol of national pride at the beginning of the nineteenth century, in the context of the revolts associated with the political emancipation of Brazil.

Currently, the presence of *aguardente de cana* in daily life is remarkably ubiquitous, since cachaça is the third most produced distilled drink in the whole world, surpassed only by vodka and Korean *soju*.[5] However, outside of Brazil, cachaça is often confused with rum, which is reflected in international commerce.[6] In the United States and the European Union, for example, cachaça mandatorily has to include the denomination of origin "Brazilian rum," hindering its recognition as a distinct beverage.[7] In spite of both being made from sugarcane, cachaça and rum are truly different drinks. Brazilian law demands that cachaça be prepared from fermented sugarcane juice, while the use of molasses is prohibited. Rum can be produced from fermented and boiled sugarcane juice, molasses, or a combination of both.[8] Chemical composition, then, as well as flavor, distinguishes these two distilled beverages.[9]

Aside from the commercial labeling difficulties, the historiographical interest in cachaça is almost nonexistent.[10] This disinterest belies the fact that the commerce and consumption of alcoholic beverages, especially distilled ones, are essential in understanding the colonial world.[11] Sadly, historical studies have advanced little beyond the lone classic by Luís da Câmara Cascudo, *Prelúdio da Cachaça*, from 1968.[12] The best and fullest work about cachaça since then was not even written by a Brazilian but by the Canadian historian José C. Curto. Furthermore, it is about the important role of the drink in the trafficking of slaves from Africa, and not about the history of cachaça in Brazil.[13]

Among the various underexplored themes, thanks to the disinterest of historians, is the very origin of the beverage. Although sugarcane had been established in Brazil in the early 1530s (becoming the principal export good in the colonial period), it is unlikely that the production of aguardente began in this era, because sources do not mention stills or any distilled beverages throughout the sixteenth century.[14] The first concrete reference to the existence of stills comes from a 1611 São Paulo inventory and will.[15] According to Câmara Cascudo, the French navigator François Pyrard de Laval, who was in Salvador Bahia in 1610, was the first to use the word *aguardente*. It is certain, however, that Laval did not refer to aguardente itself but to the juice or molasses of the fermented cane, which the Frenchman called "wine." After affirming that European goods, especially wine, were quite expensive in Brazil, the Frenchman wrote that the Brazilians made "wine from sugarcane, which is cheap, but only to serve to the slaves and to the indigenous."[16] It is important to note here that Laval observed that this drink made from sugarcane was exclusively for the lower classes in society.

Câmara Cascudo's mistaken interpretation, much like that of modern historians,[17] reveals one of the major difficulties for the study of Brazilian aguardente: the identification of words to designate alcoholic beverages in the colonial period. The documents freely use such expressions as "vinho de mel" (honey wine), "vinho de canna" (sugarcane wine), "aguardente da terra" (aguardente from the land), "licor de canna" (sugarcane liquor), and others to designate both fermented and distilled beverages. Sometimes the term *aguardente* was used to refer to indigenous fermented drinks that were not distilled whatsoever. For example, a 1793 account about the Gauicuru Indians says, "They all get intoxicated on a type of aguardente that is made from honey and water."[18]

The word *cachaça*, during most of the colonial period, was not related to sugarcane aguardente. In fact, *cachaça* referred to the foam that arose from the cauldrons when the sugarcane was boiled into a broth at the beginning of the process of sugar production. It was full of impurities and thus was usually fed to the animals.[19] The foam product of the subsequent boiling, which was less impure, was fermented by the slaves who worked in the sugar mills. This foam was kept "in jars until it lost its sweetness and became sour, because then it is said that it is ready to drink"[20] This foam, or *cachaça*, was made by adding water to *garapa*, or the "sugarcane wine" mentioned by Pyrard de Laval. *Garapa* is a word that reveals the great degree of exchange of knowledge and techniques during the formation of the colonial Atlantic world. Probably of Spanish origin (from *garapiñar*, "to solidify a liquid, freezing it in another form, so that it forms lumps"),[21] it was identified for the first time in Puerto Rico (1596), spreading through the sugarcane-producing regions in the Americas. In Spanish the word was *guarapo*, in French, *grappe*, and in English (in Barbados), *grippo*.[22]

This fermented beverage, garapa, was extremely popular in Brazil in the seventeenth century. It was traded by sugar mill slaves to other slaves and free men who did not have direct access to the production of sugar. These slaves traded it for foods like manioc flour, bananas, and black beans, in addition to drinking it themselves, "hopefully in moderation and not until they become drunk."[23] This popularity extended to poor, free men and to the *indios* (native peoples), who considered it a "marvelous" drink, as Ambrósio Fernandes Brandão, a sugar mill owner, wrote in an important account of the wealth of Portuguese America in 1618.[24] Europeans also admired the qualities of garapa. One of the major producers of sugar in colonial Brazil, João Fernandes Vieira, ordered the administrator of his mill, in 1663, not to fail to provide garapa to the slaves, in order to maintain their health and ability to work. In the winter, he said, the slaves should not be woken up in the early morning and only should begin to work after they received "their ration of foam (cachaça) and honey when available, and make sure it is not lacking for any reason."[25] The author of one of the first historical works about Brazil, Friar Vicente do Salvador, proposed substituting garapa for grape wine. "Wine? From sugar it is made very smooth, for whoever wants it stronger, upon boiling it for two days, it is as intoxicating as the wine from grapes."[26]

Besides the Portuguese, other Europeans left accounts about garapa, pointing out its character as a beverage of the poor and slaves. The Dutch, whose West Indies Company dominated a large part of the northeast of Brazil and notably was the largest regional producer of sugar from Pernambuco between 1630 and 1654, described garapa as a "cheap drink, the 'negros' use it in their parties which last twenty-four hours and consist of dances, songs, and concoctions."[27] The soldiers of the West Indies Company themselves, mercenaries recruited from various countries in Europe, were fond of the fermented sugarcane, and when they received their "money . . . put it towards garapa to drink, because beer and wine are expensive for them."[28]

The expansion and popularization of garapa prepared and permitted the development of the distillation of sugarcane, in a process similar to what happened with Caribbean rum.[29] It is almost impossible to know the exact date of the first production of aguardente, since the process could be carried out in various regions in an independent manner. What is certain is that the history of aguardente in Brazil is marked, from its beginning, by its popularity and identification with the slaves and the poorest strata of the population, as well as with numerous attempts to prohibit it.

One of the reasons for the restriction of aguardente was the danger coming from excess consumption by slaves and the poor in general. In 1636, the governor-general of Brazil, Pedro da Silva, released a provision prohibiting sugarcane aguardente. This is a very interesting document because, among other reasons, it shows that the production of aguardente was already commonplace, because "many stills" existed, and numerous people "benefited from the trade (that is, sale) of it."[30] At the same time, the document clearly identifies the drink with the popular classes, because it was seen as "very harmful to the people" and caused "many deaths among the slaves" (because of the fights provoked by intoxication), who "committed thefts against their owners" in order to buy aguardente. It was not always necessary for the slaves to buy this distilled beverage because we know that one of the principal sugar mills in Bahia, Sergipe do Conde, was distributing the drink (called "augua ardente" [burning water]) to the African slaves and the "negros da terra" (literally, "slaves of the land," but meaning the natives) already by 1622 or 1623.[31]

The document from 1636 is also important because it shows that the word *cachaça* still was not used to the designate the distilled beverage but only the original froth from the boiling of the sugarcane. The governor-general said that the drawbacks of aguardente were "greater than those that motivated the prohibition of Cachaça, and wine of the said honey," and that the punishment to those that produced the sugarcane aguardente ought to be the same "one applied to those accused of selling Cachaça or honey-wine."[32] In these early times, the word *cachaça* always appears associated with "honey-wine," or garapa, and separated from "agoardente": in 1646, "agoardente and honey-wine" and "agoardente and cachassa" were said.[33]

More important than the concern with the social control of the slave population, the prohibition of aguardente was related directly to the fiscal needs of the Crown. Revenues from regional monopolies and direct taxes on production and commerce were the principal instrument of colonial exploration, and they sustained the military and bureaucratic structure of the colony. The tax income originating from Brazil also was vital for the proper existence of the metropolitan state. After the death of the young king Dom Sebastião in 1578, and the end of the Avis dynasty, Portugal was forced to be united with Spain, whose king, Felipe II (Sebastião's uncle), was the only legal heir to the throne. It was the period known as the Iberian Union (1580–1640), marked by the decline of the Portuguese overseas empire, as it was attacked around the world by the many enemies of Spain, especially Holland. In 1640, a national revolt enthroned the Duke of Bragança, Dom João IV, reestablishing Portuguese independence, but in a situation of extreme military and economic fragility.[34]

It was a moment of harsh economic crisis in the Portuguese world. The loss of many overseas possessions drastically diminished the revenues of the Crown. The latter also was shaken by the costs of the wars of independence from Spain and various other powerful European conflicts, like with the Dutch West Indies Company in northeast Brazil. Problems like these led to the imposition of more taxes. One of the main taxes was upon Portuguese wine, the collection rights of which were farmed out to individuals, powerful men who were prejudiced against the sale of local beverages like garapa and sugarcane aguardente. Besides, the taxes on wine sustained the military bodies of the colony, a large part of which, especially in the sugar-producing region, was under the control of the Dutch West Indies Company, which excessively increased the expenses for the troops.[35]

These interests united to prompt the Crown and its colonial representatives to establish a series of prohibitions against honey-wine and aguardente. In 1649 a monopolistic business was created, the Companhia Geral de Comércio do Brasil (General Trade Company of Brazil), which exclusively held the right in the colony to supply the principal basic foodstuffs: wine, wheat flour, olive oil, and codfish.[36] However, the company never was capable of supplying Brazil with a sufficient quantity of wine at a price that was compatible with the income of the colony's inhabitants. Moreover, the taste of slaves and poor free men for sugarcane aguardente, and the personal interest of its producers, proved to be more powerful than any attempt at prohibition.

On the other hand, the increase in sugar production in the Caribbean lowered the price of the product on a global scale, which strongly damaged the interests of the Brazilian producers. In this context, producing aguardente represented an invaluable source of revenue for the sugar mill owners, especially in those areas, like Rio de Janeiro, where the sugar produced was of inferior quality and of little value commercially.[37] For this reason, the governor of Rio de Janeiro, Luís de Almeida Portugal (1652–1655), refused to prohibit aguardente, saying that this would ruin the local producers. For Governor Portugal, it was "the lack of money" that impeded the sale of Portuguese wine, and not the rivalry with sugarcane aguardente. He said, also, against the argument that aguardente caused deaths among the colonists, that "which white person that dies drinking, does not die from drinking wine in excess?"[38] In other words, any beverage could be harmful, even a "sophisticated" one like wine, if consumed in large measures.

Little by little, the municipal councils gave up trying to impede the expansion of the consumption of aguardente, establishing their own local taxes on the beverage. In the case of Salvador, its council, in 1654, declared itself incapable of paying the soldiers with the revenue from wine taxes, because the Companhia Geral de Comércio do Brasil did not succeed in supplying the consumption needs of the population. For the councilmen, the prohibition was damaging because "there were many stills that distilled aguardente and many houses selling cachaça," which could be taxed, and which effectively happened.[39]

As these types of occurrences happened throughout the colony, King Afonso VI, in 1661, finally lifted the general prohibition, as it had become useless and counterproductive.[40] Local restrictions, which were also not very effective, continued until the end of the colonial period, but this time to impede the irregular fabrication of aguardente, preserving the profits for the tax collectors, or in order to prevent the production of distilled beverages being seen as more important than foodstuffs. As colonization advanced into the interior of Brazil, especially in the gold-mining regions of Minas Gerais, Goiás, and Mato Grosso, the local councils sought to control the production and consumption of aguardente, but the repetition of these measures reveals the impossibility of effectively attaining this control.[41] Therefore, the use of aguardente became more common, until it developed into a necessity.

The popular character of the drink was reflected in the use of the word *jeribita* (or *geribita*) to designate it. The term *jeribita* was used until the middle of the eighteenth century, when it was replaced by the current word, *cachaça*.[42] The word *jeribita* very probably originated from the Tupi word *jeribá*, a species of palm tree. These indigenous people customarily made fermented beverages from the sap of various types of palm trees.[43] It is possible that a type of semantic "contamination" occurred in relation to sugarcane aguardente,[44] which reveals the identification of the natives with the distilled items of the Europeans, and also the roots of the construction of the figures of the "drunken Indian," and the cachaceiro, so typical of Brazil and other colonial contexts.[45]

It would be a mistake, however, to imagine that aguardente was promoted only by the lower classes, the poor, and slaves. It is clear that the consumption of the beverage provoked concern among the colonial authorities, especially when there were possible tumults that affected the control of the slave population. At any rate, it was impossible to prohibit it among the African slaves, even because, for many *fazendeiros* (large estate owners) and royal bureaucrats, cachaça was an essential way to maintain the happiness and health of the slaves. In 1780, for example, the governor of Minas Gerais, Rodrigo José de Meneses, stood up for the removal of any restriction against aguardente, especially because of the slaves, for whom aguardente was a "drink of basic foodstuffs," and that "with this help, they [are able to] bear with such a great labor, live healthier, and a longer time."[46]

The importance of aguardente extended well beyond the boundaries of Portuguese America. Brazilian cachaça totally dominated slave trafficking between Brazil and Africa, dislodging Portuguese wine and aguardente and rendering Brazilian merchants the masters of trafficking in Western Africa, notably in the Congo and Angola.[47] The Portuguese Crown tried to outlaw the sale of cachaça in Africa, with the objective of protecting its own producers and merchants of wine, aguardente, and slaves. Such measures never succeeded, as the slave markets in the interior of Africa demanded jeribita. In 1695, the prohibition was extinct, and aguardente, especially from Rio de Janeiro, together with tobacco from Bahia, became the principal means of obtaining slaves for Brazil.[48] In this way, aguardente transformed into a central factor in the creation of a commercial network between Portuguese America and Africa. It created a class of merchants based in Brazil that came to control the trade with Africa, practically excluding the Portuguese merchants. The realities of this trade also oppose the traditional definitions of Atlantic commerce in terms of a "Triangle Trade."[49]

Thanks to studies about slave trafficking in Africa, as well as culture and daily life of Afro-Brazilians,[50] cachaça is beginning to emerge from the historiographical shadows. In contrast, the relationship between distilled beverages and indigenous peoples remains practically unexplored, even though it is a theme so well studied in other societies and colonial contexts.[51] Although the impact of distilled beverages on natives certainly has been enormous and destructive, it is important to perceive the differences between what occurred in Brazil and in other regions that suffered from the impact of European colonization. In contrast with what happened in present-day Canada, the United States, and Australia, where the indigenous people did not know alcoholic beverages, the indios of Brazil made an infinite number of fermented drinks, and drunkenness was a fundamental part of their ritual life.

The Tupinambá, for example, who inhabited the Brazilian coastline, and who were the first to enter into contact with European colonization, possessed a profound knowledge about the techniques of fermentation and of production of alcoholic beverages, made from manioc, corn, and many types of fruits and saps of vegetables. Called *cauim* (a Portuguese word, originating from the Tupi *ca'o-y*, or "drunken water"), these concoctions were not consumed daily but, rather, in festive drinking sessions called *cauinagens*. These events brought together members of various villages to celebrate marriages and rites of passage, mourn the dead, decide about wars, or receive illustrious visitors. Moreover, the cauinagens were the setting for the principal ritual of Tupinambá society: sacrificing and devouring captured enemies. These cannibalistic feasts took place only after the production of great quantities of cauim, which could take many days or even months. On the day of the ritual itself, all of those present, including the prisoner, had to drink all of the available cauim, and only after this was the execution carried out.[52]

The cauinagens were one of the principal targets of the colonial authorities' and missionaries' repressive and catechistic action. The Crown as well as the colonists saw the cauinagens as abominable or dangerous customs, like cannibalism and the constant wars against other tribes and the Europeans themselves. The Jesuits strongly fought these celebrations and the consumption of the traditional fermented beverages that sustained them with varying degrees of success. The missionaries not only tried to co-opt women, who produced the drinks and who were also the most disposed to accept the Christian teachings, making them break the *igaçabas* (large jugs destined for fermentation), but also got them to strongly indoctrinate their children against ritual drunkenness.[53]

It is possible that the indios not only were consumers but also participated actively in the invention of cachaça itself. The natives, and their mestizo descendants, formed an important portion of society in those regions most linked to the commercial production of sugar, and in which cachaça was made for the first time. Moreover, we know that the Amerindians were the first workers on the sugar mills, before African slaves became more common in the second half of the sixteenth century.[54] These natives were great specialists in the art of fermentation and might have been the first to point out the value of the cane juice as the base for the concoction of alcoholic beverages. The sugar mill owner Ambrósio Fernandes Brandão pointed out that the indigenous, in their "drunken binges," which were "their most ordinary custom," prepared "many wines that they make from sugarcane which they get from the sugarmills."[55]

The successful struggle of the missionaries against the cauinagens left a lacuna that was rapidly filled by the new distilled beverage. In 1653, Antônio Vieira, one of the most important Jesuit missionaries of Brazil, and his peers, traveling along the banks of the Tocantins River, in the center-west of the colony, observed the impact of cachaça on the Amerindians, upon finding some natives who were in the process of being fought and enslaved by the Luso-Brazilian colonists. The Jesuit described one of the most common practices of the colonizers, before engaging in direct war, which was trying to attract the indios with presents. Since the mid-seventeenth century, cachaça transformed from being part of these presents into an excellent means of facilitating contact with the natives. When the indigenous people arrived, said Vieira, "we honored them and toasted," and then they were given cachaça, "the sugarcane wine, which is used here," and with which the natives were unfamiliar. According to the Jesuit, the indios found aguardente "to be strange" but affirmed, "with a good deal of grace," that they would get used to it.[56] It is important to note that the offering of cachaça on the part of the missionaries was not an isolated incident and was not exclusive to relations with the indigenous people. In Africa, missionaries always gave Brazilian cachaça to the natives to facilitate the process of conversion.[57]

The strong effect of distilled drinks, and the ease with which one can get drunk in drinking them, caused a great impact on indigenous societies. Happily, we have access to a firsthand account about this impact, left by the French Franciscan Yves d'Evreux, who presided in Brazil between 1612 and 1615, during the French occupation of Maranhão. Although he does not refer to cachaça, but French *eaux-de-vie* (wine aguardente), this passage shows us how the natives reacted to *cauim-tata* ("fire cauim"), the name given to all distilled drinks. After a long conversation, an important Tupinambá warrior asked the Father for a "good French wine" or a "cauim that burns"—that is, aguardente. The Amerindian had already experienced the distilled liquor, considering the drink to be "very good and very strong." Rubbing his stomach, he said that he still felt the heat of the eaux-de-vie, saying, "Oh! How good, very good, is the *vinho de fogo* (fire wine)." He also said to him that the cauim-tata was not similar to what they had drunk formerly and that it clouded the head of those who consumed it abundantly.[58]

Upon being exposed to aguardente, the natives began to demand it in their relationships with the Luso-Brazilians, as the Jesuit João Daniel observed. He lived in the Amazon rainforest between 1741 and 1757 and wrote a long description of the state of Portuguese colonization in that region. According to Daniel, the missionaries themselves largely used presents of aguardente in their contacts with the indios, with the object of attracting their friendship and good will. It was such a successful practice that the already "pacified" natives protested against the Fathers for the lack of cachaça in the villages run by the Jesuits.[59]

In order to guarantee the supply to the village Amerindians, and in order to participate in a clearly expanding market, the Society of Jesus created their own aguardente factories, destined for the consumption of the city and village populations.[60] Producing and distributing cachaça were also ways to avoid the colonists supplying the natives' demand, which threatened the missionaries' control of the villages. The Jesuits constantly solicited the colonial authorities to halt this practice, but generally without success.[61] In 1679, for example, Governor-General Roque da Costa Barreto prohibited the sale of aguardente in the villages controlled by the Jesuits, because this practice caused, "among them [the indios], deaths and other evils that are not of less importance." The colonists looked to attract through the use of cachaça, the valuable village natives, who had already been "pacified" by the missionaries, for the purpose of their labor.[62]

The problem of aguardente was a source of permanent conflict between the missionaries and colonists. In 1683, Father João Duarte do Sacramento, an Oratorian missionary in the captaincy (administrative division) of Ceará, solicited the Overseas Council, the principal organ leading the colonization of Brazil, that soldiers and merchants be prohibited from negotiating with the natives using wine or aguardente. He argued that cachaça provoked "great offenses to God as well as ruins," among them the fact that the soldiers attracted indigenous women to their quarters with the incentive of the beverage. The Father related to the council that upon complaining about these practices, the soldiers "put rifles to their chests putting themselves at risk of being made martyrs at the hands of the Catholics."[63]

Cachaça remained an important instrument of interaction between the Amerindians and colonizers for all of the colonial period, especially where a first contact was concerned. Henrique João Wilkens, a soldier who wrote various accounts about the natives of the Amazon, knew much about this when, in 1781, he used aguardente to reinforce relationships with the Cuaruna in the Amazon jungle. Frequently, the indios appeared, at night, in the camps of the travelers, which always provoked tensions. In this case, though, the indigenous people demonstrated themselves to be friendly, and requested cachaça: "The two visiting Indios were leaving . . . and I gave them a bottle of aguardente that their Chief had sent them to request from me."[64]

In 1810, traveling along the Paraná River, the treasurer of the see of São Paulo, João Ferreira de Oliveira Bueno, encountered a group of Caiapós, Amerindians unanimously recognized as ferocious and unapproachable. In spite of this, the contact, lubricated by aguardente, was surprisingly friendly. Bueno requested that the chiefs of the group come to a meeting, afterward giving them knives and food. The following day, the chiefs came, accompanied by a large number of men, women, and children. Upon distributing new presents, Bueno invited the chiefs to eat at his table. The natives "uninhibitedly made use of the forks, spoons, and knives, drinking with satisfaction, and even making toasts to me." At their departure, Bueno "gave them some bottles of aguardente and spirits," with which the indios left, saying that Bueno was "a very good white (man)."[65]

The natives who were approached were not always satisfied with the new beverage. Captain-General João da Silva Santos could verify this upon traveling in remote areas of the captaincy of Porto Seguro in 1804. Having found "wild" indios and deciding to not confront them, Santos sought to use the experience of previous explorers with presents and aguardente. He gave them flour and fresh fish, "and a knife to each one, with which they became very happy." But the Amerindians were not pleased with the cachaça, "the first sticking his finger in the cup, and putting it on his tongue, he did not like it, and rejected it, and the others did the same."[66]

Although it is impossible to generalize, it is a fact that the introduction of the distilled beverages caused a series of social problems for the indigenous peoples, repeating a process that occurred with many other natives affected by colonial expansion. It ought to be noted, though, that the introduction of aguardente to the Amerindians represented, many times, a direct threat to the interests of the colonial powers. In the war between the Dutch and the Luso-Brazilians in the northeast of Brazil (1630–1654), the military force of indios was fully utilized by both the contenders. But drunkenness provoked by the distilled beverages at times disturbed military actions. According to Johannes Listry, an official of the Dutch West Indies Company, the native chief allied with the Dutch, Pedro Poti, was a "habitual drunk, because rarely or never was he sober," which influenced his fighting abilities.[67] Felipe Camarão, a major indigenous chief who defended the Portuguese side, also was an adherent to ethylic excesses. According to an anonymous Portuguese account, Camarão did not participate in an important battle (Porto Calvo, in 1637) because he was drunk. His intoxication then limited the participation of his peers in the combat, a decisive factor in the Portuguese defeat: "Camarão did not do anything that day other than get drunk with the aguardente they gave him, he did not do a thing, and with that none of his people did anything."[68]

It is not surprising, therefore, that the main judicial document destined to regulate interactions with Amerindians during the colonial period, the *Directório que se deve observar nas povoações dos índios do Pará e Maranhão* [*Directorate That Ought to Be Observed in the Indio Villages of Pará and Maranhão*] (1757), dedicated special attention to the control of aguardente among the natives. Possessing a markedly "civilizing" nature, the *Directório* looked to transform the indigenous Brazilians into something like Iberian peasants, devoted to agriculture and directed by the Christian religion. It sought to restrain the "vices and customs" that supposedly impeded the civilization of the indios, especially drunkenness, "a vice so dominant and universal among them."[69] In order to attain this objective, the *Directório* totally forbade the "unjust and harmful trade of aguardente," instituting serious penalties "to all of those who are used to introducing this incredibly pernicious commodity in the villages."[70]

This legislation has two interesting aspects. On the one hand, it reveals the disinterest of the Crown for the living conditions of the indios, as it justifies the prohibition of cachaça only because it inconveniences their "civilizing" efforts. On the other hand, it also points toward the contradictions among the desires of the Portuguese bureaucrats and jurists and the realities of colonial life. The officials created by the *Directório* to oversee the villages, the Diretores de Índios, facilitated as well as controlled the trade of aguardente with the natives.[71]

The use, or abuse, of aguardente was crucial in the construction of the figure of the "drunken Indian," which added to the figures of "weak" and "fainthearted" indio[72] in the construction of a paradigm of racial inferiority. The act of drinking, understood not as an illness but as immorality or a sign of weakness, became a fundamental part of the discourse and images constructed by the Europeans regarding the Amerindians. One of the consequences of the conquest of the native peoples of the Americas was the emergence of a colonial narrative, which contributed to the creation of a series of stereotypical categories that placed the colonizers and the conquered peoples in two opposite poles, markedly hierarchical: civilized/savage, clean/impure, and temperate/intemperate, among others.[73] In this sense, the drunkenness associated with the indigenous, especially that caused by distilled sugarcane, was an essential element in the formation of this colonial narrative. The French naturalist Charles-Marie de La Condamine, who descended the Amazon River in 1743, defined the Amerindians by their "insensitivity," "apathy," and "stupidity." These natives, he said, are "incapable of precaution and reflection," being "lily-livered and cowardly to the extreme, if drunkenness does not make them bolder."[74]

The relationship between the indigenous people and drunkenness was a constant topic during the colonial period. Manuel Aires de Casal, a cleric, geographer, and historian who wrote one of the first books published in Brazil, insisted on placing drunkenness as one of the principal characteristics of the natives: "Inconstant, distrustful, and enthusiasts of all kinds of strong liquor, which they drink without measure, and with which they usually are furious and frightening while they remain intoxicated."[75] In a similar manner, the German naturalists Johann von Spix and Carl von Martius, who explored the Brazilian forests at the beginning of the nineteenth century, affirmed that the indios only abandoned their "natural" coldness and idleness in order to dedicate themselves to alcohol, "in regard to drinking, he is fond of his vinhaça or cachaça, when he can get it."[76]

At the end of the colonial period, cachaça had become the national beverage par excellence, since it was consumed by the poorest strata of society and by the ethnic groups most affected by the colonial experience. However, cachaça hardly was consumed by the members of the middle and elite social classes, who mostly drank European wine or port. The line that separated the *homens bons* (literally "good men," as the colonial elite called themselves) from the *cabras* (a racially mixed category) and *negros* overlapped with the line that separated cachaça drinkers from those who appreciated European beverages. Foreign travelers in Brazil at the end of the eighteenth century and the beginning of the nineteenth century are practically unanimous in declaring that Brazilians (understood here as free men and descendants of Europeans) were very moderate,[77] which contrasted with the opinion that the natives, black slaves, and the poor in general were frequently drunk from cachaça.[78]

This social differentiation, however, was not perceived, or forged, only by foreigners, but was also the basis from which the poorer strata constructed their own identity. *Quadras* (popular poems) frequently refer to cachaça as a social and ethnic marker, always relating the consumption of the drink to the social division between the "whites" and the educated, and the mulatos, caboclos, and cabras, common terms for the lower-class mestizos. In these quadras, the cabras are seen as great drinkers, even more than the black slaves: "The mulatto does not let go of the knife / nor the white, 'wisdom' / the cabra does not leave cachaça / nor the black, witchcraft." This poem reveals well the central stereotypes of colonial Brazil: the aggressiveness of mulatos, the cunning and treachery of the European, the "witchcraft" or religions of the Afro-Brazilians, and the identification of the majority of the poor, or cabras, with drunkenness and cachaça.

However, slaves also were seen as great drinkers, which is revealed in innumerable quadras dedicated to them: "Caiana [a town in the state of Minas Gerais] sugarcane juice put through our mill / it may be prejudicial / but I drink it all week long." One of the most interesting poems is one that shows Saint Benedict as a drinker of garapa. Benedict, "the Moor" or "the Black," was a Sicilian descendant of slaves and always was represented by black skin. His cult was very popular in colonial Brazil, especially among slaves. "My Saint Benedict / is saint of the black / he drinks garapa / he *ronca* [coughs] in the chest."[79]

The popular character of cachaça ended up influencing the members of the elite that rebelled against the colonial metropole in the first years of the nineteenth century. These men, who included many estate owners, military officers, and priests, looked to associate themselves with symbols that differentiated them from the Portuguese. Consumption of the national distilled beveraged served this objective well. An example of the change in the appreciation for cachaça was given by the participants in the Pernambucan Insurrection of 1817, one of the main revolts against colonial domination in Brazil. In a meeting, upon raising toasts to "revolution," one of the leaders of the insurrection refused to consume port and suggested the use of cachaça, obtaining enthusiastic support.[80]

In this way, the beverage that began as a tool of colonial exploration, a means of slave trading, a form of dominating the indigenous peoples, and a symbol of social and cultural division between the colonial elite and their subjugated peoples, became a revolutionary symbol of that very same elite. The drink that had taken its name from the impure foams made from the boiling of sugarcane, which was given to animals and slaves, came to be used in the parlor toasts of intellectuals and estate owners who looked to build a new political identity. They did this not around the drink of the colonizer but around one now qualified as "patrician," "patriotic," and "glorious."

The new condition of cachaça did not transform it into an item of habitual consumption of the elite, who continued to be faithful in their daily use of wine and port. Rather, it became a symbol in a moment when, at least in the socially dominant discourse, the term *Brazilians* seemed, for the first time, to unify in spite of enormous social differences. As always, the popular poems offer us a record of this change, indicating cachaça to be a marker of differentiation between the new country and the ex-metropole: "May the irrational masses scoff / at those who wore their lives down getting drunk, laughing at the world, / with a swig of the *Brasileira* [the Brazilian cachaça]!"[81]

Notes

1. José C. Curto, *Álcool e Escravos: O comércio luso-brasileiro de álcool em Mpinda, Luanda e Benguela durante o tráfico atlântico de escravos (c. 1480–1830) e seu impacto nas sociedades da África Central Ocidental* (Lisboa: Vulgata, 2002); Luiz Felipe de Alencastro, *O Trato dos Viventes: Formação do Brasil no Atlântico Sul—Séculos XVI e XVII* (São Paulo: Compahnia das Letras, 2000), 307–25.

2. John Hemming, *Red Gold: The Conquest of Brazilian Indians* (Chatham, Canada: Papermac, 1995), 6; João Azevedo Fernandes, "Cauinagens e bebedeiras: os índios e o álcool na história do Brasil," *Revista Anthropológicas* 13, no. 2 (2002), 39–59.

3. Roberto C. Simonsen, *História Econômica do Brasil, 1500–1820* (Brasília: Senado Federal, 2005 [1937]), 465–540; Luciano Rodrigues Figueiredo and Renato Pinto Venâncio, "Águas Ardentes: o nascimento da cachaça," in *Cachaça: alquimia brasileira*, ed. Luciano Figueiredo, Heloisa Faria, et al. (Rio de Janeiro: Design, 2005), 12–57.

4. João Azevedo Fernandes, "Cachaça, a rainha do Sul," *Revista Atlântica de Cultura Ibero-Americana* 2 (2005), 84–87. *Negro* was the term used in the colonial period to refer to African slaves. *Caboco* (or *caboclo*) was a word used to identify acculturated natives, or mixtures of Europeans and indigenous people, while *mulatto* designated the mixture of Europeans and Africans (blacks)—the two categories formed the major part of the free, poor population.

5. Soju (literally "burned water") is a distilled beverage made from various types of grain, especially rice. Henrique Carneiro, *Pequena Enciclopédia da História das Drogas e Bebidas* (Rio de Janeiro: Campus/Elsevier, 2005), 63.

6. Only 1 percent of the 1.5 billion liters produced annually is exported, which makes its consumption almost exclusively by Brazilians themselves. Adriana Renata Verdi, "Dinâmicas e Perspectivas do Mercado de Cachaça," *Informações Econômicas* 36, no. 2 (2006), 93.

7. Brian Morgan, "Cachaça From Brazil and Protected Geographic Indication," *TED Case Studies* 14, no. 2 (2004), http://www1.american.edu/TED/cachaca.htm.

8. Daniel Cardoso et al., "Comparison Between Cachaça and Rum Using Pattern Recognition Methods," *Journal of Agricultural and Food Chemistry* 52 (2004), 3429.

9. Francisco Aquino et al., "Amino Acids Profile of Sugar Cane Spirit (Cachaça), Rum, and Whisky," *Food Chemistry* 108 (2008), 784–93. In the colonial period, sugarcane juice, like molasses, was distilled. André João Antonil, *Cultura e Opulência do Brasil* (São Paulo: Companhia Editora Nacional, 1967 [1711]), 216.

10. Alencastro, *O Trato dos Viventes*, 310.

11. David T. Courtwright, *Forces of Habit: Drugs and the Making of the Modern World* (Cambridge, MA: Harvard University Press, 2001), 9–30; Peter C. Mancall, *Deadly Medicine: Indians and Alcohol in Early America* (Ithaca, NY: Cornell University Press, 1995); Sherry Saggers and Dennis Gray, *Dealing with Alcohol: Indigenous Usage in Australia, New Zealand and Canada* (Cambridge, MA: Cambridge University Press, 1998), 41–45; Michael Dietler, "Alcohol: Anthropological/Archaeological Perspectives," *Annual Review of Anthropology* 35 (2006), 237–40; Frederick H. Smith, *Caribbean Rum: A Social and Economic History* (Gainesville: University Press of Florida, 2008), 6–40.

12. Luís da Câmara Cascudo, *Prelúdio da Cachaça: etnologia, história e sociologia da aguardente no Brasil* (Belo Horizonte, Brasil: Itatiaia, 1986 [1968]).

13. Curto, *Álcool e Escravos*. Obviously, we cannot forget Joseph C. Miller's classic *Way of Death: Merchant Capitalism and the Angolan Slave Trade, 1730–1830* (Madison: University of Wisconsin Press, 1988), which also provides a lot of information about the role of cachaça (which he calls "Brazilian rum") in the African trafficking of slaves.

14. Figueiredo and Venâncio, "Águas Ardentes," 15.

15. "Inventário de Maria Jorge" (1611), in [Arquivo do Estado de São Paulo], *Inventários e testamentos*, vol. 3, *1603–1648* (São Paulo: Publicação Oficial do Arquivo do Estado de São Paulo, 1920), 208.

16. François Pyrard de Laval, *Viagem de Francisco Pyrard, de Laval: contendo a noticia de sua navegação às Indias Orientaes, ilhas de Maldiva, Maluco, e ao Brazil, e os differentes casos, que lhe aconteceram na mesma viagem nos dez annos que andou nestes paizes: (1601 a 1611) com a descripção exacta dos costumes, leis, usos, policia, e governo: do trato e commercio, que nelles há; dos animaes, arvores, fructas, e outras singularidades, que alli se encontram,* vol. 2 (Nova Goa: Imprensa Nacional, 1862), 273; Câmara Cascudo, *Prelúdio da Cachaça,* 15.

17. Leila M. Algranti, "Aguardente de cana e outras aguardentes: por uma história da produção e do consumo de licores na América portuguesa," in *Álcool e drogas na história do Brasil,* ed. Renato P. Venâncio and Henrique Carneiro (São Paulo/Belo Horizonte: Alameda/ Editora Pontifícia Universidade Católica de Minas Gerais, 2005), 73.

18. Francisco Rodrigues do Prado, "Historia dos Indios Cavalleiros ou da Nação Guaycuru," *Revista do Instituto Historico e Geographico do Brazil* 1, no. 1 (1839 [1793]), 32.

19. Antonil, *Cultura e opulência do Brasil,* 201–2.

20. Ibid., 202.

21. Antônio Houaiss, Mauro Villar, and Francisco Manuel de Mello Franco, eds. "Garapa," in *Dicionário Houaiss da Língua Portuguesa,* CD-ROM (Rio de Janeiro: Editora Objetiva, 2009).

22. Smith, *Caribbean Rum,* 11–12.

23. Antonil, *Cultura e opulência do Brasil,* 203.

24. Ambrósio Fernandes Brandão, *Diálogos das Grandezas do Brasil* (Recife: Fundação Joaquim Nabuco/Editora Massangana, 1997 [1930]), 147.

25. João Fernandes Vieira, "Regimento que há de guardar o Feitor-mor de engenho para fazer bem sua obrigação" (1663), in *Fontes para a História do Brasil Holandês,* vol. 1, *A Economia Açucareira,* ed. José Antônio Gonsalves de Mello (Recife: Compahnia Editora de Pernambuco, 2004), 258.

26. Vicente do Salvador, *História do Brasil, 1500–1627* (São Paulo/Brasília: Melhoramentos/ Instituto Nacional do Livro, 1975 [1627]), 83.

27. Johan Nieuhof, *Memorável Viagem Marítima e Terrestre ao Brasil* (Belo Horizonte/São Paulo: Itatiaia/Editora da Universidade de São Paulo [hereafter Edusp], 1981 [1682]), 341.

28. "Relatório sobre o Estado das Capitanias conquistadas no Brasil, apresentado pelo Senhor Adriaen van der Dussen ao Conselho dos XIX na Câmara de Amsterdã, em 4 de abril de 1640," in *Fontes para a História do Brasil Holandês,* vol. 1, 210.

29. Smith, *Caribbean Rum,* 12.

30. "Registo de uma Provisão do Governador Pedro da Silva sobre se não fazer aguardente (12 de outubro de 1636)," in *Documentos Históricos da Biblioteca Nacional,* vol. 16, *Patentes, Provisões e Alvarás, 1631–1637* (Rio de Janeiro: Biblioteca Nacional, 1930), 396–99.

31. Carlos Eduardo S. Gravatá, *Almanaque da Cachaça* (Belo Horizonte: Formato, 1990), 15–16; See Câmara Cascudo, *Prelúdio da Cachaça,* 18.

32. "Registo de uma Provisão do Governador Pedro da Silva."

33. "Requerimento que fizerão os misteres Antonio da Fonsequa e Domingos Gonçalvez juiz do povo Manoel Gonçalvez Camanho aos officiaes da Camera para se auer de estinguir a agoardente, e Cachassa pellas rezoens abaixo nomeadas," 8 de agosto de

1646, in *Documentos Históricos do Arquivo Municipal*, vol. 2, *Atas da Câmara, 1641–1649* (Salvador: Prefeitura do Município de Salvador, 1949), 313. On the same problem of terminology for Caribbean rum, see Smith, *Caribbean Rum*, 13.

34. Wilma Peres Costa, "Do domínio à nação: os impasses da fiscalidade no processo de independência," in *Brasil: Formação do Estado e da Nação*, ed. István Jancsó (São Paulo: Editora Humanismo, Ciência e Tecnologia [hereafter Hucitec]/Editora Unijuí/Fundação de Amparo à Pesquisa do Estado de São Paulo [hereafter FAPESP], 2003), 149–55.

35. Thales de Azevedo, *Povoamento da Cidade do Salvador* (Salvador: Itapuã, 1969 [1949]), 300–17.

36. Frédéric Mauro, *Portugal, o Brasil e o Atlântico, 1570–1670*, vol. 2 (Lisboa: Editorial Estampa, 1988), 93. See Simonsen, *História Econômica do Brasil*, 453–59; Alencastro, *O Trato dos Viventes*, 315; Figueiredo and Venâncio, "Águas Ardentes," 17–20.

37. Stuart B. Schwartz, *Segredos Internos: Engenhos e escravos na sociedade colonial, 1550–1835* (São Paulo: Compahnia das Letras, 1988), 112–3; Alencastro, *O Trato dos Viventes*, 310.

38. Figueiredo and Venâncio, "Águas Ardentes," 19–20; Alencastro, *O Trato dos Viventes*, 315. The interest of the aguardente producers in Rio de Janeiro, among other reasons, incited the region to rebel against the prohibitions in the 1660 Revolta da Cachaça (Revolt of Cachaça). Luciano Figueiredo, *Rebeliões no Brasil Colônia* (Rio de Janeiro: Jorge Zahar Editor, 2005), 52–54; Alencastro, *O Trato dos Viventes*, 314–17.

39. "Termo da resolusão do povo en que determinarão se lancaçe na cachaça e agoardente tributo para o sustento da enfantaria (12 de novembro de 1654)," in *Documentos Históricos do Arquivo Municipal*, vol. 3, *Atas da Câmara, 1649–1659* (Salvador: Prefeitura do Município de Salvador, 1949), 275–78.

40. Câmara Cascudo, *Prelúdio da Cachaça*, 25.

41. "Registro de um bando sobre o não haver engenhocas de aguardente, e canaviais nas minas dos Guayaz (22 de agosto de 1732)," in *Documentos Interessantes para a História e Costumes de São Paulo*, vol. 22 (São Paulo: Typographia da Companhia Industrial de São Paulo, 1896), 4–5; "Parecer enviado aos oficiais da Câmara de Vila Rica sobre a ereção de engenhos de açúcar na Capitania de Minas, onde se fabrica a aguardente proibida (6 de abril de 1755)," in Gravatá, *Almanaque da Cachaça*, 46–47, among many other examples.

42. Figueiredo and Venâncio, "Águas Ardentes," 18.

43. João Azevedo Fernandes, *Selvagens Bebedeiras: Álcool, Embriaguez e Contatos Culturais no Brasil Colonial (Séculos XVI–XVII)* (São Paulo: Alameda, 2011), 55–58.

44. Alencastro, *O Trato dos Viventes*, 313.

45. Gilbert Quintero, "Making the Indian: Colonial Knowledge, Alcohol, and Native Americans," *American Indian Culture and Research Journal* 25 (2001), 57–71; Fernandes, *Selvagens Bebedeiras*, 33–34.

46. Cited by Virginia Valadares, "O consumo de aguardente em Minas Gerais no final do século XVIII: uma visão entre os poderes metropolitano e colonial," in Venâncio and Carneiro, *Álcool e drogas na história do Brasil*, 133–34.

47. On this topic, besides the already-cited works of J. Curto and L. F. de Alencastro, other works are Alberto da Costa e Silva, *A Manilha e o Libambo: A África e a es-*

cravidão de 1500 a 1700 (Rio de Janeiro: Nova Fronteira-Fundação Biblioteca Nacional, 2002), 865; Roquinaldo Ferreira, "Dinâmica do comércio intracolonial: Geribitas, panos asiáticos e guerra no tráfico angolano de escravos (século XVIII)," in O Antigo Regime nos Trópicos: A Dinâmica Imperial Portuguesa, ed. João Fragoso, Maria F. B. Bicalho, and Maria de Fátima S. Gouvêa (Rio de Janeiro: Civilização Brasileira, 2001), 339–78; and Jaime Rodrigues, De Costa a Costa: Escravos, marinheiros e intermediários do tráfico negreiro de Angola ao Rio de Janeiro (1780–1860) (São Paulo: Companhia das Letras, 2005).

48. Curto, Álcool e Escravos, 123–200; see also Pierre Verger, Fluxo e refluxo do tráfico de escravos entre o golfo do Benin e a Bahia de Todos os Santos do século XVII a XIX (São Paulo: Corrupio, 1987).

49. Alencastro, O Trato dos Viventes, 116.

50. For example, Marina de Mello e Souza, Reis Negros no Brasil Escravista: História da Festa de Coroação de Rei Congo (Belo Horizonte: Editora Universidade Federal de Minas Gerais, 2002).

51. For example, among many others, Mancall, Deadly Medicine; Saggers and Gray, Dealing with Alcohol; and William B. Taylor, Drinking, Homicide, and Rebellion in Colonial Mexican Villages (Stanford, CA: Stanford University Press, 1979).

52. João Azevedo Fernandes, De Cunhã a Mameluca: A Mulher Tupinambá e o Nascimento do Brasil (João Pessoa, Brasil: Editora Universidade Federal da Paraíba [hereafter UFPB], 2003), 99–198.

53. João Azevedo Fernandes, "Feast and Sin: Catholic Missionaries and Native Celebrations in Early Colonial Brazil," Social History of Alcohol and Drugs 23, no. 2 (2009), 111–27; Ronald Raminelli, "Da etiqueta canibal: beber antes de comer," in Venâncio and Carneiro, Álcool e drogas na história do Brasil, 29–46. The majority of the current indigenous peoples in Brazil still possess their own native drinks, which are produced, many times, with the same techniques used by the Tupinambá. On the role of alcoholic beverages in contemporary native peoples, see, among many others, Tânia Stolze Lima, Um peixe olhou para mim: O povo Yudjá e a perspectiva (São Paulo/Rio de Janeiro: Editora Universidade Estadual Paulista, Instituto Socioambiental, Núcleo de Transformações Indígenas, 2005); Márnio Teixeira-Pinto, Ieipari: Sacrifício e Vida Social entre os índios Arara (Caribe) (São Paulo: Hucitec/Associação Nacional de Pós-Graduação e Pesquisa em Ciências Sociais/Editora Universidade Federal do Paraná, 1997); Marco Antônio Gonçalves, O Mundo Inacabado: Ação e Criação em uma Cosmologia Amazônica. Etnografia Pirahã (Rio de Janeiro: Editora Universidade Federal do Rio de Janeiro, 2001); Susana de Matos Viegas, Terra Calada: Os Tupinambá na Mata Atlântica do Sul da Bahia (Rio de Janeiro/Lisboa: 7Letras/Almedina, 2007).

54. Schwartz, Segredos Internos, 40–73.

55. Brandão, Diálogos das Grandezas do Brasil, 233.

56. "Carta ao padre provincial do Brasil (1654)," in Antônio Vieira, Cartas do Brasil, 1626–1697 — Estado do Brasil e Estado do Maranhão e Grã Pará (São Paulo: Hedra, 2003), 151.

57. Curto, Álcool e Escravos, 103–4.

58. Yves d'Evreux, Viagem ao norte do Brasil feita nos anos de 1613 a 1614 (São Paulo: Siciliano, 2002 [1864]), 362–63. The Dutch also furnished the indios with their aguardente, obtaining similar results: "These barbarians really enjoy our alcoholic beverages which they give the name of cauitata and when it is given to them, they become

enormously drunk." Jorge Marcgrave, *História Natural do Brasil* (São Paulo: Imprensa Oficial, 1942 [1648]), 274.

59. João Daniel, *Tesouro Descoberto no Máximo Rio Amazonas*, vol. 2 (Rio de Janeiro: Contraponto, 2004 [1820]), 320.

60. Ibid., 380, 443.

61. "Ordem para os Juizes dos Ilhéos não consentirem se venda aguardente aos Indios da administração dos Padres da Companhia (20 de agosto de 1692)," in *Documentos Históricos da Biblioteca Nacional*, vol. 32, *Provisões, Patentes, Alvarás, Mandados, 1651–1693* (Rio de Janeiro: Biblioteca Nacional, 1936), 299; in the same volume "Portaria para se tomarem por perdidas as aguardentes que se venderem aos Indios da Aldeia do Espirito Santo (7 de setembro de 1691)," 302–3. These same measures were repeated during the following century, showing that the repression was ineffective: "Portaria para não se vender aguardente aos indios que administra o Padre José de Araujo, da Companhia de Jesus (1° de março de 1714)," in *Documentos Históricos da Biblioteca Nacional*, vol. 53, *Provisões, 1717–1718 — Portarias, 1711–1715* (Rio de Janeiro: Biblioteca Nacional, 1941), 262.

62. "Portaria que se passou ao Pe. Jacobo Cocleo, Religioso da Companhia de Jesus (25 de abril de 1679)," in *Documentos Históricos da Biblioteca Nacional*, vol. 32, 126.

63. Maria do Céu Medeiros, *Igreja e Dominação no Brasil Escravista: O caso dos Oratorianos de Pernambuco, 1659–1830* (João Pessoa, Brasil: Centro de Ciências Humanas, Letras e Artes-UFPB/Idéia, 1993), 72–73.

64. Henrique João Wilkens, "Diário da Viagem ao Japurá," in *Relatos da Fronteira Amazônica no Século XVIII, Documentos de Henrique João Wilkens e Alexandre Rodrigues Ferreira*, ed. Marta R. Amoroso and Nádia Farage (São Paulo: Núcleo de História Indígena e do Indigenismo/Universidade de São Paulo/FAPESP, 1994), 28.

65. João Ferreira de Oliveira Bueno, "Simples narração da viagem que fez ao Rio Paraná o thesoureiro-mór da Sé d'esta cidade de S. Paulo . . . ," *Revista do Instituto Historico e Geographico do Brazil* 1, no. 3 (1839 [1810]), 145–46.

66. João da Silva Santos, "Descripção diaria do Rio Grande de Belmonte desde o Porto grande desta Villa até o fim delle ou divisão de Villa Rica . . . (1804)," *Anais da Biblioteca Nacional* 37 (Rio de Janeiro: Biblioteca Nacional, 1915), 261.

67. Johannes Listry, funcionário (Diretor dos Índios) da Companhia das Índias Ocidentais (1642), cited by Marcus P. Meuwese, "'For the Peace and Well-Being of the Country': Intercultural Mediators and Dutch-Indian Relations in New Netherland and Dutch Brazil, 1600–1664" (PhD diss., University of Notre Dame, 2003), 177.

68. Anonymous account, in José Antônio Gonsalves de Mello, *Restauradores de Pernambuco: Biografias de figuras do século XVII que defenderam e consolidaram a unidade brasileira* (Recife: Imprensa Universitária, 1967), 27.

69. "Diretório que se deve observar nas povoações dos índios do Pará e Maranhão (1757)," in Rita Heloísa de Almeida, *O Diretório dos Índios: Um projeto de "civilização" no Brasil do século XVIII* (Brasília: Editora Universidade de Brasília, 1997), 380–81.

70. Ibid., 392.

71. Ibid., 333–35.

72. Antonello Gerbi, *O Novo Mundo: história de uma polêmica — 1750–1900* (São Paulo: Companhia das Letras, 1996).

73. Quintero, "Making the Indian," 57–71.

74. Charles-Marie de la Condamine, *Viagem pelo Amazonas — 1735–1745* (Rio de Janeiro/São Paulo: Nova Fronteira, 1992 [1745]), 55.

75. Manuel Aires de Casal, *Corografia Brasílica ou Relação Histórico-Geográfica do Reino do Brasil* (Belo Horizonte/São Paulo: Itatiaia/Edusp, 1976 [1817]), 36.

76. Johann B. von Spix and Carl F. von Martius, *Viagem pelo Brasil — 1817–1820*, vol. 1 (São Paulo: Melhoramentos/Instituto Histórico e Geográfico Brasileiro/Imprensa Nacional, 1976 [1828–1829]), 203.

77. Câmara Cascudo, *Prelúdio da Cachaça*, 33–35.

78. Mary C. Karasch, *A vida dos escravos no Rio de Janeiro, 1808–1850* (São Paulo: Companhia das Letras, 2000), 242–57.

79. Câmara Cascudo, *Prelúdio da Cachaça*, 43–50. The "ronco" in the chest refers to the respitory diseases, such as tuberculosis, endemic in the slave population. On general folklore about cachaça and garapa, see Luís da Câmara Cascudo, *Dicionário do Folclore Brasileiro* (São Paulo: Global, 2000), and Mário Souto Maior, *Dicionário Folclórico da Cachaça* (Recife: Fundação Joaquim Nabuco/Editora Massangana, 2004).

80. Figueiredo and Venâncio, "Águas Ardentes," 30.

81. Câmara Cascudo, *Prelúdio da Cachaça*, 45.

CHAPTER THREE

Drunkenness and Interpersonal Violence in Colonial Michoacán

Aaron P. Althouse

The role of alcohol in colonial Mexican rural society has been examined along several related lines of inquiry over the past half-century since Charles Gibson's trailblazing study of central Mexican indigenous life after the conquest. The general development of research has been well documented elsewhere to the extent that a detailed recounting of such scholarship here is unnecessary, although a brief discussion of this work serves to locate the present chapter in the broader historiographical context. By and large, Gibson's work placed native village alcohol use squarely in the realm of passive response to the loss of political, ethnic, and religious self-determination owing to Spanish occupation originating in the first half of the sixteenth century. In this light, Gibson portrayed alcohol consumption as indicative of a collectively flagging hope and depression concomitant with diminished native cultural autonomy.[1]

Written more than a decade after Gibson's opus, William Taylor's equally classic work on central and southern Mexican village life analyzed alcohol consumption to arrive at a much different interpretation of colonial native society. Taylor responded to Gibson's arguments by applying theories of peasant agency and action, contending that, far from "losing" culture and turning to alcohol use as a salve for the collective hopelessness in the face of the dramatic and multifaceted changes that accompanied Spanish colonialism, native peoples in central Mexico and Oaxaca continued preconquest patterns of alcohol consumption in ways that revealed tension between native landholding villages and Hispanic cultural and functional hegemony. In this context, alcohol use and associated violence indicated community attempts to preserve, protect, and modify—in native terms—localocentric collective identity and social relations.[2]

The publication of Taylor's work in the late 1970s encouraged additional work by scholars curious to learn how native cultural forms were continued, preserved, and modified throughout the colonial period. Significantly, although this research followed in the footsteps of Gibson and Taylor, little of it focused on the role of alcohol in native society, and only recently have scholars employed new approaches in order to revisit the topic of alcohol use in colonial society, with the richest of this recent work examining ritual use of alcohol by various native ethnic groups.[3] However, very little research has considered alcohol consumption at the subcollective level and in a context beyond the *milpas* (communally held fields) that surrounded native villages. In fact, aside from work such as Steve Stern's on gendered violence in central Mexico, or Michael Scardaville's on regulation of alcohol production and consumption under the Bourbons, the ways that alcohol use functioned in individual social relations and in society "at large" are starkly absent from the historiography.[4]

This chapter addresses this situation by examining the role of alcohol consumption in facilitating rural peoples' willingness to express visions of society along lines they may have been reluctant to share while sober. Specifically, speech associated with instances of drunkenness and interpersonal violence from rural Michoacán recorded from the late seventeenth century until the middle of the eighteenth century reveals patterns of face-to-face contact and conflict that differ significantly from those documented for urban settings. Superficially, many of these allegedly intoxicated encounters appear spontaneous and fueled by little beyond mundane personal grievances. Yet, closer inspection of the details surrounding drunken fights suggests the existence of broadly shared notions of civility in rural areas that were tied to a quasi-egalitarian sense of fair and decent treatment expressed through courteous and expected salutation and nonthreatening posture, rather than more typically urban concerns over the Iberian-inspired honor complex.[5] Thus, the instances of drunkenness and interpersonal strife utilized for this study rarely, if at all, contain language indicating preoccupation with lost, damaged, or threatened honor, and instead contain speech regarding "poor" or "unfair" treatment inflicted by one party upon the other, with these breaches of conduct instigating sometimes lethal violence.

In addition to drunken speech articulating rural people's sense of fair treatment at the hands of their fellow country dwellers, some instances of drunken speech also illuminate the intriguing possibility that rural people harbored a highly individualistic streak, which though not representing a direct challenge to Spanish hegemony, nonetheless suggest that, by the late seventeenth and early eighteenth century, the Spanish dominion over Mexico's rural spaces may have been fading figuratively in the minds of country people of mixed or native identity.[6] The examples are not numerous enough to allow much beyond speculation, yet such pondering stands as potentially significant given events that occurred with the rise of Father Miguel Hidalgo's rebellion in the early nineteenth century, when poor and dispossessed country folk ransacked several key cities in Mexico's agrarian heartland before the movement both lost force and was terminated by royalist forces.

Importantly, these conditions emanated in part from rural Michoacán's spatial development, and this chapter gives specific consideration to how the texture of interpersonal relations developed in such environments and how alcohol use motivated behavior that expressed individual sentiments about correct and incorrect manners, and the need to violently respond to digressions when they occurred. From the outset of Spanish colonialism in Mexico, the incomplete conquest of the countryside shaped the character of personal interaction, as many areas outside cities received little more than the veneer of a colonial administrative structure, and so Spanish power remained regionally variable. Consequently, in areas subjected to attenuated Spanish administrative force, opportunities arose for exercising individual agency through the violent resolution of personal disputes before crime-control authorities could intervene and alleviate tensions.

Thus, in a climate defined by more sparse and scattered human habitation, less centralized crime-control machinery—few justices to serve large tracts of land—and sometimes hard-to-locate spatial reminders of Spanish rule, conflict resolution was often, by default, managed by the participants.[7] In this light, individuals depended upon visual cues to identify and interpret the motives of potential adversaries. Thus, factors such as corporal bearing, salutation (or lack thereof), and physical appearance (including skin color) provided identifying markers, indicated friendly or significantly less benevolent intentions upon approach and served as the impetus to act in the interest of self-preservation. Consequently, individuals depended upon their readings of potentially dangerous situations, with such interpretations leading to the use of both proactive and reactive tactics.

In this environment, witness testimony often illustrated the importance of expected salutations in personal encounters, with rural people noting that the omission of greeting rituals portended bad things to follow. In bringing such issues to light, these individuals revealed that friendly—or at least expected—greetings served as admissions that the person under approach faced no peril, even if the parties in question had no prior knowledge of each other. Thus, wishing someone a good day, removing a hat, or even waving upon approach not only were expected acts but also could prove determinative in avoiding or intensifying tension and conflict. Although such practiced greetings were not meaningful exclusively in the rural sphere, what vested them with such determining power in such areas was their sequential placement in unfolding personal contacts, as they signaled an approach toward, and preceded access to, self-perceived and unofficially constructed individual space. In rural areas, where the institutional imprint of the colonial judicial system was profoundly less visible (including the attenuated oversight of justice officers) than in urban areas, the "civilizing" logic and attendant social order of Iberian-led city planning loosely elaborated, the physical boundaries between different land parcels not always obvious (and largely unguarded), and individual Spaniards present yet more dispersed than in cities, the difference between life and death could boil down to accurately reading the potentially harmless or malevolent motives of an approaching person.[8] Given such conditions, rural people considered greetings—or the lack thereof—serious matters.

Criminal suits associated with alcohol use from the Pátzcuaro region during the late seventeenth century through the middle stages of the eighteenth century compose the documentary base of the project, and these cases provide interesting perspectives on rural social relations. Since drunkenness and drunken speech appear to reveal individual ideas about appropriate interpersonal conduct, analysis also delves into several key cases in which alcohol was not a factor. Importantly, these cases buttress the findings gleaned from instances of alcohol-driven conflict, particularly in the sense that alcohol provided the impetus to express sentiments that, though characteristic of rural society, may have been largely repressed during periods of sobriety.

As a routine afternoon in June 1727 crept toward conclusion in the small pueblo of Numarán (rural northern Michoacán), the discordant sounds of violence precluded a tranquil end to the day.[9] The clatter drifted to the town's administrative buildings, where it drew the attention of the local lieutenant, don Sebastián Sánchez Ramírez (don is an honorific title for men denoting status), who departed the government offices, followed the racket down a central street and arrived at a spot where he encountered some town *indios* (native persons) engaged in a brawl and others spectating. His presence probably hastened the incident toward closure, as shortly after his arrival the fighting abated. Although peace was restored,

one of the combatants, a town Indian named Francisco Xavier, remained—
in the words of don Sebastián—on the ground and "senseless." After di-
recting Francisco's removal so that he could receive the minimal available
medical attention, don Sebastián questioned the remaining onlookers
concerning their recollections of the incident. Based on their information,
he soon apprehended a primary suspect, Numarán resident Salvador Tolento, and several others known to have taken part in the battle, and "se-
cured" them in the town jail.[10]

Witness statements pointed the finger at an "inebriated" Tolento, first
for assault, and second for homicide, as Francisco Xavier soon died from
his injuries. According to the collected testimony, Tolento both instigated
the disturbance and delivered the death blow. This bit of information
proved important to don Sebastián, since determining responsibility for
crimes of this nature as well as suitable punishment was one of the principal goals of a colonial criminal administration that stretched from rural
settings like Numarán all the way to the colonial high court in Mexico
City and, in theory, across the Atlantic to the Iberian Peninsula.[11] Salvador
Tolento's crimes highlight how alcohol use exposed the ways rural people
interpreted greeting practices and the implicit messages revealed by omit-
ting such rituals. Six days after the fracas, the (by then) deceased Xavier's
brother and widow submitted a preliminary petition to the criminal courts,
blaming Tolento, described as the town *prioste* (the head of a religious
confraternity), for both initiating the altercation and killing Xavier. The
basis of the disagreement that escalated into the mortal scuffle apparently
had little to do with Francisco and instead stemmed from a dispute initiated earlier in the day by Tolento and another indio from Numarán named
Nicolás Lango. That morning, an inexplicably angry Tolento appeared at
Francisco's house, looking for Lango. Though the records do not indicate
the origin of the dispute, witnesses noted that they knew Tolento arrived
with bad intentions because he failed to "greet" Lango. Tolento's failure to
provide the anticipated salutation prompted Lango to ask why he had dispensed with the expected gestures, and why he (Lango) deserved such
treatment. Tolento retorted, "Who are you?" and struck Lango, who recip-
rocated by slapping his assailant. Even with this ominous beginning, tensions eased temporarily, and Tolento left the site for several hours. By the
middle of the afternoon, however, Tolento's anger returned, and he re-
newed the argument emphatically, revisiting Francisco's house (with Lango
still present) armed with a bull's horn and, in Tolento's own words, "ca-
liente por haber beber [sic] charape" ("mad because of having drunk *charape*," a fermented beverage made with barley or pineapple and sugarcane

molasses). In the course of this rekindled conflict, before striking Lango with his makeshift weapon, Tolento utilized quasi-treasonous speech, saying his assault was "from the king," he was the "judge," and "here, there is no other king than I."[12] Francisco then inserted himself into the feud, telling Tolento that he was not going to "govern" Francisco's house. These threats and retorts ignited a skirmish among not only Tolento and Lango but also several other pairs of individuals, and when Francisco entered the fray in order to defend his friend Lango, Tolento informed him that "today we are going to eat life" ("hoy tenemos de comer la vida"), before inflicting what proved to be the fatal blow.

Although Tolento's drunken words may appear little more than an attempt to psychologically intimidate his adversary during a street fight, his pointed language, along with his prior omission of greeting, suggests there is more to the story—specifically, notions of individual autonomy at work. In particular, Tolento's calculated disregard for anticipated greetings and his explicitly seditious speech suggest a dual-faceted articulation of his individual agency that was lodged squarely in the rural social context. First, he gained the upper hand in his encounter with Lango through the manipulation of expected behavioral norms, refusing to perform commonly practiced salutations. Second, he took advantage of the relative spatial autonomy provided by the rural setting to assert self-perceived authority by claiming powers in theory reserved for the Crown and colonial judicial institutions. In this particular case, his assessment may not have been too far from the truth. After all, he was able to barge into Francisco's house in the morning, snub and strike Lango, drink for a few hours, and return later as self-anointed local royalty ("aquí yo soy el Rey" [Here I am King]) armed to kill, without facing interference from crime-control officers.[13]

Another case, from May 1689, also illustrates alcohol's role in interpersonal violence, how such violence was associated with omission of civility, and the way that rural individuals might assume informal policing powers to settle disputes. On the eighteenth day of the month, Baltasar de los Reyes, a mestizo (a racial mixture consisting of European and indigenous heritage) worker from the hacienda of Pomacuaro in northern Michoacán, attended Mass in the nearby pueblo of Aguanuato. Following the service, Reyes continued to the small rural town of Panindícuaro, searching for his Indian friend Pedro Rincón, who possessed a *garrocha* (an object akin to a sharpened pole sometimes used in ranching) he borrowed from Reyes during a visit to Pomacuaro. After arriving in Panindícuaro, Reyes found Rincón at his house, "wounded" and no longer with the garrocha, which, he explained, had been removed from his care by another

Panindícuaro resident, Francisco Pérez. By this point in the day Reyes was drunk—by his own admission—and he angrily pressed Rincón for details about his injuries and what became of the garrocha.

Rincón explained that late in the afternoon, he (with the garrocha in tow) went looking for an acquaintance at the house of Andrés Moreno, a mestizo who also lived in Panindícuaro. When Rincón arrived at Moreno's house, he entered and found Moreno in the company of several other men. Rincón made certain to mention in his official statement that he greeted all of those present, yet still received poor treatment, as following his courtesies, one of Andrés's guests, Francisco Pérez, inquired of Rincón, "How's it going, indio, and what about the five *reales*?" referencing a debt that Rincón owed Pérez. Rincón responded that he did not have the money, which prompted Pérez to attack Rincón and seize the garrocha from him. Soon after, Pérez's nephew, Pedro González, arrived at the house and congratulated his uncle on taking the pole from the "slow-paying indio" before grabbing a stick and hitting Rincón on the head hard enough to draw blood. At that point, Rincón returned home and soon after crossed paths with Reyes.[14]

Significantly, Reyes's response to this news demonstrated the sense of individualism revealed by Salvador Tolento's case. In this situation, however, while alcohol consumption may have vested him with sufficient courage to follow a particular course of autonomous violent action, at least his motives appeared less intentionally malicious than those of Salvador Tolento. Reyes's testimony to the *alcalde* (minister) of the Santa Hermandad (Saint Brotherhood) and the witnesses who accompanied him to Panindícuaro demonstrated a genuine interest in obtaining his absent garrocha, yet the strongest sentiment revealed by his words was indignation about Rincón's treatment by Pérez, González, and company.[15] Thus, after discovering that Pérez could be found in the home of Andrés Moreno (along with several other mestizos), the drunken Reyes expressed his anger by barging into Moreno's place of residence, withholding all pleasantries, and demanding to know who had injured Rincón and taken the garrocha. Pérez admitted that he had committed the act as a means of collecting the five reales of debt Rincón could not compensate, which led Reyes to question him as to "what cause [Pedro] Rincón had given him" to warrant the assault. Following this abrupt discussion, both men left the residence on horseback, Pérez following Reyes, with Pérez striking Reyes with a pole and Reyes stabbing his adversary with a knife during their initial altercation. Reyes added that he was uncertain as to who administered his most serious wounds, due to both his drunken state and the fact that he fell to the ground at a point in the fight when the other men from Moreno's house joined the action.

On one hand, this case could be read as simple vengeance—Reyes, inflamed with alcohol, defending the welfare of his acquaintance Rincón and paying a heavy price for his involvement. On the other hand, events surrounding the case and the nuanced statements delivered by Reyes and Rincón suggest that hearty consumption of alcohol likely empowered Reyes to pursue an apparently simple outcome—recovery of his garrocha and avenging the injuries to his friend—based on more complex motivations. In this situation, he took matters into his own hands by displaying no interest in notifying municipal officials of the incident and overtly eschewing customary greetings (which Rincón, for his part, had been careful to mention) when walking into Moreno's house and demanding an explanation from the guilty parties.

In 1694, again in Numarán, yet another instance of violence—this time combined with seditious speech—hinted at the intersection of alcohol, conflict, and rural individualism. This particular occasion, also seemingly brought to a crisis point by the reckless consumption of alcohol, points up the potential tug-of-war between compliance with colonial administrative regulations and the thirst for individual autonomy. One day in May, the town *teniente* (lieutenant), Juan de Maza, learned that a mestizo named Joseph de Cáceres roamed the dirt streets of town in a drunken state, causing quite a stir. In order to (in his words) "remedy this," Maza departed the *casas reales* (town hall) in search of Cáceres, whom he found drunk and up to no good. Upon being informed of Maza's appearance by some bystanders, Cáceres stood unperturbed by the arrival of official justice, saying he "gave little [notice] to the lieutenant." For his part, Maza acted as if he were capable of subduing Cáceres with persuasion rather than force, invoking the "name of royal justice" at his arrival and explaining that he planned to apprehend and imprison Cáceres. Despite these declarations, his quarry remained unimpressed and responded that he "gave little [credence] to the King" and that he would not cooperate because "there were few who came for him" and "he would kill" those who dared any attempt to imprison him. Unperturbed by the threats, Maza forged forward in his attempt to apprehend the troublemaking Cáceres, yet due in part to Cáceres's well-armed status—both sword and knife—the situation turned into a standoff enduring nearly half of an hour and ending only when Maza, acting with the assistance of two mestizos and a *ladino* (Spanish-speaking) indio named Diego Zavala (who claimed to be a "minister" of the teniente) finally subdued Cáceres.

Shortly after Cáceres's reluctant submission, Maza transported him to Pátzcuaro, where, he believed, the suspect could be more securely held. This was not merely idle speculation on Maza's part, as Cáceres had already escaped from Numarán's jail two years earlier in 1692, when he had been apprehended at the request of Numarán resident don Juan de Nieve, who complained that an armed Cáceres entered his house by force and absconded with Nieve's female servant. In this previous brush with the law, Cáceres was also credited with harassing the town's indios, as well as stealing other women from the local countryside.[16]

Based on the above, it seems clear that Cáceres did not launch his criminal career that particular May afternoon after imbibing too much of the local liquor, yet in his statement made after transportation to Pátzcuaro, he blamed the "evil" of alcohol for his behavior and resulting incarceration and claimed that he went to Numarán only to hear mass (that being the closest service to where he lived) and that it was his "disgrace" that he had remained after mass, drinking to the point of inebriation. Interestingly, Cáceres lacked evidence of collective ties in his apparently common and unoriginal, but nonetheless unique, existence. For example, he claimed the small northern town of La Piedad as home yet was a *vecino* (householder) of the jurisdiction of Tlazazalca—something much less locationally specific. In addition, Cáceres listed muleteer as his occupation (in theory, a job entailing significant physical mobility) and said that he was married to a *mulata* (a person of mixed African and European heritage) named Lorenza Zavala. Thus, in all likelihood he moved around quite a bit while at work and married across caste lines. This information creates a composite image of Cáceres as a man leading an existence almost entirely defined by his individual circumstances—no clear place of origin, no "ethnic" support network, no local church, and probably irregular work wherever it could be found. Even though nothing in his life story indicates anything approaching kingly power, it should also come as no surprise that, with his tongue loosened by heavy drinking, he boasted that he took orders only from himself.

Another situation from 1740 and the latter stages of the study resonates similar themes—a drunken crime suspect who overtly challenged colonial justice personified but, once in captivity and sober, expressed contrition. One afternoon during the highland hamlet of Nahuatzen's August fiestas for San Luis, the community's patron, Joseph Guzmán, generated quite a commotion among natives and nonnatives gathered at the town's bull ring. In all likelihood, both groups joined in the festivities—or at the least enjoyed the leisurely pace of a fiesta day—until, that is, Guzmán turned up—drunk, armed, and full of insults. The perpetrator, described as a free mulato and vecino from Coeneo (some miles northeast of Nahuatzen), arrived at the royal offices in fine form, showering those present—including several women—with taunts so impressively rude that witnesses noted their scandalous nature but refrained from mentioning the specific content in their affidavits.[17]

Word soon reached the town teniente, don Juan de Lujar—who had been relaxing at the home of don Matías González de Aguirre—that an "armed mulato" on horseback hovered near the casas reales, insulting the women there. Subsequently, Lujar returned to the town hall, where he found Guzmán still engaged in his verbal barrage. Lujar then, "in the name of the King," ordered Guzmán to cease his activity, yet three separate warnings went unheeded, and Guzmán's only response to these cautions was his retort that he would not listen to Lujar, "a shitty little teniente." Guzmán then unsheathed his sword and, during a grand closing flurry of insults crafted in the presence of Lujar, don Matías, the town priest, and "many other people," told Lujar that he would kill him rather than leave Nahuatzen and he did not respect the King nor anyone else. This proved to be Guzmán's last stand of the day, for, after this finale, several of those present overpowered him and left him in Lujar's custody.

On the heels of this incident, Guzmán testified in Nahuatzen's jail that he was thirty years old, currently an unemployed muleteer, and that he had no prior cause for his actions against Lujar. Instead, he blamed alcohol for his behavior. Alone, this information would suggest that Guzman's deteriorating material existence built sufficient pressure upon him that he simply slipped into a show of emotionally venting extreme misconduct after a day of drinking—and in the process targeted the casas reales and teniente Lujar. However, there is more to the story, as additional evidence shows that Guzmán knew Lujar prior to their run-in and that Guzmán did not consider his unruliness as insubordination. Rather, he implied that the exchange reflected conflict between racial peers, since Guzmán claimed that both his mother and father were considered to be Spaniards. While Guzmán's behavior does not follow a strict pattern of social inversion, he nonetheless viewed things so as to make himself a powerful individual who took orders only from himself and would kill any dissenters. Yet, once transported to Pátzcuaro, where the magnitude of his actions likely appeared graver than they had while in Nahuatzen, Guzmán turned contrite when explaining the events that occurred during the San Luis fiesta. In particular, while testifying from Pátzcuaro's jail, Guzmán highlighted that before his run-in with Lujar, he saw the teniente and properly greeted both

Lujar and his wife—showing good intentions. In effect, the alcohol was to blame, as Guzmán characterized himself as peaceful, respectful, and in accordance with expected behavior.

Another case, this one from 1735, details the death of Joseph Tiburcio de Vargas, the Spanish *mayordomo* (overseer) of the hacienda of Patuan, who mistakenly, and with dire consequences, assumed ostensible authority over non-Spaniards beyond the boundaries of the hacienda where he worked.[18] The case contains only oblique reference to alcohol use and so can be taken as an indication of how the values expressed by drunken speech in the prior cases may have typified rural social relations. Specifically, the incident in question demonstrates the conjunction of greeting protocol in rural space with the egalitarian interpersonal violence of the countryside. In this particular incident, Vargas ranged from Patuan one February afternoon in order to locate several cattle that had gone missing from the estate the previous day. Accompanied by his brother-in-law, co-worker Nicolás de Garibay, he traveled a few miles to the northeast of the hacienda, heading for the nearby Indian pueblo of San Angel Zurumucapio, where, Vargas had been informed, several natives had slaughtered what likely was one of the missing animals. On the road to Zurumucapio, Vargas crossed paths with an acquaintance—a mulato named Nicolás Navarro—and, as Navarro noted to the investigating teniente, both Vargas and his companion saluted him. It is significant that Navarro believed this information important enough to report in his statement, since, from the teniente's perspective, it probably had little bearing on the case. Yet, the unfolding chain of events tied to the case would soon reiterate the gravity (already addressed here) that country people attached to the provision and receipt of appropriate greetings in personal interactions, and how dispensing with such acts could be considered both offensive and an indication of trouble on the horizon.

At any rate, now riding three abreast, they entered into conversation during which Vargas informed Navarro that he rode for Zurumucapio to question the suspected rustlers. As they approached Zurumucapio, Navarro again voiced issues that highlighted specific aspects of rural society related to this study, for, as he counseled Vargas regarding his planned course of action, he explicitly warned him that "friend, we are going badly, it seems certain to me that we should see the alcalde [in this case, magistrate] of the pueblo and together with him arrive at the house" where the indios lived. Importantly, Navarro predicted the danger awaiting Spaniards who assumed implicit measures of cultural or administrative authority over rural non-Spaniards, particularly when such contacts occurred in small outlying settlements that, though literally only miles away from Hispanic estates, were figuratively much more distant. In this case, Navarro believed the intervention of the village's indigenous alcalde would assist his friend's cause and, perhaps, curtail any overt conflict. Vargas responded that there was no need to do so, for he did not have any problem with the natives in question. Despite this admission, Vargas clearly sought to handle matters on his own, and unfortunately, it soon became clear that Navarro's estimation of the inherent danger was nothing less than prophetic.

Upon reaching Zurumucapio, the three men arrived at the house where one of the indios, Juan Roque, lived with his two sons, Joseph Roque and Antonio Lucas. In his testimony, Vargas claimed that, at this juncture, he waved to the natives and greeted them "with all familiarity [and] in this fashion, 'Hail Mary comrades, I am coming to see the hide of the steer that you slaughtered last night.'" Juan Roque and his sons responded to this request by asking why he sought the inspection, to which Vargas (by his account) said that some animals were missing from the hacienda where he served as mayordomo and he sought information on their whereabouts. After some initial haggling, and Vargas's demand that he be allowed to enter the house to verify whether the animal's remains were indeed present, Roque permitted Vargas to enter his dwelling. Here, events took a turn for the worse, as Garibay documented in his statement, recounting that once inside, Vargas and Juan Roque began to argue, and soon Vargas emerged from the hut, pulling Roque by the hair with one hand and wielding a small sword (or perhaps large knife) in the other. When Roque's sons grabbed makeshift weapons (clubs and sticks) and aimed to intervene, Garibay and Navarro quickly dismounted from their horses and relieved them of their weapons. This, however, did not end the skirmish, as the natives (with Juan Roque free from Vargas's grasp by this point) resorted to even more makeshift weaponry, grabbing rocks and pelting their three unwelcome visitors. This barrage, Garibay said, was "impossible" to resist, and one of the numerous rocks found its mark, striking Vargas with what would prove to be fatal impact. Reeling from the wound incurred in this disastrous meeting, Vargas and his compatriots fled from Zurumucapio on foot, since the indigenous men had either ridden away on their horses or, at the very least, driven them away so they were temporarily unavailable for purposes of retreat.

The testimony provided to the investigating justices by Juan Roque and his sons merits mention, since their violent retaliation and apparent lack of concern over the consequences of events in Zurumucapio quickly disappeared once they were placed in custody, first in San Ildefonso Taretán and later in Pátzcuaro. Importantly, none of the three mentioned Vargas's claim that he provided friendly greeting. Perhaps they all forgot to mention this point, yet their blanket omission of the initial contact leading to Vargas's death suggests either that Vargas's lack of protocol or his insistence in looking for the missing animals proved insulting and consequent implication of their guilt broke an unwritten law of rural life. Furthermore, finding themselves before official colonial representatives in Pátzcuaro, the three painted themselves as drunken victims. Juan Roque claimed that Vargas had not only grabbed him by the hair but also hit him with the short sword and knocked him to the ground. He further added that he had no idea whose rock projectile hit Vargas since, at the time, he was drunk. Joseph Roque claimed to have seen nothing, although he somehow still managed to participate in the dispute, and Antonio Lucas admitted that his rock connected with Vargas, but that he resorted to such action only after desiring to "correct" Vargas with a club yet having the weapon lifted from his grip by Navarro. Whether due to the weight of evidence, testimony, or the portrait of passivity forced into action crafted by Roque and his sons, the three were absolved of their crimes and allowed to go free roughly half a year after the event and their initial incarceration.

Several more incidents of interpersonal violence demonstrate rural individuals' sensitivity to perceptions of both fair treatment and proper salutation to indicate harmless intentions. Importantly, these cases were not— at least according to case testimony—characterized by drunken speech. Yet, they prove important to the central issues of this chapter along two interwoven threads. First, they further corroborate that some individuals in rural areas maintained defined notions of individualism in terms of expectations for fairness from both acquaintances and strangers and that violations of such norms were taken seriously since they might foreshadow danger. Second, the previous examples of drunken speech and interpersonal violence show that alcohol may have held a significant role in enabling rural non-Spaniards to articulate what may well have been a nascent sense of "equality" with Spaniards, at least in rural places where Iberian social hierarchies were less well defined. Drunken speech expressing such ideas as "Here, I am the king" mesh well with the violent responses of sober non-Spaniards against their Spanish instigators, as these victims of violence explained that they were merely defending themselves from excessive physical force. In some sense, these extreme responses of people under extreme duress echo the sentiment of individual autonomy expressed by drunken speech.

So, these two instances of criminal acts not overtly tied to alcohol consumption suggest that Spaniards who were not official authority figures, and who violated expected rural behavioral norms, could be the targets of physical force from sober non-Spaniards who explained their victims had not appropriately observed their informal individual rights when placing them in physical danger. When exhibiting what could be taken as violent "insubordination" against Spaniards, rural non-Spaniards justified their actions by citing breaches of conduct committed by Spaniards—lack of proper greeting, excessive or unreasonable verbal abuse. For example, in 1693, Joseph Calderón and Joseph de la Cruz, mulato slaves from an estate in the Numarán area, were cited for removing cattle from another estate and selling one of the animals to an *india* (female native) from the nearby village of Conguripo. According to rumor, after committing the alleged crime, de la Cruz fled southwest toward Colima, while Calderón remained and fended off several attempted arrests before capture. Case proceedings indicate Calderón's complicity in this and other unlawful acts, yet the testimony he supplied once in custody was not crafted to elicit absolution from his activities. Instead, he seemed to be more interested in explaining that he violently fought Spanish attempts to apprehend him because, in essence, his pursuers did not follow correct protocol when approaching his person.

During questioning after his arrest, Calderón appealed to informal rural codes of conduct in what seems to have been a ploy to shift the interrogation from the subject of his guilt to how he had been wronged through the violation of regular norms of behavior by his would-be captors. When workers at Aramútaro, the estate in question, noticed the disappearance of the cattle, they initiated the process of sending word to the local magistrate, who then commenced his investigation and soon received information that Calderón was hiding in an acquaintance's house in the small village of Conguripo.[19] Consequently, the magistrate sent Juan Baraja, Aramútaro's mayordomo, to arrest Calderón. Rather than return with Calderón in tow, Baraja came back with wounds inflicted by Calderón. Finally, the magistrate tried his luck with Calderón, who continued to resist even after being informed several times that he must submit to royal justice. At last, the magistrate appealed to several witnesses for assistance, at which point Calderón was subdued and later incarcerated. During subsequent questioning regarding the theft and his resistance, Calderón provided little information capable of exonerating himself, but he did raise the issue of proper respect for greeting and space in rural areas by claiming that when Baraja and his companion encountered him in Conguripo, they did not identify themselves but instead moved immediately to the task of apprehending him. At this point, Calderón insisted that he did not understand their motives and asked them "why they mistreated him." As they continued to provide no response to his inquiries, Calderón defended himself and in the process wounded Baraja several times. While this testimony appears suspect in light of the fact that Baraja's arrest attempt was not the first that Calderón evaded, Calderón nonetheless chose specific language to explain his actions, and his words played upon the theme of offering proper and nonthreatening salutation—whether verbal or demonstrative—in rural areas before commencing a breach of another's self-defined domain.[20]

The last case, from 1731, finds another apparently sober non-Spaniard taking unilateral action through physical contestation of Spanish authority and shows that even on a hacienda near Pátzcuaro, challenges to Spanish "authority" could be swift, forceful, and predicated upon unseemly behavior by Spanish instigators. Late one March afternoon in 1731, Joseph Vicente, the mayordomo of the hacienda of Chapultepeque (roughly two leagues from Pátzcuaro), completed the work of seeding the fields and began returning supplies to one of the estate's storage outbuildings. With a sack of corn in tow, Vicente encountered one of the estate workers, an Indian named Anselmo Clemente, whom Vicente had previously directed to retrieve the corn and return it to storage. Frustrated that Anselmo had not fulfilled his daily work obligations with (in Vicente's opinion) sufficient alacrity, and also was engaged in altogether undirected activity—corralling livestock—Vicente expressed his displeasure by striking Anselmo with a club he employed "to govern the people." Rather than submit to such corporal discipline, Anselmo reacted violently and without concern that he might seriously injure or even kill the estate mayordomo, who also happened to be "Spanish." In later testimony before criminal authorities, Anselmo explained that he had merely forgotten to go after the sack of corn, and so when Vicente hit his head and back with the club, he "was obligated to pull his knife" and inflict various stab wounds to Vicente's face. Had Ignacio Martínez, a Spanish-speaking native who also worked on the hacienda, not been present, Vicente's wounds might have been worse and even fatal. Given the scandalous nature of Anselmo's actions in light of Vicente's superior caste and occupational status, Anselmo's estimation of his innocence in the matter and Vicente's role as perpetrator were supported by three indigenous estate workers called to testify. By July of that same year, the case closed with Vicente pardoning Anselmo.[21]

In conclusion, the drunken speech associated with incidents of alcohol-related violence, as well as the motives for the violence itself, likely more accurately reflect the values, beliefs, and frustrations expressed by rural people in the course of quotidian affairs. Thus, the presence of and sometimes excessive taste for alcohol in rural Michoacán was probably not unique on a world scale in the late seventeenth and eighteenth centuries. Rather, given the context of Spanish attempts to tighten administrative and institutional control through the eighteenth century, as well as the human powder keg building toward nineteenth-century combustion in Mexico's fertile crescent (which included much of the northern Michoacán countryside), it is interesting to note that, at least in terms of how individuals may have viewed their informal expectations for self-perceived decent and fair treatment, drinking was associated with expressions of such values, and these values differed significantly with those articulated by people who lived in urban centers.[22]

Finally, whereas colonial Mexican cities were often dens of criminal activity, little of this activity has been shown to be targeted against Spaniards. Although the sample of cases employed for this study is small (not by design, but rather due to the difficulty in encountering intact criminal suits connected to such acts), the material suggests that non-Spaniards acting under the influence of alcohol were less inhibited in terms of expressing their contempt for both Spanish rule and official representatives of the colonial state. Even sober non-Spaniards might lash out at Spaniards who did not represent the Crown in official capacity but who nonetheless occupied social standing theoretically (and practically) greater than their own. And, in the drunken and sober variations on this theme, those who committed the violence explained—at least in their initial statements—that they were defending their person, space, or property, and their Spanish adversaries were at fault for the altercations due to their failure to observe informal and anticipated boundaries of proper conduct. This situation does not singularly explain why individuals who faced grave crises of subsistence in 1810 may have chosen to lash out violently against the symbols of colonial hegemony, but it does indicate that rural culture was moving along a different trajectory than its urban cousin in this crucial period in Mexico's historical development.

Notes

1. Charles Gibson, *The Aztecs Under Spanish Rule: A History of the Indians of the Valley of Mexico, 1519–1810* (Stanford, CA: Stanford University Press, 1964).

2. William B. Taylor, *Drinking, Homicide, and Rebellion in Colonial Mexican Villages* (Stanford, CA: Stanford University Press, 1979).

3. See, e.g., John F. Chuchiak, "'It Is Their Drinking That Hinders Them': Balché and the Use of Ritual Intoxicants Among the Colonial Yucatec Maya, 1550–1780," *Estudios de Cultura Maya* 24 (Fall 2003), 1–43.

4. Steve J. Stern, *The Secret History of Gender: Women, Men, and Power in Late Colonial Mexico* (Chapel Hill: University of North Carolina Press, 1995), presents a somewhat contrary assessment of alcohol's role in gendered interpersonal violence. Stern does not cast aside the connection between alcohol and violence but, rather, argues that violence associated with alcohol consumption was typical, rather than an expression of deviance. Thus, Stern claims that "the data corroborate social science studies that undermine the presumption that the physiological effects of drinking lead to deviant outbursts by individuals uncontrolled by social convention" (50). See also Michael C. Scardaville, "Alcohol Abuse and Tavern Reform in Late Colonial Mexico City," *Hispanic American Historical Review* 60, no. 4 (November 1980), 643–71, for discussion of alcohol regulation policies under the Bourbons.

5. For a regional example of urban ideas about race and identity, see Aaron P. Althouse, "Contested Mestizos, Alleged Mulattos: Racial Identity and Caste Hierarchy in Eighteenth Century Pátzcuaro, Mexico," *The Americas* 62, no. 2 (October 2005), 151–75. Furthermore, Cheryl English Martin demonstrates that even in "peripheral" cities like San Felipe el Real de Chihuahua, which really did not gain relevance until the eighteenth century, well after the conquest and initial phase of importing European social values to the colonies, elite preoccupation over outward demonstrations of authority, and connection to the Iberian Peninsula, remained strong. In *Governance and Society in Colonial Mexico: Chihuahua in the Eighteenth Century* (Stanford, CA: Stanford University Press, 1996), Martin argues that "ritual acts of deference to royal authority afforded the *cabildo* members a tangible reminder of their own importance in a chain of command that reached from the dusty streets of San Felipe directly back to the king himself. In the performance of their duties they frequently invoked this connection, asking local citizens to cooperate with them 'in the name of the king'" (74).

6. The significance of this possibility merits examination since Spanish administration spent considerable effort establishing and sustaining a legal and institutional structure as a symbol and means of control over its overseas empire. Brian Owensby, *Empire of Law and Indian Justice in Colonial Mexico* (Stanford, CA: Stanford University Press, 2008), summarizes this policy well, stating, "Perhaps no other conquest and colonization, certainly none in modern European history, made such a point of its laws and judicial institutions as did Spain in America during and after the sixteenth century" (3).

7. Colonial administrators were not blind to this situation and, in fact, attempted to strengthen rural crime control with reforms in the eighteenth century. See Colin M. MacLachlan, *Criminal Justice in Eighteenth Century Mexico: A Study of the Tribunal of the Acordada* (Berkeley: University of California Press, 1974), for a detailed study of the development and effectiveness of the Real Acordada.

8. Much has been made of the "civilizing" intention of urbanization during Spanish colonization in the Americas, particularly in terms of the well-known utilization of the Spanish grid plan as a structurally logical template for new and already existing cities and towns. For an interesting discussion of the range of changes associated with Spanish-style urbanization, see Jacqueline Holler, "Conquered Spaces, Colonial

Skirmishes: Spatial Contestation in Sixteenth-Century Mexico City," *Radical History Review* 99 (Fall 2007), 107–20.

9. Probably no more than a few hundred people claimed Numarán as their home, yet the small rural settlement on the northern fringes of the Pátzcuaro region still had its own resident royal official and documented Spanish and *casta* residents in addition to its Indian majority. A seventeenth-century ecclesiastical survey of Michoacán noted that Numarán had thirty vecinos. If multiplied by a factor of either four or five, this would place the village's total population at roughly one hundred to two hundred individuals. Ramón López Lara, *El Obispado de Michoacán en el Siglo XVIII: Informe Inédito de Beneficios, Pueblos y Lagunas* (Morelia, Mexico: Fimax Publicistas, 1973), 143.

10. Archivo Histórico del Ayuntamiento de Pátzcuaro (hereafter AHAP), caja 25, expediente (hereafter exp.) 3, fojas (hereafter f.) 549–67.

11. A detailed layout of Spanish colonial administration—via the *audiencia*, an administrative unit and court—is available in Eduardo Martiré, *Las Audiencias y la Administración de Justicia en las Indias* (Madrid: Ediciones Universidad Autónoma de Madrid, 2005).

12. This exclamation appears to echo—no offense to Tolento—a less complex sentiment than the collective notions of kingship and popular sovereignty espoused by eighteenth-century Andean indigenous rebels. For more on collective notions of kinship, the "rey común," see S. Elizabeth Penry, "The Rey Común: Indigenous Political Discourse in Eighteenth-Century Alto Perú," in *The Collective and the Public in Latin America: Cultural Identities and Political Order*, ed. Luis Roniger and Tamar Herzog (Brighton, UK: Sussex Academic Press, 2000), 219–37.

13. In this light, Tolento's speech under duress, although still just a view through the keyhole, serves much the same purpose to historians as the menacing language accompanying indigenous community-based tumults and the blasphemous oaths made by Afro–Latin American slaves enduring corporal discipline. In such instances, speech expressed during moments of intense mental or physical strain revealed values that typified society in more mundane, routine, quotidian—and ultimately more representative—terms. Taylor's *Drinking, Homicide, and Rebellion* examines village-based tumults, demonstrating that speech utilized by participants indicated indigenous peasants' conceptions of the social order and the relationship between Crown, colonial state, and semiautonomous Indian corporate community. For non-Indians, Javier Villa-Flores, "'To Lose One's Soul': Blasphemy and Slavery in New Spain, 1596–1669," *Hispanic American Historical Review* 82, no. 3 (August 2002), 435–36, examines cases of individual slaves, arguing that slaves' utterances of blasphemous oaths and claims of losing their souls due to often extreme physical punishment allowed Afro-Mexican bonds people to effect "an inversion of the colonial discourse that justified slavery by predicating the Christian salvation of African souls upon the servitude of their bodies."

14. "Causa criminal que se ha seguido de oficio de la real justicia contra Andrés Moreno, Baltasar de los Reyes, Pedro Rincón, Pedro González, Juan de la Vega, Nicolás Guillén, Lorenzo de Loya por la pendencia de cuchilladas que tuvieron en el pueblo de Panindícuaro, todos reos ausentes," AHAP, caja 16, exp. 4, f. 576–81.

15. The Santa Hermandad, or Saint Brotherhood, was an "organization supposedly entrusted with the administration of justice in rural areas." Martin, *Governance and Society*, 93.

16. AHAP, caja 18, exp. 1, f. 32–49.

17. "Contra Joseph Guzmán mulato que dijeron ser por la novedencia y resistencia que estando ebrio tuvo con Juan de Lujar teniente de Paracho," AHAP, caja 35, exp. 1, f. 40–49.

18. "Causa criminal contra Antonio Lucas, contra Juan Roque, y contra Joseph Roque, todos tres indios naturales del pueblo de San Angel Zurumucapio fecha en 23 de febrero año de 1735. Comenzada por Joseph de Medina y Herrera teniente del pueblo de Taretan," AHAP, caja 28, exp. 4, f. 658–727.

19. According to sources pertaining to the seventeenth century, Conguripo's population could not have been more than a few hundred at the most. According to López Lara (*El Obispado de Michoacán en el Siglo XVII*, 81), the village was a joint *cabecera* (municipality), along with Puruándiro, of the *partido* (administrative area) of San Juan Puruándiro, and was home to twenty Indian vecinos.

20. AHAP, caja 18, exp. 2, f. 288–309.

21. AHAP, caja 30, exp. 2, f. 265–75.

22. See Althouse, "Contested Mestizos," for anecdotes regarding Spanish versus non-Spanish violence. The cases cited for Pátzcuaro proper show non-Spaniards as more passive receptors of informal punishments meted out by Spanish aggressors.

PART TWO

The Long Nineteenth Century (1820s to 1930)

The period from the 1820s through 1930 brought major changes to the region as new nations struggled to forge their identities. In the several decades that followed independence, leaders, who mainly identified as either liberal or conservative, fundamentally disagreed about how to shape their new countries. Liberals tended to prefer a federalist republic, with a laissez-faire economy and limited power for the Catholic Church. Conservatives, on the other hand, wanted to maintain closer ties to the Church, as well as Spain and Portugal, some even going so far as to invite European monarchs to rule countries organized on centralist principles. One area that both groups agreed on was that women and the masses, largely of indigenous, African, or racially mixed descent, and whom they often labeled as drunkards, ought to be excluded from the benefits of citizenship.

By the 1880s, liberals had come to power in most countries, and they began rebuilding economies that had been beset by decades of warfare, often by courting foreign investment to industrialize and build infrastructure, such as railroads and ports. Another way of raising revenue was to tax cantinas and other such establishments, as well as alcohol production. Inspired by the French philosophy of positivism, liberal leaders believed that to attain such European-style progress, they must first create an orderly, crime-free society. Once again, this meant controlling the masses, which they perceived to be unruly and detriments to progress. Often elites sought to distinguish themselves from these groups by their consumption habits—wearing French fashions, listening to Austrian waltzes, and drinking Spanish wines or German beers. According to the aspirations of modernity and industrialization, wine, beer, and tequila producers in places like Argentina, Brazil, and Mexico used the language of progress to advertise their industrially produced spirits in the late nineteenth and early twentieth centuries.

In this section, Nancy Hanway (chapter 4), Áurea Toxqui (chapter 5), and David Carey Jr. (chapter 6) explore the challenges and methods employed by nineteenth-century politicians in the development and modernization of their nations. Hanway examines this formative period through the analysis of the introduction of French grapes and production techniques in the countryside of Argentina. Toxqui studies women's participation in the production and consumption of alcohol in Mexico City and their responses to liberal policies and taxation. Carey analyzes Guatemalan efforts in creating a nonnative nation free of social evils such as drunkenness that supposedly characterized the native Maya population. Gretchen Pierce, José Orozco, and Steve Stein also contribute to the discussion of these issues in their respective chapters included in part 3 of this book.

CHAPTER FOUR

Wine Country

The Vineyard as National Space in Nineteenth-Century Argentina

Nancy Hanway

At a weak moment the idea came to me of producing a bottle of San Juan wine. They acted as if I had tried to poison them, the best of our wines cutting such a poor figure alongside those of Oporto, Bordeaux, Burgundy, etc.

— DOMINGO FAUSTINO SARMIENTO

Statesman-author Domingo Faustino Sarmiento (1811–1888) was governor of the province of San Juan, Argentina, in 1862, when he related this story of enological embarrassment. Considered one of the fathers of the modern Argentine nation and, at the time, its most prominent intellectual, Sarmiento eventually became its president as well, holding office from 1868 to 1872. He was also the author of one of nineteenth-century Latin America's most foundational literary texts. His 1845 *Facundo o Civilización y Barbarie* (*Facundo, or Civilization and Barbarism*) set forth Sarmiento's theories, based on scientific racism, that Argentina was a "barbaric" territory and that people could be "civilized" only through European immigration and progress.

Less well known is Sarmiento's involvement in the Argentine wine industry. Starting in the 1850s, Sarmiento, a native of San Juan, set out to improve and modernize viticulture in the Cuyo region—which included back then the wine-producing provinces of San Juan, San Luis, and Mendoza—, and he is held indirectly responsible for the introduction of French wine varietals to Argentina.[1] Sarmiento's interest in viticulture was not, however, simply an expression of his interest in agriculture and commerce; rather, it sprang from his deeply rooted social and political ambitions.

This chapter argues that for Sarmiento the vineyard represented a national space in which his ideals for the new Argentine nation played out— a space in which modern, imported know-how would be put to work to rid outmoded colonial ways from the territory. Like the pampas (the vast grasslands in the central part of the country) of his classic work, *Facundo*, the vineyard figured symbolically as a space of conflicting struggles regarding the nation and served as the nexus of Sarmiento's beliefs about education, Europeanization, and progress. Unlike the pampas, however, Argentina's wine country was Sarmiento's home region, and he understood the economic and regional loyalties there only too well. The reorganization and advancement of this particular territory were truly personal, as this affected the livelihood of his home and, during his time as a provincial politician, of his constituents. The vineyard also appeared in Sarmiento's work as a place of regional and political struggle, an overdetermined space where wine country sometimes stood for the nation (with its capital in Buenos Aires) and sometimes stood apart from it. This uneasy negotiation in Sarmiento's writings about wine, between core and periphery, nation and province, would never be resolved discursively, even by the end of his long career.[2]

The story of Argentina and wine is a complex and somewhat tortuous one that, over its nearly five-century history, has been hampered by changes in government, the wars of independence, civil wars and unrest, devastating earthquakes, a cholera outbreak, military dictatorships, poor government oversight, short-sighted economic policies, and a lack of organized cooperation in the industry.[3] Winemaking in Argentina began in the 1550s, when vines were brought from Chile by Jesuit priests.[4] The original grape was, without doubt, the *uva Criolla*, the Mission grape, described by an early twentieth-century observer as "a high-yielding, very rustic crop . . . that produces an alcoholic wine of a yellowish pink color and with a disagreeable smell and taste."[5] Although its original purpose was to provide wine for Catholic mass, winemaking eventually became an important economic activity for the region, particularly in Mendoza, which sent wine overland to Córdoba and Buenos Aires.[6] While winemaking did not become the central industry of the region until centuries later, recent research has shown that winemaking was already thriving by the eighteenth century, during which time there were more than forty bodegas (wineries) of importance in Mendoza alone.[7]

In the early nineteenth century, however, viticulture in Cuyo began to decline. Mendoza served as the staging ground for José de San Martin's army in the Wars of Independence, the first blow among many to follow for viticulture.[8] The years from 1829 to 1851 were punctuated by civil unrest, internal struggles, and the increasing economic and political stranglehold of the Juan Manuel de Rosas dictatorship, with a brief period of peace in the 1840s.[9] Many influential Cuyan winemakers were forced into exile. The earthquake of 1861, which leveled Mendoza, was the final indignity. The industry in Mendoza and San Juan suffered so many shocks to its system during the nineteenth century that, by 1870, it was mostly focused on local production.[10] As a result, the wine industry in Argentina experienced its real boom only in the 1880s, when the arrival of train lines to Mendoza, combined with a wave of European immigrants, produced what might be considered Sarmiento's dream come true: an avalanche of European laborers, an influx of European winemaking knowledge, and a way for producers to ship their wines safely to the exterior.[11]

More than most agricultural products, wine is inextricably linked to the land in the public imagination. Wine enthusiasts speak confidently of *terroir* (a word that refers to how the place in which wine grapes are grown affects the characteristics of the wine), and the study of enology involves detailed knowledge of soil composition and rainfall patterns. Something that everyone, experts and enthusiasts alike, seems to agree upon is that the Argentine territory hugging the Andes—a rugged arid region of semi-desert, over four thousand miles from France—is perfect for making wine and, in fact, is ideal for producing a certain Bordeaux grape, the Malbec. This is the result of "optimal soils, a dry climate with marked variations in temperature from day to night, and a progressive use of waters from the rivers that helped organize the landscape into a productive space [for winemaking]."[12]

It is easy to see how the vineyard became a space for Sarmiento to locate the nation: wine country in Argentina was a perfect natural landscape for wine, as long as it was combined with changes to the land, plus technical know-how and plants brought from Europe and the United States. Fixated on the idea that only European progress would bring about national unity, Sarmiento had already expounded on the symbolic connection between land and nation in his influential work, *Facundo*, a thinly veiled attack on dictator Rosas, who is personified as a "barbarous" gaucho associated with the vast pampas. Like other nineteenth-century politicians, Sarmiento believed that the Argentine nation should be white, Europeanized, and "civilized," something that would be achieved through immigration from Europe.

In Argentina, the struggle between core and periphery that plagued all the young republics of Latin America can be described as a double conflict, at once between Buenos Aires and the provinces, and between the two parties at that time battling for control over the nation: the Federalists and the Unitarists. On issues of trade, the split involved Buenos Aires and the provinces. Politicians of both parties in Buenos Aires wanted open markets that would maintain the singular advantages the city had held as the territory's port since late colonial times (and which, afterward, it sometimes protected by force). Provincial politicians, of course, wanted the sharing of trade revenues. A second political struggle complicated the first: the Federalist Party supported a federal-style government giving more power to provincial military authorities (or *caudillos*), whereas the Unitarists supported a strong centralized government with its capital in Buenos Aires.[13]

The phenomenon of *caudillismo*, or rule by provincial military leader, which emerged during the Wars of Independence in the early nineteenth century, was another factor in the bumpy road to national unity. The caudillos effectively stepped into the power vacuum caused by the end of colonial rule. This was true throughout many countries in Latin America, as the struggle between Federalists and Unitarists (referred to as centralists in most other countries) was a common feature of the new republics,[14] as Áurea Toxqui discusses in chapter 5. Sometimes allied with political parties, sometimes working against them, the political conflicts caused by caudillos differed from one country to the next, but in these struggles generally, though not always, the caudillos often represented traditional, conservative values associated with rural life.[15] And although they are usually understood to oppose centralized rule, caudillos like Argentina's Juan Manuel de Rosas (who ruled almost continuously from 1829 to 1852) sometimes strengthened the rule by the center.

The struggle between Buenos Aires and the provinces eventually led to a divided nation in 1854, as the result of actions by one of those caudillos. José de Urquiza, a military leader from Entre Ríos, defeated Rosas on the battlefield, an event that eventually sparked the separation of Buenos Aires province from the rest of Argentina. This division persisted politically until 1861 and psychologically for much longer. The issue of unity, therefore, was paramount for the generation that was building the new nation. And during the period of national consolidation, Argentina's national founders believed that, for the nation to succeed, there must be a discursive remapping of those lands as well. The land had to become national space, "imagined" as belonging to the new nation of Argentina, something accomplished through a diverse set of texts, in new "national" novels and in speeches, essays, and other forms of public discourse.[16] Many nineteenth-century writings reflected the fact that Argentine statesmen believed they must sever the link to what they perceived as both an outmoded colonial past and a "barbaric" way of life.[17] The interior of the country, therefore, had to be Europeanized; the caudillo (and his foot soldier, the gaucho) had to be tamed.

Sarmiento, in particular, saw the future of Argentina as coming from Europe and the United States, believing that the nation would need to remake its territory through a process that required both new labor and new technology imported from abroad. While this would be exactly the model Sarmiento used in remaking the vineyards of his native region, his place as a self-educated man from the interior, part of the intellectual class of Buenos Aires but geographically and economically apart from it, complicated the way in which he formulated the vineyard as a national space. Speaking sometimes as a man from San Juan and sometimes as a liberal politician from Buenos Aires, Sarmiento's personal and political connections to winemaking also led him to pursue a curious and often overdetermined rhetorical strategy when writing and speaking about the region.[18]

In his ruminations on "the Argentine gourmet world" in *La Argentina fermentada*, Matías Bruera focuses on the personal link between Sarmiento and wine, discussing how both "the vine and its juice form a recurring part of [Sarmiento's] pragmatic and symbolic meditations."[19] Referring to the fact that the word *sarmiento* in Spanish refers to the vine shoots, Bruera discusses wine as one of the ways in which Sarmiento collapses the notion of nation and self, a function of Sarmiento's self-aggrandizing, bombastic style, all the while pursuing the ideal of Argentina as an industrialized nation.[20] It should come as no surprise that Sarmiento, a relentless self-promoter sometimes mocked by his peers as "Don Yo" ("Mr. Me"), would delight in the linguistic coincidence that enabled him to connect himself to what he viewed as his homeland's agricultural future. However, the spatial element of this coincidence goes deeper, in that Sarmiento made himself part of the beginnings of the winemaking process and dug deep into the terroir of his native land.

The decades prior to 1880 were when Sarmiento and other Cuyan politicians and winemakers were setting the stage for the eventual success of

Argentine wines. And this was where Sarmiento emerged as the hero of this particular national narrative. In 1852 Sarmiento was already well known as an author and journalist who had worked tirelessly and, to some, tiresomely against the Rosas dictatorship while in exile in Chile, writing such fiery denunciations of the dictator that the Rosas government demanded, unsuccessfully, that Sarmiento be extradited to face trial. While in Chile, Sarmiento became aware of the experiments in Chilean viticulture. He had recently traveled to Europe, where—although he was somewhat disappointed by French civilization—he had drunk French wine in situ. And, while in exile, he was responsible for convincing Mendozan authorities to hire Michel Aimé Pouget, a French agronomist, to take charge of the newly established Quinta Normal, an institute founded for the betterment of Mendozan agriculture in general, which would have an enormous impact on the region's viticulture.[21]

Not only did Pouget bring (according to Sarmiento) "one-hundred and twenty varieties of grape vines," but he also remained in the province as a winemaker even upon resigning from his post, after Mendozans rejected both the idea of new plants and the expense related to maintaining the Quinta Normal.[22] While Pouget's official tenure was brief, he continued to experiment with new varietals and techniques as a private citizen, promoting, as Pablo Lacoste has stated, "the culture of quality wines in Argentina."[23] Most significant, Pouget helped establish French grapes to replace the uva Criolla.

It is easy to see why the idea of the Quinta Normal—and scientific viticulture—was so appealing to Sarmiento. Best known in Argentina as the educator president, he would, during his term in office, bring a group of teachers from the United States to found teaching colleges throughout Argentina. The Quinta Normal combined his belief in education, immigration (in the form of plants, experts, and laborers), and progress, all doing their work in Argentine soil. In his self-serving autobiography, *Recuerdos de Provincia* (*Recollections of the Province*), Sarmiento had linked his family history to the idea of both the founding of the nation and the need to embrace agricultural science. In a famous scene, his mother's beloved fig tree (associated with his mother's colonial traditions and clearly meant to symbolize the colonial past because the fig was brought by the Spaniards to the Americas) is chopped down on the insistence of his modernizing sisters. Sarmiento tells us that he replaced the fig tree with an orchard, a space that was "worthy of her advanced knowledge of agricultural science."[24]

The casting off of colonial ways had additional significance for Sarmiento. Several writers, including Bruera, refer to Sarmiento's fear of alcoholism, based, it is suggested, on the sad example of his undependable father, along with other important male figures, such as his beloved uncle, José de Oro.[25] Sarmiento clearly associated drunkenness with an unproductive colonial past. And for Sarmiento, drunkenness was also a precursor to violence and solitude, the same vices he links to the gauchos of the pampas in *Facundo*.[26] Furthermore, centuries of bad habits, enforced by the expansiveness of the land and the supposed "barbarism" of what was called "miscegenation," had led to this state of affairs, which Sarmiento and other Argentine leaders eventually helped to "cure" in a forced resettlement of the gauchos and the extermination of the native peoples of the pampas.

It should be noted that the Cuyo region had long ago "resettled" its native population, the Huarpe people. Sarmiento devoted a chapter to the Huarpes in *Recuerdos de Provincia*, in part, it seems, to demonstrate how, like the Huarpes, the "indolent Spanish colonists" too might someday be "wiped from the roster of nations," intoning, "Woe to the nations that fail to march forward!"[27] As a result of his belief in this natural indolence of the Spaniards, Sarmiento described the lack of natural resources in San Juan to be a blessing. "[San Juan's] population would have degenerated by now into brutishness, had not the need to exercise man's physical and moral strengths been born from that very scarcity of natural resources."[28] In *Recuerdos de Provincia*, alcoholism was seen as a sickness coming from the old vineyards, representing a lack of modern progress and the failure to create a civilized government: "In San Juan, this is a disease that takes hundreds of people, who—as they grow old, disenchanted with life, without hopes, without theaters, without movement, for there is neither education nor liberty—often retire early to their vines. Loneliness and spiritual emptiness bring on this tedium, this calls them to wine as an antidote, and they end by withdrawing from society and giving themselves up to a misanthropic, solitary and perennial drunkenness."[29] Here, the vineyards of San Juan became representative of the worst of the old colonial regime and of the Rosas dictatorship (the "lack of democracy" in this statement); the vineyard is the seat of "spiritual emptiness." Collapsing the provincial and the national, the vineyards of his forefathers in San Juan demonstrated a reason for the new nation Sarmiento envisioned: an educated and "civilized" one, with a new government run by white, privileged men like Sarmiento himself. Like the pampas, the vineyard represented the potential of the new Argentina; it had to be "marched forward" for the good of the nation. Sarmiento ignored the fact that a modern vineyard might also produce drunkenness—this piece of logic is pushed aside by the ideas of modernity, Europeanization, and national unity.

Complicating Sarmiento's own unstable discourse about the vineyard as a national space is the fact that—prior to this period—the winemaking provinces had developed their own, autonomous identity, based in part on viticulture.[30] On several occasions, from colonial times onward, what historian Pablo Lacoste calls "the Cuyan winemaking bourgeoisie" worked to separate the region from its contemporaneous government.[31] Originally part of the Kingdom of Chile, in 1700 Mendozan elites petitioned the Spanish Crown to remove Mendoza and San Juan to what would become Argentina. This would eventually happen with the reforms that led to the creation of the Viceroyalty of Río de la Plata in 1776. After the fall of Mendoza to the forces of dictator Juan Manuel de Rosas in the 1830s, influential Mendozans tried to convince the Chilean government to partition the Cuyo region back to Chile. According to Lacoste, Cuyans saw themselves as much allied with their winemaking peers on the other side of the Andes as they were with their troubled new nation. It could be argued, therefore, that the vineyard represented an unstable national/regional identity and that Sarmiento's wish to have the vineyard stand for the nation was an exercise in wish fulfillment. In speaking of Mendoza, in particular, architect and scholar Eliana Bórmida maintains that winemaking has long been an essential part of Mendoza's identity: "Viticulture is understood to mean an agro-industrial activity, but it is much more than that: it is a form of culture in a deep sense, that strongly marks and distinguishes the identity of Mendoza."[32]

The vineyard as a problematic nexus for Sarmiento's regional and political views could also be seen in 1853, when Sarmiento wrote mournfully of the problems with the Quinta Normal in Mendoza—the institute that was meant to revolutionize Argentine viticulture. Here, Sarmiento articulated the geographical determinism seen previously, but also used language that called into question Mendoza's patriotism. Sarmiento had been disappointed by the angry reaction to this first pet project—Mendozans immediately vilified their minister Vicente Gil for his creation of the Quinta Normal. In an article in the newspaper *La Crónica*, Sarmiento linked the failure of Mendozans to support the Quinta Normal to what he believed was their lack of national spirit during recent political turmoil in favor of a selfish provincialism that threatened the nation. Moving rapidly from agriculture to national politics, Sarmiento raged against the events following the defeat of the dictator Rosas by the caudillo José Justo de Urquiza, a military leader Sarmiento once supported but whom he now saw as a tyrant whose rule would destroy national unity. He thundered: "Mendoza was, from the first, the complacent executor of the will of

General Urquiza." Sarmiento claimed that, at some moment in the future, with the success of Mendoza's agricultural riches, "the Minister Gil will be avenged, with the only vengeance to which good patriots should aspire."[33] It is clear, from his language, that the "patriotic" Gil was a patriot not only for Mendoza alone but also for Argentina. Sarmiento was linking the idea of the homeland to agricultural progress, at the same time that he was settling old provincial scores with his inflammatory language. In an essay titled "Political Capital" in the newspaper *El Nacional* in 1856, he complained again about the ungrateful and politically selfish Mendozans, who did not recognize that as the result of the Quinta Normal "you can already taste Bordeaux in Mendoza that is finer and more pure than the brew of the same name that is drunk in Buenos Aires."[34] Clearly, Sarmiento's fury over the divided nation can also be read into this comment.

In 1862, when Sarmiento became governor of San Juan province, one of his first tasks was the creation of a Quinta Normal for San Juan. He hired a German agronomist who brought grape vines: "Four thousand new plants . . . to form part of the catalog of the Quinta Normal, of the varieties that serve to make wines of Bordeaux, of Burgundy, etc." In his speech on opening day, Sarmiento referred to the "sterile" land that would be made fruitful by the establishment of the Quinta Normal: "I have had the honor of inviting you to sanction with your presence the opening of the first branch, that from these sterile fields will become the first educational agricultural institute devoted to the science that today honors all civilized peoples, agriculture, the culture of the earth that, [even] without science is, however, until now the only source of wealth in San Juan."[35] While San Juan had been lucky, Sarmiento seemed to suggest, the people still needed this "culture of the earth" and science in order to become truly civilized, repeating the theme he had begun in *Recuerdos de Provincia*. He then blamed the absence of good wine on bad habits, suggesting that the poor quality of the wines made from the uva Criolla is the result of a lack of education: "Why are there no good wines, in a country so favorable to the culture of the vine? Because [the vine] whose first shoots were introduced three centuries ago, has perhaps degenerated, losing color or acquiring a disagreeable flavor from bad cultivation."[36] The uva Criolla now represented idleness and ignorance, thereby using the Mission grape as another example of an outmoded colonial past, like the gauchos of the pampas and his drunken, elderly neighbors in San Juan. The uva Criolla grape, in this formulation, has been destroyed by the outmoded colonial citizen, and the poorly tended "sterile" lands of the Quinta Normal of San Juan now stood in for the pampas.

It was in this same speech that Sarmiento recounted his tale of enologi-cal humiliation, cited in the epigraph, about serving San Juan wines to Bartolomé Mitre (a general and future president of Argentina), Urquiza, and other "illustrious" personages to celebrate the signing of a pact mark-ing the unification of the country after nearly a decade—a moment Argen-tines incorrectly assumed was the end to the long civil war. Sarmiento's motive was simple: he wanted to convince his audience that the Quinta Normal was sorely needed in San Juan. In Sarmiento's typical, overdeter-mined style, he used the competition between Mendoza and San Juan as part of his ammunition, dropping famous names freely and invoking European culture, national pride, patriotism, and provincial competition, in an anecdote that, also typically, made Sarmiento himself the central figure.

Introducing the anecdote with, "Two years ago, while General Mitre celebrated the peace of November with General Urquiza," Sarmiento dis-cussed the horrified reaction of his audience, who "acted as if I had tried to poison them, the best of our wines cutting such a poor figure alongside those of Oporto, Bordeaux, Burgundy, etc." He then made a telling confes-sion: "At my own table I generally drink Mendozan wine, because the love of one's country cannot lead one to the extreme of drinking such a brew on a daily basis."[37] The anecdote referred to the opposing generals of the recent civil wars, following the signing of a pact in November 1859 that would eventually lead to the reunification of Argentina in 1861. At the time that Sarmiento opened his infamous bottle of wine, Urquiza had just defeated Mitre's forces in Buenos Aires, and the two sides had negotiated a fragile pact over a period of weeks.

Sarmiento's audience, in September 1862, knew that this was not the end of the story. Urquiza would eventually retreat from the battlefield at Pavón in 1861, and it was a foregone conclusion for Sarmiento's listeners that Mitre would become president of the newly united republic. This was a dramatic moment in Argentine history—involving tense political nego-tiations that would decide the fate of the nation—and yet Sarmiento men-tioned it in an almost off-hand way, as if the event was simply setting the stage for a wine tasting. Of course, he knew his audience: this wine tasting had international, national, and regional implications for his listeners. San Juan wines would be representing Argentina for the foreign guests and provincial wines for the *porteños* (residents of Buenos Aires) and were spe-cifically regional for Sarmiento's contemporary audience from San Juan. Wine—specifically, "their" wine—was playing a role in national history. For Sarmiento, it was vital to his message that this particular negotiation failed: San Juan viticulture, he was saying, needed technical knowledge from abroad, in order to take its place alongside its European and Argentine peers on a national stage.

What was also significant from this anecdote is the way in which Sarmiento navigated, yet again, the national and the provincial, this time creating yet another division for his audience in a way that suggested his partisanship. San Juan wines were first compared unfavorably with European wines (it was suggested that foreign wines were the only wines drinkable to a porteño), but Sarmiento then ranked Mendozan wines above those of San Juan. But while diminishing his own province's wines, Sarmiento used the word *país* (country) here to mean San Juan and not Argentina. In Spanish, of course, he would use *nación* (nation) to refer to the republic and *país* when talking about the territory. The vineyard, for Sarmiento, continued to have a dual identity, now representing both the *sanjuanino* (individual or item from San Juan) and the Argentine.

The conflation of the regional into the national, however, was happening even before the rise of the wine industry, through the expositions that were such a ubiquitous part of nineteenth-century national cultures. As scholar Jens Andermann has written, the importance of such expositions in Argentina and Brazil in the nineteenth century resided in being "as instances of visual education that turned local audiences into consumers, were a first step towards making viable a 'national industrialization.'"[38] Within Argentina, Cuyan wines were making a statement at agricultural expositions in Buenos Aires and Córdoba, beginning to represent the nation for other Argentines. And as early as 1867, these same wines had begun to win international prizes, something that was a source of great pride for Sarmiento. By 1882, when he wrote "Vinicultura Argentina," Sarmiento had served as president of the republic. Discussing the state of the wine industry, in *El Nacional*, Sarmiento referred to Pouget as a "known vintner who brought a collection of 120 varieties of vines, going later personally to France to exhibit his Bordeaux wine of Mendoza, which won a copper [*sic*] medal, and to bring new varietals."[39] The title of the article is not "Vinicultura Cuyana" ("Viniculture of Cuyo") but "Vinicultura Argentina" ("Argentine Viniculture"). When writing for a national newspaper, Sarmiento turned the provincial industry into a matter of pride for the nation.

Sarmiento returned to the subject of San Juan wines in 1884, this time at the opening of the Government House in San Juan. Unlike the old vineyard of *Recuerdos de Provincia*, the vineyard was no longer cast as the space of solitude and misanthropy: "Among the many difficulties that oppose its development, San Juan has an anchor of salvation, which is the cultivation of wine, whose products are measured not as much by the originating goodness of the grape, as by the level of intelligence that has been devoted to making it. The wine that distorts reason is the work of that same reason."[40] In a neat play on words that almost defies logic, the drunkenness that may come with wine was now, somehow, a trait positively associated with reason. Sarmiento invoked both Roman historian Suetonius on French wine and Julius Caesar on the beer of Germanic tribes to demonstrate the many generations of experience that other nations have had in the cultivation of their native brew. Again, he elided San Juan and, by extension, the rest of Argentine wine country into the nation, when he claimed that "it is to contemporary science to which we must ask advice about the making of our wines, since in order to export them with success in the markets we have to stand shoulder to shoulder with science and the experience of all the nations of the world."[41] Only four years before his death, the vineyard was now the space through which both the heroic ancient cultures and scientific prowess would enter Argentina from other nations.

Defending the advantages of wine to other agricultural exports, Sarmiento extolled the fact that it would end up in the hands of a "civilized" man: "A load of wheat exported from San Juan to the coast, even in a train, will avoid surcharges, but a bottle of Château-Lafitte or of Veuve Cliquot can arrive at the Poles, cross the seas, and scale mountains, finally arriving in the hands of a civilized man who will drink it."[42] Argentine wines, Sarmiento implied, could also take the same globe-trotting expeditions; the economic advantage of wheat was now seen as a dull commercial one, the product lacking any heroic, historical drama for the nation. Representing the culture of the civilized, scientific nation he imagined, wine, like Sarmiento himself—the sanjuanino turned national citizen— could "cross the seas and scale mountains." The vineyard was where this drama must begin: a space where this link between Argentina and the "civilized" world would be forged.

Sarmiento identified wine as a national industry long before the future of Argentina as a wine powerhouse was assured. His devotion to supporting the industry never wavered, a fact that was well illustrated in "Vinicultura Argentina." Writing about the phylloxera virus, he asserted that every official power in the nation must "pursue like the most abominable infection, just like syphilis, the introduction of any vine plant from any part of Europe to America, from any part of America to another."[43] Sarmiento's language contained more than a few echoes of the language of the public hygiene movement of his day: unlike European know-how and (white) immigrants, European viruses should be treated like unwashed travelers. And he presented the prospect of the invading virus as a tragedy for his home region that would have national implications: "By not taking these safeguards, we are going to lose the future of the region bordering the Andes . . . whose climate lends itself exclusively and favorably to the cultivation of the grape vine."[44] The vineyard regions, deemed "Argentine" by Sarmiento in the article's title, clearly represented the future of the nation, deserving every protection that every national agency can muster. Yet, despite Sarmiento's devotion to the industry, and despite signs of promise for the region during his lifetime, it is only in the twentieth century that Argentina's wines have received the kind of respect that Sarmiento desired, as discussed by Steve Stein later in this collection.[45]

The Argentine wine industry did not develop in exactly the way Sarmiento envisioned. Argentina may be the fifth leading producer of wine in the world currently, but its wines have only recently received accolades from the international wine world. Despite the many fine wines produced in Argentina for decades, the country still suffers from a reputation for producing thin reds of poor quality. This reputation seems to be changing, finally, along with the culture of Mendoza and San Juan. Now part of the "Great Wine Capitals Global Network," Mendoza is a popular destination for international wine tourists.[46] French travelers can book the *route du vin argentin* (Argentine wine route) to taste Malbecs and Spaniards can find Argentine Tempranillo wines. In both Mendoza and San Juan, tourists can visit historic sites devoted to wine and wine architecture, as part of the national patrimony. And Argentina's vineyards are attracting not only wine-tasting visitors but also winemaking immigrants. While some contemporary Argentines see these new immigrants as invaders, some of these vineyards are producing wine that is internationally regarded as Argentine wine. Sarmiento would have been pleased, convinced as he was that Argentina could join European nations as a wine-producing powerhouse and that his country was capable of producing wines that even the enophiles of Buenos Aires could love.

Notes

1. More recently, the Cuyo region has also included La Rioja province.
2. Many scholars have commented on the difficulties in analyzing the contradictory, self-fictionalizing, and often unlikable Sarmiento. He should be seen in his

context as the ultimate politician, crafting his discourse according to his reading (and misreading) of the political moment, combined with a messianic sense that he knew what was right for the nation.

3. For more on the lack of cooperation between the industry and experts hired to help them, see Ana María Mateu and Steve Stein, "Diálogos entre sordos, los pragmáticos y los técnicos en la época inicial de la industria vitivinícola argentina," *Historia agraria: Revista de agricultura e historia rural* 39 (2006), 267–92. Mateu and Stein discuss the long conflict between quantity and quality that has plagued the Argentine wine industry.

4. Pablo Lacoste, *El vino del inmigrante: los inmigrantes europeos y la industria vitivinícola argentina* (Mendoza, Argentina: Universidad del Congreso/Consejo Empresario Mendocino, 2003), 281.

5. Pedro Arata, *Investigación Vinícola: Informes presentados al Ministro de Agricultura por la Comisión Nacional* (Buenos Aires: Talleres de la Oficina Meteorológica, 1903), 134, qtd. in Steve Stein, "Grape Wars: Quality in the History of Argentine Wine," in *Wine, Society, and Globalization: Multidisciplinary Perspectives on the Wine Industry,* ed. Gwyn Campbell and Nathalie Guibert (New York: Palgrave Macmillan, 2007), 104.

6. Estela del Carmen Premat, "La Bodega Mendocina en los siglos XVII y XVIII," *Revista Universum* 22, no. 1 (2007), 118–35.

7. Ibid.

8. Pablo Lacoste, "Viticultura y Política Internacional: El intento de reincorporar a Mendoza y San Juan a Chile (1820–1835)," *Historia* 39 (2006), 170.

9. Luis Alberto Coria López, "El siglo anterior al boom vitivinícola mendocino (1780/1883)," *Revista Universum* 21, no. 2 (2006), 100–24.

10. Rodolfo Richard-Jorba, "Los empresarios y la construcción de la vitivinicultura capitalista en la provincia de Mendoza (Argentina), 1850–2006," *Scripta Nova. Revista Electrónica de Geografía y Ciencias Sociales* 12, no. 271 (2008), http://www.ub.edu/geocrit/sn/sn-271.htm.

11. Ana María Mateu and Hugo Ocaña, "Una mirada empresarial a la historia de la vitivinicultura mendocina (1881–1936)," *Boletín Americanista* 59 (2009), 52–53.

12. Mateu and Stein, "Diálogos entre sordos," 270.

13. Sujay Rao, "Arbiters of Change: Provincial Elites and the Origins of Federalism in Argentina's Littoral, 1814–1820," *The Americas* 64, no. 4 (2008), 512–14.

14. Jeremy Adelman, *Sovereignty and Revolution in the Iberian Atlantic* (Princeton, NJ: Princeton University Press, 2006), 382–92.

15. Charles F. Walker, *Smoldering Ashes: Cuzco and the Creation of Republican Peru* (Durham, NC: Duke University Press, 1999), 122–23.

16. Nancy Hanway, *Embodying Argentina: Body, Space and Nation in 19th Century Narratives* (Jefferson, NC: McFarland, 2003).

17. Ibid., 19–20.

18. William H. Katra, "Rereading *Viajes*: Race, Identity and National Destiny," in *Sarmiento: Author of a Nation,* ed. Tulio Halperín Donghi et al. (Berkeley: University of California Press, 1994), 73–75.

19. Matías Bruera, *La Argentina fermentada: vino, alimentación y cultura* (Buenos Aires: Paidós, 2006), 56

20. Ibid., 55.

21. William H. Beezley, "La senda del Malbec: la cepa emblemática de Argentina," *Revista Universum* 20, no. 2 (2005), 288–97.

22. Domingo Faustino Sarmiento, "Vinicultura Argentina," in *Obras Completas, 51 vols., ed. A. Belín Sarmiento* (Buenos Aires: Mariano Moreno, 1899), 42:109; Lacoste, *Vino del inmigrante,* 95.

23. Lacoste, *Vino del inmigrante,* 112.

24. Domingo Faustino Sarmiento, *Recuerdos de provincia* (Buenos Aires: Editorial de Belgrano, 1981), 235; see also Hanway, *Embodying Argentina,* 69–70.

25. Bruera, "Sarmiento, la fermentación del país," 63.

26. Depending on the rhetorical needs of the moment, in *Facundo* wine is consumed to excess or rarely. Gauchos are seen either avoiding drink because of their "Arab-like" nature or choosing to spend the day on a drunken binge.

27. Domingo Faustino Sarmiento, *Recollections of a Provincial Past* (London: Oxford University Press, 2005), 23.

28. Domingo Faustino Sarmiento, *San-Juan, sus hombres i sus actos en la rejeneración Arjentina* (1851), qtd. in Elizabeth Garrels, introduction to Sarmiento, *Recollections of a Provincial Past,* xl.

29. Sarmiento, *Recuerdos de provincia,* 49.

30. Lacoste, "Viticultura y Política Internacional," 170.

31. Ibid.

32. Eliana Bórmida, "Patrimonio de la industria del vino en Mendoza," paper presented at the Jornadas de Trabajo *Patrimonio industrial. Fuerza y riqueza del trabajo colectivo* of the Centro Internacional para la Conservación del Patrimonio (Buenos Aires, Argentina, July 1–2, 2003), 143.

33. Sarmiento, "La Quinta Normal de aclimatación de plantas en Mendoza," *Obras Completas,* 10:224.

34. Sarmiento, "Capital Política," *Obras Completas,* 25:93.

35. Sarmiento, "Quinta Normal: Discurso pronunciado en la inauguración de la Quinta Normal en San Juan, 7 de septiembre de 1862," *Obras Completas* 21:165.

36. Ibid.

37. Ibid.

38. Jens Andermann, "Tournaments of Value: Argentina and Brazil in the Age of Exhibitions," *Journal of Material Culture* 14, no. 3 (2009), 357.

39. Sarmiento, "Vinicultura Argentina."

40. Faustino Sarmiento, "Discurso en la inauguración de la casa del gobierno, 10 de mayo de 1884," *Obras Completas,* 22:260.

41. Ibid.

42. Ibid.

43. Sarmiento, "Vinicultura Argentina."

44. Ibid.

45. Martin de Moussy, *La Confederation Argentine a l'Exposition Universelle de 1867 a Paris: Notice Statistique Generale et Catalogue* (Paris: Bouchard-Huzard, 1867), 48.

46. Great Wine Capitals Global Network, "Mendoza," http://greatwinecapitals .com/capitals/mendoza/introduction, accessed August 27, 2013.

CHAPTER FIVE

Breadwinners or Entrepreneurs?

Women's Involvement in the *Pulquería* World of Mexico City, 1850–1910

Áurea Toxqui

Although *pulque* and *pulquerías* have been the topic of many studies, mostly focusing on economics, little attention has been given to women's active participation in this trade.[1] In the second half of the nineteenth century, while elite white women owned large landholdings producing pulque and pulquerías, poor women of indigenous descent sold different meals outside these taverns. The former became involved in the trade as the daughters, wives, or widows of pulque entrepreneurs; the latter, lacking skills and capital, found a way to put bread on their family's table through cooking. Well-to-do female producers supervised their businesses from the privacy of their houses by hiring male administrators who ran the daily operations. Food vendors, instead, had to sell their products in the street themselves and faced all the inconveniences that this implied. The social connotations of pulque, due to its identification as an indigenous, artisanal, unhygienic product, heavily impacted the perception of female participation in the trade. Furthermore, in the late nineteenth century, liberalism expanded women's rights and roles as responsible and productive members of society, although it also expected them to maintain honor through domesticity. For those women publicly participating in the economy, mainly working in the street and highly condemned places such as taverns, these contradictory expectations represented a challenge and made it difficult to maintain an honorable reputation.

Through the analysis of municipal and notary records as well as contemporary narratives, this chapter studies the pulquería world as an arena where the economic and political activities of women of different classes and races intersected. It compares their experiences in the pulque trade and their participation in the local and national economy and politics based on their ethnic and social background. In addition, it analyzes how their activities were shaped and perceived by social norms and contemporary understandings of patriarchy, honor, and progress. This chapter draws on the extended scholarship on women's dominant role in alcohol trade in other times and parts of the world, as well as on gender and contestation in Mexico and Latin America,[2] and benefits particularly from studies on the tensions developed by liberalism and women's influence on social change and the economy and politics of their society.[3]

The chapter focuses on the second half of the nineteenth century and the first decade of the twentieth century as the period in which these women continually defended their enterprises from the discourse and actions of liberal governments. Taxes from estate property, pulque, and pulquerías represented significant revenues for the national treasury, which granted large producers political lobbying power. In contrast, the food sellers' small capital and tax contributions to the municipal economy caused the city council to perceive their enterprises as petty trade. Therefore, authorities disregarded the food sellers' interests when they interfered with larger business owners and taxpayers. Because of the profitability of the trade and the lack of federal and local reserves, authorities constantly increased taxes on pulque and pulquerías. Moreover, urbanization and beautification programs led the government, following principles of order and progress, to issue strict legislation intended to control hygiene and behavior in pulquerías and eradicate the sale of food in the streets.

Under this context and framework, this chapter argues that although the economic activities of pulque and food producers intersected in the pulquería world, this did not imply a social exchange. Their lives were parallel without intersecting due to the geographical, social, economic, racial, and cultural separation between them. However, all of them became political actors who defended their trade from the government's impositions by using different strategies, according to their class and resources. Appealing to their status as taxpayers, breadwinners, single mothers, or widows, as well as to notions of equality, self-sufficiency, and free trade, these women, by themselves or through their male representatives, demanded that the government change its policies. In some cases, but not all, they succeeded in convincing authorities to repeal some regulations. Despite their exclusion from political citizenship at the time due to their gender, through their economic activities and their defense, these women contributed to the politics of modern Mexico.

The Intersection of Women and Pulque: The Origins

Women's involvement in the realm of pulque did not begin with the emergence of the pulquería in the sixteenth century but, rather, dated back to the pre-Hispanic period. In Aztec mythology, women and pulque were related.[4] The groups living in the arid areas of the High Plateau relieved their lack of drinking water with *aguamiel*, the clear and refreshing unfermented sap of the maguey. Soon they noticed the sap fermented in a day or two, acquiring a white viscous consistency, a rotten smell, and, more important, intoxicating and nutritional qualities. Mayahuel, the first woman who found out how to get the sap from the plant, became the goddess of aguamiel, the maguey, and fertility, while pulque got a sacred connotation. The beverage was a status marker but also a potential source of drunkenness and social disorder; therefore, its consumption was highly regulated and its sale was forbidden among the Aztecs.[5] Only pregnant and nursing women, as well as elders of both sexes, could have a small amount of pure pulque daily.[6] Apparently selected women from towns surrounding Tenochtitlan, the Aztec capital, were in charge of the production of pulque for the elite's consumption. But they were not allowed to sell it; otherwise, they could receive capital punishment.

With the Spanish conquest, pulque, free from previous regulations, lost its sacred character and became a widely demanded commodity. A few years after the fall of the Aztecs in 1521, some native females started selling it in the streets and plazas of México-Tenochtitlan. In contrast to the mutual distaste for wheat bread and corn tortillas by Native Americans and Europeans, respectively, pulque appealed to Africans, castas, poor Spaniards, and the indigenous people alike.[7] By origin, pulque was a beverage of the southern section of the High Plateau. The maguey plant only grew in the cold and arid highlands of the current states of Hidalgo, Tlaxcala, México, and Puebla. Despite the resilient nature of the plant, its sugary sap, aguamiel, and the fermented concoction, pulque, did not withstand long trips. Soon, the pulquería, or *casilla*, came out as a local phenomenon of the multiethnic Mexico City, where demand for the beverage was particularly high.[8] Later, pulquerías spread to the surrounding cities and towns of the region, but the capital kept the lead.

Figure 5.1. Interior of a Pulquería, José Agustín Arrieta, ca. 1850, one of the earliest depictions of pulquerías, which shows the active presence of women as bartenders and cooks. (Museo Nacional de Historia, Mexico City. CONACULTA-INAH-MEX. Authorized reproduction by Instituto Nacional de Antropología e Historia)

Since the creation of casillas, women had an active input, not only as customers interacting with their male peers but also as pulque and food sellers (figure 5.1). While peddling was not a new activity for the native women of central Mexico, who before the conquest had worked outside the home as marketplace vendors and administrators, working in pulquerías certainly represented a new occupation. Although taverns have been commonly understood as male sites, especially because of gendered ideas of proper female and male behavior, as well as private and public spaces, casillas became sites in which both men and women belonged. The main attraction became the free interaction among them, from the exchange of gazes to courtship and physical contact, which was further promoted by the crowds, the music and dances, the presence of young women as bartenders, and the intoxicating nature of the beverage.[9] The Church and the Crown tried to stop this interaction, which they equated with sex, adultery, and prostitution. Yet, pulque production and commercialization delivered significant revenues to the royal treasury; therefore, authorities merely regulated the customers' behavior. To do so, at the beginning of the colonial period the Spanish Crown allowed only old native women to sell pulque. Female producers living closer to Mexico City took advantage of the regulations and requested permits to open inns and taverns on the roadways.[10] In contrast with *chicha*, the production and sale of which has been a female task from the pre-Hispanic period until today, women were displaced from pulque production in Mexico. Once the beverage became an important trade item in the seventeenth century and entire large landholdings were allocated to its production, pulque production fell into the hands of men.

Afterward, women were involved only in retailing, and many of them were no longer indigenous. By the late eighteenth century, women ran almost half of the 850 illegal taverns in service in the outskirts of the city.[11] Most of them were lower-class, married Spanish women who had opened a tavern in their homes, a practice very common across cultures because it required a small investment.[12] They were commonly called *cuberas*, because they managed only small quantities of pulque, a few *cubos* (7.23 gallons each). They generally bought it from customs officials, who kept a portion of the incoming product in the city, and from native producers who, under the excuse that it was for their personal consumption, sold it clandestinely. These women also bought leftover pulque from casillas and made it into the more palatable *tepache* by adding sugar, pineapple, and some *aguardiente*. At the end of the eighteenth century, strict surveillance over pulquerías made patrons prefer these improvised taverns.

The Essential Accompaniment to Pulque:
Food and Its Producers

If the presence of young pretty women as bartenders was a great marketing strategy, the offering of cheap or free food exceeded it. In agreement with the casilla-keeper, some women, commonly called *chilmoleras* (*mole* makers), installed their portable braziers in or outside the establishments (see figure 5.1). They offered different dishes such as *mole* (meat in a sauce made of peppers and spices), broths, enchiladas, tacos, *chalupitas* (small fried tortillas stuffed with salsa, onion, cheese, and shredded meat), and other meals that were part of the diet of the southern section of the High Plateau.[13] In some cases, keepers requested spicy meals on the menu to promote a larger consumption of pulque. The sale of food became so popular that some businesses became famous not because of their beverages but because of their food. Between the mid-1500s and the mid-1900s, the presence of these female cooks around the casillas led Mexico City residents to associate these taverns with the *enchiladera* (enchilada maker) or the chilmolera and the delicious meals they prepared.

Since the colonial period, food peddlers proliferated in the Mexican capital because it was easier for the urban poor to buy their meals in the street stalls, markets, or *fondas* (small eateries) rather than cooking in their own places. Many members of the lower classes lacked steady housing or cooking utensils, lived in rooms with no kitchens in overcrowded tenements, or had to share a rudimentary stove with other families. In many cases, female members of the family had to contribute to the household income by working outside the house and could not invest extended periods of time in cooking.[14] Just making tortillas could take them two to four hours a day, depending on the size of the family, because of the need to prepare the corn, precook and grind it on the grindstone, and make the tortillas by hand. With the rapid urban growth and industrialization that Mexico experienced in the late nineteenth century, more women entered the labor force. In 1811, women constituted almost one-third of the labor force in Mexico City.[15] The majority worked as domestic servants (54 percent) or in activities related to the food industry (20 percent), and the rest were involved in different trades. In 1895, women represented almost half of the total economically active population, and 21 percent of them worked in processing industries.[16] Despite the increasing participation in factory labor and arts and sciences, a good number of women were still involved in food production and had found their niche by satisfying the broad working classes' basic need for meals.

Participation in the food industry represented a valuable option for many women who had recently migrated to the city or lacked the skills to work in factories or workshops but who had learned to cook since their childhood.[17] Cooking and housework had been part of women's identity since pre-Hispanic times, especially among rural and lower-class urban families, and demonstrated an acceptance of traditional gender roles.[18] Cooking as livelihood also suited women's busy schedules of taking care of several children, aging relatives, and household chores. In many cases, it was seen as a suitable female activity that did not compromise womanhood in the way factory work did, even if it was related to food processing.[19]

Working outside the home within the urban context provided these women some sort of temporary escape from family authority and surveillance, but it also threatened their honor for the very same reasons. Society in general questioned working-class women's honor, especially those involved in peddling, as people tended to assume that working in a public space made them "public" women.[20] As breadwinners, they were also seen as a threat to family values in a period of men's declining economic status. Industrialization offered opportunities to women at the expense of displacement of skilled male workers and perpetuated the uncertain labor conditions of unskilled ones.[21]

Because of the ambiguity of being independent breadwinners who worked on the streets, chilmoleras were the target of several criticisms. Writers, while recognizing the delicious food these women prepared, did not forget to remark on their behavior and personality. Enchiladeras were described as mestizo or native women with abundant black hair, black eyes, and wide noses, who dolled themselves up with lots of jewelry (see figure 5.2).[22] Intellectuals qualified them as gossipy individuals with loud and sharp tongues. They made fun of chilmoleras' readiness to defend their property, lovers, and partners, if needed, and who did not hesitate to scratch, bite, or tear out their rivals' hair. But these men failed to acknowledge that this was these women's way to defend their honor and that the location of their stands, outside markets, by pulquerías, or in the middle of squares and sidewalks, kept them informed.

The freedom of mobility and action food peddlers enjoyed differentiated them from elite and middle-class women who were tied to rigid gender codes.[23] In contrast to the enchiladeras, who risked their reputation by working on the streets, female pulque producers and pulquería owners did not compromise their honor despite the reputation of the beverage and the taverns, because they were scarcely visible in the trade.

Figure 5.2. *Lunch on a Street of Mexico*, Charles B. Waite, ca. 1905, showing chilmoleras' customers enduring the sun in their faces in order to enjoy the food prepared by these women. (CONACULTA-INAH-MEX. Authorized reproduction by Instituto Nacional de Antropología e Historia)

The Nineteenth-Century Ladies of Pulque and Their Power

Soon after the emergence of pulquerías, Spaniards and mestizos noticed the profitability of the pulque trade and began participating in it. By the second half of the eighteenth century, many members of the nobility were involved, too. Among them was the marchioness of Selva Nevada, Antonia Gómez de Bárcena, who owned three major estates, largely producing pulque, and four pulquerías.[24] Noble families had an advantage over native towns and small producers by owning haciendas allocated to mostly planting maguey plants and producing pulque. They aided the commercialization of the beverage by leasing pulquerías and forcing renters to buy their product.

The nobility of European descent controlled the trade in Mexico City, and almost no small producer could open a casilla in the city. Instead, in exchange for their contribution or services to the monarchy, the Crown granted these aristocrats permission to open new pulquerías. The fact that the Spanish legal system granted similar rights in ownership and succession for men and women allowed elite colonial females in New Spain to achieve financial and social independence. One of them was María Micaela Romero de Terreros, oldest daughter of the count of Regla. Upon his death, she succeeded him in the pulque business, despite being single and younger than twenty-five, the age of legal majority.[25]

Aristocratic families intermarried in order to consolidate their power, and the pulque nobility were no exception. The daughter of the second count of Xala, María Josefa Rodríguez de Pedroso, married the son of the count of Regla, Pedro Ramón Romero de Terreros. Between both of them, they owned thirteen pulquerías and twenty-one pulque haciendas.[26] The count of Xala's granddaughter married the count of Tepa, and by 1800, they owned five casillas and six pulque ranches. This custom of marrying among pulque entrepreneurs persisted into the late nineteenth century. In 1879, the owner of the hacienda of San Antonio Ometusco, José Torres Adalid, married Pilar Sagaseta, whose father owned the hacienda of San Antonio Xala.[27]

After Mexico got its independence in 1821, the trade continued in the hands of the aristocratic oligopoly, and some of its female members actively participated in the administration of their businesses. These ladies were well known for their determination, strong character, and entrepreneurial skills.[28] However, like many other elite women, despite actively participating in financial activities, according to notary records, they did not identify themselves as having an occupation in censuses.

The great-granddaughter of the count of Xala embodies perhaps one of the most interesting cases of aristocratic women involved in the pulque trade.[29] Josefa Adalid y Gómez de Pedroso was a young widow and mother of three. Besides raising her children, Josefa ran her four haciendas and several taverns that she had inherited from her father.[30] She also sold pulque to other pulquería owners; among those was doña Guadalupe Sánchez, who received forty-five *cargas* (2,439 gallons) weekly from doña Josefa's estates. The section on pulque retailers in the traveler's guide of 1852 listed only her business and remarked that high-quality bottled pulque could be purchased at her house on Espíritu Santo Street, one of the most elegant streets in Mexico City.[31] By noting the quality and packaging of the beverage, the editor separated her from any negative connotation that pulque and pulquerías had acquired, such as being filthy and smelly, suggesting instead hygiene and modernity. The fact that the beverage could be purchased at her home implied that she was a homemaker whose entrepreneurial activities did not compromise her honor or gender roles. Although there is evidence that she owned several casillas, there are no records at the municipal archive under Josefa's name requesting a business license for them.[32] As many other members of the aristocracy, she needed to be careful with questions of propriety and femininity; therefore, she hired a manager to run her pulquerías.

It was a common practice among elite women to rely on representatives when dealing with municipal taxation or administration.[33] Men acting as their legal guardians or administrators filed applications for pulquería licenses in their name. That was the case for Josefa Adalid's granddaughters, Concepción and Luz Torres Sagaseta, who by 1901 were underage and had inherited the business—fifteen casillas and some pulque estates— from their parents.[34] Their uncle Ignacio Torres Adalid acted as their legal guardian, submitting applications for pulquería licenses and other transactions in their name. The practice of having male representatives became more common during the second half of the nineteenth century, when the bourgeois society adopted even more rigid gender codes in order to separate itself from the lower classes and justify the latter's political exclusion. In some cases female names did not appear in municipal records, but their partnership or stake of a family property was recognized under the terms *testamentaría* (estate), *negociación* (business), *compañía* (company) and its abbreviation *y cía.* (and Co.), or Sociedad (company) Concepción and Luz Torres Sagaseta.[35] This procedure helped these women to maintain their honor. Concepción later on became a nun[36] and most likely renounced her share in the trade when she took the veil. In 1909 her name no longer appeared among the pulquería owners, only the name of her sister, Luz, who then owned fourteen casillas, one hacienda, and three ranches.

In the Adalid clan, Josefa was not the only woman with entrepreneurial skills; her daughter-in-law, Leonor Rivas de Rivas, followed in her footsteps. Born as Leonor Rivas Mercado, she married Javier Torres Adalid, who, as Josefa's son, had inherited the hacienda of San Miguel Ometusco. When Javier died in 1893, Leonor inherited the pulque business. By 1901 she had married her cousin Carlos Rivas Gómez, and a year later they bought the hacienda Bocanegra.[37] In 1905, Leonor owned thirty-five pulquerías in Mexico City, besides pulque haciendas and some other properties. By 1910, Carlos had died, and Leonor joined the recently founded Compañía Expendedora de Pulques (Pulque-Selling Company).[38] This was a wholesaler created by powerful pulque producers or retailers with the intention of controlling the trade in Mexico City and other cities. She joined the group owning 930 shares. Her brothers Luis and Juan Rivas Mercado owned 1,785 and 1,140, respectively; her niece Luz Torres owned 720.

Leonor's active management of her business in her later years proved how older married women or widows enjoyed more freedoms than did younger married or single females. While Leonor was a widow for the first time, her brother Luis submitted license applications in her name. Her children were grown when she remarried; she then started filing petitions and signing instruments under her married name. After Carlos died, she signed as a widow. Another example was Gerarda Pardo, who also signed documents in her own name. At the time of her death, in 1902, she owned twenty-four casillas under the mercantile name of Negociación Mazapa.[39]

In 1909, when the Compañía Expendedora de Pulques was created, several elite women participated as shareholders because they owned either pulquerías or haciendas. Compared to men, women owned fewer shares; still, some of them owned thousands of stocks. Among them were the widow Dolores Sanz, who inherited thirty-nine pulquerías, one hacienda and adjacent ranches, and 3,270 bonds from her husband, Luis G. Lavie; and Trinidad Scholtz de Iturbe, owner of twelve casillas, one hacienda and adjacent ranches, and 4,500 bonds.[40]

Besides controlling the pulque trade, this group intended to create a unified front against the train company in charge of shipping the beverage to Mexico City and the government's taxation and regulations, which they saw as excessive. Producers constantly complained about the lack of support from the federal or local government for their industry, which manifested in their policies toward pulque. According to them, this affected the trade and gave a larger advantage to imported beverages, hurting national industry.[41] Since the 1850s, the Mexico City government had issued several pulquería regulations, intending to improve hygiene and customers' behavior. In 1903, modifications required the installation of sinks and urinals with running water, floors, window shutters, and plastered walls, among other improvements.[42] Some pulquería owners came together and complained about the costs of these improvements, arguing that the price of pulque was very low and that their customers were members of the lower classes who would not know how to take care of the new improvements.[43] Among the signatories were female entrepreneurs or their representatives. The lobbying power of these people became evident when the government either lessened the requirements or granted extensions to fulfill them.

The profitability of pulque made it a target of taxation beginning in the colonial period. The lack of resources due to civil wars, foreign invasions, and constant political turmoil that Mexico experienced since 1810 encouraged the government to keep these policies, particularly in the second half of the nineteenth century. In 1857, liberal president Ignacio Comonfort created a tax of 3 percent over pulque production that was added to its *alcabala* (customs duty) of 26.66 percent. The same year, he announced a new tax for pulquerías in Mexico City in order to provide the municipality with funds.[44] A group of pulque producers, among them Josefa Adalid, complained that aguardiente had an alcabala of 14 percent and that other national products paid only 8–10 percent.[45] According to these producers, their pulque estates had a total value of 2.7 million pesos, and the annual alcabala came to 178,000 pesos, 6.5 percent of the value of their estates. They argued that the new fee on casillas in Mexico City, ranging from five to twenty-five pesos per business, to be paid every three months in advance, would damage their industry. These charges were separate from the taxes paid for business licenses and renewals. The fall of Comonfort and the beginning of another civil war, rather than the lobbying power of the pulque producers, led to the repeal of this new tax.

Very often state governors and mayors in central Mexico applied similar policies and pulque producers lobbied against them. Under the excuse that there were many bandits on the roads and pulque shipments needed protection, Agapito de la Barrera, political boss of Otumba, imposed a tax on muleteers and shipments. Producers pressured the Ministry of Interior and got a revocation on the measure.[46] In January 1873, Rafael Madrid, mayor of Apan—an important pulque county in the state of Hidalgo—imposed a tax on aguamiel extraction.[47] Soon, Governor Tagle, who was related to some producers, revoked this tax. From the 1870s to the 1890s, the liberal newspaper *Monitor Republicano* constantly published letters from pulque producers and editorials criticizing the increase or creation of new taxes, as well as the high prices and poor service that the railway companies offered them.[48] Producers justified their claims with the fact that promotion of national industries would keep the good credit reputation that Mexico wanted to achieve.[49] Their trade also would represent higher revenues for the treasury if it had fewer restrictions.

Despite the inexpensive price of pulque, it represented important contributions to the national economy. In 1896, around 128,000 people participated in the pulque industry throughout its different stages of production, distribution, and commercialization.[50] Compared with export goods such as minerals or textiles, pulque did not represent a high percentage of national tax collection, but within the domestic sectors of food and beverage production it did. In 1900, the production of pulque represented 2.38 percent of the entire value of the agricultural production for domestic consumption, and 3.35 percent of the production of food and beverages.[51] In comparison, corn, the largest crop produced for domestic consumption, made up 40.11 percent of the entire value of the agricultural production, but only 5.64 percent of food and beverages. Tequila and mezcal together represented 3.27 percent of food and beverages, but they were much more expensive than pulque. These numbers do not include the amounts of beverages clandestinely produced.

Mexico City and surrounding municipalities together encompassed the Federal District, and taxes collected there directly contributed to the federal treasury. It was publicly acknowledged that among all the alcabalas collected in the city, pulque and tobacco were the most significant. In July 1856, the pulque alcabala represented 6.13 percent of all the taxes collected in the Federal District, including customs, sales, property, and other venues.[52] During the Porfiriato, the oligarchic regime of Porfirio Díaz (1876–1911), the collection system improved, and pulque revenues increased even more. In 1903, pulque sale taxes collected in the city represented 8.81 percent, while taxes on pulquerías and other taverns made up another 1.9 percent.[53]

Besides all the taxes on sales and pulquerías, pulque estates also reported important tax revenues. By 1870, the 278 pulque haciendas located in the states of Hidalgo, México, Puebla, and Tlaxcala had increased their value to more than ten million pesos.[54] In 1891, they reached fourteen million pesos, and their value doubled by 1896. In the fiscal year 1896–1897, property taxes—excluding mines—represented 2.19 percent of all revenues collected throughout the nation that year.[55] In 1901, with the introduction of the railway throughout the pulque region, the estates achieved a value of almost one hundred million pesos.[56] With the creation of the Compañía Expendedora de Pulques and the consolidation of the monopoly on the beverage, the value of pulque haciendas reached two hundred million pesos in 1909.[57]

The different revenues generated by the pulque trade, from taxes on the estates, sales, and its dispensaries, and their important contribution to the national coffers and economy, demonstrate why female producers, in conjunction with their male peers, were able to lobby and negotiate with the government. In contrast, taxes collected from fondas and *figones* (smaller eateries) were insignificant. Their owners paid less than 1 percent of the annual collection in the branch of domestic trade in 1903.[58] Enchiladeras, like many other peddlers, avoided paying taxes, but they did have to pay a very small monthly fee for a sales license. Although food taxes could not compete with pulque taxes, the sale of food in general contributed to the city's economy.

The Economic and Political Power of the Poor

Chilmoleras greatly contributed to the informal economy of Mexico City. They controlled the food market among the urban masses, but their role in the development of the urban economy has not been studied in detail because of the lack of sources. Compared with other informal sectors of the economy, these entrepreneurs had a steadier income because of the heavy reliance on their products among the lower classes. Moreover, they had some kind of control over their hours of work and the merchandise they sold. Chilmoleras' day started in the morning when they got their ingredients, set up their stalls, and began cooking on braziers on the sidewalks. It ended either when their merchandise was gone or by sunset. Every day they reinvested their daily earnings in stock, buying produce and meats from other small merchants.

Female petty traders in other parts of Latin America, such as Bolivian *chicheras* (corn-beer producers and sellers), wool weavers, and store owners, engaged in their trade by relying on family and social ties.[59] They developed credit systems at the local level based either on these relationships or merely on economic connections. The lack of evidence hinders the possibility of knowing whether or not Mexico City food vendors engaged in the trade because they already had relatives or acquaintances from their hometown working in it. The same applies to the potential networks and credit systems at the local level that these women developed among one another and with the neighborhood as a consequence of their daily inter- actions. However, based on observations of twentieth- and twenty-first- century practices in Mexico City's informal economy, some patterns can be deduced. Most likely these women would have extended credit to regu- lar customers, who, as members of the working class, paid their bill once a week after receiving their weekly wages. At the same time, these women would have relied on credit to purchase their supplies from local shop owners and market vendors. At the local sphere of the neighborhood, peo- ple relied on trust and good credit history known as *fiado*.

Food in general was inexpensive compared with other products. The daily minimum wage for an average worker in Mexico City by 1900 was thirty cents; factory workers made forty-two, and army members, 37.5.[60] Upscale fondas charged at least 12.5 cents for a three- to five-course meal. In 1852, for 37.5 cents, people could get a five-course meal that included soup, rice, veal or mutton stew, an entrée or a steak with salad, and des- sert.[61] In contrast, by the 1900s, the urban masses could have a couple of lamb or beef tacos for four cents on the street. For three to seven cents, individuals could savor a bowl of broth, an entrée cooked with peppers and meat, and lots of tortillas, which were used as spoons and forks.[62] How- ever, they had to eat while standing, squatting, or sitting on the floor, as figure 5.2 shows.

Food peddlers' trade became endangered by liberal governments, which banned seats, music, dancing, and food sales in pulquerías. Conse- quently, chilmoleras working inside the casillas had to move their braziers to the street. Soon, they again became the target of the government as it intended to rid public space of peddlers and rowdy lower classes, who threatened public order. Authorities justified their actions, such as the dis- cipline and surveillance of the poor and their vices, because they suppos- edly obstructed national development.[63]

The city government, intending to reverse underdevelopment, pushed for urbanization and public health campaigns that included the relocation of street vendors into municipal markets. Enchiladeras and many others did not have a place in a city undergoing modernization, unless they were concealed from the public gaze. Leaders believed they should be inside markets where they could not block the movement of pedestrians and offend the gaze of the upper and middle classes, who considered them and their products disgusting and unhygienic.[64] Some intellectuals, in fact, attributed the lower classes' backwardness and behavior to the inadequate corn-based diet they consumed.[65] Journalists endorsed these ideas by condemning the presence of chilmoleras and their equipment on the street. In 1868, a newspaper reported that at the entrance of a pulquería an enchiladera was frying food in a portable brazier. A child was passing by when the boiling lard splashed his face, "causing some painful burns."[66] The lard also reached the expensive dress of a lady walking by and ruined it. The reporter mentioned that the woman "lost more than 100 pesos in seconds." By emphasizing the damage to the expensive dress rather than the physical and psychological harm to the boy, he was valuing the material goods of a wealthy lady over the health of a child, who most likely was poor. His words made evident the mentality of the upper and middle classes, who called themselves *gente decente* (decent people). The journalist urged the authorities to clean the streets of those disgusting braziers, "whose female owners were not more attractive than them." He suggested moving them into the pulquerías because the meals prepared with these devices were a natural match with pulque. He closed his article by mentioning that "the decency of the population suggested these measures."[67] His statements echoed the gente decente's perception of enchiladeras, describing them as ugly and disgusting beings whose products and livelihoods were stopping progress and impeding the correct use of the street. These comments were based not only on the unhygienic working clothes of these women but also on the elite's repugnance for natives' diet, livelihood, and ethnic features.[68] By 1907, perceptions about these women had not changed. The government intended to remove peddlers from their customary location because "their dirty clothes" ruined "the clothes of the young ladies" buying flowers there.[69] These statements made evident the mentality of the elite and how they justified the hiding of the urban poor from public sight for cultural and aesthetic reasons.

During the Porfiriato, when stronger strategies to promote modernity were applied, chilmoleras faced increasing difficulties in making a living. In 1904, the city council made food sales in doorways and entrances illegal, particularly outside of pulquerías (see figure 5.3). The municipal government hired several inspectors to enforce the law and remove trespassers. Authorities justified the measure by again emphasizing public order and hygiene. Shop owners complained about the buildup of garbage around the booths and the bad behavior of the chilmoleras' customers.[70] Rulers supported these merchants, arguing that street vendors blocked the

Figure 5.3. Pulquería Waterloo, Casasola, ca. 1905. Despite the regulations, multiple street vendors peddled in the street, particularly outside pulquerías. (Courtesy of the Archivo General de la Nación, Fondo Instrucción Pública y Bellas Artes, Propiedad Fotográfica Artística y Literaria)

sidewalks and the entrances of established businesses, which paid higher contributions, and as a consequence, their interests were more relevant to the city.[71]

With the aforementioned regulation, the authorities tried not only to enforce public order but also to disassociate women from the pulquería world. Authorities believed the presence of working women in the street was unsightly and closely related to moral degeneracy. Thus, these men materialized the elite's concepts of femininity and womanhood, broadly spread by intellectuals and journalists.[72] To them, pulquerías were unhygienic, immoral places, and there was nothing less feminine and more morally degrading than women around these taverns.

Enchiladeras responded to the threat to their livelihood by engaging in resourceful confrontation and resistance with the authorities. At the beginning most of them simply dodged the municipal regulations and continued working in their customary locations. Along with food, some of them sold pulque without any kind of license. To do so, they carefully monitored the steps of the police officers and inspectors.[73] The traveler Adolfo Dollero noticed that in some neighborhoods there were lookouts, mostly children, who with a whistle advised the neighborhood of the arrival of the police.[74] Sometimes the gendarmes allowed lawbreaking as long as they received bribes, as newspapers of the time denounced.[75]

Other enchiladeras resorted to legal means by exercising their right "to petition authorities and to get a response" granted by the 1857 constitution.[76] They turned to public scribes, who wrote letters for them asking the city government for a license to sell in the streets. In their petitions, chilmoleras and other food peddlers claimed to be extremely poor and had several family members to provide for, as Gretchen Pierce also describes in chapter 7. They alleged they had no capital or any other resources to honorably and lawfully provide for their families other than their work.[77] They introduced themselves as honest, caring, and hardworking single heads of households and invoked patriarchal hierarchies by stressing their condition as "weak and defenseless women" and calling the governor the father and protector of the poor.

These ladies appealed to custom and based their right to sell in the streets on their collective and individual history. They emphasized the fact that they had worked in the same location "since time immemorial without blocking the passage of people or offering a bad appearance."[78] They had done so for many years without any government interference; now with the new regulations their source of livelihood became an illegal activity. Petra Carrillo explained that she had sold *pambazos* (fried bread stuffed with potatoes and sausage) for eight years at Portal de Santo Domingo without ever being fined, until recently, when she was fined for being "near a cantina and a pulquería."[79] She worked as a food vendor to provide bread and instruction to her multiple children. By appealing to her customary rights of having sold in the same location for several years and emphasizing her virtuous motivation, she justified working in a recently forbidden location. She closed her letter by appealing to the benevolence of the authorities and asking them to save her family from indigence. Carrillo and many other women had learned how to use the discourse of hardworking breadwinners and invoke justice and the government's paternalism to ground their rights to keep working in unlawful locations.[80]

Many of these women, using the discourse of "defenseless women," also confronted the government's right to question their morality. According to them, moral arguments and slander were no reason to be denied their right to work in the streets. In 1904, seventy-three women working around the Buenavista train station received the order to move two blocks away to avoid blocking the traffic of people, cars, and trains. In their plea to the government, they argued that even though people denigrated and spoke badly of them, they were "widows, heads of big families, and defenseless women" who had "no other means . . . by which . . . [their] families [could] subsist."[81] Many enchiladeras who worked in front of a casilla, knowing the disorderly reputation of pulquerías, backed up their petition arguing that they had worked in a "quiet and peaceful" way in that location for several years and that no reports of immorality had been filed against them.[82] For these women, morality meant striving for an honorable life.

Some of the petitioners referred to their rights and held authorities accountable for protecting these freedoms. They claimed the right of free trade, justice, and equality before the law—compared with other merchants—and accused the government of violating the principles of liberalism, despite having emerged from the Liberal Party. The owners of fondas and figones, among them several women, complained that restrictive regulations openly violated rights granted by the constitution.[83] With their letters, these working women engaged in a dialogue with the local authorities that constituted their legitimate and accessible form of making politics given the exclusion of illiterate men and women from political citizenship in this period. Through the defense of their interests and honor, the chilmoleras confronted the state and the upper and middle classes, who criticized and threatened the life-style of the working classes. By stressing gender roles, patriarchal notions, and civil rights, these women influenced political strategies among the peddlers, a practice that has remained until the twenty-first century.

Conclusions

Elite female owners of pulque haciendas and pulquerías did not have anything in common with the enchiladeras selling their food at the entrance of these taverns other than gender and honor constraints. While some had the means to fulfill the expectations and gender codes of their society, and therefore preserve their honorability, others constantly saw theirs affected by societal views. Criticisms of their physical appearance and morality due to their peddling activities represented a direct blow for chilmoleras, whose jobs represented an honest source of income to their families.

Because of their geographical and cultural separation, these women experienced dissimilar housing, as well as different networks and places of sociability. The functions of urban space separated them; while some used the street to promenade on, others used it as working place. Pulquería owners lived in elegant houses on the beautiful and prosperous west side of the city and socialized in exclusive clubs. Chilmoleras, instead, dwelled in overcrowded and ruined tenements near downtown or in squatters' shacks in the swampy eastern and southern periphery, socializing in the patios of those houses or at the plaza, the pulquerías, or the market.[84] However, the pulquería as a business, workspace, or place of social interaction represented a virtual spatial intersection among them.

This intersection by no means was a friendly one. Cleansing the streets of peddlers became a constant goal during the Porfiriato. The threat chilmoleras faced with the city's plans, based on issues of health and policing, embodied one of the many examples of confrontation between elite projects and the poor's use of the street.[85] While female pulque producers supported the government's urbanization campaigns, the enchiladeras suffered the consequences of those campaigns. Moreover, the lobbying and monopolistic power of producers proved detrimental for female owners of small eateries, who could not sell pulque without meals or had to reduce their business hours to the minimum.

The Mexican Revolution brought several changes for all these women. It put an end to the Porfiriato, the regime that large landowners, among them pulque entrepreneurs, had openly supported. However, the incipient collective action of many disenfranchised groups like food vendors undermined the legitimacy of the Porfiriato and its achievements. The defense of their trade and culture triggered the emergence of a new sense of collectivity and political power based on new networks and common demands that later on became difficult for revolutionary governments to ignore.[86] Chilmoleras' food became glorified as the "authentic mestizo cuisine" under the nationalistic discourse of these governments. More important, their actions represented an unintentional step in the struggle for universal suffrage in Mexico, although women did not get that right until decades later. But by remarking on their decent occupation, they were challenging the constitutional requirement that voting citizens should "possess an honest livelihood."[87] Their political actions fostered a popular liberalism that contemporary organizations of workers and popular groups draw on. Their demands and awareness of their condition as political actors planted the seed for further mass political activity that characterized postrevolutionary governments.[88] Since then, any political party, from the right to the left, interested in winning local or federal elections looks for the support of these kinds of political organizations and their display of popular mobilization. Thus, with their strong political and economic power from the privacy granted by the use of administrators and representatives or through their public presence, collective actions, and the help of public scribes, all of these women played a historical role in the formation of contemporary Mexico.

Notes

1. William B. Taylor, *Drinking, Homicide, and Rebellion in Colonial Mexican Villages* (Stanford, CA: Stanford University Press, 1979); John Kicza, "The Pulque Trade of Late Colonial Mexico City," *The Americas* 37, no. 2 (1980), 193–221; Michael C. Scardaville, "Alcohol Abuse and Tavern Reform in Late Colonial Mexico City," *Hispanic American Historical Review* 60, no. 4 (1980), 643–71; Juan Pedro Viqueira Albán, *Propriety and Permissiveness in Bourbon Mexico* (Wilmington, DE: SR Books, 1999); Áurea Toxqui, "Taverns and Their Influence on the Suburban Culture of Late Nineteenth Century Mexico City," in *The Growth of Non-Western Cities: Primary and Secondary Urban Networking, c. 900–1900,* ed. Kenneth R. Hall (Lanham, MD: Lexington Books, 2011), 241–69. Among the Mexican historiography can be mentioned Marco Bellingeri, *Las haciendas en México. El caso de San Antonio Tochatlaco* (Mexico City: Secretaría de Educación Pública, Instituto Nacional de Antropología e Historia, 1980); José Jesús Hernández Palomo, *La renta del pulque en Nueva España, 1663–1810* (Seville: Escuela de Estudios Hispano-Americanos de Sevilla, 1979); Mario Ramírez Rancaño, *Ignacio Torres Adalid y la industria pulquera* (Mexico City: Plaza y Valdés-Instituto de Investigaciones Sociales, Universidad Nacional Autónoma de México, 2000); Ricardo Rendón Garcini, *Dos haciendas pulqueras en Tlaxcala, 1857–1884* (Mexico City: Gobierno del Estado de Tlaxcala-Universidad Iberoameri-

cana, 1990); Ernest Sánchez Santiró, ed., *Cruda realidad. Producción, consumo y fiscalidad de las bebidas alcohólicas en México y América Latina, siglos XVII–XX* (Mexico City: Instituto Mora, 2007). Among the few studies exploring female participation in pulque trade are Edith Couturier, "Women in a Noble Family: The Mexican Counts of Regla, 1750–1830," in *Latin American Women: Historical Perspectives*, ed. Asunción Lavrín (Westport, CT: Greenwood Press, 1978), 129–49; Couturier, "Micaela Angela Carrillo: Widow and Pulque Dealer," in *Struggle and Survival in Colonial America*, ed. Gary B. Nash and David G. Sweet (Berkeley: University of California Press, 1980), 362–75; and María Áurea Toxqui Garay, "'El Recreo de los Amigos': Mexico City's *Pulquerías* During the Liberal Republic (1856–1911)" (PhD diss., University of Arizona, 2008).

2. Selected works focusing on Latin America include David Carey Jr., ed., *Distilling the Influence of Alcohol: Aguardiente in Guatemalan History* (Gainesville: University Press of Florida, 2012); Gina Hames, "Maize-Beer, Gossip, and Slander: Female Tavern Proprietors and Urban, Ethnic Cultural Elaboration in Bolivia, 1870–1930," *Journal of Social History* 37, no. 2 (2003), 351–64; Pablo Lacoste, "Wine and Women: Grape Growers and *Pulperas* in Mendoza, 1561–1852," *Hispanic American Historical Review* 88, no. 3 (2008), 361–91; Jane E. Mangan, *Trading Roles: Gender, Ethnicity, and the Urban Economy in Colonial Potosí* (Durham, NC: Duke University Press, 2005). Selected works for the rest of the world include Thomas E. Brennan, *Burgundy to Champagne: The Wine Trade in Early Modern France* (Baltimore: Johns Hopkins University Press, 1997); Barbara A. Hanawalt, "The Host, the Law, and the Ambiguous Space of Medieval London Taverns," in *Medieval Crime and Social Control*, ed. Barbara A. Hanawalt and David Wallace (Minneapolis: University of Minnesota Press, 1999), 204–23; A. Lynn Martin, *Alcohol, Sex, and Gender in Late Medieval and Early Modern Europe* (New York: Palgrave, 2001); Sarah Hand Meacham, *Every Home a Distillery. Alcohol, Gender, and Technology in the Colonial Chesapeake* (Baltimore: Johns Hopkins University Press, 2009); Diane Kirkby, *Barmaids. A History of Women's Work in Pubs* (Cambridge: Cambridge University Press, 1997); Sharon V. Salinger, *Taverns and Drinking in Early America* (Baltimore: Johns Hopkins University Press, 2002); Peter Scholliers, ed., *Food, Drink, and Identity. Cooking, Eating, and Drinking in Europe Since the Middle Ages* (Oxford: Berg, 2001).

3. Silvia Marina Arrom, *The Women of Mexico City, 1790–1850* (Stanford, CA: Stanford University Press, 1985); Sueann Caulfield, Sarah Chambers, and Lara Putnam, eds., *Honor, Status, and Law in Modern Latin America* (Durham, NC: Duke University Press, 2005); Sarah C. Chambers, *From Subjects to Citizens: Honor, Gender, and Politics in Arequipa, Peru 1780–1854* (University Park: Pennsylvania State University Press, 1999); Heather Fowler-Salamini and Mary Kay Vaughan, eds., *Women of the Mexican Countryside, 1850–1990* (Tucson: University of Arizona, 1994); John D. French and Daniel James, eds., *The Gendered Worlds of Latin American Women Workers* (Durham, NC: Duke University Press, 1997); William French and Katherine Elaine Bliss, eds., *Gender, Sexuality, and Power in Latin America Since Independence* (Lanham, MD: Rowman and Littlefield, 2007); Kimberly Gauderman, *Women's Lives in Colonial Quito. Gender, Law, and Economy in Spanish America* (Austin: University of Texas Press, 2003); Susan Kellogg, *Weaving the Past. A History of Latin America's Indigenous Women from the Prehispanic Period to the Present* (New York: Oxford University Press, 2005); Mangan, *Trading Roles*; Jocelyn Olcott, Mary Kay Vaughan, and

126 • *Áurea Toxqui*

Gabriela Cano, *Sex in Revolution. Gender, Politics, and Power in Modern Mexico* (Durham, NC: Duke University Press, 2006); Susie S. Porter, *Working Women in Mexico City: Public Discourses and Material Conditions, 1879–1931* (Tucson: University of Arizona Press, 2003); Susan Migden Socolow, *The Women of Colonial Latin America* (Cambridge: Cambridge University Press, 2000).

4. Oswaldo Gonçalves de Lima, *El maguey y el pulque en los códices mexicanos* (Mexico City: Fondo de Cultura Económica, 1956), 24–33.

5. Bernardino de Sahagún, "About the Punishment They Gave to Those Who Were Intoxicated," in *Florentine Codex* or *Historia General de las Cosas de la Nueva España* (Mexico City: Editorial Nueva España, 1946), vol. 1, book 3, appendix, chapter 3, 324; Taylor, *Drinking, Homicide,* 28–34.

6. Agustín de Vetancurt, "Manifiesto del celo de un religioso ministro de los naturales a cerca de el estado de la República de los Indios con el pulque, que beben, y la perdición que tienen," in *Teatro Mexicano* (Mexico City: Editorial Porrúa, 1971 [1697]), 95; Sonia Corcuera de Mancera, *El fraile, el indio y el pulque. Evangelización y embriaguez en la Nueva España (1523–1548)* (Mexico City: Fondo de Cultura Económica, 1991), 62, 110–28; Taylor, *Drinking, Homicide,* 30.

7. Corcuera de Mancera, *El fraile, el indio,* 110–28; Sonia Corcuera de Mancera, *Entre gula y templanza. Un aspecto de la historia mexicana,* 3rd ed. (Mexico City: Fondo de Cultura Económica, 1990), 65–66; Jeffrey M. Pilcher, "Tamales or Timbales: Cuisine and the Formation of Mexican National Identity, 1821–1911," *The Americas* 53, no. 2 (1996), 196; Taylor, *Drinking, Homicide,* 35, 40, 45; Vetancurt, "Manifiesto del celo," 95.

8. Spanish officials used the term *casilla* to designate the taverns and tent-like stalls selling pulque. In this chapter, *pulquería* and *casilla* are used interchangeably. Auguste Génin, *Notes sur le Mexique* (Mexico City: Imprenta Lacaud, 1910), 77.

9. Manuel Payno, *Memoria del maguey mexicano y sus diversos productos* (Mexico City: A. Boix, 1864), 78; Taylor, *Drinking, Homicide,* 38; Vetancurt, "Manifiesto del celo," 96–97; "Law 37, Title I, Book VI," in [Consejo de Indias], *Recopilación de leyes de los reinos de las Indias,* vol. 2 (Mexico City: Librería de Miguel Ángel Porrúa, 1987 [1681]); Elías Loyola Montemayor, *La industria del pulque* (Mexico City: Departamento de Investigaciones Industriales del Banco de México, 1956), 266–68.

10. Taylor, *Drinking, Homicide,* 36–37; Pomar y Zurita, qtd. in Corcuera de Mancera, *El fraile, el indio,* 123.

11. Scardaville, "Alcohol Abuse," 653–54.

12. Mangan, *Trading Roles;* John DeFelice, *Roman Hospitality. The Professional Women of Pompeii* (Warren Center, PA: Shangri-La Publications, 2001), 4–14, 30–38; Hanawalt, "The Host, the Law," 204–23; Martin, *Alcohol, Sex, and Gender,* 70–73; Meacham, *Every Home a Distillery,* 64–81.

13. Guillermo Prieto, *Memorias de mis tiempos. Obras Completas de Guillermo Prieto,* vol. 1 (Mexico City: Consejo Nacional para la Cultura y las Artes, 1992), 84–86, 112–13, 316; Manuel Payno, *Los bandidos de Río Frío,* 16th ed. (Mexico City: Porrúa, 1996 [1891]), 89–91; "Gacetilla. Denuncio a la policía," *Monitor Republicano* (hereafter *MR*), March 19, 1868, 3; Jeffrey M. Pilcher, *¡Que vivan los tamales! Food and the Making of Mexican Identity* (Albuquerque: University of New Mexico Press, 1998).

14. Arrom, *Women of Mexico City,* 155; Marie Eileen Francois, *A Culture of Everyday Credit: Housekeeping, Pawnbroking, and Governance in Mexico City* (Lincoln:

University of Nebraska Press, 2006), 95; John Lear, *Workers, Neighbors, and Citizens. The Revolution in Mexico City* (Lincoln: University of Nebraska Press, 2001), 50; Porter, *Working Women in Mexico City*, 136.

15. Arrom, *Women of Mexico City*, 157–69; Porter, *Working Women in Mexico City*, 8–14.

16. Lear, *Workers, Neighbors, and Citizens*, 50, 60, 73–75; Francois, *A Culture of Everyday Credit*, 163–65, 330–36; Porter, *Working Women in Mexico City*, xiii, 19–46, 200n39; Pablo Piccato, "Urbanistas, Ambulantes, and Mendigos: The Dispute for Urban Space in Mexico City, 1890–1930," in *Reconstructing Criminality in Latin America*, ed. Carlos A. Aguirre and Robert Buffington (Wilmington, DE: Scholarly Resources Books, 2000), 120.

17. Arrom, *Women of Mexico City*, 192; Dawn Keremetsis, "Del metate al molino. La mujer mexicana de 1910–1940," *Historia Mexicana* 33, no. 2 (1983), 285–302; Porter, *Working Women in Mexico City*, 133–38, 145–47.

18. Steve Stern, *The Secret History of Gender: Women, Men, and Power in Late Colonial Mexico* (Chapel Hill: University of North Carolina Press, 1995), 382; Louise M. Burkhart, "Mexica Women on the Home Front. Housework and Religion in Aztec Mexico," in *Indian Women of Early Mexico*, ed. Susan Schroeder et al. (Norman: University of Oklahoma Press, 1997), 25–54; Susan Kellog, *Weaving the Past*, 23–25, 35, 39.

19. Ann Farnsworth-Alvear, *Dulcinea in the Factory. Myths, Morals, Men, and Women in Colombia's Industrial Experiment, 1905–1960* (Durham, NC: Duke University Press, 2000), 28–30; John D. French and Daniel James, "Squaring the Circle: Women's Factory Labor, Gender Ideology, and Necessity," in French and James, *The Gendered Worlds*, 1–30; Porter, *Working Women in Mexico City*, xv–xvii, 63–72, 119–32; Joel Wolfe, *Working Women, Working Men. São Paulo and the Rise of Brazil's Industrial Working Class, 1900–1955* (Durham, NC: Duke University Press, 1993), 12–13, 23–39; María Teresa Fernández-Aceves, "Once We Were Corn Grinders. Women and Labor in the Tortilla Industry of Guadalajara, 1920–1940," *International Labor and Working-Class History* 63 (2003), 81–101; Heather Fowler-Salamini, "Gender, Work, and Working-Class Women's Culture in Veracruz Coffee Export Industry, 1920–1945," *International Labor and Working-Class History* 63 (2003), 102–21.

20. Porter, *Working Women in Mexico City*, 134–35, 139–45.

21. The questioning of the honor of food peddlers and market women because of their work in public spaces was very common throughout Latin America since the colonial period. Among those scholars exploring this topic are Florence E. Babb, *Between Field and Cooking Pot. The Political Economy of Marketwomen in Peru* (Austin: University of Texas Press, 1989); Chambers, *From Subjects to Citizens*; Gauderman, *Women's Lives in Colonial Quito*; Laura Gotkowitz, "Trading Insults: Honor, Violence, and the Gendered Culture of Commerce in Cochabamba, Bolivia," *Hispanic American Historical Review* 83, no. 1 (2003), 83–118; Hames, "Maize-Beer, Gossip, and Slander."

22. Prieto, *Memorias de mis tiempos*, 251; Payno, *Bandidos de Río Frío*, 89; Carlos Macazaga Ramírez de Arellano, *Las calaveras vivientes de José Guadalupe Posada* (Mexico City: Editorial Cosmos, 1976), 51.

23. Arrom, *Women of Mexico City*, 151–52, 157–74, 201–5.

24. Taylor, *Drinking, Homicide*, 35–39; Kicza, "Pulque Trade," 203–15; Scardaville, "Alcohol Abuse," 650.

25. Couturier, "Women in a Noble Family," 135.

26. Ibid., 141–42; Kicza, "Pulque Trade," 204, 209.

27. Ramírez Rancaño, *Ignacio Torres Adalid*, 37.

28. Arrom, *Women of Mexico City*, 172.

29. Madame [Frances Erskine] Calderón de la Barca, *Life in Mexico During a Residence of Two Years in That Country* (New York: E. P. Dutton, 1954), 154–55; Ramírez Rancaño, *Ignacio Torres Adalid*, 20–22.

30. Archivo Histórico del Distrito Federal, Ayuntamiento Gobierno del Distrito, Pulquerías (hereafter AHDF-AGD-P), vol. 3719, expediente (hereafter exp.) 48, 1818; Arrom, *Women of Mexico City*, 329.

31. Juan Nepomuceno Almonte, *Guía de forasteros y repertorio de conocimientos útiles* (Mexico City: Imprenta de Ignacio Cumplido, 1852), 464. The guide of 1854 includes several retailers, and Josefa is the only woman mentioned among them.

32. AHDF-AGD-P, vol. 3719, exp. 70 and 71, 1845.

33. Arrom, *Women of Mexico City*, 172–73.

34. Archivo Histórico del Distrito Federal, Ayuntamiento Gobierno del Distrito, Gobierno del Distrito Pulquerías (hereafter AHDF-AGD-GDP), vol. 1771, exp. 126 and 132, December 1901, and exp. 309, October 1903; Archivo Histórico del Distrito Federal, Ayuntamiento Gobierno del Distrito, Policía en general, AHDF-AGD-PG, vol. 3637, exp. 983, October 1890; Ramírez Rancaño, *Ignacio Torres Adalid*, 37.

35. Arrom, *Women of Mexico City*, 166; AHDF-AGD-GDP, vol. 1771, exp. 309, October 1903.

36. Ramírez Rancaño, *Ignacio Torres Adalid*, 147, 151, 271.

37. AHDF-AGD-GDP, vol. 1769, exp. 26, March 1901; vol. 1771, exp. 263, May 1903; vol. 1772, exp. 376 and 377, November 1904, and exp. 399, January 1905.

38. Ramírez Rancaño, *Ignacio Torres Adalid*, 55–56, 188, 328.

39. AHDF-AGD-GDP, vol. 1769, exp. 95, August 1901; vol. 1770, exp. 151, January 1902; and vol. 1771, exp. 295, October 1903.

40. Ramírez Rancaño, *Ignacio Torres Adalid*, 146–55, 188, 328–33.

41. AHDF-AGD-PG, vol. 3634, exp. 604, April 1870.

42. Toxqui Garay, "'El Recreo de los Amigos,'" 136–56.

43. AHDF-AGD-GDP, vol. 1771, exp. 295, September 1903, and exp. 309, January 1904.

44. "Oficial. Ministerio de Hacienda," *MR*, September 26, 1857, 1–2.

45. *Representación al Exmo. Sr. Presidente de la República por los hacendados de los Llanos de Apan y tratantes en el ramo de pulques, para que se suspenda la ley sobre aumento de fondos municipales* (Mexico City: Establecimiento Tipográfico de Andrés Boix, 1857), 6–11.

46. Agapito de la Barrera, "Avisos," *MR*, November 17, 1862, 4.

47. Juvenal, "Boletín del Monitor," *MR*, January 17, 1873, 1; "Gacetilla. Pulques," *MR*, February 7, 1873, 3.

48. Some examples are "El Ferrocarril de México a Veracruz. Los contratistas de pulque" and "Gacetilla. La cuestión de pulques," *MR*, August 29, 1871, 2 and 4; "Gacetilla. El ferrocarril de México a Puebla," *MR*, October 31, 1871, 2; "Gacetilla. Hidalgo," *MR*, February 17, 1872, 3; "Gacetilla. Efectos del Estado de Sitio," *MR*, March 9, 1872, 3; "Gacetilla. El Ramo del Pulque," *MR*, May 7, 1872, 3; "Remitidos"

MR, February 8, 1873, 3; "Gacetilla. A las 8 de la Mañana," *MR*, August 7, 1873, 3. Benigno Zamudio, "Remitidos," *MR*, September 18, 1873, 2.

49. "Remitidos," *MR*, December 2, 1873, 3.

50. Ramírez Rancaño, *Ignacio Torres Adalid*, 74.

51. Seminario de Historia Moderna de México, *Estadísticas económicas del Porfiriato. Fuerza de trabajo y actividad económica por sectores*, vol. 2 (Mexico City: El Colegio de México, 1960), 63, 67–69, 119.

52. "Administración principal de rentas del distrito y departamento de México," *MR*, August 11, 1856, 6; Salvador Novo, *Cocina Mexicana. Historia gastronómica de la Ciudad de México* (Mexico City: Pórtico de la Ciudad de México–Estudio Salvador Novo, 1993).

53. Seminario de Historia, *Estadísticas Económicas*, 221–23.

54. Ramírez Rancaño, *Ignacio Torres Adalid*, 76–77.

55. Seminario de Historia, *Estadísticas Económicas*, 200, 204.

56. Ramírez Rancaño, *Ignacio Torres Adalid*, 77–78.

57. Ibid., 78.

58. Seminario de Historia, *Estadísticas Económicas*, 223.

59. Hames, "Maize-Beer, Gossip, and Slander," 251; Bianca Premo, "From the Pockets of Women: The Gendering of the Mita, Migration, and Tribute in Colonial Chuchuito, Peru," *The Americas* 57, no. 2 (2000), 88–90; Babb, *Between Field and Cooking Pot*, 53–65, 148–56.

60. Seminario de Historia, *Estadísticas Económicas*, 147–52.

61. Almonte, *Guía de forasteros*, 458–59.

62. Archivo Histórico del Distrito Federal, Ayuntamiento Gobierno del Distrito, Gobierno del Distrito Mercados (AHDF-AGD-GDM), vol. 1728, exp. 178, August 1904; Archivo Histórico del Distrito Federal, Ayuntamiento Gobierno del Distrito, Gobierno del Distrito Fondas y Figones (AHDF-AGD-GDFF), vol. 1620, exp. 30, December 1901; AHDF-AGD-GDP, vol. 1769, exp. 22, March 1901; Payno, *Bandidos de Río Frío*, 90.

63. Piccato, "Urbanistas, Ambulantes, and Mendigos," 113–48.

64. AHDF-AGD-GDM, vol. 1727, exp. 70, February 1902; AHDF-AGD-PG, vol. 3640, exp. 1222, December 1898.

65. Pilcher, "Tamales or Timbales," 206.

66. "El chisporroteo de la manteca, alcanzó en parte a la cara del niño, ocasionándole algunas dolorosas quemaduras, cayendo en abundancia sobre el rico vestido de la señora, quien ha perdido en un momento más de cien duros" ("Gacetilla. Denuncio a la policía").

67. "¿No sería posible que esos braceritos, de aspecto repugnante (sin que sea más atractivo el de las mujeres que de ellos se sirven), se colocaran en el interior de las pulquerías, ya que las tales chalupitas son el acompañamiento obligado de los sendos jarros de pulque con que allí se obsequian a los amigos? Ya que no otras consideraciones, la decencia de la población aconseja esta medida." Ibid.

68. Despite the public display of repugnance against the natives' diet, which was based on corn and pulque, many members of the upper and middle classes enjoyed these foods in their privacy of their homes. Pilcher, "Tamales or Timbales," 204; Novo, *Cocina Mexicana*, 204.

69. AHDF-AGD-GDM, vol. 1729, exp. 197, May 1907.

70. AHDF-AGD-GDM, vol. 1728, exp. 140, January 1905, and exp. 150, May 1905.

71. AHDF-AGD-GDM, vol. 1727, exp. 94, July 1903, and vol. 1728, exp. 150, May 1905.

72. Porter, *Working Women in Mexico City*, 134, 140; Francois, *A Culture of Everyday Credit*, 152–55.

73. AHDF-AGD-GDM, vol. 1728, exp. 150, May 1905; AHDF-AGD-PG, vol. 3641, exp. 1266, 1899.

74. Adolfo Dollero, *México al día. Impresiones y notas de viaje* (Paris: Librería de la vda. de C. Bouret, 1911); AHDF-AGD-GDM, vol. 1728, exp. 150, May 1905.

75. "Gacetilla. Quejas contra los gendarmes," in *MR*, March 20, 1884, 3.

76. Several authors have analyzed the use of the law as a common practice throughout Latin America since the colonial period among street vendors, market women, and other urban dwellers, who relied on public scribes to engage in a dialogue with local authorities about their rights and claims. Interesting examples are Christina M. Jiménez, "From the Lettered City to the Sellers' City: Vendor Politics and Public Space in Urban Mexico, 1880–1926," in *The Spaces of the Modern City. Imaginaries, Politics, and Everyday Life*, ed. Gyan Prakash and Kevin M. Kruse (Princeton, NJ: Princeton University Press, 2008), 214–46. David Carey Jr., "'Hard Working, Orderly Little Women.' Mayan Vendors and Marketplace Struggles in Early-Twentieth-Century Guatemala," *Ethnohistory* 55, no. 4 (2008), 579–607.

77. A few examples of these letters can be found in AHDF-AGD-GDM, vol. 1727, exp. 17, June 29, 1901, and exp. 94, July 1903; vol. 1728, exp. 111 and 126, July 1904, and exp. 178, August 1904; vol. 1730, exp. 232 and 242, March 1908, exp. 283, 288, and 290, April 1908, and exp. 317 and 329, May 1908.

78. AHDF-AGD-GDM, vol. 1727, exp. 94, July 1903.

79. AHDF-AGD-GDM, vol. 1733, exp. 625 bis, 1908–1909.

80. AHDF-AGD-GDM, vol. 1730, exp. 329, May 1908.

81. AHDF-AGD-GDM, vol. 1728, exp. 126, 1904.

82. AHDF-AGD-GDM, vol. 1730, exp. 329, 1907–1908.

83. AHDF-AGD-GDFF, vol. 1620, exp. 33, January 1902.

84. Lear, *Workers, Neighbors, and Citizens*, 9.

85. Piccato, "Urbanistas, Ambulantes, and Mendigos," 131.

86. Lear, *Workers, Neighbors, and Citizens*, 89–142.

87. Congreso Constituyente de 1857, *Constitución federal de los Estados Unidos Mexicanos sancionada y jurada por el congreso general constituyente el día 5 de febrero de 1857*, article 34, http://www.agn.gob.mx/constitucion1857/constitucion1857.html, accessed June 30, 2012.

88. Jiménez, "From the Lettered City," 217–18; Lear, *Workers, Neighbors, and Citizens*, 4–12.

CHAPTER SIX

Drunks and Dictators

Inebriation's Gendered, Ethnic, and Class Components in Guatemala, 1898–1944

David Carey Jr.

The bottle of aguardiente *is his consolation, his happiness, the true companion of his life. The Indian learns to drink since his childhood and to that can be attributed a great part of his degeneration. He does not have ambitions nor does he even know how to improve his miserable state; in addition he works only to obtain a plate of beans with chili, some tortillas and money to buy* aguardiente *. . . it is rare to meet [an Indian] that is not in a state of inebriation.*

    —JORGE GARCÍA GRANADOS, GUATEMALAN INTELLECTUAL

What pains me most . . . is that k'uxa *[homebrew made from sugarcane] is so cheap. Many people have died from* guaro *[moonshine] from cirrhosis, but the people who sell* guaro *don't care. . . . When a twelve year old boy gets drunk, the government is at fault because there is no law to prohibit it. . . . Before it was prohibited to make* k'uxa *for this reason.*

    —IX'EYA', KAQCHIKEL MAYA (HEREAFTER KAQCHIKEL) ELDER[1]

While these people [Mayas] undoubtedly suffer from drunkenness, one would hesitate to remove the bottle from them until the entire pattern of their lives is changed. They are an introverted people, consumed by internal fires which they cannot or dare not express, eternally chafing under the yoke of conquest, and never for a moment forgetting that they are a conquered people. In occasional drunkenness, in dancing, and in the more elaborate ceremonies with the pageantry they find a much-needed release.

    —OLIVER LA FARGE, ETHNOGRAPHER

For a postcolonial nation like Guatemala, whose early twentieth-century leaders were trying to present it as modern in the eyes of the Atlantic World, alcohol's social ills were problematic. Inebriated men and women yelling, carousing, and fighting in the streets belied claims of public order and progress. With their self-proclaimed "Indian problem," *criollo* (Spanish-descent elite) and *ladino* (nonindigenous) Guatemalan leaders and intellectuals claimed they faced a great obstacle to modernization. Creating a more productive nation was contingent upon righting the moral compass and addressing the supposed afflictions—laziness, ignorance, alcoholism—of the indigenous population. In short, nation-building was enmeshed with alcohol.

As one aspect of Guatemala's state formation process, the administrations of Manuel Estrada Cabrera (1898–1920) and General Jorge Ubico y Casteñeda (1931–1944) poured money into a national facelift. Like their liberal counterparts in other areas of Latin America, they called upon architects to design grand buildings and other public works that would attract tourism and foreign investment. Since appearing weak or backward made Latin American nations vulnerable to foreign domination and intervention, such investments were as much about keeping foreign dignitaries at bay as enticing foreign capitalists. By the end of the nineteenth century, large urban centers like Guatemala City and Quetzaltenango enjoyed electric lights, telegraph services, wide boulevards, refashioned central plazas, and indoor markets, all of which conveyed a sense of progress.[2] In some ways their strategy worked; Estrada Cabrera and Ubico both enjoyed some success at attracting foreign capital.[3]

Like the nation-building process, perceptions of alcohol use and abuse reflected prejudicial notions of race and gender. To understand the relationship between alcohol consumption and race, this chapter focuses on several Kaqchikel towns in the highland departments of Chimaltenango and Sacatepéquez. Even as leaders and intellectuals portrayed *indígenas* (indigenous people) as drunks to justify their marginalization or assimilation, national police records indicated that they were no more inclined to inebriation than ladinos. The racist roots of such false perceptions notwithstanding, at times indigenous litigants used these stereotypes to their advantage in the courtroom. Gendered patterns of consumption also contributed to nation-building. Allowing few releases under dictatorial rule, the Estrada Cabrera and Ubico regimes generally ignored, if not condoned, drunken men who beat their wives. Even if they were fortunate enough to avoid violence, females often had to support families whose alcoholic husbands or fathers contributed little. But women were not merely victims of alcoholic consumption. Many drank with great vigor, at times causing "scandals" and occasionally becoming violent. Whether celebrating or venting, these women evinced female freedom and autonomy at a time when patriarchs from dictators to husbands were bent on circumscribing women's mobility.

With its ethnic, class, and gendered components, the consumption of alcohol was an axis around which modern Guatemala was formed. Alcohol consumption facilitated such social ills as poverty and violence, but it also served many purposes from filling coffers to maintaining community identities and upsetting social norms. It both upheld and exacerbated such hegemonic relations as men's exploitation of women and the state's attempt to control its population. It also defied the status quo when, for example, women flouted society's and the state's expectations of them with drunk and disorderly behavior. More than any other commodity, alcohol left few lives untouched. By facilitating the perseverance of Maya rituals that stood in the face of the state's effort to assimilate indígenas, providing a source of revenue for the state and a trope around which to excoriate indigenous and working-class people, bringing together very different social actors in one place, and allowing consumers to discard their inhibitions enough to act in ways, whether conciliatory or confrontational, that both upset and reinforced social norms and expectations, alcohol consumption helped to shape the nation.

Alcohol's Influence

Like in contemporary Mexico, where critiques of alcohol consumption focused on indigenous people and the working classes, moral reform, racial assimilation, and worker productivity went hand in hand.[4] Eliminating excessive alcohol consumption, Guatemalan authorities and intellectuals purported, could only advance *ladinoization* (the process of forcing native peoples to adopt ladino culture). To their minds, such broad cultural changes were a crucial step toward Guatemala's modernization. In addition to redefining the national character, temperance would produce a healthier and more vigorous rural workforce, leaders claimed. Plantation owners and even some foreign observers disagreed: only by plying indígenas with booze could contractors, foremen, and owners secure their labor.[5] One coffee plantation owner quipped, "Take *aguardiente* away from the Indian and what will become of coffee? Coffee plantations run on *aguardiente* as an automobile runs on gasoline."[6]

Indígenas did little to dissuade assumptions that alcohol was central to their lives. Like in other parts of Latin America, alcohol routinely was offered as a ceremonial gift in Guatemala. Although its significance changed over time, drinking was an important part of many Maya community and family rituals over several centuries.[7] Because its traditional uses helped to create and reconstitute community, alcohol was vital to the preservation of local culture and religion. In response to authorities' efforts to criminalize the production, trade, and consumption of alcohol in the nineteenth century, for example, Q'anjob'al Mayas highlighted the paramount role ritualized drinking played in their communities and culture. Even if they seldom convinced authorities of their position, indígenas' negotiations with the state in which they emphasized alcohol's cultural and customary primacy reveal much about the "highly divergent interpretations of alcohol use."[8]

In addition to Maya ceremonies and patron saint festivals, market days were also venues for drinking. Even though few people were complete strangers, the anonymity of these occasions, where even "respectable housewives"[9] drank "as freely as the men,"[10] helped drunks distance themselves from their actions once they were sober.[11] Because quarreling was so common among drunks, indígenas generally avoided drinking in private settings with family, neighbors, or old rivals, except of course for special celebrations such as baptisms and weddings. The seventy-five-year-old Kaqchikel weaver Ix'aj explains, "Women a long time ago made *k'uxa*. I was a child then. They made it for baptisms, weddings, and other celebrations. . . . Then people would drink and dance to pure *marimba* [a musical instrument similar to a xylophone]. The *Guardia* [Police] took both men and women to jail."[12] Like other Guatemalans, indígenas routinely prescribed alcohol to cure fevers and other ills.[13] As one public health official noted in 1923: "It is a very old custom to sell legal aguardiente . . . for medicinal use in pharmacies."[14] And of course, quotidian consumption kept cantinas and speakeasies busy.

Yet as the second epigraph on the opening page of this chapter attests, some Mayas were critical of excessive drinking. Kaqchikel conscripts complained about soldiers who drank excessively.[15] Even though they generally treated drunks kindly and many Mayas considered drunkenness a weakness rather than a vice,[16] they were apprehensive about inebriation since it could lead to fighting, infidelity, and financial loss. Based on judicial records, such fears were warranted. Perhaps the frequency of these transgressions explains why some K'iche'-Mayas considered excessive drinking a crime.[17] As historian David McCreery points out, "Drunkenness exposed the Indian to a variety of hazards, from fighting and violence to accidental injury or exposure to chills, insect bites, and disease or to the enticements or threats of the unscrupulous *habilitador* [loan shark] and local official."[18]

Since *chicha* (generally made from fermented maize or fruit), k'uxa, and aguardiente were blamed for everything from sloth to murder, alcohol consumption was problematic for another reason: crime. On the eve of Estrada Cabrera's rule, the historian, jurist, and critic Antonio Batres Jáuregui (1847–1928) purported that alcohol contained the "elements of destruction, poverty, and debasement for the unfortunate aborigines" and led them to crime.[19] Law enforcement personnel held similar notions about the relationship between crime and alcohol. As the National Police emphasized in 1933, "Alcoholism, under its influence are committed the majority of criminal acts."[20]

The early twentieth-century legal system reinforced this view. Since justices often considered inebriation an extenuating circumstance and reduced sentences accordingly, many indigenous defendants exaggerated their attitudes about alcohol as a cause of crime. Of course, alcohol often did play a role in altercations and behavior that landed indígenas in jail. For example, while serving his five-day sentence, Narciso Esquit admitted he was drunk when he insulted his brother Domingo on February 17, 1928. About a month later, Juan de la Cruz Corona was in a similar state (and ended up in the same jail) when he insulted his in-laws at a family gathering.[21] Whether sincere or contrived, their courtroom testimonies reinforced authorities' perceptions about drinking, ethnicity, and crime.[22]

Successfully deploying elite stereotypes was but one example of the way indígenas' agency emanated from their subjectivity. As a way of trying to lessen their potential sentence, some male and a few female defendants, such as Rita Simolif, claimed they drank to the point of unconsciousness and memory loss.[23] Martín Choc's assertion on July 30, 1943, that he had no idea why he was in jail was not unusual: "In the state they found me, I was not conscious of anything."[24] To cite another example, when he awoke in jail on a June morning in 1931, José Morales Lima asked his cellmate what had happened. Overhearing the question, the guard informed Morales that he had stabbed a police officer in a cantina the previous night. Upon hearing this, Morales returned to his "unconscious state."[25] Even when they clearly recalled events, indígenas often blamed inebriation for their transgressions. If the record of domestic violence is any indication, such assertions could reduce their sentences.[26]

With less success, lawyers also used this rhetoric. When José María Yal killed his two-week-old stepdaughter in 1911 on the way home from a baptism, he claimed he was drunk; witnesses testified that he was not. His lawyer, the forty-four-year-old farmer Pedro Ruiz, refuted their testimonies, explaining that "it is inconceivable that 'los indios' [the Indians] can give up getting drunk with any pretext and baptisms are always very festive occasions for them."[27] Ruiz argued that his client should not be held accountable for the crime to the full extent of the law because "'los indígenas' don't labor in their activities with full and complete discernment, well the shameful labors to which their lives are subjected; the precarious life they lead; the habit of inebriation and principles of doubtful morality that are inculcated in them from childhood, make them beings very susceptible to crime."[28] Unfortunately for Yal, playing upon these racist stereotypes did not help his cause. Though the judge did not take exception to the description, he insisted those traits did not constitute extenuating circumstances and sentenced Yal to fifteen years in jail.[29]

Guatemalan elites from the colonial era to the twentieth century associated indígenas with alcohol.[30] One journalist writing in 1892, for example, considered chicha the Indian's "natural beverage."[31] By the 1920s, ladino writers began to emphasize ethnicity more than class as they conflated indigeneity with inebriation.[32] The first epigraph on the opening page of this chapter offers one example. Nobel Prize laureate Miguel Angel Asturias was an early proponent of this view: "Alcoholism is the factor that has most characterized the degenerative defects of the Indian. It is well known to what extent brandy is consumed among the population, whose poverty and debasement are drowned in order to give way to a hurricane of rejoicing that blows fiercely over the last ruins of indigenous life . . . where clouds of brandy and corn beer extend over rotting flesh and numb organs gasping in the throes of a slow death."[33] As the twentieth century wore on, popular imagination so conflated inebriation, poverty, and ethnicity that some poor drunk ladinos were identified as indígenas.[34]

Ethnic Consumption and Perceptions

To capture the state's attention, as historian Virginia Garrard-Burnett points out, intellectuals deployed a national paradigm that "credited Guatemala's 'drunken' and 'racially degenerate' indigenous majority with the nation's underdevelopment."[35] In 1894, Batres Jáuregui identified alcoholism as the "single most important reason for the decline of the indigenous race." He also observed, "The income from alcohol sales is among the most valuable to the national treasury. . . . The more the vice spreads, the more income grows . . . and the more the race deteriorates."[36] Guatemalan intellectual J. Fernando Juárez Muñoz similarly chided, "If we complain that this race is the heavy burden that weighs down the nation threatening to drown it and impeding its full development, it is more rational to blame the singular act of maintaining as state income, the alcohol tax. . . . [W]e are poisoning the population."[37] Ethnographic studies too suggested that efforts to boost national coffers often came at the expense of highland economies and people.[38] Even some scholars have accepted the idea that indígenas drank more than other segments of the population. A number of academics have purported that alcohol abuse among indigenous people increased dramatically during the late nineteenth and early twentieth centuries in response to liberal reforms and natives' increased access to cash via wage labor.[39]

Contrary to ladino (and some foreigners' and contemporary scholars') assertions, indígenas did not dominate national inebriation. Annual police reports reveal that ladinos often were arrested in larger numbers than natives for public inebriation. A representative glance from the 1930s underscores this phenomenon (see table 6.1). In 1934, the police arrested more ladinos than indígenas for drunkenness. In 1935 and 1936, the latter slightly bested the former. Beginning in 1937, ladinos again outnumbered indígenas. By 1938 and 1939, about 60 percent of those arrested for public inebriation were ladinos, a pattern that continued throughout the Ubico years, with the exception of 1943, when 70 percent of those arrested were ladinos.[40] Though at first glance the data seem slanted toward police activity in Guatemala City, where ladinos predominated, the annual reports incorporated information from police activity in the Maya highlands.

When one considers census data, these numbers become even more striking. Even by the government's figures, which almost assuredly undercounted natives, ladinos comprised 35 and 44 percent of the population in 1921 and 1940, respectively.[41] That ladinos equaled and often outnumbered indígenas in public inebriation arrests means that a far greater percentage of the ladino than the indigenous population was involved in such transgressions. Using the 1940 census population figures to contextualize the 1940 data reveals a striking contrast between the two groups. Within their own populations, the percentage of ladinos arrested for public inebriation was nearly twice that of indígenas.[42] Although these reports were public information, ladino intellectuals writing about indios and alcohol never referred to them. And since most indígenas were unaware of their

Table 6.1. Arrests for Public Inebriation in Guatemala, 1931–1944

Year	Total	Indígenas		Ladinos		Women	
		Number	Percent of total pop.	Number	Percent of total pop.	Number	Percent of total pop.
1931	8,513						
1932	8,818					3,158	35.8
1933	6,905	4,012	58.1	2,893	41.9	1,343	19.5
1934	6,974	3,250	46.6	3,724	53.4	1,540	22.1
1935	7,697	3,992	51.9	3,705	48.1	825	10.7
1936	8,970	4,713	52.5	4,257	47.5	1,060	11.8
1937	7,835	3,580	45.7	4,255	54.3	710	9.1
1938	4,105	1,636	39.8	2,469	60.2	495	12.1
1939	4,196	1,695	40.4	2,501	59.6	487	11.6
1940	5,018	1,929	38.4	3,089	61.6	549	10.9
1941	5,975	2,523	42.2	3,442	57.6	566	9.5
1942	7,164	2,595	36.2	4,569	63.8	509	7.1
1943	9,055	2,910	32.1	6,145	70.8	684	7.6
1944	7,502	2,991	40.0	4,511	60.1	592	7.9

Source: *Memoria de los trabajos realizados por la dirección general de la Policía Nacional* (Guatemala: Tipografía Nacional, 1931–1944).

existence (even if they happened to be literate in Spanish and had the time to read them), the popular image of drunken indio undermining national progress took hold. Nineteenth- and twentieth-century travelers and ethnographers present a more balanced view; most observed both natives and ladinos getting drunk or made note of indígenas who eschewed alcohol. But of course, few of these accounts were translated into Spanish.[43]

Like the campaign against the production of *aguardiente clandestino* (moonshine), efforts to curtail inebriation (or at least public acts associated with it) and thus modernize the nation were informed and organized by racial bias, not data. Reflecting elite perceptions, Ubico focused his rhetoric and policies on the indigenous people: "It is necessary to eradicate, to the maximum, the affection for liquor among the Indians. . . . When we achieve a reduction of alcohol consumption among the Indians we will have better workers and healthier generations."[44] Convinced that "Indians" were the primary consumers of alcohol and aware that they comprised the majority of laborers on coffee and other plantations, he passed a law in 1940 prohibiting the sale of alcohol at *finca* (large landed estate) stores.[45]

With an emphasis on indigenous consumption, the frequency with which Kaqchikel and other Maya towns appear in the criminal record is not surprising. For some authorities, this attention was bothersome. Although respectful and quick to address superiors' queries and mandates, local leaders developed strategies for deflecting the state's attention. In his response to the aforementioned 1940 law about the sale of alcohol on fincas, the *intendente municipal* (municipal intendant) of San Antonio Aguas Calientes (hereafter Aguas Calientes) insisted there were no fincas in his town.[46] Therefore, he implied, there was no need to enforce the law there.

Class Acts

Even as ethnicity colored perceptions of alcohol use and abuse, some intellectuals viewed alcohol consumption through a class lens. Editorialists contrasted images of laborers getting drunk on moonshine with depictions of elites sipping imported cognac and brandy. Advertisers perpetuated these distinctions. In an image familiar to drinkers (and readers) today, Johnnie Walker appeared in a 1937 edition of *La Gaceta: Revista de Policía y Variedades* as an elite male with his top hat, bowtie, long coat, high boots, and walking stick (see figure 6.1). In contrast to poor and indigenous people's consumption of alcohol, elite drinking was refined. Underscoring that Ron Amaja (Amaja rum) was too expensive for indígenas and poor ladinos, whose wages in the 1930s averaged ten cents a day, the company insisted its rum was only sold at "good establishments," suggesting it would not be available at lower-class or indigenous ones (see figure 6.2). While intellectuals vilified the lower classes and indígenas for getting drunk, elites maintained both the privilege of drinking alcohol and the profits from its sales.

Like in contemporary Mexico, public drunkenness was a crime of the poor; unless they were driving, elites were seldom arrested for inebriation.[47] A few single men and women notwithstanding, most offenders were either married or widowed. Almost all were illiterate.

Although determining class from the criminal record can be difficult, Clara Partenal's ability to commute her five-day sentence for public inebriation on June 20, 1927, with 1.25 *quetzales* (Guatemalan currency) set her apart from the majority of defendants whose poverty condemned them to incarceration.[48] At times incarceration could be expensive. After a police officer remanded three illiterate indigenous *jornaleros* (day laborers) to jail for inebriation and vagrancy on March 13, 1928, they tried to break down

Figure 6.1. Johnnie Walker advertisement, 1937, depicting whisky, an elite libation, as elegant. (Image courtesy of The Latin American Library, Tulane University)

their cell door; the judge assessed them each a fifty-peso fine for the damage.[49]

With rumors of guards raping women in prison, women like Partenal and the thirty-five-year-old indígena Valentina Miculax were more likely than men to commute their sentences.[50] Because such arrests could dam-

Figure 6.2. 1936 advertisement for Ron Amaja, another elite drink, which could be found at "all the good establishments." (Image courtesy of Hemeroteca Nacional de Guatemala)

age reputations, occasionally the accused attempted to contextualize their behavior. Perhaps because she was married and could commute her sentence, the thirty-six-year-old Kaqchikel woman Rita Simolif wanted the record to reflect that "this was the first time she committed [this crime] and for her drunkenness she was unaware of her scandals."[51]

The Gendered and Legal Components
of Inebriation

In contrast to their focus on the ethnic and class dimensions of alcohol consumption, authorities and elites seldom addressed its gendered components. Indicating that some women—both married and single—enjoyed mobility outside their homes late into the evening, police reports disclose that women regularly drank and disturbed the peace. Often their husbands or common law partners accompanied them, but sometimes men were absent from these incidents. Although the overwhelming majority of women arrested in the highlands were indigenous, in Guatemala City many were ladinas. Unfortunately, neither the archives of the Kaqchikel town of Patzicía nor the national police records elaborate on what comprised "scandalous behavior," which in other places such as contemporary Mexico, suggested sexual relations and prostitution.[52]

A number of factors contributed to perceptions that women rarely drank. Scholars often assume that women seldom became drunk publicly because such behavior was less socially acceptable for women than for men. The focus on men's role in the *cargo* system (politico-religious offices and burdens) and the concurrent paucity of literature on *texela'* (religious sisterhoods) has obscured women's ritual drinking.[53] For reasons of propriety, Kaqchikel oral histories similarly downplay women's consumption of alcohol. As such, women tend to be portrayed as victims of men's drunken behavior as opposed to drunks themselves. While it is difficult to overstate the deleterious effects of the former, certainly the historiography of the latter calls for revision.

To be sure, women drank less frequently than men. Social pressures likely dampened female intoxication. Urban elites often associated female alcoholics with prostitution. When referring to brothels, Juárez Muñoz observed, "There we will find unhappy women abandoned by society to the sad condition of carnal sin, drowning in alcohol their misfortune of having fallen so far."[54] For most women, poverty was the most significant deterrent to drinking. Poor and working-class women were often the sole providers for their children. When struggling to feed, clothe, and shelter their dependents, these women could ill afford to spend money on alcohol.

Despite the aforementioned social, economic, and familial pressures and their limited mobility compared with men, the frequency with which women were cited for public inebriation in the archival record reveals that many poor and working-class women were not teetotalers. During Estrada

Cabrera's reign and throughout the 1920s, women comprised 6–27 percent of those arrested for public inebriation and the scandalous behavior generally associated with it.[55] *Patzicianas* (female residents of Patzicía), for example, were regularly arrested for public inebriation and "scandalous behavior" during the first three decades of the twentieth century.[56] As table 6.1 reveals, this female drinking pattern continued nationally throughout Ubico's dictatorship, when women made up between 7 and 35 percent of those arrested for intoxication.[57]

Although their arrests were immediately confining, the poor and working-class indigenous and ladino women who got drunk and behaved in ways that contravened the state's and broader society's expectations of them betrayed the relative autonomy and mobility they enjoyed, especially compared with the lives of their elite counterparts. In communities where according to some ethnographers, women seldom left their courtyards, and members of the opposite sex were rarely together in the streets, drunken women carousing on their own or in large groups with men upset social norms.[58] If community members associated autonomous, quarrelsome women with the "absence of masculine control over the household," as historian Pablo Piccato purports,[59] then women who were arrested for drinking, fighting, and disrupting public order late into the night upset patriarchal authority in their homes and communities.

Like men, women too were protagonists in drunken altercations.[60] The tragic events of April 8, 1914, are illustrative. Already inebriated when she arrived at the home of Vicenta Luis at 11 a.m., Regina Taquiej demanded a drink. Luis's twelve-year-old daughter informed Taquiej that Luis was sleeping off a drinking binge. This news only infuriated Taquiej, who pulled a knife out of her belt and stabbed Luis in the throat, killing her.[61] Whether Luis sold alcohol from her home or Taquiej simply knew her to have alcohol on hand is difficult to discern, but her daughter's casual observation of her mother's inebriated state betrayed a familiarity with Luis's drinking habits. Although such fatalities at the hands of inebriated women were uncommon, women who drank did occasionally become violent.[62] When Isabel Medina and Cayetana Batres got in a fight in a cantina, it took four agents to break it up and bring them into custody. Sentenced to ten days in prison, both women sustained injuries serious enough to require five days to recover.[63]

The frequency with which alcohol consumption, whether their own or someone else's, jeopardized women's well-being cautions against celebrating inebriation as a sign of women's liberation. When women drank, they were particularly vulnerable to rape. Unable to recall how they got there, some awoke in another man's bed.[64] Often in these situations, women explained they had not intended to get drunk but had been compelled to in ways that ranged from gentle cajoling to physical coercion.[65] In domestic violence incidents, victims and perpetrators regularly identified alcohol as a factor in the crime.[66] Knowing their husbands well, many women sought shelter elsewhere until drinking binges subsided. Such was the case in 1916, when Raymunda Chicol fled, explaining, "when [my husband] drinks [he] is dangerous."[67] Other women confronted their husbands directly. When María Jesús Saj refused to give her husband, Florentín Roquel, money to continue his drinking binge in 1904, he attempted to hit her, striking and killing their infant son instead. Buttressed by the testimonies of his character witnesses who portrayed him as a chronic drunk, Roquel readily admitted that he was intoxicated.[68] Fatalities were not unusual when alcohol blurred domestic disputes. Jealous, drunken rages often ended tragically. Such was Fernando Rabinal Ordoñez's state in Tecpán in 1942 when he killed his lover Feliciana López Chanay with a machete.[69] Like elsewhere in the Americas, police blotters and judicial records are filled with women who met similar fates at the hands of drunken men they knew well.

For many women whose husbands routinely drank, poverty accompanied violence. When the twenty-two-year-old Francisca Chiroy de Sutuj denounced her husband for beating her and threatening to kill her, she also explained that his constant drinking "has deprived me of what is necessary for my son and I to eat, well he only gives us five pesos a week for these expenses, he has not given me clothes for my son and I to dress."[70] In addition to such privations becoming apparent in domestic violence cases, women often identified inebriation as a problem when they sued their husbands for child support. Since such neglect flew in the face of socially mandated expectations that patriarchs provide for their families, alcoholics risked losing their patriarchal privileges. The 1927 civil codes set forth that *patria potestad* (a father's control over and responsibility for his children) could be suspended or terminated if he was a habitual drunk.[71] At times local magistrates freed wives from their responsibilities toward drunken husbands.[72] Although few would have framed it this way, it is ironic that alcohol abuse could provide some (albeit relative) relief to the drinker's victims. Alcohol's ability to shape ethnic, class, and gender identities, to explain if not excuse violent behavior and crime, and produce profits placed it at the heart of Guatemala's nation-state formation process.

Drunks and Dictators

The government's handling of alcohol laws and violations reflects some of the contradictions inherent in the nation-building process. Its temperance rhetoric notwithstanding, throughout the first half of the twentieth century the Guatemalan government, like other Latin American countries, was dependent on alcohol income.[73] With legal alcohol revenues funding the military, police, and public works projects aimed at "modernizing" the country, Estrada Cabrera prioritized the prosecution of bootleggers and moonshiners.[74] Their paltry wages financed partly by alcohol revenues, soldiers in the lowland departments of Izabal and Zacapa enforced liquor laws by arresting disorderly drunks.[75] In Guatemala City, such responsibilities fell to police officers, who pursued these transgressions with great zeal. In 1899, the year after Estrada Cabrera assumed office, for example, the police arrested 5,347 people for public drunkenness.[76] The following year they arrested 4,598 people for the same crime.[77]

Even in the rural highlands where national authorities had less control, they took drunken disorderly conduct seriously. Police in Patzicía, for example, regularly detained those who had been drinking, yelling, or otherwise disturbing the peace. A snapshot from 1916 is illustrative. Late at night on March 4, Patzicía authorities arrested two Kaqchikel couples, one married and the other not, who they found yelling in "a state of scandalous inebriation." Their five-day sentences were commutable by three pesos a day.[78] In an apparent attempt to curb such behavior, the Patzicía justice of the peace increased the commutation rate to four pesos a day by May and then five pesos a day by August.[79] According to the criminal record, this deterrent had little effect.

Throughout the 1920s, national administrations continued their campaigns against public inebriation to varying degrees. Aware that Estrada Cabrera's overthrow was largely a rejection of his repressive tactics and politics, General José María Orellana's government (1921–1926) intervened less in daily affairs. As one example of the notable decline in arrests during his term, in 1923, the Guatemala City police arrested only 2,944 people for inebriation.[80] During General Lázaro Chacón's rule (1926–1930), however, arrests for scandalous drunken behavior rebounded. When he assumed office, the National Police both increased their campaign against public intoxication and began keeping statistics for the whole country. During his first year, the police arrested 4,097 men and 258 women for inebriation and 1,849 men and 226 women for public scandals, most of which involved alcohol.[81] By 1928, the numbers increased to 6,067 men and 459 women for public intoxication and 501 men and 185 women for scandalous behavior.[82] Whether the sudden increase the following year was a reflection of people's responses to the Great Depression or the government's attempts to buoy its finances during it is unclear, but in 1929 the police arrested 18,987 people for public intoxication![83] As evidenced by the growing number of arrests, Chacón's campaign against intoxication was both a reflection of and response to the attention intellectuals increasingly drew to alcohol abuse among the poor and indígenas.

Like his predecessors who desperately needed the income, Ubico had to balance the demand to eradicate alcohol's social ills with the need for alcohol's revenue. The pressure on Ubico to control consumption was even greater than that faced by previous administrations. By 1930, writers were increasingly calling for solutions, some even recommended prohibition, holding up the US experiment as a model.[84] Against this backdrop, upon taking office in February 1931, Ubico immediately cracked down on public inebriation. During the first two years of his administration, police arrested over seventeen thousand people for it.[85] Some local authorities welcomed these efforts. Within weeks of Ubico assuming office, the mayor of Santiago Zamora assured his superior that his town was actively working to eradicate "vagrancy and inebriation, because they are the sources from which emanate so many acts that hurt the reputation of one's own pueblo."[86] Ubico's policy also resonated with many Kaqchikel, particularly women, who lamented the way alcoholism destroyed families, engendered violence, undermined public health, and impoverished individuals.[87] Reflecting the broader support among Mayas for his harsh approach,[88] two Kaqchikel elders recalled, "Ubico straightened everything out. He was tough but good. . . . He sent thieves and drunks to jail."[89]

One reason Mayas remember Ubico's strong-armed rule so vividly (and with greater accord than might be expected) is that he employed public punishment, whether it be lashings or labor such as cleaning the plaza and streets.[90] As Michel Foucault points out, such displays were aimed more at the broader community than the individual criminal. As they bore their transgressions through their sentences, publicly punished criminals became signifiers of their crimes. In this way, the power to punish manifested in the minds of the population more so than on the body of the criminal.[91] One Kaqchikel ajq'ij (Maya ritual spiritualist or shaman) from Tecpán recalled: "Under Ubico, the police hit drunkards between 150 and 300 times according to the severity of their crime."[92] Located right off the Pan-American Highway, Tecpán was one Kaqchikel town where the National Police focused their efforts and regularly arrested locals for "scandalous inebriation."[93] Neighboring Comalapa, too, developed a reputation for alcohol production and consumption. Even when *Comalapenses* (residents of Comalapa) traveled, they attracted authorities' attention. Such was the case in April 1943 when the thirty-five-year-old *soltera* (single woman) Narcisa Colaj López was arrested for being scandalously drunk and fighting with another woman in Chimaltenango.[94] Not surprisingly, elders from Comalapa also have vivid memories of Ubico's alcohol policies and punishments. One farmer from a Comalapan village explained, "If people were drinking aguardiente, they were sentenced to only three days in jail, but you would also get 200 lashes . . . from a big stick with thorns. You were all bruised on the backside."[95] Despite these varied attempts to curb alcoholic consumption, drinking patterns changed little.

Since eradicating alcohol consumption held the potential to bankrupt the state, most administrations were ambivalent about their alcohol campaigns. For local officials, discerning the priority in the state's contradictory policies of cracking down on consumption and expanding alcohol revenues was not difficult. In 1930, for example, Chimaltenango's *jefe político* (governor) reminded mayors in his jurisdiction: "The more aguardiente consumed from [official] depositories, the greater the income the municipality will receive from the taxes. For each bottle sold . . . its tax is evidence of the investment in works of progress and utility."[96] Plying local officials with promises of improved infrastructure and other public works highlighted the state's hypocritical stance. The memorandum implicitly encouraged leniency with drunks—after all, each bottle they purchased contributed to national income. From this perspective, drunks were crucial to the nation's progress! True to their mantra of "progress and order," early twentieth-century administrations were more concerned about discouraging the adverse public effects of inebriation than curtailing consumption.

Intellectuals, however, were quick to point out the social costs of enriching the state and municipalities through these revenues. Writing in 1927, Jorge García Granados decried, "The state contributes to the depravation of morals by making popular alcoholization one of its elements of life."[97] A few years later, Juárez Muñoz noted, alcohol "produces an enormous earnings for the state and its production and consumption is demanded in many ways, without ever thinking that it results in an anachronism that claims to banish its ingestion and on the other hand demands its consumption." He concluded, "The result is an impossible paradox that preaches that the alcoholic vice is harmful, atrophies organic functions and mental mechanisms . . . [and] debases the race and on the other hand" enriches "the public treasury."[98] He was convinced that as long as the state depended on alcohol income, any effort to restrict alcoholism "would be like pounding cold iron."[99] Such admonishments had little influence; the Estrada Cabrera, Orellana, Chacón, and Ubico administrations all granted liquor licenses liberally.[100] Alcohol was too profitable a vice to eradicate.

Conclusions

In light of García Granados's assertion that "one could assert without any risk of being wrong, that there are more liquor vendors than bakeries in this country," cantinas, speakeasies, and other drinking establishments offer a metaphor for alcohol's role and influence in late nineteenth through mid-twentieth-century Guatemala.[101] With their mix of indigenous and ladino, female and male clients, proprietors and workers from different socioeconomic backgrounds, cantinas were a microcosm of the broader highland society. They were sites of celebration, sorrow, companionship, lust, and violence where highland neighbors engaged with one another and often brushed up against the state (particularly when officials sauntered in to have a drink). Generally, owners and clientele understood that a certain level of decorum and respect should be maintained in these establishments, partly because news of what transpired in them often spread throughout the community. In this way, hanging out in a cantina was much like living under dictatorships that demanded social order and gave the impression that people were being watched.

Despite this sense of scrutiny, cantinas and other drinking venues provided some shelter from hegemonic influences. Political scientist James Scott observes, "Here subordinate classes met offstage and off-duty in an atmosphere of freedom encouraged by alcohol. Here was also a privileged site for the transmission of popular culture—embodied in games, songs, gambling, blasphemy, and disorder—that was usually at odds with official culture."[102] Fueled by inebriation, challenges to social norms and mores, however subtle, at times led to unrest and violence.[103]

The expectations and experiences in cantinas often put proprietors in a tough spot. Dependent on loyal customers, owners sought to shield these patrons from the authorities.[104] Regularly attacked and in rare cases even

killed, bartenders, cantina owners, aguardiente vendors, and other purvey-
ors of alcohol were frequently compelled to seek aid from authorities.[105]
Like their poor and working-class counterparts, those involved in this
aspect of the alcohol economy were generally ambivalent about the
state because it could both undermine and facilitate their goals and
livelihoods.

The interactions that took place around alcohol consumption both reinforced old social patterns and forged new ones. In amicable relationships that defied both Guatemalan historiography and contemporary authorities' and intellectuals' assumptions, for example, at times indígenas
and ladinos got drunk together.[106] Gendered networks can also be dis-
cerned where people gathered to drink. The archival record abounds with
examples of male camaraderie in these locales.[107] Although the evidence
is not as clear as historian Sarah Chambers's observations for early Republican Peru,[108] archival materials also intimate that women felt safe in
female-owned and run cantinas because they enjoyed the protection and
solidarity of other women there. To cite but one example of altered gender
relations in these venues, when Manuel Meses entered Nicolasa Corona's
cantina in 1923, Corona called him a *sinverguenza* (shameless scoundrel)
for trying to take advantage of the inebriated woman who had accompanied him the night before. Meses sued her because even in a cantina, this
"accusation threatens . . . my . . . social position."[109] Enjoying the upper
hand at her cantina, Corona used it to defend the honor of her friend. The
places where alcohol was dispensed and consumed were reflective of the
broader nation where ethnic, class, gender, and state-subaltern relations
could be cooperative or confrontational.

As these relations were upheld, shaped, shattered, and reconstructed by
the many social actors who drank alcohol or addressed the consequences
of inebriation, alcohol consumption became an axis around which modern Guatemala was formed. Indeed, it revealed many of the contradictions
in this process, such as the state's need to both profit from alcohol consumption and curtail the way drunken poor and working-class men and
women upset its image as an orderly, civilized nation. Although many
people drank without confronting the state, inebriation often facilitated
people's willingness to behave and speak in ways that contravened official
culture, norms, and power. Whether they did so in cantinas or the street
while drunk or attributed their actions to inebriation thereafter in court-
rooms or private homes, they influenced social relations in a nation whose
ethnic, gender, and class tensions frustrated attempts to impose what early
twentieth-century dictators defined as "order and progress."

Notes

1. The oral history interviews, which date from 1997 to 2005, were conducted in Kaqchikel. Due to Guatemala's continued political volatility and recurrent human rights abuses, I have preserved the anonymity of my sources. For the most part, I have used names that derive from the Maya calendar. Female informants can be recognized by the "Ix" prefix to their one-word names. In contrast, male names have two words. A name in parentheses after the informant's citation indicates that my research assistant Ixch'onïk (also a pseudonym) performed the interview. I conducted all other interviews.

2. Greg Grandin, *The Blood of Guatemala: A History of Race and Nation* (Durham, NC: Duke University Press, 2000), 162–64; David McCreery, *Rural Guatemala 1760–1940* (Stanford, CA: Stanford University Press, 1994), 171; Pablo Piccato, *City of Suspects: Crime in Mexico City, 1900–1931* (Durham, NC: Duke University Press, 2001); Walter E. Little, "A Visual Political Economy of Maya Representations in Guatemala, 1931–1944," *Ethnohistory* 55, no. 4 (Fall 2008), 633–63; Sueann Caulfield, "Getting into Trouble: Dishonest Women, Modern Girls, and Women-Men in the Conceptual Language of 'Vida Policial,' 1925–1927," *Signs: Journal of Women in Culture and Society* 19, no. 1 (Autumn 1993), 166.

3. Paul Dosal, *Power in Transition: The Rise of Guatemala's Industrial Oligarchy, 1871–1994* (Westport, CT: Praeger, 1995), 43, 68–77.

4. Pablo Piccato, "'El paso de Venus por el disco del sol': Criminality and Alcoholism in the Late Porfiriato," *Mexican Studies/Estudios Mexicanos* 11, no. 2 (1995), 208–29, 241; Robert Buffington, "Prohibition in the Borderlands: National Government-Border Community Relations," *Pacific Historical Review* 63, no. 1 (1994), 24–25; Jeffrey Pilcher, *¡Que vivan los tamales!: Food and the Making of Mexican Identity* (Albuquerque: University of New Mexico Press, 1998), 83; Piccato, *City of Suspects*, 54; Stephen Lewis, "Mexico's National Indigenist Institute and the Negotiation of Applied Anthropology in Highland Chiapas, 1951–1954," *Ethnohistory* 55, no. 4 (Fall 2008), 609–32.

5. VERA, "A los indios muertos," *La República*, January 30, 1919; Ruth Bunzel, "The Role of Alcoholism in Two Central American Cultures," *Psychiatry* 3 (1940), 363; Bunzel, *Chichicastenango: A Guatemalan Village* (Seattle: University of Washington Press, 1959), 259; Robert Burkitt, "Explorations in the Highlands of Western Guatemala," *Museum Journal (University of Pennsylvania)* 21, no. 1 (1930), 59; Oliver LaFarge, *Santa Eulalia: The Religion of a Cuchumatán Indian Town* (Chicago: University of Chicago Press, 1947), 7. Historian Aviva Chomsky points out alcohol abuse also served planters' interests by "turning dissatisfaction and resentment inward, or onto other workers, instead of organizing for any kind of effective change in the unsatisfactory situation." See Chomsky, *West Indian Workers and the United Fruit Company in Costa Rica, 1870–1940* (Baton Rouge: Louisiana State University Press, 1996), 175.

6. Bunzel, "Role of Alcoholism," 363.

7. Carlos Enrique Reiche C., "Estudio sobre el patrón de embriaguez en la región rural Altaverapacense," *Guatemala Indígena* 5 (1970), 103–27; Bunzel, "Role of Alcoholism," 384; Stephen E. Lewis, "La guerra del posh, 1951–1954: Un conflicto decisivo entre el Instituto Nacional Indigenista, el monopolio del alcohol y el gobierno del estado de Chiapas," *Mesoamérica* 46 (2004), 111–34; Ben Fallaw, "Dry Law, Wet Poli-

tics: Drinking and Prohibition in Post-Revolutionary Yucatán, 1915–1935," *Latin American Research Review* 37, no. 2 (2001), 37–64; E. Michael Mendelson, "Religion and World-View in Santiago Atitlán" (PhD diss. University of Chicago, 1956), long version: 61.

8. Stacey Schwartzkopf, "Consumption, Custom, and Control: *Aguardiente* in Nineteenth-Century Maya Guatemala," in *Distilling the Influence of Alcohol: Aguardiente in Guatemalan History*, ed. David Carey Jr. (Gainesville: University Press of Florida, 2012), 29.

9. Bunzel, *Chichicastenango*, 255, 258.

10. Bunzel, "Role of Alcoholism," 366.

11. Ibid., 367–69, 370–71; Bunzel, *Chichicastenango*, 257–58; Christine Eber, *Women and Alcohol in a Highland Maya Town: Water of Hope, Water of Sorrow* (Austin: University of Texas Press, 2000), 34–35.

12. Ix'aj, Comalapa, August 5, 2005.

13. Schwartzkopf, "Consumption, Custom, and Control."

14. Archivo General de Centro América (hereafter AGCA), Jefatura Política, Sacatepéquez (hereafter JP-S) 1923, carta de Administración de Rentas al Jefe Político e Intendente de Hacienda, February 5, 1923.

15. David Carey Jr., *Our Elders Teach Us: Maya-Kaqchikel Historical Perspectives. Xkib'ij kan qate' qatata'* (Tuscaloosa: University of Alabama Press, 2001), 179; Carey, "Maya Soldier-Citizens: Ethnic Pride in the Guatemalan Military, 1925–1945," in *Military Struggle and Identity Formation in Latin America: Race, Nation, and Community During the Liberal Period*, ed. Nicola Foote and René D. Harder Horst (Gainesville: University Press of Florida, 2010), 147.

16. Charles Wisdom, *Chorti Indians of Guatemala* (Chicago: University of Chicago Press, 1940), 301.

17. Bunzel, "Role of Alcoholism," 386.

18. McCreery, *Rural Guatemala*, 294.

19. Antonio Batres Jáuregui, *Los indios: Su historia y su civilización* (Guatemala City: Tipografía La Unión, 1894), 13.

20. Policía Nacional de Guatemala. *Memoria de la Dirección General de la Policía Nacional* (hereafter MDGPN) 1932, (Guatemala City: Tipografía Nacional, 1933), 11. Mexican authorities were coming to similar conclusions. In 1900 nearly 70 percent of all crime in Mexico City was committed by individuals while drunk. See Pablo Picato, *The Tyranny of Public Opinion: Honor in the Construction of the Mexican Public Sphere* (Durham, NC: Duke University Press, 2010), 197.

21. Archivo Municipal de Patzicía (hereafter AMP), paquete (hereafter paq.) 24, March 15, 1928.

22. See, e.g., AGCA, índice 116, Chimaltenango 1911, legajo (hereafter leg.) 12f, expediente (hereafter exp.) 25.

23. AMP, paq. 24, August 13, 1929.

24. AMP, paq. 107, Libro de Sentencias Económicas (hereafter LSE) 1943, Máxima Gómez contra Martín Choc, July 30, 1943.

25. *La Gaceta: Revista de Policía y Variedades*, June 14, 1931.

26. AMP, paq. 24, August 13, 1929; David Carey Jr. and Gabriela E. Torres, "Precursors to Femicide: Guatemalan Women in a Vortex of Violence," *Latin American Research Review* 45, no. 3 (2010), 142–64. For colonial Mexico, William Taylor, too,

152 • *David Carey Jr.*

found defendants commonly invoking inebriation and memory loss to explain their crimes. See Taylor, *Drinking, Homicide, and Rebellion in Colonial Mexican Villages* (Stanford, CA: Stanford University Press, 1979), 64–65.

27. AGCA, índice 116, Chimaltenango 1911, leg. 12f, exp. 25. *Indio* was a pejorative term used to denigrate Mayas, though at times indigenous litigants and their lawyers used it to play upon the very stereotypes it conjured.

28. Ibid.

29. Ibid.

30. McCreery, *Rural Guatemala*, 87–89; Alvis Dunn, "'A Sponge Soaking Up All the Money': Alcohol, Taverns, *Vinaterías*, and the Bourbon Reforms in Mid-Eighteenth Century Santiago de los Caballeros," in *Distilling the Influence of Alcohol*, 71–95; Stacey Schwartzkopf, "Maya Power and State Culture: Indigenous Politics and State Formation in Nineteenth-Century Guatemala" (PhD diss., Tulane University, 2008).

31. *Diario de Centro América*, April 19, 1892. For an earlier association (1829) of Maya with alcohol from the newly arrived Dutch consul to the Republic of Central America, see Jacobo Haefkens, *Viaje a Guatemala y Centroamerica*, ed. Francis Gall (Guatemala: Editorial Universitaria, 1969), 290, 293.

32. Virginia Garrard-Burnett, "Indians Are Drunks, Drunks Are Indians: Alcohol and *Indigenismo* in Guatemala, 1890–1940," *Bulletin of Latin American Research* 19, no. 3 (2000), 345–46.

33. Miguel Angel Asturias, *Sociología Guatemalteca: El problema social del indio*, trans. Maureen Ahern (Tempe: Arizona State University, 1977 [1923]), 92.

34. Garrard-Burnett, "Indians Are Drunks," 345–46; Reiche C., "Estudio sobre el patrón," 103, 105.

35. Virginia Garrard-Burnett, "Conclusion: Community Drunkenness and Control in Guatemala," in Carey, *Distilling the Influence of Alcohol*, 163.

36. Batres Jáuregui, *Los indios*, 191.

37. J. Fernando Juárez Muñoz, *El indio Guatemalteco: Ensayo de sociología nacionalista* (Guatemala City: Tipografía Latina, 1931), 159.

38. Benjamin Colby and Pierre L. van de Berghe, *Ixil Country: A Plural Society in Highland Guatemala* (Berkeley: University of California Press, 1969), 72–73; Bunzel, *Chichicastenango*, 259.

39. Garrard-Burnett, "Indians Are Drunks," 348–49, 354–55; Sol Tax, *Penny Capitalism: A Guatemalan Indian Economy* (Chicago: University of Chicago Press, 1963); Bunzel, *Chichicastenango*; Norman B. Schwartz, "Drinking Patterns, Drunks and Maturity in a Petén Town (Guatemala)," *Sociologus* 28, no. 1 (1978), 35–53. For a similar conclusion regarding southern Mexico, see Robert Wasserstrom, *Class and Society in Central Chiapas* (Berkeley: University of California Press, 1983), 107–56.

40. *MDGPN, 1934*, 137; *MDGPN 1935*, 159; *MDGPN 1936*, 170; *MDGPN 1937*; *MDGPN 1938*; and *MDGPN 1939*.

41. Dirección General de Estadística, *Censo de la república levantado el 28 de agosto de 1921. 4o Censo, Parte II* (Guatemala City: Talleres Gutenberg, 1926); Dirección General de Estadística, *Quinto censo general de población levantado el 7 de abril de 1940* (Guatemala, June, 1942), 214.

42. The 1940 census counted 1,457,122 ladinos and 1,820,872 indígenas. The 3,809 ladinos arrested for public inebriation made up 0.21 percent of the population.

In contrast, the 1929 Maya natives arrested for the same crime made up only 0.11 percent of their population.

43. John Stephens, *Incidents of Travel in Central America, Chiapas, and Yucatán*, vol. 2 (New York: Dover, 1969 [1841]), 105, 165, 200, 235; Robert Glasgow Dunlop, *Travels in Central America, Being a Journal of Nearly Three Years' Residence in the Country. Together with a Sketch of the Republic, and an Account of Its Climate, Productions, Commerce, Etc.* (London: Longman, Brown, Green, and Longmans, 1847), 337–38; G. F. von Tempsky, *Mitla: A Narrative of Incidents and Personal Adventures on Journey in Mexico, Guatemala, and Salvador in the Years 1853 to 1855* (London: Longman, Brown, Green, Longmans, and Roberts, 1858), 330, 373; LaFarge, *Santa Eulalia*, 7; Ruben Reina, *The Law of the Saints: A Pokoman Pueblo and Its Community Culture* (New York: Bobbs-Merrill, 1966); Burkitt, "Explorations," 57–59. For a study of drinking in a ladino town, see Schwartz, "Drinking Patterns," 40–41.

44. Federico Hernández de León, *Viajes presidenciales: breves relatos de algunas expediciones administrativas del General D. Jorge Ubico, presidente de la República*, vol. 2 (Guatemala: Tipografía Nacional, 1940), 49.

45. *El Imparcial*, October 14, 1940. Concerns about alcoholism detracting from laborers' productivity preoccupied leaders during the colonial and early national periods as well. See McCreery, *Rural Guatemala*, 87, 128; Garrard-Burnett, "Indians Are Drunks," 355.

46. AGCA, JP-S 1940, carta al jefe político de San Antonio Aguas Calientes, June 8, 1940.

47. Piccato, *City of Suspects*, 54. For examples of efforts to stamp out drunk driving, see *La Gaceta*, February 14, 1937.

48. AMP, paq. 24, LSE 1927, June 20, 1927, juzgado de paz, detención a Clara Partenal. Of course, drinking itself was expensive. Charles Wagley found that one man spent 10 percent ($5–6) of his family's annual income to purchase alcohol for the three-day festival of Santiago in 1937. See Wagley, *Economics of a Guatemalan Village. Memoirs of the American Anthropological Association* 43, no. 3, pt. 3 (1941), 51–52. In contemporary Panajachel, Sol Tax calculated that Kaqchikel families spent 40 percent of their cash on alcohol. See Tax, "Changing Consumption in Indian Guatemala," *Economic Development and Cultural Change* 5, no. 2 (1957), 157; Tax, *Penny Capitalism*.

49. AMP, paq. 24, juzgado 1o municipal Patzicía, March 13, 1928.

50. AMP, paq. 24, July 18, 1929, detención de Valentina Miculax.

51. AMP, paq. 24, juzgado 1o municipal Patzicía, August 13, 1929.

52. Katherine Elaine Bliss, *Compromised Positions: Prostitution, Public Health, and Gender Politics in Revolutionary Mexico City* (University Park: Pennsylvania State University Press, 2001), 89–90. In his study of El Petén (Guatemala), Norman Schwartz found that female drunks were labeled as such less for their consumption than for their behavior, including sexual promiscuity. See Schwartz, "Drinking Patterns," 48.

53. Susan Migden Socolow, *The Women of Colonial Latin America* (Cambridge: Cambridge University Press, 2000), 163; Reina, *Law of the Saints*, 141; Walter Randolph Adams, "Guatemala," in *International Handbook on Alcohol and Culture*, ed. Dwight B. Heath, 99–109 (Westport, CT: Greenwood Press, 1995); Garrard-Burnett, "Indians Are Drunks," 347; Schwartz, "Drinking Patterns," 35, 43, 48. During his early nineteenth-century travels in Guatemala, John L. Stephens encountered inebriated

females. See Stephens, *Incidents of Travel*, 105, 200, 219. Similarly, Taylor found evidence of women (and children) drinking in colonial Mexico. At the same time, women who drank without their husband's or lover's consent were severely punished. See Taylor, *Drinking, Homicide, and Rebellion*, 35, 45, 58, 62, 87–88. During his research in 1932, Oliver LaFarge noted that during fiestas it was common to see men and women "so drunk they could hardly walk." See LaFarge, *Santa Eulalia*, 91. Carlos Enrique Reiche noted similar behavior among Altaverapaz women in the 1960s. See Reiche, "Estudio sobre el patrón de embriaguez," 117.

54. Juárez Muñoz, *Indio Guatemalteco*, 166.

55. *MDGPN, 1899; MDGPN 1900*, 14; *MDGPN 1922 y 1923*, 8; *MDGPN 1926*, 61; *MDGPN 1928*, 60; *MDGPN 1929*, 27. In southern Mexico, anthropologist Christine Eber found that Mayan women often kept up with men in ritual, if not informal, drinking. See Eber, *Women and Alcohol*, 7.

56. For many examples of scandalous behavior see AMP, paq. 24, LSE 1906 and LSE 1927; AMP, paq. 24, LSE 1927, June 20, 1927, contra Clara Partenal; AMP, paq. 24, July 18, 1929, detención de Valentina Miculax; AMP, paq. 24, August 13, 1929.

57. *La Gaceta*, January 12 and March 2, 1941; *La Gaceta*, April 25, 1943.

58. Mendelson, "Religion and World-View," short version: 7–8.

59. Piccato, *Tyranny of Public Opinion*, 215–16.

60. AMP, paq. 237, Bernardo Can y la mujer Gregoria Ajsivinac, December 1, 1948. For an example of a drunken altercation involving women (including one who was too drunk to remember what happened) on the eve of Estrada Cabrera's dictatorship (1897), see the inset (Diriaco Chamali, June 28, 1897) in AGCA, índice 116, Chimaltenango 1901, leg. 2f, exp. 40.

61. AGCA, índice 116, Chimaltenango 1914, leg. 15D, exp. 53.

62. *La Gaceta*, April 25, 1943.

63. AGCA, Jefatura Política, Chimaltenango (hereafter JP-C) 1937, December 18, 1937.

64. AGCA, índice 116, Chimaltenango 1901, leg. 2f, exp. 45; AGCA, índice 116, Chimaltenango 1911, leg. 12, exp. 44.

65. AMP, paq. 24, February 24, 1923.

66. See, e.g., AMP, paq. 24, LSE 1906, juzgado municipal de Patzicía, July 30, 1916; AMP, paq. 24, LSE 1929, juzgado municipal de Patzicía, August 1, 1929; AMP, paq. 127, LSE 1935, juzgado municipal de Patzicía, January 3, 1935; AMP, paq. 107, LSE 1943, Maxima Gómez contra Martín Choc, July 30, 1943. This pattern of alcohol and domestic violence has been documented throughout Latin America. See, e.g., Tanja Christiansen, *Disobedience, Slander, Seduction, and Assault: Women and Men in Cajamarca, Peru, 1862–1900* (Austin: University of Texas Press 2004), 73–74; Lola Romanucci-Ross, *Conflict, Violence and Morality in a Mexican Village* (Palo Alto, CA: National Press Books, 1973), 136; Olivia Harris, "Complementaridad y conflicto: Una vision andina del hombre y la mujer," *Allpanchis* 25, no. 21 (1985), 17–42; J. J. Gayford, "Battered Wives," in *International Perspectives on Family Violence*, ed. Richard J. Gelles and Flaire Pedrick Cornell, 123–37 (Lexington, MA: Lexington Books, 1983); Kristi Anne Stølen, "Gender, Sexuality and Violence in Ecuador," *Ethos* 56, nos. 1–2 (1992), 82–100.

67. AGCA, índice 116, Chimaltenango 1916, leg. 17b, exp. 6.

68. AGCA, índice 116, Chimaltenango 1904, leg. 5D, exp. 18.

69. *La Gaceta*, April 19, 1942. For another example, see *La Gaceta*, July 4, 1943.

70. AGCA JP-C 1926, petición de Francisca Chiroy de Sutuj, December 6, 1926.

71. *Código Civil de la República de Guatemala, Libro Primero del año 1927* (Guatemala City: Tipografía Nacional, 1927), 61. In certain extenuating circumstances, Guatemalan law allowed mothers to assume patria potestad. See David Carey Jr., *I Ask for Justice: Maya Women, Dictators, and Crime in Guatemala, 1898–1944* (Austin: University of Texas Press, 2013).

72. Reina, *Law of the Saints*, 266.

73. McCreery, *Rural Guatemala*, 176–79; Buffington, "Prohibition in the Borderlands," 25, 26, 28; Garrard-Burnett, "Indians Are Drunks," 350–53; James Alex Garza, *The Imagined Underworld: Sex, Crime, and Vice in Porfirian Mexico City* (Lincoln: University of Nebraska Press, 2007); David Carey Jr., "Distilling Perceptions of Crime: Maya Moonshiners and the State, 1898–1944," in Carey, *Distilling the Influence of Alcohol*, 120–56. Even before the Liberal Revolution, perhaps as much as 25 percent of the government's income was generated by alcohol taxes. See René Reeves, *Ladinos with Ladinos, Indians with Indians: Land, Labor, and Regional Ethnic Conflict in the Making of Guatemala* (Stanford, CA: Stanford University Press, 2006), 116, 227n47.

74. Frederick Douglass Opie, "Adios Jim Crow: Afro-North American Workers and the Guatemalan Railroad Workers' League, 1884–1921" (PhD diss., Syracuse University, 1999), 141–43. In contrast to assertion by historians Ana Carla Ericastilla and Liseth Jiménez that Estrada Cabrera "did not persecute drunkenness but rather the commercialization [of alcohol] outside of the state's fiscal control," other research including my own indicates that Estrada Cabrera's security forces regularly arrested drunks. See Ericastilla and Jiménez, "Las clandestinistas de aguardiente en Guatemala a fines del siglo XIX," in *Mujeres, género e historia en América Central durante los siglos XVIII, XIX, XX*, ed. Eugenia Rodríguez Sáenz (San José, Costa Rica/Burlington, VT: United Nations Development Fund for Women/Plumsock Mesoamerican Studies, 2002), 21.

75. Frederick Douglass Opie, "Alcohol and Lowdown Culture in Caribbean Guatemala and Honduras, 1898–1920," in Carey, *Distilling the Influence of Alcohol*, 96–119.

76. *MDGPN*, 1899.

77. *MDGPN*, 1900, 14

78. AMP, paq. 24, LSE 1906, March 5, 1916.

79. AMP, paq. 24, LSE 1906, May 16, June 2, and August 1, 1916.

80. *MDGPN 1922 y 1923*, 8.

81. *MDGPN 1926*, 61.

82. *MDGPN 1928*, 60.

83. *MDGPN 1929*, 27.

84. *La Gaceta*, May 3, 1931, and January 22, 1933. One exception to this trend was J. Fernando Juárez Muñoz, who argued against prohibition, citing other nations such as Germany, France, and England that had not banned alcohol. He simply advocated restricting its consumption. Juárez Muñoz, *Indio Guatemalteco*, 160. In truth, as a Catholic nation, Guatemala was far more tolerant of alcohol consumption than many of its Protestant counterparts.

156 • *David Carey Jr.*

85. *MDGPN*, 1932, 99.

86. AGCA, JP-S 1931, carta de alcalde de Santiago de Zamora, Marcelo Miranda al jefe político de Sacatepéquez, February 21, 1931.

87. Ixrusal, Comalapa, June 28, 2001 (Ixch'onïk); Ixtol, Comalapa, June 26, 2001, (Ixch'onïk); Ixkawoq, Pamamus, Comalapa, June 25, 2001; Bunzel, "The Role of Alcoholism," 386; McCreery, *Rural Guatemala*, 293–94. For an example from the archives of a family torn apart by aguardiente, see AGCA, JP-C 1925, leg. 68, Herlinda García carta a jefe político de Chimaltenango.

88. B'eleje' Kawoq, Tecpán, June 9, 1998; Ixch'op and Ixmes, San Antonio Aguas Calientes, January 18, 1998; Junlajuj Kame, Pachitur, Comalapa, April 12, 1998; Wo'o' Iq', Panicuy, Comalapa, December 2, 1997; Kab'lajuj Ajpu', Comalapa, November 14, 1997.

89. Wo'o' Kawoq and Waqi' Kawoq, Kojol Juyu', Comalapa, March 3, 1998.

90. Wisdom, *Chorti Indians of Guatemala*, 214.

91. Michel Foucault, *Discipline and Punish: The Birth of the Prison* (New York: Pantheon, 1977).

92. B'eleje' Kawoq, Tecpán, June 9, 1998.

93. *La Gaceta*, January 3, 1943.

94. *La Gaceta*, April 25, 1943.

95. Oxi' Kame, Chi Chalí, Comalapa, March 4, 1998.

96. AGCA, JP-C 1930, leg. 73, carta de jefe político de Chimaltenango al alcalde de San Martín Jilotepeque, October 11, 1930. In a marked departure from his colleagues, one departmental governor tried to convince his superiors that drunken behavior ultimately cost the state more money than it made through monopolies and taxes. See Reeves, *Ladinos with Ladinos, Indians with Indians*, 128.

97. Jorge García Granados, *Evolución sociológica de Guatemala/Ensayo sobre el gobierno del Dr. Mariano Gálvez* (Guatemala: Sánchez and de Guise, 1927), 74.

98. Juárez Muñoz, *Indio Guatemalteco*, 82, 86.

99. Ibid., 163.

100. See, e.g., AGCA, JP-C 1927, leg. 70A, licencias para tocar marimba en establecimiento de licores: Marcela viuda de Rodríguez, January 9; José Ángel Gálvez, February 26; Soledad Morales, March 12, April 9; José Ángel Galores, April 10; AGCA JP-C 1930, leg. 73, memorandum de jefe político de Chimaltenango al alcalde de San Martín de Jilotepeque, April 11; memorandum de jefe político de Chimaltenango al alcalde de San Martín de Jilotepeque, September 1; carta de Depósito de licores, San Martín de Jilotepeque al alcalde de San Martín de Jilotepeque, April 2, June 30; AGCA, JP-C 1944, leg. 88A, Sanidad no. 72, María Rogelia Gálvez Roca, March 17; Roselia Ruano de Roca, January 27; Paula Hernández, April 20; Beatriz Álvarez, April 16.

101. García Granados, *Evolución sociológica de Guatemala*, 74. Ethnographic accounts also point to the proliferation of bars. In his study of Nebaj in the 1940s, Jackson Steward Lincoln counted nearly eighty in that town alone. See Lincoln, "An Ethnographic Study of the Ixil Indians of the Guatemalan Highlands," Microfilm Collection of Manuscripts on Middle American Cultural Anthropology, University of Chicago, no. 1, 1945.

102. James C. Scott, *Domination and Arts of Resistance: Hidden Transcripts* (New Haven, CT: Yale University Press, 1990), 121.

103. AMP, paq. 107, LSE 1943, September 6, 1943; AMP, paq. 24, Manuel Meses contra Nicolasa Corona, February 24, 1923.

104. AGCA, índice 116, Chimaltenango 1900, leg. 1F, exp. 47; AGCA, índice 116, Chimaltenango 1907, leg. 8E, exp. 17. See also *La Gaceta*, January 1, 1933, 30, for an example of a *cantinera* (female cantina owner) whose reaction to a customer who threatened to kill her on various occasions intimated that she had become accustomed to violence.

105. *La Gaceta*, January 1, 1933; *La Gaceta*, March 26, 1933; AGCA, índice 116, Chimaltenango 1914, leg. 15D, exp. 53.

106. *La Gaceta*, May 1, 1941.

107. The same was true in Mexico, where Piccato found that "bars were essential places of comradeship." See Piccato, *Tyranny of Public Opinion*, 77.

108. Sarah C. Chambers, "Private Crimes, Public Order: Honor, Gender, and the Law in Early Republican Peru," in *Honor, Status and Law in Modern Latin America*, ed. Sueann Caulfield, Sarah C. Chambers, and Lara Putnam (Durham, NC: Duke University Press, 2005), 40.

109. AMP, paq. 24, Manuel Meses contra Nicolasa Corona, February 24, 1923.

PART THREE

The Twentieth and Twenty-First Centuries

During the twentieth century, Latin America experienced a broad range of changes in political and economic systems and strong participation of the disaffected in them. Between 1910 and 1930, groups including male and female peasants, urban workers, and the middle class joined together to overthrow liberal oligarchs. New leaders—some of them revolutionary, some reformist, and some merely strategically adopting populist rhetoric— often garnered support with a nationalist message. By expropriating land, infrastructure, and other resources, actively promoting domestic economic development, providing political and socioeconomic benefits for the masses, and celebrating the nation's African or indigenous roots, these authority figures worked to counter some of the more damaging elements of the nineteenth century. At times, this nationalism was expressed by a newfound interest in traditional, fermented beverages like *pulque* or *chicha*. Other leaders couched temperance rhetoric in the desire to uplift the masses.

By the 1960s, thanks in part to the Cold War and reactions to the Cuban Revolution, many of these progressive policies were beginning to disappear. Several democratically elected leaders were overthrown by military regimes that used torture and the suppression of civil liberties to eliminate suspected communist subversives. Particularly in Central America, civil wars also pitted right against left. The extreme political polarization of society has begun to subside since the 1990s, but the region continues to face challenges, including globalization and the loss of centuries-old traditions to the spread of mass culture, a neoliberal economic system coupled with an increase in extreme poverty, a rising foreign debt, environmental degradation, and the escalation of violence in countries connected to the worldwide drug trade. As economies have been privatized, manufacturers of distilled beverages and wines have increasingly abandoned a nationalist marketing strategy and have directed their wares to foreign consumers. The resulting high prices for these beverages mean that, once again, poorer members of society have remained loyal to cheaper drinks such as chicha, pulque, and beer.

In this section, Gretchen Pierce (chapter 7) explores the reaction of small producers, among them women, who defended themselves from the attacks of temperance and revolutionary reformers who sought to restrict alcohol consumption. When producers saw their businesses being attacked, they questioned the government's revolutionary and nationalistic nature. José Orozco (chapter 8) and Steve Stein (chapter 9) explore the targeted markets and strategies that tequila and wine producers have chosen throughout the twentieth and twenty-first centuries. Their studies provide an overview of the strong connection between alcohol, national development, and globalization. Finally, Anton Daughters (chapter 10) closes this anthology with the remarkable account of the role of *chicha de manzana* in contemporary rural Chile. This hard apple cider and its communal production represent an act of solidarity and identity reinforcement in the face of economic change and globalization, showing in this way that despite centuries of political, economic, and social changes, alcohol at the local level continues to reinforce communal bonding, identity, and reciprocity.

CHAPTER SEVEN

Pulqueros, Cerveceros, *and* Mezcaleros

Small Alcohol Producers and Popular Resistance to Mexico's Anti-Alcohol Campaigns, 1910–1940

Gretchen Pierce

In May 1922, M. Luna y Menocal and José María Montaño, president and secretary, respectively, of the Sindicato de Trabajadores de la Industria Magueyera (Union of Maguey Industry Workers), wrote to President Álvaro Obregón, complaining about the Clausura Dominical, a mandatory closing of businesses on Sundays in Mexico City. The city's town council had taken this measure to prevent employees from being overworked and to contribute to the nation's anti-alcohol campaign, which aimed to keep workers, who they believed to be most susceptible to the vice of alcoholism, from spending their day off drinking. This forced closure negatively affected eateries, *pulquerías*, and their employees, Luna y Menocal and Montaño claimed, because *pulque* is a beverage that needs to be consumed quickly or it will go bad. But the closure harmed more than just the sellers of the beverage; they estimated hundreds of thousands of other families involved in the trade "without capital [and] that needed to work" would be hurt as well. They did not necessarily disapprove of the anti-alcohol campaign. In fact, they reasserted that pulque had less alcohol per volume than other drinks, even beer, and thus the government should support it to help promote sobriety. However, they did question revolutionary leaders' intent, arguing that forcing businesses to close one day per week and thus reducing their sales, was doing anything but helping workers.[1]

More than a decade later, in March 1938, and eighty miles away, in Jojutla, Morelos, Engracia Posas wrote to President Lázaro Cárdenas with similar concerns. She occasionally sold pulque and said she did so in a law-abiding manner, paying her taxes on time and making sure that her customers took the beverage home so as to avoid disorder. However, in the prior month, the governor had forbidden the sale of all alcoholic beverages in the state, and therefore she had to shut down her operations. Dismayed, she explained that she was a poor, single mother and needed the small but regular source of income. She asked that the president, who admittedly had "bigger things to deal with," find it in his heart to help her reopen her business and "better her life."[2]

These two stories reveal several issues about Mexico's anti-alcohol campaigns. First, leaders from town councilmen to presidents during the Revolution of 1910–1940 perceived alcoholism to be a problem, especially among the working class. In carrying out anti-alcohol campaigns over this thirty-year period, they tried various solutions, such as raising taxes on alcoholic beverages, requiring drinking establishments to close on certain days or times, and even occasionally prohibiting the consumption of all intoxicants. Second, in spite of the government's attempt at moralizing and uplifting workers, temperance-related policies negatively impacted poor *pulqueros, cerveceros,* and *mezcaleros* (producers of pulque, beer, and mezcal, a distilled beverage similar in composition to tequila), as well as other employees of the alcohol industry. This was especially true for women, many of whom had been made widows during revolutionary fighting and now had to support families on their own. Third, these small entrepreneurs and laborers should not be considered immoral or recalcitrant for refusing to stop producing or selling alcohol. Often, it was the only decent way for them to make a living. Many supplicants explained this using gendered language, emphasizing that they were trying merely to fulfill their duties as good mothers and fathers. Fourth, their claims demonstrated that they were not passive members of society. Rather, they actively took part in the state-building process by resisting unpopular measures and demanding that the revolutionary government live up to its name and truly pursue measures that would help the working class.

This chapter focuses on the hundreds of thousands of small pulque, beer, and mezcal producers, transporters, and sellers, men and women, in Mexico from 1910 to 1940. Pulque was produced mainly in the central part of the country, especially the states of Hidalgo, México, Puebla, and Tlaxcala. Since the nineteenth century, wealthy landowners with ties to the pre-revolutionary regime dominated this industry,[3] as Áurea Toxqui demonstrates in chapter 5. It was not these men and women, though, who were responsible for the actual production of pulque. Contemporary observers suggested that between a few thousand to over a hundred thousand people tended the plants, harvested and fermented the *aguamiel*, transported the drink to be sold, or served it in pulquerías. The number grew to over six hundred thousand once the laborers' families who depended on their wages were included.[4]

The number of workers in the beer industry was considerably smaller. In the first half of the twentieth century, the major breweries were spread throughout the country, including the states of Chihuahua, México, Nuevo León, Sonora, and Veracruz. Although in the late nineteenth century foreigners owned many of them, by the twentieth century they came to be dominated by powerful Mexican families who could afford the large capital investment needed to open such a factory. As the newspaper *El Nacional* estimated in 1937, these breweries employed 2,665 people who, depending on the size of the brewery, either made the beer by hand or tended the machinery that did. Surely this number is low, though, because it does not include auxiliary laborers who toiled in bottling, boxing, or malt plants, as well as those who transported or sold the final product.[5]

The number of mezcaleros is harder to determine because the mezcal industry was smaller. Situated in several states, including Chihuahua, Oaxaca, and Sonora, production was often unofficial and clandestine. The planting, harvesting, distilling, and bottling of the beverage, although not all done by the same people, was typically performed by families or small enterprises with only a few employees each. It is these thousands to hundreds of thousands of workers from each industry, as well as those who packaged, transported, and sold the drinks on a small scale, that this chapter examines.[6]

The Mexican Revolution and the Anti-Alcohol Campaigns, 1910–1940

The Mexican Revolution is well known for its overthrowing of the dictatorial regime of Porfirio Díaz (1876–1911), redistribution of land, nationalization of key industries, and progressive labor legislation. Less well documented are its anti-alcohol campaigns. In fact, all revolutionary presidents expressed concern with the problem of alcoholism. They feared that chronic intoxication caused a number of problems for the drinker, ranging from diseases like cirrhosis to ones they supposedly became more susceptible to, such as tuberculosis and syphilis. Alcoholism affected even the nation, because drunkards could not contribute to the revolutionaries' nation-building goals. They could not be productive workers or participate in the political process, and their "backward" practice of drinking seemed to imply a rejection of the modernity and progress that the Revolution strove for. Indeed, alcohol consumption seemed to be taking Mexico in the opposite direction its leaders wanted to see it go.[7]

Temperance advocates argued that the anti-alcohol campaign was the height of revolutionary reform because it directly helped the poor and women in general. Political leaders and reformers alike believed that male workers and, to a lesser extent, indigenous men were the most likely to fall into the snares of alcoholism. These drunken men's actions negatively affected their family as well, for wives and children lost their monetary support to the cantina and lived in fear of domestic violence.[8] Reformers further claimed that intoxicating beverages had long been used to take advantage of the less powerful, beginning during the colonial period and continuing into the present day. There were a variety of reasons for this. The legislator Dr. José Siurob y Ramírez explained in 1917 that when an *hacendado* (hacienda owner) wanted to prevent his workers from organizing and demanding a higher salary, he would give them pulque or other alcoholic beverages to pacify them. It was also common practice for hacendados to pay their workers in drink, rather than in cash, which established a system of debt servitude. Other reformers pointed out that if urban workers stopped visiting cantinas, they could save more money and work their way out of poverty. Indeed, as Siurob argued, "Pulque is opposed to the principal idea of the Revolution, which is to raise up the spirit of the masses."[9] The same could be said of other types of drinks.

Presidents employed a variety of techniques to combat this problem. From 1910 to 1920, they employed a hands-off approach, mirroring their laissez-faire states, encouraging drinkers to give up their vice and requesting that governors, legislators, and bureaucrats in the Department of Public Health deal with the issue.[10] From 1920 to 1932, as the country moved toward increasing stability after the military phase of the Revolution ended, leaders' techniques became more diverse. They increased taxes on alcoholic beverages, hired inspectors to ensure that said drinks were at least sanitary, and provided more of a budget to the Department of Public Education to teach children about the dangers of alcohol consumption. The most significant step in this phase came in 1929 when President Emilio Portes Gil created the Comité Nacional de Lucha contra el Alcoholismo (CNLCA), or the National Committee of Struggle Against

Alcoholism.[11] This body used mostly cultural techniques, organizing parades, distributing propaganda, and presenting speeches on the radio. Between 1932 and 1940, the campaign intensified. With an even stronger state backing it, the CNLCA increased its cultural work, putting on several temperance-themed events each week and working closely with schools. Presidents also took a more active role, creating corps of inspectors to monitor drinking establishments, issuing decrees that limited when and where alcohol could be consumed, and following up on complaints from regular citizens about violations of local dry laws. In the latter two stages, reformers specifically solicited women's help, asking them to join anti-alcohol leagues that would persuade their husbands not to drink and petition local authorities to close cantinas in their neighborhoods.[12]

The anti-alcohol campaign was not waged just on the national level. Many governors, mayors, policemen, teachers, and ordinary citizens also strove to keep their communities sober. Several governors enacted restrictive measures that limited the production, distribution, or consumption of beverages with high levels of alcohol and, in the case of Sonora from 1915 to 1919, all intoxicating drinks.[13] It was up to lower-level political officials, policemen, and alcohol inspectors to see that these measures were carried out, and some did so quite enthusiastically and effectively. Loreto Valenzuela, for example, the mayor of Guaymas, Sonora, in 1918 and 1919 worked closely with an alcohol inspector and a police captain. Together, on trains, on boats, and in cars, they discovered and poured out a plethora of illegal beverages nearly every day. Many teachers, as well, diligently informed students about the dangers of alcohol consumption, put on temperance-themed festivals for their school districts, and protested to authorities when cantinas opened up too near their schools. Finally, regular men and women joined thousands of temperance leagues that distributed propaganda or, as members of labor unions and neighborhood organizations, wrote letters to officials complaining about high levels of vice.[14] These cases demonstrate that the anti-alcohol campaign was not merely a project imposed from above but, rather, one that had support that cut across various levels of society.

Poor Pulqueros, Cerveceros, and Mezcaleros
Resist the Anti-Alcohol Campaigns

In spite of this widespread support, there was also a significant percentage of the population that did not approve of attempts to limit alcohol production and consumption. In states that passed restrictive legislation against intoxicants, some of the biggest violators of the law were elected and appointed officials, even policemen and alcohol inspectors. These figures either accepted bribes and allowed people to sell alcohol or participated in the trade themselves, directly benefiting from this forbidden activity.[15] For instance, in 1922 the mayor of Ticul, Yucatán, Santiago Barbosa, permitted illegal cantinas to remain open for a fee. José R. Berlanga, General Treasurer of Sonora, was supposedly the principal distributor of alcohol that arrived from the neighboring state of Sinaloa, and yet he managed not to pay any taxes.[16] The opportunism of these individuals constantly frustrated dedicated reformers.

More important for this study, regular people at times also resisted the anti-alcohol campaign. When Sonora passed its Dry Law in 1915, honest authorities had their hands full. In the town of Cananea alone, over 60 percent of incidents that police handled in 1918 were related to drunkenness. More numerous still were the producers and sellers of intoxicants who continued to operate. Large businesses, like the Cervecería de Sonora (Sonora Brewery), shut down rather quickly, but smaller operations found it easier to continue production. Mezcal could be made easily on isolated rural properties, far away from the eyes of authorities. Indeed, in 1917, Interim Governor Cesáreo G. Soriano reported that more than sixty stills were located near the border with the state of Chihuahua. This liquor, in turn, could be sold clandestinely at bordellos, restaurants, or homes. These infractions took place despite the fact that the repercussions were harsh: they included fines, jail time, military service, or, as some critics suggested, execution.[17]

Alcohol producers and vendors throughout the country resisted less restrictive measures as well. Luna y Menocal and Montaño were not the only ones to complain about weekend closures; cantina and pulquería owners petitioned officials to let their businesses be closed on any other day. Many of them explained that they could not earn enough during the rest of the week to pay their rent.[18] Numerous owners of small alcohol dispensaries as well as workers in beer factories and on pulque haciendas often wrote to presidents and governors, asking that tax rates be reduced.[19] Finally, many teachers noted the difficulties of trying to shut down cantinas in their region. In doing so they stepped on the toes of the locals, who refused to show up to anti-alcohol festivals or did so drunk, demanded that the teacher be replaced, or would not send their children to school. Miguel Angel Martínez of Gochico, Sonora, even mentioned that because of his promotion of sobriety, he feared for his life and had to work with a gun in his hand.[20]

If the anti-alcohol campaign was meant to help the masses, why did many of them seem to reject it? Why would alcohol producers and sellers risk incarceration and maybe even execution to make and sell prohibited wares? Why did they threaten the life of a teacher who tried to teach their children a temperate lifestyle? Some contemporary officials, teachers, and other reformers believed that these people were uneducated and just providing them more lessons in the dangers of alcohol consumption would change their minds. Others claimed that peasants, workers, and natives were set in their ways and simply refused to abandon alcohol. In 1919, the mayor of Tacupeto, Sonora, went further, positing that his townspeople were lazy and preferred to spend their lives dedicated to making intoxicating beverages. For all of these reasons, Juan F. Márquez, a school director in Nogales, Sonora, argued that the anti-alcohol campaign would not be useful "while the life of this pueblo is the cantina."[21] According to all of these assertions, if the temperance crusade failed, the fault would lie largely with the masses and their rejection of the benefits of the Revolution and modernity.

Only a few studies examine the reasons for the ultimate failure of the anti-alcohol campaign in depth. In an earlier work, I argued that the weakness of the government at various levels prevented leaders from utilizing more resources to fight vice.[22] Several authors showed that the movement was hampered by officials who considered the alcohol business to be too lucrative to liquidate, as David Carey also found in chapter 6 in this volume.[23] Others demonstrated that even when regular people enthusiastically joined temperance leagues, legally they were limited in their abilities to fight alcoholism and were often frustrated by the corruption they experienced.[24] When it comes, though, to the question of why more ordinary Mexicans did not work with these reformers and, in fact, resisted them, one historian seemed to echo his sources when he claimed that people were just "recalcitrant" and rejected the revolutionaries' cultural reforms.[25] More generous observers simply stated that most Mexicans were not as concerned about vice as officials were.[26] Other scholars reminded us that alcohol served a cultural and religious role for some native peoples and that peasants often found alcoholic beverages to be the ideal substitute for less-than-secure sources of food, water, and medicine.[27]

Another factor needs to be considered: for the thousands of men and women employed in some way by the alcohol industry, the temperance movement was damaging to their economic interests—it only made sense for them to resist it. Dozens of people who violated alcohol laws asked to have their fines reduced because they could not afford them; some even claimed to be "notoriously poor." Often, friends and family members wrote to authorities to verify these assertions.[28] As long as the person was not a repeat offender, the government was usually sympathetic to such claims and lowered the fine. It is hard to know, then, if poverty merely became an excuse to have a punishment forgiven. However, given that several outside observers asserted that many of those who broke the law did so out of economic necessity, it is likely that many of the lawbreakers told the truth.[29]

Those small-time producers and sellers who opposed closures, taxes, and even the imposition of reformist teachers, often did so, like Posas, Luna y Menocal, and Montaño, for economic reasons as well. These measures made it difficult for their businesses to function; they feared losing their jobs and being unable to support their families. Such a prospect caused José León of the Unión de Contratistas y Expendedores Pulque (Union of Middle Men and Sellers of Pulque) to feel "desperate and demoralized."[30] In 1925, Juan Saint Martín [sic], president of the Convención de Cerveceros de la República Mexicana (Convention of Beer Producers of the Mexican Republic), claimed that increased taxes were affecting beer producers negatively, especially smaller ones, forcing them to raise their prices and lose sales. The breweries had to reduce their workforce, and for those workers who remained, they "could not attend to their most important needs, to the education of their children," leaving both them and their children as "defects" that the nation would have to bear.[31] Truly, these men and women do not seem recalcitrant.

The poor must have been even more desperate than normal from 1910 to 1940, because the economy was incredibly weak. Revolutionary fighting destroyed fields, mines, and railroads. Every general issued his own set of bills, and people often ended up being paid in script that would later become useless. Large business owners, many of them foreign, fled the country and took their expertise with them. As the fighting slowed in 1920, the economy began to improve, but it was weakened once again after the stock market crash of 1929.[32] Women were particularly vulnerable in such a climate. Widows and the unmarried had to support themselves and their families, while others may have found it necessary to take on employment to supplement their husbands' wages. In a relatively patriarchal society that was only slowly offering opportunities for women to work in skilled positions or receive an education, finding a lucrative job could be difficult.[33]

One image in particular demonstrates the lengths that the impoverished went to make ends meet (see figure 7.1). Sometime between 1919 and 1933, the brothers Ponsiano and Cresensio Sanches [*sic*] commissioned an *ex-voto*, a piece of devotional art, typically painted by an academically untrained artist on a piece of wood or tin, thanking a religious figure for a miracle performed in the commissioner's life. According to the text on this ex-voto, the Sanches brothers were grateful for the US Prohibition of alcohol, for it had allowed them to sell contraband tequila and *aguardiente*. One can assume that these brothers were poor: the image depicts them wearing the white cotton trousers and sombrero typical of peasants, and they are barefoot. Furthermore, what they were doing—producing alcohol to be sold in the United States—was risky, for it was illegal in both countries. The fact that they had not been caught and were profiting seemed miraculous enough to them that they ought to thank a saint, in this case, El Niño de Atocha. Thus, the image clearly shows that

Figure 7.1. This ca. 1920s–1930s *ex-voto*, or popular devotional item, thanks a saint for the US Prohibition of alcohol. (Image from author's collection)

poor men and women were willing to engage in risky behavior, defying international law, if it meant they might survive or even prosper.

In some parts of the country, especially the deserts of Sonora, Zacatecas, or Hidalgo, producing and selling alcohol were two of the only sure ways of making a living. School inspector Juan G. Oropeza's 1936 report was typical. He said that in his zone of Arizpe, Sonora, all of the residents, except one or two, survived by making and distributing mezcal. This happened in part because the maguey, the genus of plants from which pulque, mezcal, and tequila come, thrives in dry climates. Its hearty nature allows it to grow in places where little other agriculture can be sustained.[34] Indeed, in the ex-voto, the Sanches' land seems fairly barren, with only one maguey and two trees. In December 1929, Jesús Teutimer and Espíritu Babiche, who were in jail for distilling mezcal in Cerro Prieto, Sonora, claimed that, at least in their community, the "cattle-men have fired their cowboys, the farmers their peons, and the mines their miners."[35] They felt they had no other option but to do what they did. As the beer industry was one of the first in the manufacturing sector to recover from its slump in the 1920s, and the other alcohol businesses had remained intact, although weakened, throughout the period, it should come as no surprise that both the urban and rural working class would look to the production and sale of intoxicating beverages to provide a steady income.[36]

Poor women likely found selling alcohol to be an ideal occupation as well. Not only was it difficult for them to secure jobs in agriculture, industry, or the professions but also they might have to worry about how they could both work and take care of young, aging, or ill relatives. Herminia Duarte of Nogales, Sonora, who sold individual cups of alcohol, had a sick son that needed to be seen by a doctor, while in Guaymas, Sonora, Bethsabe Contreras, who clandestinely trafficked bottles of liquor, watched over a deaf-mute aunt. Peddling pulque, mezcal, or other beverages, which could be done from one's home at any time, must have seemed like the perfect answer. It allowed these women to earn fairly decent money, and they could balance their labor with their other responsibilities.[37]

Those people who protested measures of the anti-alcohol campaign were careful to mention that they were not stubborn, immoral, or supporters of vice but only opposed to measures that impacted their ability to survive.[38] The vast majority of those who asked to have fines reduced, have taxes lowered, or not have their business closed explained that they had a family (thus implying that they were honorable) and that they were struggling to feed them. In doing so, supplicants often made reference to traditional gender roles, although not always explicitly. For instance, Carmen

Rivera, who was discovered making mezcal secretly in the Sonora country-side in July 1919, said he had to do this because he had a large family to support. Community members wrote to the governor on behalf of Miguel Altamirano, who was caught along with Rivera. They pleaded that he be released from prison or have his fine lowered because he was a "good family man" with a wife and four young children.[39] Rivera, Altamirano, and their friends would have agreed that it was men's responsibility to provide for their wives and children. In their minds, when the law prevented them from acting as good husbands and fathers, and thus men, it was justified to break it.

Women who broke the law by selling alcohol relied on gendered stereo-types to justify their actions as well. They highlighted the need to care for their families, but unlike the men, they also emphasized their vulnerability. Of nine women who claimed to violate restrictive alcohol laws for reasons of economic necessity, four were widows. This included Belén Camarero Vda. de Maza[40] of Coxcatlán, San Luis Potosí, who argued that the aguardiente she produced and peddled supported twenty-five families. Five women, like the aforementioned Contreras, cared for ill or disabled family members, rendering their lives even more difficult. These suppli-cants certainly hoped to elicit sympathy from the paternalistic state by re-lying on the common notion that women were naturally weak and needed protection, and that their situations made them even needier. Without husbands, they were forced to make ends meet on their own.[41] At the same time, they were careful to point out their honor. Camila Retes Vda. de García said that she had not paid enough in taxes on her alcohol dispen-sary not because she was a contrabandist but, rather, because she had no sons to earn her an income, and her only daughter had died and left her with three small grandchildren. She explained that she was a respectable, educated person from a high social position who had merely fallen on tough times. This distinction was an important one, for people often looked at working women as not only physically weak but also morally questionable, as Áurea Toxqui explains in chapter 5.[42]

Other suppliants were careful to note that they supported the anti-alcohol campaign in general, and they actually believed their business could help to achieve a temperate nation. Pulque and beer workers were quick to point out that the beverages they produced and sold had low alco-hol contents and were much safer to drink than mezcal, tequila, or other drinks. Saint Martín suggested that President Plutarco Elías Calles work with him and other cerveceros to promote the beer industry and temper-ance and thus create a "true Era of Progress and Civilization."[43] Some people noted that if legitimate businesses like their own were closed, clandestine ones would pop up in their place and sell harder, and perhaps even adulterated, beverages.[44] By appropriating the government's moralizing rhetoric, relying on traditional notions about gender, and emphasizing their own poverty and decency, these supplicants had a better chance that their voices would be heard and respected. Had they appeared to be immoral or reactionary, it might have been easier to ignore their petitions.

One begins to wonder how revolutionary the anti-alcohol campaign actually was, in spite of all of the rhetoric. It is prejudiced and myopic to single out the working class and indigenous as the only people in society who abuse alcoholic beverages, as David Carey also notes in chapter 6. Evidence also suggests that leaders pursued poor violators of the law more tenaciously than they did rich and powerful ones. As explained above, some of the worst violators of alcohol legislation were officials who sold or consumed alcohol illegally. Calles, the governor of Sonora who presided over the state's prohibition from 1915 to 1919, was himself a well-known dipsomaniac and may even have had a bottle of cognac at his side as he signed the measure into effect.[45] Other leaders accepted bribes from well-placed individuals in the beverage industry. For instance, members of the Compañía Expendedora de Pulques (Pulque-Selling Company), a monopolistic operation run by wealthy landowners with social and political ties to the Díaz regime that existed from 1909 to 1916, opposed small establishments they did not control selling pulque in and around Mexico City. They tried to force them out of business by paying inspectors to fine the owners arbitrarily.[46] Data suggest that the wealthy and powerful also found it easier to consume alcohol in their homes even when the law forbade it. During Sonora's prohibition, people could petition to purchase or consume alcohol for reasons like Catholic mass or medicinal use. Strangely, wealthy petitioners also argued, successfully, that they should have access to the beverages that they were accustomed to drinking domestically.[47] Not only did the elite find it easier to evade the law, but powerful offenders seemed to avoid harsh punishments. Several observers claimed that Calles had a few public drunkards executed, all of whom were poor. The less powerful also might be sentenced to military conscription, a fate that did not seem to befall their more influential peers.[48] This evidence, although cursory at this point, seems to reinforce the suggestion that the anti-alcohol campaigns were not as revolutionary as their promoters claimed them to be.

Furthermore, some temperance reformers, like the revolutionaries in general, acted in a paternalistic and patriarchal manner. In the same speech where the legislator Siurob argued that alcohol taxes would help society's less fortunate members, he also characterized them as unintelligent and in need of guidance. According to him, it was up to the Revolution to convert "this flock of pariahs" into "honorable citizens."[49] Like Siurob, many reformers claimed to want to help the masses, whether by sobering them up, teaching them the rudiments of hygiene, or secularizing them, but they often attempted to do so without much input from the very people they wanted to change. For instance, the CNLCA officially encouraged women, peasants, and workers to form temperance leagues to assist them in the struggle against alcoholism, but very few of these types of people were on the CNLCA's governing board.[50] Although leaders in some ways empowered women to improve their lives by trying to domesticate their husbands and rid their neighborhoods of vice, many of these officials still held on to traditional notions of gender. They continued to view these women primarily as wives and mothers who ought to look to male reformers and leaders for guidance.[51]

Additionally, as we have seen, the anti-alcohol campaign may actually have hurt more workers than it helped by attacking some of the most secure jobs they could find. To be fair, a handful of reformers did recognize this. Dr. José María Rodríguez, a constitutional delegate in 1917 and a former head of the Department of Public Health, fully supported the idea of suppressing alcoholism, but he realized the problems that a national prohibition would cause for hundreds of thousands of regular people. He said:

> What are we going to do with these unfortunate Indians . . . that do not live on more than this [pulque production], that in this moment cannot dedicate themselves to agriculture, because the indispensable elements for this labor have been destroyed . . . by the necessities of war? What, will it be possible to feed them with air, with the decrees that we give in this Constitution? . . . What, does it not occur to you . . . that a measure so violent and radical [a proposed prohibition] in these moments, instead of being a benefit, would be a major detriment to an immense quantity of the population?[52]

Rodríguez's reasoned opinion, although not unique, was not in the majority, either. One senior member of the CNLCA, Enrique Monterrubio, said in 1930 that the committee should ignore this economic issue, as the workers "chose" to be employed in a "clandestine [*sic*] business."[53] When one is poor and has a family to support, though, there is often little choice in the type of job one takes.

The anti-alcohol campaign would have been more effective and revolutionary had it tried harder to solve some of the socioeconomic causes of alcoholism. Temperance reformers were not unaware of these problems; they spent countless meetings and conferences discussing them.[54] One factor that experts pointed to was the lack of potable water in many communities; it was simply safer to drink an alcoholic beverage. The teacher Manuel Vélez Andrade explained that this problem was common in the Hidalgo desert, the Valle del Mezquital. He claimed that a public health official there had said to a thirsty newcomer looking for water, "You have to boil it; boil it again; throw it away and drink beer." Andrade went on to argue that if teachers like himself and other reformers were going to reduce alcohol consumption because of the physical damage it could do to a person, "at least we need to change our moral attitude to those who drink, we ought to and are obliged to give them something as a substitute, that is to say; potable water, complete nutrients, bodily protection and comfort, happiness and optimistic faith for the spirit."[55] Obviously, these were goals that teachers and the bureaucrats at the CNLCA could not achieve on their own, but had the various branches of the government worked more in concert, both expanding the supply of potable water and reducing alcoholism might have been achieved. Nor would the alcohol industry have been as lucrative. This would have meant that closing pulquerías or taxing breweries might not have been so onerous for the working class.

Another measure that leaders should have pursued more earnestly was investing in utilizing the maguey for other products. Dozens of experts (and even primary school students!) wrote to presidents suggesting ways that this might be done. The chemist Elie Delafond spent several years of the 1920s in such correspondence with President Obregón. In 1922, he claimed to be overseeing experiments in the states of Tlaxcala and Yucatán that would convert the maguey into industrial alcohol, twine, paper, sugar, and a fuel. Delafond even said he had a patent along with the chemist Donaciano Morales for a healthy, noninfectious drink that would replace pulque.[56] Wealthy owners of pulque haciendas worked on similar projects beginning in the late nineteenth century, briefly producing honey, syrup, vinegar, and medicinal tonics.[57] In spite of the enthusiasm, though, it seems very little was ever done to follow through with these leads at the governmental level. Given that the maguey plant thrived in otherwise sterile land, the suggested substitutions could have kept people employed, expanded the country's industry, and combated alcoholism all at the same time.

Resistance and the State-Building Process

In the last fifteen years, historians have demonstrated that although some of the Revolution's social programs were indeed paternalistic and misguided, ordinary citizens were not naïve dupes. Rather, they actively fought back against policies they did not like, such as socialist and sexual education, as well as anticlericalism. By keeping their children from school, demanding that the subject matter be changed, or actively picking up arms so that they could practice their religion freely, they forced revolutionaries to scale back on their educational and secularizing goals.[58] In doing these things, as scholars have argued, regular people have actively played a role in the state-building process.[59] After all, these protests, in their various forms, helped to shape the revolutionary government and its actions.

Examining the complaints of alcohol producers and vendors also shows that the lower classes were actively involved in the state-building process. The poor were not helpless victims of a government that did not always act in their best interests. Rather, as we have seen, these people demanded that the government help them by reducing or forgiving a fine for breaking alcohol-related legislation, not closing their bars, or lowering their taxes. Many supplicants went so far as to challenge the revolutionary nature of their leaders. For instance, sixteen owners of small cantinas in Hermosillo, Sonora, in 1920 signed a petition protesting against high taxes. They explained that the exorbitant rate favored large businesses, while small ones like theirs struggled. They called this situation "anti-commercial, anti-social, and anti-constitutional."[60] Manuel Portugal of Mexico City ventured further than this in his complaint in 1911. He had applied for a license to open a *fonda* (a small eatery that often sold pulque), only to have it denied by the governor of the Federal District. Portugal suspected that the governor was working with the Compañía Expendedora de Pulques. Not only did this company use bribes to try to harass their competitors, but they also distributed free pulque to fondas' potential customers.[61] Although the first elected revolutionary president, Francisco Madero, had been in office for less than a month, Portugal did not hesitate in criticizing his

cia Posas were typical ones. These small producers and sellers of pulque

administration for not eviscerating the monopoly yet. In a letter to a newspaper, he wrote, "The current government is not adjusting to the circumstances of the time: small businessmen and the poor have not found any
advantages in the triumph of the Revolution, because Porfirian methods
reign."[62] In demanding that their leaders look out for the interests of the
working class, and in questioning their motives for not doing so, small alcohol producers and vendors demonstrated their involvement in the state-
building process.

Conclusions

The stories of M. Luna y Menocal and José María Montaño and of Engracia Posas were typical ones. These small producers and sellers of pulque
found their livelihoods at risk because of measures that aimed to reduce
alcohol consumption. These were not immoral people who hoped to
profit off of others' vices. Rather, they wanted to be sure they earned
enough money to care for their children and give them decent educations.
The Clausura Dominical in Mexico City and the prohibition of alcohol in
Morelos were preventing them from doing that, and so they wrote to their
leaders, asking for help, often using gendered language. Nor were they
alone. Perhaps hundreds of thousands of other working-class men and
women suffered because of measures carried out during the anti-alcohol
campaigns of 1910 to 1940 that resulted in their businesses closing or in
them paying high taxes or fines. Although this revolutionary project was
enacted in large part to help Mexico's poor workers, native peoples, and
women, this often was not the result because they depended on the well-
being of the alcohol industry to survive. However, by writing to the authorities and requesting assistance, or even criticizing them for not acting
as progressively as they should, these small entrepreneurs and workers
were actively participating in the state-building process. Although they
were not always successful in having their demands met, they should not
be seen as helpless victims of an insensitive government, either.

Notes

1. M. Luna y Menocal and José María Montaño to Álvaro Obregón, May 24, 1922,
Archivo General de la Nación, Fondo Administración Pública, Obregón-Calles (hereafter AGN-FAP-OC), expediente (hereafter exp.) 802-D-9.

paper, he wrote, "The current government is not adjusting to the circum-

2. Engracia Posas to Lázaro Cárdenas, March 5, 1938, Archivo General de la Nación, Dirección General de Gobierno (hereafter AGN-DGG), series (hereafter ser.) 2/015.4(14)31539, caja 7, exp. 16.

3. Mario Ramírez Rancaño, *Ignacio Torres Adalid y la industria pulquera* (Mexico City: Plaza y Valdés and Instituto de Investigaciones Sociales, Universidad Nacional Autónoma de México, 2000), 31, 43, 58–59, 61, 137–41.

4. "El monopolio del pulque en auge. Los explotadores empiezan a tomar vuelo," *Diario del Hogar* (hereafter *DH*), November 26, 1911, 1; "Continua la discusión del proyecto de ley de ingresos," July 16, 1917, in *Memoria de la Secretaría Hacienda y Crédito Público*, vol. 3, *16 de abril de 1917 a 21 de mayo de 1920* (Mexico City: Talleres Gráficos de la Nación, 1959), 397–98, 416; *Congreso Constituyente 1916–1917: Diario de Debates*, tomo 2 (Mexico City: Instituto Nacional de Estudios Históricos de la Revolución Mexicana, 1985), 939; "Razones en que se fundan los productores e introductores de pulque en el DF para solicitar la revocación del decreto que ordenó cerrar la mitad de los sábados y todo el domingo las pulquerías en la ciudad" [ca. September 15, 1920], AGN-DGG, ser. A.200.162, caja 5, exp. 22; "Ligeros apuntes sobre el pulque," March 1925, AGN-FAP-OC, exp. 104-P-2; José María Montaño to the Chief of the Secretaría de Industria, Comercio y Trabajo (hereafter SICT), December 28, 1925, AGN-DGG, ser. 2/015.3.(5–1)1, caja 2, exp. 12; Mariano Muñoz et al. to Cárdenas, January 7, 1935, Archivo General de la Nación, Fondo Administración Pública, Lázaro Cárdenas (hereafter AGN-FAP-LC), exp. 564.1/50; José Paz, *En defensa del pulque: 668,677 viven de la industria pulquera: el medio de vida de estos proletarios debe respetarse* (Mexico City: n.p., 1935), 73–76.

5. "Hablan los números," *El Nacional* (hereafter *EN*), October 13, 1938; Nora Hamilton, *The Limits of State Autonomy: Post-Revolutionary Mexico* (Princeton, NJ: Princeton University Press, 1982), 310–11; Gabriela Recio, "El nacimiento de la industria cervecera en México, 1880–1910," in *Cruda realidad. Producción, consumo y fiscalidad de las bebidas alcohólicas en México y América Latina, siglos XVII–XX*, ed. Ernest Sánchez Santiró (Mexico City: Instituto Mora, 2007), 164, 172–73, 175, 178–80.

6. I am using the term *mezcal* here loosely. Sources refer to the distilled product of the maguey as mezcal as long as it was not produced in Jalisco, particularly in the Tequila region, where tequila is the denomination of origin. Today, various terms, such as *mezcal*, *bacanora*, and *sotol*, are used to distinguish among the various types of liquors and where they originated. Jorge Quiroz Márquez, *Mezcal: Origin, Elaboration, and Recipes* (Oaxaca: Códice Ediciones, 1997), 12–13, 16–18.

7. Gretchen Kristine Pierce, "Sobering the Revolution: Mexico's Anti-Alcohol Campaigns and the Process of State-Building, 1910–1940" (PhD diss., University of Arizona, 2008), 145–46, 151–54, 162–67.

8. Ibid., 134–44, 147–51.

9. "Reglamento de la ley sobre el impuesto del timbre a las bebidas fermentadas llamadas pulque y tlachique," August 24, 1916, in *Memoria de la Secretaría Hacienda y Crédito Público*, vol. 1, *23 de febrero de 1913 a 15 de abril de 1917* (Mexico City: Talleres Gráficos de la Nación, 1952), 746–47; "Continua la discusión del proyecto de ley de ingresos," 396–98; circular, April 22, 1929, Archivo General de la Nación, Fondo Administración Pública, Emilio Portes Gil (hereafter AGN-FAP-EPG), exp. 3/669, legajo (hereafter leg.) 2; "Festival en contra del alcoholismo," *EN*, March 1,

1936; "Decálogo antialcohólico," *El Maestro Rural* (hereafter *EMR*) 11, no. 9 (September 1938), 34.

10. *Laissez-faire* is French for "let do" or "let it be." Associated with the eighteenth- and nineteenth-century ideology of liberalism, a laissez-faire state was one that relied on free market principles and tried not to apply the power of the national government to make socioeconomic change. The first few revolutionary presidents resisted using the executive branch to solve the problems associated with alcoholism.

11. The CNLCA changed names several times from 1929 to 1940, but for simplicity's sake, in this chapter I refer to it as CNLCA.

12. Pierce, "Sobering the Revolution," chaps. 1–3.

13. Carlos Martínez Assad, *El laboratorio de la revolución: el Tabasco garridista* (Mexico City: Siglo Veintiuno Editores, 1979), 141–51; Ben Fallaw, "Dry Law, Wet Politics: Drinking and Prohibition in Post-Revolutionary Yucatán, 1915–1935," *Latin American Research Review* 37, no. 2 (2001), 40–42; Christopher R. Boyer, *Becoming Campesinos: Politics, Identity, and Agrarian Struggle in Postrevolutionary Michoacán, 1920–1935* (Stanford, CA: Stanford University Press, 2003), 133, 188; Pierce, "Sobering the Revolution," 192–223.

14. Loreto Valenzuela to various, Archivo Histórico del Estado de Sonora, Ramo Ejecutivo (hereafter AHES-RE)-1918, tomo 3202: September 18, 1918; September 29, 1918; November 21, 1918. Mary Kay Vaughan, *Cultural Politics in Revolution: Teachers, Peasants, and Schools in Mexico, 1930–1940* (Tucson: University of Arizona Press, 1997), 41–42, 45, 58–60; Guillermo Palacios, *La pluma y el arado: Los intelectuales pedagogos y la construcción sociocultural del "problema campesino" en México, 1932–1934* (Mexico City: Colegio de México, 1999), 106–7, 180, 186–87, 192–93; Fallaw, "Dry Law, Wet Politics," 43–47, 61; Boyer, *Becoming Campesinos*, 206–7, 220–21; Patience A. Schell, *Church and State Education in Revolutionary Mexico City* (Tucson: University of Arizona Press, 2003), 34, 57, 87–88; Jocelyn Olcott, *Revolutionary Women in Postrevolutionary Mexico* (Durham, NC: Duke University Press, 2005), 64, 72–76, 80–89, 138–47; Stephanie Mitchell, "Por la liberación de la mujer: Women and the Anti-Alcohol Campaign," in *The Women's Revolution in Mexico, 1910–1953*, ed. Stephanie Mitchell and Patience A. Schell (Wilmington, DE: Rowman and Littlefield, 2007), 173–85; Pierce, "Sobering the Revolution," chaps. 1, 2, 4, 5. For information on temperance activities in Colombia, Uruguay, and Guatemala, also at multiple levels of society, see Óscar Iván Calvo Isaza and Marta Saade Granados, *La ciudad en cuarentena: Chicha, patología social y profilaxis* (Bogotá: Ministerio de Cultura, 2002); Daniela Bouret, "El consumo de vinos en el Uruguay del novecientos. El desarrollo de la industria vitivinícola vrs. campañas antialocoholistas," *Boletín Americanista* 59 (2009), 155-76; René Reeves, "From Household to Nation: The Economic and Political Impact of Women and Alcohol in Nineteenth-Century Guatemala," in *Distilling the Influence of Alcohol: Aguardiente in Guatemala*, ed. David Carey Jr. (Gainesville: University Press of Florida, 2012), 48–49.

15. Ben Fallaw, *Cárdenas Compromised: The Failure of Reform in Postrevolutionary Yucatán* (Durham, NC: Duke University Press, 2001), 93, 103–4; Fallaw, "Dry Law, Wet Politics," 48–49; Boyer, *Becoming Campesinos*, 54–55; Félix Brito Rodríguez, "La cultura política en el Sinaloa posrevolucionario: elecciones, alcohol, y violencia," paper presented at the thirtieth Simposio de Historia y Antropología de Sonora (Hermosillo, Mexico, February 25, 2005), 6–8, 15, 19; Stephen E. Lewis, *The Ambivalent*

Revolution: Forging State and Nation in Chiapas, 1910–1945 (Albuquerque: University of New Mexico Press, 2005), 102, 104–5, 115; Olcott, *Revolutionary Women*, 145, 154; Pierce, "Sobering the Revolution," chap. 4; Andrae M. Marak, "Portes Gil's Anti-Alcohol Campaign in Ciudad Juárez, 1929–1934," paper presented at the American Historical Association (New York, 2009), 6, 13.

16. List of confidential facts, July 1937, Archivo Histórico de la Secretaría de Educación Pública, Dirección General de Educación Primaria en los Estados y Territorios, Dirección de Educación Federal, Sonora (hereafter AHSEP-DEFS), caja 8401, exp. S/N-2; Fallaw, "Dry Law, Wet Politics," 49.

17. The evidence seems to indicate that Governor Plutarco Elías Calles at the very least approved executions on three different occasions, but it is unclear if this was standard procedure. Decree no. 1, August 8, 1915, AHES-RE-1916, tomo 3062. In AHES-RE-1917, tomo 3124, see: Adolfo De la Huerta to the mayor of Nogales, July 16, 1917; Cesáreo G. Soriano to Calles, August 18, 1917; A. R. Cárdenas to Soriano, August 25, 1917; Soriano to unknown, November 17, 1917. Calles to Arnulfo R. Gómez, December 6, 1917, Fideicomiso Archivos Plutarco Elías Calles y Fernando Torreblanca, Archivo Plutarco Elías Calles, Fondo Elías Calles (hereafter FAPECyFT-APEC-FEC), fondo 03, ser. 0202, exp. 78, inv. 933; report, [Rinabemba?] M., August 26, 1918, AHES-RE-1918, tomo 3220; Antonio Cruz to unknown, February 7, 1919, AHES-RE-1919, tomo 3294; Brígido Caro, *Plutarco Elías Calles: dictador bolsheviqui de México. Episodios de la Revolución Mexicana, desde 1910 hasta 1924* (Los Angeles, CA: Talleres Linotipográficos de "El Heraldo de México," 1924), 63–64, 77–78; Enrique Ramos Bours, "El incendio de la cervecería en 1926," *El Pitic* 2, no. 24 (March 2003), 1; Pierce, "Sobering the Revolution," 220–22.

18. Manuela Jesús Montiel et al. to De la Huerta, May 20, 1922, AHES-RE-1922, tomo 3480. In AGN-FAP-OC, exp. 802-D-9, see: Luna y Menocal and Montaño to Obregón, May 24, 1922; Miguel Macedo Enciso to Obregón, November 10, 1923; José León to Obregón, November 13, 1923; J. Ramírez Cabañas to Obregón, April 9, 1924. Manuel Ortega, Francisco Cobarrubio, and Miguel Baldenegro to unknown, July 12, 1926, AHES-RE-1926, tomo 42; cantina owners to Francisco S. Elías, November 15, 1929, AHES-RE-1929, tomo 41.

19. Small business people to unknown, July 16, 1920, AHES-RE-1920, tomo 3391, 2a parte; Juan Saint Martín to Calles, July 7, 1925, AGN-FAP-OC, exp. 205-C-169. In AGN-FAP-EPG, exp. 4/321, see: Eduardo Tamariz and Gerónimo Merchán y González to Portes Gil, May 13, 1929; José Pacheco to Portes Gil, May 16, 1929; Ignacio Palencia et al. to Abelardo Rodríguez, November 5, 1932, Archivo General de la Nación, Fondo Administración Pública, Abelardo Rodríguez (hereafter AGN-FAP-AR), exp. 533.4/62; Muñoz et al. to Cárdenas, January 7, 1935.

20. Archivo Histórico de la Secretaría de Educación Pública, Departamento de Escuelas Rurales, Sonora (hereafter AHSEP-DERS), caja 5719, referencia (hereafter ref.) 19243, exp. 47: Miguel Angel Martínez to Elpidio López, April 25, 1933; J. Lamberto Moreno to López, April 30, 1933; report, Juan G. Oropeza, March 1936, AHSEP-DEFS, caja 5763, ref. 319, exp. 3; Adrian A. Bantjes, *As If Jesus Walked on Earth: Cardenismo, Sonora, and the Mexican Revolution* (Wilmington, DE: SR Books, 1998), 33.

21. Report, Jesús María Valencia, August 31, 1918, AHES-RE-1918, tomo 3220; Ygnacio Valenzuela to General Manuel Piña, May 8, 1919, AHES-RE-1919, tomo

3297; notes, Alberto M. Sánchez, November 22, 1920, AHES-RE-1920, tomo 3391, 2a parte; report, Roberto Thomson, August 4, 1927, AHSEP-DERS, caja 829 (5), ref. 19324, exp. 68; report, Juan F. Márquez, January 2, 1930, AHSEP-DEFS, caja 5507 (25), exp. 20; report, López, April 2, 1932, AHSEP-DEFS, caja 8401, exp. 20; Celerino Cano, "Hacia la nueva escuela rural," *EMR* 11, no. 10 (October 1938), 5.

22. Pierce, "Sobering the Revolution," chaps. 1, 2, and 4.

23. See note 15 for more information about how corruption challenged the success of the anti-alcohol campaigns.

24. Olcott, *Revolutionary Women*, 86, 145; Mitchell, "Por la liberación de la mujer," 167–70; Pierce, "Sobering the Revolution," 181, 285–87.

25. Alan Knight, "Revolutionary Project, Recalcitrant People: Mexico, 1910–1940," in *The Revolutionary Process in Mexico: Essays on Political and Social Change, 1880–1940*, ed. Jaime E. Rodríguez O. (Los Angeles: University of California Press, 1990), 230, 252, 255, 258.

26. Douglas W. Richmond, *Venustiano Carranza's Nationalist Struggle, 1893–1920* (Lincoln: University of Nebraska Press, 1983), 168; Alan Knight, "Popular Culture and the Revolutionary State in Mexico, 1910–1940," *Hispanic American Historical Review* 74, no. 3 (1994), 401, 426, 440–41.

27. Tim Mitchell, *Intoxicated Identities: Alcohol's Power in Mexican History and Culture* (New York: Routledge, 2004), 4, 13; Lewis, *Ambivalent Revolution*, 106.

28. Statement, José Salazar, June 26, 1916, AHES-RE-1916, tomo 3061; Mariano Urrea to Soriano, October 10, 1917, AHES-RE-1917, tomo 3124. For similar claims in Guatemala, see Stacey Schwartzkopf, "Consumption, Custom, and Control: Aguardiente in Nineteenth-Century Guatemala," in Carey, *Distilling the Influence of Alcohol*, 32.

29. Unknown to Soriano, October 1, 1917, AHES-RE-1917, tomo 3124; unknown to unknown, March 5, 1919, AHES-RE-1919, tomo 3293; unknown to unknown, June 4, 1919, AHES-RE-1919, tomo 3296; report, Alberto E. Peraza, July 20, 1920, AHES-RE-1920, tomo 3365, 2a parte; Caro, *Plutarco Elías Calles*, 77–78; "Se han hecho algunos decomisos de mezcal por inspectores federales," *El Observador* (hereafter *EO*), March 31, 1928, 1; Francisco Romero to Elías, November 19, 1929, AHES-RE-1929, tomo 50; Emilio Hoyos to Elías, December 18, 1929, AHES-RE-1929, tomo 47-2; report, Lewis V. Boyle, October 2, 1933, Records of the Department of State Relating to the Internal Affairs of Mexico, 1930–1939, 812.114 Liquors/92, Regenstein Library, University of Chicago; Posas to Cárdenas, March 5, 1938.

30. León to Obregón, November 13, 1923; Ortega et al. to unknown, July 12, 1926; Tamariz and Merchán y González to Portes Gil, May 13, 1929; Palencia et al. to Rodríguez, November 5, 1932; Paz, *En defensa del pulque*, 179.

31. Saint Martín to Calles, July 7, 1925.

32. Caro, *Plutarco Elías Calles*, 77–78; Paz, *En defensa del pulque*, 53–55; José C. Ramírez, Ricardo León, and Oscar Conde, "Una época de crisis económica," in *Historia general de Sonora*, vol. 5, *1929–1984*, ed. Gerardo Cornejo Murrieta (Hermosillo, Mexico: Gobierno del Estado de Sonora, 1985), 53–66; Ramírez, León, and Conde, "La estrategia económica de los Callistas," in *Historia general de Sonora*, 69–77; Thomas Benjamin, "Rebuilding the Nation," in *The Oxford History of Mexico*, ed. Michael C. Meyer and William H. Beezley (Oxford: Oxford University Press, 2000), 470.

33. Caro, *Plutarco Elías Calles*, 77–78; report, Alberto E. Peraza, July 20, 1920; Boyer, *Becoming Campesinos*, 209; Mitchell, *Intoxicated Identities*, 101; Susie S. Porter, *Working Women in Mexico City: Public Discourses and Material Conditions, 1879–1931* (Tucson: University of Arizona Press, 2003), 6–8, 20–46.

34. Canuto Ortega to Calles, September 25, 1918, AHES-RE-1918, tomo 3205; report, Peraza, July 20, 1920; memorandum, "Ligeros apuntes sobre el pulque," March 1925; Belén Camarero Vda. de Maza to Calles, April 29, 1925, AGN-FAP-OC, exp. 104-E-23; Jesús Castro Torres to Elías, June 8, 1929, AHES-RE-1929, tomo 41; Moreno to López, April 30, 1933, caja 5719, ref. 19243, exp. 47; Mariano Muñoz to Cárdenas, January 7, 1935; Paz, *En defensa del pulque*, 47; report, Oropeza, March 1936; Quiroz Márquez, *Mezcal*, 16; Vaughan, *Cultural Politics in Revolution*, 86.

35. Jesús Teutimer and Espíritu Babiche to Elías, December 18, 1929, AHES-RE-1929, tomo 47-2.

36. Recio, "Nacimiento de la industria cervecera," 182.

37. Josefa Cosío to unknown, January 22, 1919, AHES-RE-1919, tomo 3297. In AHES-RE-1919, tomo 3296 see: report, June 5, 1919; F. E. Ochoa to Piña, June 9, 1919. Josefina Robles to unknown, November 19, 1919, AHES-RE-1919, tomo 3294; unknown to De la Huerta, February 14, 1920, AHES-RE-1920, tomo 3362, 2a parte; employees of Restaurant Sonora, June 15, 1920, AHES-RE-1920, tomo 3365, 2a parte; Camarero Vda. de Maza to Calles. In AHES-RE-1929, tomo 50, see: twelve women to unknown, November 23, 1929; Camila Retes Vda. de García to Elías, December 29, 1929; Posas to Cárdenas, March 5, 1938; Porter, *Working Women in Mexico City*, 146, 148, 154–55. For examples of women in other times and places who turned to the alcohol industry economic for support, see Jane E. Mangan, *Trading Roles: Gender, Ethnicity, and the Urban Economy in Colonial Potosí* (Durham, NC: Duke University Press, 2005), 57, 60, 86, 89; Pablo Lacoste, "Wine and Women: Grape Growers and *Pulperas* in Mendoza, 1561–1852," *Hispanic American Historical Review* 88, no. 3 (2008), 383, 387, 390; Schwartzkopf, "Consumption, Custom, and Control," 32; Reeves, "From Household to Nation"; David Carey Jr., "Distilling Perceptions of Crime: Mayan Moonshiners and the State, 1898–1944," in Carey, *Distilling the Influence of Alcohol*, 126, 136.

38. Poor alcohol vendors made similar assertions in nineteenth-century Guatemala. See Schwartzkopf, "Consumption, Custom, and Control," 32.

39. Statement, Salazar, June 26, 1916; Filiberto Lung to Calles, October 6, 1917, FAPECyFT-APEC-FEC, fondo 03, ser. 0202, exp. 27, inv. 882, leg. 1; José Galaz to Soriano, October 8, 1917, AHES-RE-1917, tomo 3125; Urrea to Soriano, October 10, 1917. In AHES-RE-1919, tomo 3293, see: Luis Basso to Calles, February 22, 1919; Jesús Elías to Calles, March 20, 1919; Petra Ancelmo de Rivera to Piña, June 4, 1919; community members to unknown, July 8, 1919; employees of Restaurant Sonora to unknown, June 15, 1920; Luna y Menocal and Montaño to Obregón; Saint Martín to Calles, July 7, 1925; Teutimer and Babiche to Elías, December 18, 1929. For an example of men in colonial Potosí appealing to authorities as poor heads of households to prevent their businesses being closed, see Mangan, *Trading Roles*, 64, 67, 73. David Carey Jr. finds that male violators of alcohol laws in late nineteenth- through early twentieth-century Guatemala emphasized poverty in their defense, but rather than focusing on family, they cited tradition and custom as reasons they ought to be allowed

to continue to sell their wares, and they also noted the vulnerability of their businesses. Carey, "Distilling Perceptions of Crime," 144.

40. Vda. de stands for "widow of." Therefore, this women's name is Belén Camarero widow of Maza.

41. Ochoa to Piña, June 9, 1919; unknown to unknown, June 14, 1919, AHES-RE-1919, tomo 3296; Robles to unknown, November 19, 1919; employees of Restaurant Sonora to unknown, June 15, 1920; Camarero Vda. de Maza to Calles, April 29, 1925; Romero to Elías, November 19, 1929; Posas to Cárdenas, March 5, 1938. For women in other times and places who appealed to authorities based on gendered economic necessity and vulnerability, see Calvo Isaza and Saade Granados, *La ciudad en cuarentena*, 175–76; Porter, *Working Women in Mexico City*, 154–56; Mangan, *Trading Roles*, 57; Carey, "Distilling Perceptions of Crime," 139, 142–43.

42. Retes Vda. de García to Elías, December 29, 1929. For accusations of other working women as immoral, and their assertions that they were not, see Katherine Elaine Bliss, *Compromised Positions: Prostitution, Public Health, and Gender Politics in Revolutionary Mexico City* (University Park: Pennsylvania State University Press, 2001), 1–2, 9, 159, 175, 196–202; Gina Hames, "Maize-Beer, Gossip, and Slander: Female Tavern Proprietors and Urban, Ethnic Cultural Elaboration in Bolivia, 1870–1930," *Journal of Social History* 37 (2003), 355–57; Porter, *Working Women in Mexico City*, 59–69, 123–25, 140, 143–45, 148–57; Mangan, *Trading Roles*, 89, 150.

43. Saint Martín to Calles, July 7, 1925. See also: small business people to unknown, July 16 1920; anonymous letter [ca. September 15, 1920], AGN-DGG, ser. A.200.162, caja 5, exp. 22; Montaño to the Chief of the SICT, December 28, 1925.

44. Anonymous letter [ca. September 15, 1920]; Montaño to the Chief of the SICT, December 28, 1925; "Se han hecho algunos decomisos de mezcal por inspectores federales," *EO*, March 31, 1928, 1; Tamariz and Merchán y González to Portes Gil, May 13, 1929.

45. Caro, *Plutarco Elías Calles*, 15–16, 20; Adolfo de la Huerta, *Memorias de Don Adolfo de la Huerta: Según su propio dictado*, trans. Roberto Guzmán Esparza (Hermosillo, Mexico: Gobierno del Estado de Sonora, 1957), 135–36; Germán Zúñiga Moreno, "Comentarios sobre la ley seca en Sonora de 1915," *Memorias del Simposio de Historia de Sonora* (Hermosillo, Sonora), 6 (1979), 265.

46. Ramírez Rancaño, *Ignacio Torres Adalid*, 216–17.

47. Petitions can be found in AHES-RE-1916, tomos 3061–62, 3071; AHES-RE-1917, tomo 3124; AHES-RE-1918, tomos 3201–2, 3204–5; AHES-RE-1919, tomos 3293–97. In particular, see petitions from the following types of people: AHES-RE-1916, tomo 3062: Fernando Chacón (Calles's relative), July 8, 1916; Otto Rademacher (German businessman), July 8, 1916; Major Manuel M. Aguirre (military officer), August 4, 1916; Rodolfo Garduño (engineer), August 28, 1916; W. Iberri (banker), July 21, 1917, AHES-RE-1917, tomo 3124; five town councilmen, March 23, 1918, AHES-RE-1918, tomo 3202; Luis Basso (alcohol inspector), January 15, 1919, AHES-RE-1919, tomo 3294. Note also that when a petition was granted to a group of poor men from Cananea, Sonora, it prompted the mayor to write to the governor and explain that because these men were so impoverished, he believed they were planning on clandestinely selling the white wine they were granted. In AHES-RE-1918, tomo 3202, see: petition, R. R. González, Ventura A. Valencia, Luis R. León, Rafael Campoy, and Rodolfo Lima, June 14, 1918; R. Rinaberky M. to governor, June 27, 1918.

48. "Un batallón de rateros, vagos, y borrachos. Las tres ventajas que pueden obtenerse con ese batallón," *Orientación* (Hermosillo), November 16, 1917; Calles to A. Gómez, December 6, 1917; J. R. Estrada to Soriano, April 23, 1918, AHES-RE-1918, tomo 3205; J. Torres to Calles, April 5, 1919, AHES-RE-1919, tomo 3296; Caro, *Plutarco Elías Calles*, 63–64, 78; Teodoro O. Paz, *Guaymas de Ayer* (n.l.: n.p., n.d.), 104–6, 216–17, 226, 231, Biblioteca del Colegio de Sonora.

49. "Continua la discusión del proyecto de ley de ingresos," 396–97.

50. Knight, "Popular Culture," 401, 412–13, 415; Palacios, *La pluma y el arado*, 71–72, 82, 188, 234; Katherine Elaine Bliss, "For the Health of the Nation: Gender and the Cultural Politics of Social Hygiene in Revolutionary Mexico," in *The Eagle and the Virgin: Nation and Cultural Revolution in Mexico, 1920–1940*, ed. Mary Kay Vaughan and Stephen E. Lewis (Durham, NC: Duke University Press, 2006), 198, 205; Pierce, "Sobering the Revolution," 186–87.

51. Pierce, "Sobering the Revolution," 180–81.

52. Ramírez Rancaño, *Ignacio Torres Adalid*, 311–12.

53. Report, Enrique Monterrubio, April 3, 1930, Archivo Histórico de Salubridad y Social Asistencia, Fondo Salubridad Pública I, Sección Servicio Jurídico (hereafter AHSSA-FSPI-SSJ), caja 18, exp. 1.

54. CNLCA minutes, June 24, 1935, AHSSA-FSPI-SSJ, caja 42, exp. 1; "Resumen del estudio sobre el alcoholismo en México," September 6, 1937, AGN-FAP-LC, exp. 553/11.

55. Manuel Velázquez Andrade, "La voz del maestro. Cuadros vivos," *EMR* 5, no. 9 (November 1, 1934), 11.

56. Elie Delafond to Obregón, January 7, 1922, AGN-FAP-OC, exp. 104-P-2; "Tlaxcala to Open Fiber and Alcohol Plant. Entire Component of Maguey to Be Utilized," *Mexico Times*, May 20, 1922, AGN-FAP-OC, exp. 808-A-35; Delafond to Obregón [1922 or 1923?], AGN-FAP-OC, exp. 808-A-35; "La industria alcoholera puede desaparecer en el país sin originar daños. El Sr. De Negri acoge con entusiasmo la idea del Sr. Presidente para combatir el vicio de la embriaguez en la república y trabajará en ese sentido," *El Universal*, April 1929, 1; Aurelio López, "El Magueyito," *EMR* 3, no. 2 (June 15, 1933), 39; CNLCA minutes, June 24, 1935; "De 'Juventudes Temperantes de México,' perfectamente documentados," *EN*, July 27, 1937.

57. Ramírez Rancaño, *Ignacio Torres Adalid*, 101–9, 209–13, 317–18.

58. Knight, "Popular Culture," 401–3, 422–23, 426, 440–41; Vaughan, *Cultural Politics in Revolution*, 33–36, 62–63, 88–96, 122, 152–56; Adrian A. Bantjes, "Saints, Sinners, and State Formation: Local Religion and Cultural Revolution in Mexico," in Vaughan and Lewis, *Eagle and the Virgin*, 145–53; Jean Meyer, "An Idea of Mexico: Catholics in the Revolution," in Vaughan and Lewis, *Eagle and the Virgin*, 283–91.

59. Gilbert M. Joseph and Daniel Nugent, "Popular Culture and State Formation in Revolutionary Mexico," in *Everyday Forms of State Formation: Revolution and the Negotiation of Rule in Modern Mexico*, ed. Gilbert M. Joseph and Daniel Nugent (Durham, NC: Duke University Press, 1994), 3–23; Elsie Rockwell, "Schools of the Revolution: Enacting and Contesting State Forms in Tlaxcala, 1910–1930," in *Everyday Forms of State Formation*, 190–99; Pierce, "Sobering the Revolution," 218, 290–95. René Reeves and David Carey. Jr. argue that small alcohol producers and vendors in nineteenth- and twentieth-century Guatemala also contributed to the state-building process in Guatemala both through their economic contributions and their defiance of

laws that they saw as unjust and exclusionary. See Reeves, "From Household to Nation," 57–61; Carey, "Distilling Perceptions of Crime," 121–23, 138–41, 150.

60. Small business people to unknown, July 16, 1920; unknown to Alberto M. Sánchez, December 11, 1920, AHES-RE-1920, tomo 3364; Montaño to the Chief of the SICT, December 28, 1925.

61. Ramírez Rancaño, *Ignacio Torres Adalid*, 216–17.

62. "El monopolio del pulque en México. Según un comerciante lo protege el Gob." *DH*, December 9, 1911, 4; "Quedó anulado el contrato de la Compañía Pulquera," *El Radical*, December 23, 1914, 3.

CHAPTER EIGHT

Tequila Sauza and the Redemption of Mexico's Vital Fluids, 1873–1970

José Orozco

> More than a drink for mere consumption, tequila has become an ele-
> ment that allows people to feel inducted into a special practice and
> made privy to a certain knowledge. . . . As tequila penetrates to the core
> of society through its history and traditions, its presence extends through-
> out, reaching from the upper to the lower classes, from the highest cul-
> tural sophistication (which can be found among the underprivileged) to
> the most unrefined manifestations of mass culture (which can pertain to
> the upper classes).[1]

Alberto Ruy-Sánchez Lacy wrote these words in 1994 for an issue of the
magazine *Artes de México* dedicated to tequila. Neither Ruy-Sánchez nor
the editors of *Artes de México* invented the discourse that linked tequila to
Mexicanness. Rather, in using poems, essays, and photographs to portray
tequila as the transclass, pan-social glue that bonds Mexicans into a peace-
able kingdom of slightly inebriated siblings, they were tapping into a nationalist narrative that over the course of the twentieth century had natu-
ralized an intimate and seemingly ahistorical relationship between tequila
and Mexican national identity.

To understand how tequila became Mexico's national drink in the post-
revolutionary era, or why other alcoholic drinks (most notably, *pulque*) lost
out on this prestigious designation, requires a lengthy study of the complex
interplay among technology, nationalist sentiment, and the vagaries of the
racial ghosts that continue to haunt the Mexican psyche. In this chapter I
narrow the focus of what is currently a book-length manuscript to analyze

the role that the owners of one of Mexico's most storied tequila companies, Tequila Sauza, had in defining and disseminating the idea of tequila as the alcoholic drink most closely identified with Mexico and revolutionary *Mexicanidad* (Mexicanness). All three members of the famous *Tres Generaciones de Sauza* (three generations of Sauza owners) and other *tequileros* (tequila producers) had a role in creating this discourse. But, as I argue, it was the last owner of the company, Francisco Javier Sauza (1946–1988), who made the most important contributions in creating an enduring and usable image of their beverage as the liquid embodiment of a modern, clean, and non-Indian nation. He did this by refining a "tequila discourse" that positioned tequila as the antithesis of pulque, the fermented, milky white, viscous beverage that is associated with Mexico's Indian rural population and their mixed-race urban counterparts.[2] In contrast with pulque's reputation as the dirty and smelly drink of Mexico's supposedly degenerate Indian past, Francisco Javier's narrative defined tequila as a clean, non-Indian fluid that excited the personal and national qualities that would bring Mexicans international respect and their nation entry into the modern world.

The First Generation: Cenobio Sauza (1873–1909)

Cenobio Sauza was born in 1842 in the village of Teocuitatlán, Jalisco, about 115 kilometers south of Guadalajara. At fifteen, in 1858, he left home and headed for the valley of Tequila. There he began a lengthy apprenticeship in the mezcal industry by working for several of the most prominent mezcal producers in the valley, including José Antonio Gómez Cuervo and Lázaro J. Gallardo.[3]

Tequila, or as it was most commonly referred to prior to the end of the nineteenth century, mezcal, or *vino de mezcal* (mezcal wine), is a distilled liquor that has been produced in Mexico since the seventeenth century. Though mezcal can be produced by distilling the fermented juice of many of the approximately 136 species of agave found in Mexico, tequila is made from the agave plant named *Agave tequilana* Weber var. azul, or blue agave, and is produced in the municipality of Tequila and several other officially recognized regions in the bordering states of Guanajuato, Michoacán, Nayarit, and Tamaulipas. The politics of naming and the distinction between tequila and mezcal are similar to those of other liquors, such as champagne versus sparkling wines and cognac versus brandy. In this chapter I employ both terms, using *mezcal* when writing about the period prior to the twentieth century, and *tequila* after that.[4]

In 1873, Cenobio Sauza purchased a mezcal *taberna* (tavern), La Antigua Cruz (The Old Cross), from Félix López. *Taberna* was the term for mezcal distilleries and their rustic, artisanal production in the nineteenth century before they became fully industrialized in the twentieth century.[5] In the decade that followed, Sauza, like many of his competitors in the industry, especially the Cuervo family, acquired land and smaller tabernas from his neighbors.[6] In 1878 don Cenobio razed the original taberna and constructed an edifice to accommodate the modern steam-powered machines he installed. Reflecting the progressive spirit of the Porfiriato, Porfirio Díaz's regime (1876–1911), he renamed his flagship distillery La Perseverancia (The Perseverance).[7]

When Cenobio Sauza transformed La Antigua Cruz into La Perseverancia he initiated the mythic genesis of the tequila-making dynasty that his grandson Francisco Javier Sauza immortalized in publicity campaigns as Las Tres Generaciones de Sauza. Much of what is known about don Cenobio is documented in the book *Historia de la Industria Tequila Sauza* (*History of the Tequila Sauza Industry*). The book was written by Gabriel Agraz García de Alba and funded by Francisco Javier Sauza through the Departamento de Investigaciones Históricas de Tequila Sauza. The book, a hagiography that privileges the place of the Sauza family in the pantheon of the tequila producers of the region, gives an inflated sense of the innovation that don Cenobio brought to the mezcal industry of Tequila. According to García de Alba, don Cenobio was the first *mezcalero* to export tequila to the United States when in 1873 he exported barrels of the liquid to El Paso del Norte in Texas. In addition, the text credits him with being the person most responsible for not only popularizing the association of the name *tequila* with the mezcal produced in the region of Tequila but also of being the first mezcalero to recognize that it was the blue agave that gave the mezcal from Tequila its distinctive taste and personality.[8] Prior to his supposed discovery, Tequila's mezcaleros, like those all over Mexico, produced their mezcal/tequila using different varieties of the agave plant. If all of these assertions are true, Tequila Sauza can legitimately lay claim to engendering Tequila's mezcal as a distinct product and setting the basis for the tequila industry as a modern and international entity.[9]

While these claims are far from being substantiated, we are on firmer ground when discussing other aspects of Cenobio Sauza's work life. First, like other mezcaleros in Tequila, don Cenobio participated eagerly in the accumulation of land and the dispossession of local land-owning communities.[10] Second, he accommodated his increased access to raw materials by expanding the physical size of La Perseverancia and replacing humans and animals with steam-powered machinery.[11] Third, while he may or may not have been the first mezcalero to export to the United States, Sauza understood the importance of enlarging the foreign and domestic market for his product and eagerly took advantage of the growing access it had to Guadalajara and the Southwest of the United States.[12] Last, he understood the importance of the symbolic power of names and reputation and was aware that without the blessings of the international community, the Mexican Europhile elite that he wanted to curry favor with would never accept mezcal as a modern and civilized spirit.

Cenobio Sauza manifested his desire for international recognition most acutely by participating in the regional industrial and commercial expositions and World's Fairs of the late nineteenth century.[13] The World's Fairs were events where nations showcased idealized versions of their achievements in culture, industry, science, and empire. Progressive nations used the fairs to imagine solutions to the social and technological problems that ailed them. While Western industrialized nations triumphantly emphasized their achievements and minimized their shortcomings, non-European nations like Mexico had a hard time following suit. Instead, nations like Mexico had little choice but to create aspirational narratives of potential and merit rather than achievement. The viability of this ambivalent discourse depended on maintaining a precarious and often dangerous balance between emphasizing difference and authenticity, requirements of nationalism, and claiming likeness, a requisite for modernity. This balance presented immense difficulties for Mexican elites because the national characteristics that made their country different, authentic, and hence, an individuated, autonomous nation (its Indian racial stock, tropical environment, cultures, etc.) were also widely considered by Westerners to be the sources of Mexican inferiority, lethargy, and dependency.

For the modernizing elite that supported Díaz's regime, redemption lay in constructing an *indigenista* (indigenous-oriented) discourse that allowed them to claim the rich (Hellenic-like) history of the Aztec and Mayan past while imagining a future where machines, education, and an infusion of European immigrant blood and culture would give lower-class Mexicans the mental, cultural, and physical energy to escape the limitations imposed by their supposedly dubious past and inferior racial stock.[14] Many mezcaleros like Sauza sympathized with the national government's modernization project because they understood how Western narratives of

Mexican degeneration affected the reputation of their product at home and abroad. Specifically, they were troubled by the fact that foreigners seemed not to distinguish between their mezcal and the alcoholic beverage that many foreign and domestic observers saw as a significant impediment to modernity, pulque.

Pulque is a fermented beverage made from the sap of the drought-resistant maguey plant, a member of the agave family. Along with corn, beans, chilies, and squash, it was one of the staples of the ancient Mesoamerican diet and a spiritually coded element central to religious rituals related to life, death, and agriculture.[15] As the part 1 introduction explains, the Aztecs highly prescribed pulque consumption. Those who could benefit from its nutritional and medicinal qualities (the young and the infirm) and those whose social role or station in life brought them in ritual or actual proximity to the sacred and/or death (priests, warriors, and the elderly) had relatively open access to it. The general populace, on the other hand, was allowed to drink pulque only during carefully prescribed rituals and celebrations. The Aztec elite did not allow unregulated drinking because they feared, as they reported to the Franciscan missionary Bernardino de Sahagún after the conquest, that it was "the cause of all discord and dissension, of every revolt and tension in each and every town and kingdom. Like a whirlwind it wreaks havoc on everything. It is a storm from hell, bringing with it every evil."[16]

Postconquest elite also saw pulque as a dangerous liquid. In contrast to wine, which they associated with the Catholic Church, its civilizing mission, and the transformative power of Jesus's blood, Mexico's colonial elite, some of whom consumed the Indian elixir, believed pulque debauched its non-Spanish consumers and stripped away the thin veneer of civilization that the Spaniards believed they had bequeathed to them.[17] Their logic was thus: if Indian and mixed-race people were slothful, sullen, profane, and violent prior to the conquest, pulque, consumed in communal rituals that lauded public drunkenness as an acceptable form of religious ecstasy and social bonding, introduced the Devil into the affairs of humans and reverted the natives back to their natural state and away from the community of Christ that was founded on Christ's blood and the Virgin mother's milk.[18]

Like preconquest narratives about alcohol, the Spanish elite's critique of pulque and non-European drinking habits was informed by archaic and magical beliefs about the power of certain significant liquids. They, like their indigenous counterparts, believed that significant liquids like blood, semen, breast milk, water, and alcohol could maintain or alter social identities, establish or destabilize political hierarchies, and transmogrify the human body.[19] While the influence of this type of magical thinking was somewhat superseded in the late nineteenth century by modern discourses, especially those emanating from the United States and Western Europe that explained difference and hierarchy with medical and scientific knowledge, it never fully disappeared.[20] Indeed, if modern nations depended on a population that was energetic, quick of mind, strong of body, and, as I emphasize below, clean, Americans like W. E. Carson believed that pulque stripped the Mexican masses of the physical and mental abilities they needed to progress: "[Pulque] acts upon [Mexicans] as a poison, and there is little doubt that by its means their natural laziness and stupidity have been increased a hundred-fold, till they have lost all ambition and have reached a point of animal degradation from which it seems almost hopeless they will recover."[21] Gilbert Haven, an American Methodist minister who tasted pulque while doing missionary work in 1874, was even more emphatic, and colorful, in his denunciation of the favorite alcoholic drink of the Mexican working class:

> The chief traffic of the road is in carrying this stuff [pulque] to Puebla and Mexico. It lies at the station in pig-skins and barrels, the pigs looking more hoggish than ever, as they lie on their backs and are tied at each leg and at the nose stuffed full of this foolish stuff. It ferments fiercely, and the barrels are left uncorked and the pigs' noses unmuzzled to prevent explosion. You will see the natives sticking their noses into the hog's nose, and drinking the milk of this swinish cocoa-nut, even as they are dumping it on the platform. Never was like to like more strikingly exhibited than in such a union of hogs and men.[22]

Man kisses pig and in the exchange of a milky-white substance is transmogrified into a hog. Haven is not finished with his insults and later in the book delivers poor Mexicans and their pulque the coup de grace when he reminds his American audience that man has yet to discover "a more disgustingly smelling and tasting substance [than old pulque]. . . . Rotten eggs are fragrant to its odor, and pigs' swill sweet to its taste."[23]

Pulque smells, and by implication, Mexicans smell also. This was not a new concept. It appears that Haven was channeling a trope that foreigners had used against pulque drinkers since the sixteenth century. Indeed, as early as 1552, Francisco López de Gómara, the first Spanish chronicler to mention the agave plant in print, remarked on the smell of pulque: "There are no dead dogs, not a bomb, tha[t] can clear a path as well as the smell of . . . this [wine]."[24] Since then, and for over three centuries before Carson or Haven had ever tasted or smelled pulque, foreigners and snooty (usually wine-drinking) Mexicans had used the supposed stench of the viscous pulque (the viscosity added another layer of repulsion) and the disgust reflex it engendered to create an almost impassable barrier between themselves and Mexico's poor pulque drinker.[25]

Mezcaleros like Sauza must have been embarrassed by how the magical thinking that linked the consumption of pulque with degeneracy sullied tequila's reputation. In this way they were no different than their elite contemporaries in Mexico City who were mortified by how the stench of their overflowing and inadequate sewer system reflected poorly on their nation, their race, and their ability to become modern.[26] The mezcaleros understood, as George Orwell knew, that once their mezcal was associated with the disgust-inducing stench of pulque and its purported filth, there was little they could do to deodorize themselves.[27] Indeed, as William Ian Miller argues, the importance of smell-induced disgust is that it creates markers of difference that are felt viscerally and have real social and psychological consequences: "[Disgust] does not admit of equitable distribution, and it works against ideas of equality. It paints a picture of pure and impure. And the compromises it makes across those lines are by way of transgression as sin, lust, or perversion. Hierarchies maintained by disgust cannot be benign; because the low are polluting they constitute a danger; a policy of live and let live is not adequate."[28]

By entering his mezcal in the World's Fair, Cenobio Sauza wanted to highlight the ways in which mezcal was simultaneously an authentic product of Mexico and a clean, non-disgust-inducing, civilized, and cosmopolitan liquor like cognac, champagne, or brandy.[29] In the same manner that Mexican modernizers hoped technology, nutritional science, education, and eugenics would refine natives into a respectable usable population, Sauza must have hoped that his presentation at Chicago's Columbian World's Fair would earn his product a small measure of respect.[30] After all, Sauza seemed to be saying, mezcal is the product of an industrial process that refines agave (an authentically indigenous raw material) into a modern, energy-giving stimulant, worthy of foreign admiration and consumption.

Sauza could not have been disappointed by the results of his efforts in Chicago. During the fair, American judges awarded Mexican spirits twenty-two awards, including a gold medal certificate for Sauza's "Mezcal Brandy." To receive a gold medal, a distilled spirit had to earn at least ninety points out of one hundred in four categories: purity, distillation, taste and appearance, and general condition. Sauza's mezcal earned ninety-one points. The head American judge, Guido Marx, was impressed enough with Mexico's distilled products to write that the ability of the distillers to purify and deodorize a range of raw materials that included sugar, mesquite, and agave showed the progress of their industry.[31] And while it could be argued that his achievements in Chicago were mostly aesthetic, understood in the context of the binding dilemma that Mauricio Tenorio-Trillo believes confounded Mexico's "wizards of progress," we can see that his gold medals and the American judge's comments were hardly insignificant: "How, in a nationalist and scientifically racist era, could a country of Indians be completely disinfected? The response of the Por-firian Científicos was to constantly look for, classify, reclassify, and adapt possible answers from international science, arts, and politics, but they found no answers. How could they? The long-standing identification of the Indians with miasma and dirt was something that neither Western ex-oticism nor scientific hygienism could overcome."[32]

Because Sauza and his fellow mezcaleros were anxious to sever the viscerally negative connection that Americans made between mezcal and pulque, Marx's praise of their product's purification and deodorization must have felt like not only an affirmation of the quality of their mezcal but also a confirmation of a larger project rooted in aspirational racial pu-rity, refined social taste, and the improved appearance and general condi-tion of the Mexican nation and its people.

When Cenobio Sauza died in 1909, he was a rich man who could right-fully feel proud of the progress he had made in modernizing his industry and bringing a measure of respect to his product. Over his long tenure, he had procured enough land to provide his distillery with a steady and reli-able supply of agave, modernized some of his machinery, extended the markets for his product within and beyond Mexico, received many med-als, ribbons, and plaques to put up on his walls, and even managed to get himself appointed mayor of Tequila on three occasions, in 1883, 1886, and 1892.

But all was not well with his industry. In spite of having experienced years of spectacular growth at the end of the nineteenth century, by the beginning of the twentieth century the tequila/mezcal industry was in cri-sis. In 1879 mezcal represented 36 percent of the agricultural production of Jalisco, but between 1901 and 1903 mezcal/tequila production de-creased by 23 percent. Indeed, with the country on the verge of a civil war that would further damage the social, economic, and political infrastruc-ture that had been developed by the Porfirian mezcaleros, the distilleries in the region were producing seven times less product than they were in 1901.[33] Luckily for Cenobio, the task of maneuvering through the minefield of the Mexican Revolution (1910–1920) and the profound changes it wrought to the tequila business was left to his son, and eventual heir, Eladio Sauza.

The Second Generation: Eladio Sauza (1909–1946)

Eladio Sauza was born in Tequila in 1883, the fifth of seven children. Though his father had died in 1909, Eladio was not named the main legal beneficiary of the Sauza estate until 1927.[34] By then, the mezcal industry had suffered through volatile market swings. Moments of expansion brought on by diverse factors, such as the outbreak of World War I (1914–1918), the popular belief that tequila could cure the Spanish influenza (1918) and arthritis, the oil boom in Tamaulipas in the 1920s, and Prohibition in the United States during the 1920s, were offset by the effects of a decade of civil war at home and the economic turbulence emanating from abroad in the 1930s. The financial well-being of Tequila's mezcaleros was also adversely affected by the state-sponsored redistribution of land during the 1920s and 1930s. Beginning in 1927, but accelerating during the presidency of Lázaro Cárdenas (1934–1940), the Mexican state redistributed the lands of large mezcal producers to the local peasantry in the form of *ejidos* (collective, state-owned land). In the municipality of Tequila alone, the government redistributed fourteen thousand hectares. The redistribution of land, while undoubtedly a social necessity, was an economic disaster for the large mezcaleros, who could ill afford to interrupt the growth cycle of their slow-growing (between seven to ten years) raw material. The crisis these changes precipitated can be measured in different ways. The production of tequila plummeted from 4.6 million liters in 1910 to 3 million in 1920 to a low of 1 million in 1935. Of the 87 distilleries extant in Jalisco in 1910, only 32 existed by 1930 and, according to the 1940 Agriculture and Livestock Census, only 2,603 hectares of land in the region were being cultivated with agave. This was only 35 percent of the land that had been cultivated in 1930 and only a tenth of the 30,000 acres (and 70 million agaves) that were being cultivated with agave in the 1880s.[35]

While the lack of capital, the instability of markets, and the diminution of available agave forced Eladio Sauza to slow the process of modernization begun by his father in the last decades of the nineteenth century, the revolutionary cultural policies initially thwarted any attempts to build on his father's crusade to create a high-brow image for the mezcal from Tequila—now more commonly known in Mexico simply as *tequila*. Rather than becoming the drink of high society that don Cenobio had hoped for, the preference for tequila on the part of the dirty and ragged men who fought the Revolution reinforced the image of tequila as a disgusting, lower-class, violence-inducing beverage.[36] On the other hand, any attempt to make tequila the drink of a respectable working class was undermined by a resurgent folkloric and indigenista populist nationalism that enhanced the reputation of Mexico's indigenous populations and mezcal's oldest and most pungent nemesis, pulque.

Indigenista muralists, poets, politicians, and filmmakers believed that Mexico's essence was rooted in its Indian past and parts of its (mostly folkloric) Indian present. As part and parcel of this ideology, indigenistas saw pulque as the liquid embodiment of Mexico's Indian soul and the drinking culture of the *pulquería* as a cultural and aesthetic source of Mexico's populist nationalism. Their sentiments were shared by the many Mexicans for whom pulque and drinking in pulquerías were routinized and culturally significant (as well as physically and emotionally pleasurable) parts of their lives.[37] Unfortunately, for pulque, *chicha, tepache, teshuino,* and other fermented drinks associated with Mexico's Indian and mestizo poor, many revolutionary cultural power brokers were, like their Porfirian predecessors, obsessed with modernity, status, race, and cleanliness as a measure of all three.[38] Yes, pulque's nationalistic bona fides were praised in verse and song as the true expression of Mexicanidad, but in spite of the nationalist turn in revolutionary culture, and pulque's thousand-year history in Mesoamerica, its historic association with filth and sloth (and drunken, dangerous, and smelly Indians) still resonated with many revolutionary modernizers who preferred that Mexico's national drink reflect its modernizing and sanitized aspirations.

Rather than embrace pulque as Mexico's national drink, some of the country's strongest economic, political, and cultural power brokers lined up to undermine pulque's symbolic and quotidian importance in Mexican life. The prejudice was ubiquitous. Sometimes it was gratuitous, such as when Manuel M. Ponce, the Mexican composer famous for taking traditional popular Mexican songs and weaving their melodies into more acceptable classical forms, described his work as removing the "smell of pulque" from the songs to make them respectable.[39] Often, though, degrading pulque was part of calculated campaigns designed by interested parties for political or economic advantage. In the 1920s the Mexican beer industry circulated the myth that pulque producers fermented their *aguamiel* by introducing a small amount of feces. There is evidence that some pulque producers, in some isolated instances, did use the *muñeca* (a piece of feces wrapped in a cloth that resembled a rag doll) to start fermentation. This would not have come as a surprise to the pulque-consuming public, some of whom preferred this type of pulque. Clearly, though, the hyperbolic claims about the prevalence of this practice were an attempt to discredit all pulqueros. Because beer has an alcohol content similar to pulque (between 4 and 8 percent) and is conducive to similar drinking/spending patterns, the campaign was intended by Mexican beer companies to leverage disgust for a greater share of a very lucrative market.[40] In their campaign, aided eventually by the Cárdenas regime on the grounds that tainted pulque posed a danger to public health, Mexico's beer producers characterized pulque as antihygienic, stupefying, and a cause of physical and social degeneration. On the other hand, they portrayed beer as "family friendly, rigorously hygienic and modern drink that promoted health as a diuretic, stimulated circulation of blood, cleansed the kidneys and was ideal for lactating women."[41]

This rhetoric, as old as it was ubiquitous,[42] was also the foundation for the tequila discourse that Eladio Sauza (and other tequileros) developed and diffused in the 1930s and 1940s. But unlike beer producers, who were selling a product introduced into Mexico by Germans and Austrians during the reign of Maximilian (1864–1867), tequila producers could claim (as they invariably did) that in addition to being hygienic, modern, and healthy, tequila was also Mexican. The nationalist advantage was not as unambiguous as it may seem. Beer companies ran the risk of highlighting the Teutonic people who brought their alcoholic beverage to Mexico. However, tequila companies continually risked reminding consumers about their product's indigenous roots and its many negative associations. Still, and very much like his father before him, Eladio Sauza set out to convince Mexican and, after the repeal of Prohibition in 1933, American consumers that tequila was a modern and clean drink whose consumption had a civilizing and salubrious effect on those discerning enough to know how to imbibe it in moderation.

This message was calibrated to resonate on slightly different cultural and emotional registers depending on the intended audience. For the US market, Sauza and his American advertising agent, L. B. Foster, crafted ads that assuaged Americans' historic fear of ingesting Mexican fluids, whether pulque, water, or blood.[43] For example, in an ad titled "Tequila Sauza, What It Is," Sauza and Foster promoted tequila as an "undoubtedly whole-some and nourishing drink" that is "nutritive, tonic, exhilarating, stom-achal, digestive, appetizing, sudorific, corroborant, healing [and] astrin-gent"—a drink that is "entirely free from fusel oil . . . [which] eats up the hydrochloric acid of the stomach lining, inflames it and causes nervous indigestion."[44] Unlike the milky, viscous, and dirty pulque that many Americans believed degenerated and softened (feminized?) the body, stu-pefied the mind, killed personal ambition, and lowered the morality of the working people who consumed it, Sauza promoted his tequila to Ameri-can consumers, who were unsure about the difference between the drinks, as a clean and modern beverage worthy of their sophisticated palate and their civilized, if not effete, stomachs.[45]

The ads Sauza aired for Mexican consumers on XED, the radio sta-tion he established in Guadalajara in 1929, also emphasized tequila's taste, cleanliness, curative power, and modernity.[46] But unlike ads aimed at American consumers, these ads were more explicit, insistent, and specific about the connection between tequila, modernity, and proper individual morality. In a series of ads written by the poet Benjamín D. Castillo, Sauza extolls his tequila as an elixir that is capable of exciting some of the personal qualities closely associated with modernity and in-dustrial capitalism. Like coffee, which was valued by enlightened eighteenth-century Protestant Europeans for its ability to achieve "chem-ically and pharmacologically what rationalism and the Protestant ethic sought to fulfill spiritually and ideologically," tequila was promoted by Sauza as a mental stimulant that vivified the body and exhilarated per-sonal ambition.[47]

As they were in eighteenth-century Europe, different liquids were linked to physical and mental transformations that were gender specific. Indeed, if tequila was analogous to the Protestant (male) coffee, pulque, as it was historically purported to make its drinkers lazy and languid, was its Catholic (female) antithesis, chocolate.[48] More specifically, Sauza ads as-sured Mexican consumers that drinking Tequila Sauza Añejo revealed and refined men's good taste, their bon vivant sociability, and middle-class respectability.[49] On the other hand, the ads encouraged Mexican women, for whom alcohol consumption was traditionally seen as both cause and effect of loose sexual morals and physical degeneration, to drink the sweeter almond liqueur Crema Sauza, a liqueur guaranteed to augment women's physical beauty and feminine morality.[50] Having nurtured all these qualities, Sauza promised Mexicans of both genders that his products would take them out into a wider world where they, or at least their national drink, would be respected and treated as civilized equals: "London! . . . Paris! . . . Berlin! . . . Rome! . . . The most elegant hotels in the most splendorous and lavish European capitals regale the palate of their aristocratic clientele with Mexico's national aperitif: Tequila Sauza."[51]

To attract consumers already living in modern nations like the United States, Sauza resorted to using advertising slogans that promoted tequila as the product of a particular exotic place and time. By lacing his ads with a bit of primitivism, Sauza was attempting to achieve a delicate balance between difference and similarity, authenticity and modernity, history and future.[52] Like his father and other Porfirian elites before him, Eladio Sauza's historical narrative was rooted in exotic, imperial notions of indigenous history. But because indigenista ideologies were in fashion during revolutionary Mexico and post-Prohibition United States, Eladio Sauza's ads were, as is highlighted in a 1933 ad campaign, less anxious and pleading than Cenobio's:[53] "It is interesting . . . that nearly every nation has evolved its own peculiar type of beverage. Thus we find wines originated in the ancient kingdoms of the Mediterranean [who possessed] the necessary grape. Scotland has achieved its fame from its whiskey, Russia for its vodka, Germany for its beer. The ancient Aztec civilization was also not without its own national distillation."[54]

While Aztec iconography was featured in some ads aired for Mexican consumers, Sauza was more interested in reminding the recently urbanized peasants who flocked to cities like Guadalajara about their past in an idyllic and romanticized countryside. In "The National Aperitif, the Exquisite Tequila Sauza," a half-hour radio musical show that Tequila Sauza sponsored, regional audiences were treated to both classical music ("Wine, Women and Song" by Johann Strauss II) and more traditional, folkloric fare ("Un Viejo Amor" [An Old Love], "Las Perlitas" [The Little Pearls], "El Zopilote" [The Vulture]). Interspersed among the music were ads for Tequila Sauza like this one: "It is neither forgotten, nor is it left behind . . . Memories, delights and joy of days gone by. Yes, Sir, a shot of the exquisite Tequila Sauza brings forth yesterday's memories. By delighting in a drink of Tequila Sauza Añejo we relive the moments of our past. Who does not like remembering the joys of our past? Next we will hear the song 'Así es la Vida' ['Such Is Life']."[55]

During his tenure as the president of Tequila Sauza, Eladio Sauza was not able to move his tequila discourse far away from the broad outlines established by his father. Nor was he able to solve the uncomfortable riddle of how to balance authenticity and modernity. Eladio's advantage over beer and other foreign drinks was a discourse that blended nationalistic imagery with a "science-speak" claim about how tequila was clean and good for the body and the mind. But as long as this nationalism linked his product to Mexico's natives, Sauza could not clearly distinguish tequila from pulque and its web of negative racial and sensory associations. Two generations of Sauzas had attempted to cleanse tequila's image and create a confident discourse, but neither had totally succeeded. It was not until Eladio's son, Francisco Javier, linked his product to a Mexican countryside purged of its indigenous genetic and cultural presence, as we shall see, that tequila was able to assume its "natural" position as the liquid embodiment of modern Mexicanidad.

The Third Generation:
Francisco Javier Sauza (1946–1988)

Francisco Javier was born in 1903 and died in 1990. After receiving his primary and secondary education in Guadalajara, Francisco Javier was sent by his father to Chicago, Illinois. Ostensibly the young heir to the Sauza empire moved to the United States to complete his education, but as he revealed later in life, his father was more concerned about keeping his pleasure-seeking son out of trouble during the religious civil war known as the Cristero Rebellion (1926–1929). The strategic exile did not work out as planned. In Chicago, Francisco Javier met and then married María Elena "Nina" Gutiérrez Salcedo. Nina, who was studying at St. Mary's College, not only was related to the Sauzas' biggest business and social competitor, the tequila-producing Cuervo family but also was a divorcee with a young child.

Eladio Sauza was scandalized by the union and ostracized his obstinate young son. Francisco Javier remained in the United States with Nina and supported his new family by working as a logger in Northern California and a folkloric singer in Chicago. He eventually moved to Mexico City, where he worked as a tour guide. After the violence of the Cristero Rebellion and his father's ire had subsided, Francisco Javier moved back to Jalisco. In 1931 his father put him in charge of the family's dairy, La Moderna, and then soon after promoted him to director of sales and promotion for Tequila Sauza. Francisco Javier, the self-acknowledged "playboy," was not entrusted with the family business until after Eladio died in 1946, but his time in the promotion department would influence the rest of his career.[56]

Francisco Javier Sauza's tenure as head of Tequila Sauza lasted until 1988, when he sold the company to the brandy conglomerate Pedro Domecq.[57] During his tenure Sauza expanded production and modernized the physical production plant of La Perseverancia. Twenty years after he took over the company, Francisco Javier had turned La Perseverancia from a factory that was producing nineteen thousand gallons of tequila a day to one that was distilling one hundred fifty thousand gallons a day in 1967. As he bragged to an American reporter at the end of his life: "I was selling more than Cuervo, and I bought tequila from everybody except Cuervo."[58]

As proud as he was of his business achievements, Sauza seemed even prouder of the fact that over his long career as a tequilero, he had worked tirelessly and successfully to promote tequila as a refined liquor equal to the best and most cultured spirits of the world. There seemed to be no medium, from the most intimate and personal to the mass media of television and radio, that he did not exploit in his efforts to propagate this image. Sauza was always on message, often writing missives to opinion makers in Mexico and abroad to thank them for promoting Tequila Sauza and the cause of friendship between Mexico and their country.[59] In 1963 he sent Antonio Armendáriz, the Mexican ambassador to England, a letter that contained the following:

> Since inheriting [Tequila Sauza] from my father, my most pressing concern has been to give tequila the universal prominence that it deserves . . . some of this has been achieved, but we must continue the fight with the help of people such as yourself who do not discriminate against our national drink and who serve it with pride at official receptions. In this way, we will succeed in having our Tequila [shine] with the dignity that it deserves as one of the best drinks in the world.[60]

Sauza also scoured the print media for articles related to tequila or the culture of Jalisco. When he liked the article, he congratulated the author. When the article contained errors of fact or interpretation, Sauza sent letters to correct the author. In 1968 *Business Week* published an article about American expatriates in Mexico titled "Old Guadalajara: Haven for Gringos and Money." The author mistakenly described tequila as "the national liqueur" and stated that it was made from "distilled pulque" and was "as rough as a Tennessee White Mule." Sauza wrote the publishers to inform them not only that tequila was not a liqueur (it was a "hard liquor") but also that it was most certainly not made from fermented pulque and that when aged in wooden barrels was "as smooth as a good vodka." After detailing the differences between pulque and tequila, Sauza, the third generation of tequileros to wrestle with *gringo* (slang for a foreigner, especially an American) ignorance and the long shadow that pulque cast over tequila, ends his letter in a more genteel manner. He hopes that his explanation has "clarified the difference between Pulque and Tequila" and states that it is an honor to be mentioned in the article of such a prestigious magazine.[61]

When he was not writing letters from his desk in Guadalajara, Sauza traveled to the United States to promote his tequila and the culture of Jalisco. In the early 1960s he promoted and funded a traveling music and dance show that brought his vision of Mexican folklore (mariachis and the "Jarabe Tapatío" traditional dance from Guadalajara) to Tucson, Arizona, during George Washington's birthday.[62] The annual event was cosponsored by the Tucson Trade Bureau and a local businessman of German-Mexican descent named Gilbert Ronstadt.[63] In the early 1970s, Sauza commissioned a statue of the Aztec goddess of pulque, Mayahuel, and presented it to the mayor of the city of Victoria in British Columbia, Canada.[64]

Like his father, Eladio, Francisco Javier used mass consumer media such as radio and television to sell his tequila and diffuse his tequila discourse. Early in his tenure, Sauza teamed up with the Spanish-expatriate advertising agent Eulalio Ferrer to create a series of uniquely powerful national and international marketing and media campaigns. These ads mined the narrative link that Mexico's most capitalized sectors of the popular culture industry, cinema and radio, had made between tequila and a particular type of Mexicanidad. From these forms of mass entertainment, especially the so-called *ranchero* movies that became popular in the late 1930s, Sauza and Ferrer borrowed a version of Mexicanness that, while acknowledging that Mexicans were the product of both Indian and Spanish cultural and genetic material, clearly favored the Spanish side of the mestizo equation.[65] Mayahuel was the lone image of indigenous origin that Sauza and Ferrer consistently used for promotional reasons. But while the motherly Mayahuel was an important deity in the Nahuatl culture and her statue graced the entrance of Tequila Sauza's main office in Guadalajara, she was clearly overshadowed in Sauza advertisements by a multitude of fair-skinned mariachis, bullfighters, horse-riding *charros* (Mexican cowboys), and raven-haired, rosy-cheeked damsels.[66] These Hispanic archetypes were the stock characters of the mythscape that Ferrer and Sauza created in the 1960s and 1970s and propagated in print, radio, and after 1956 in the television program *Noches Tapatías* (*Tapatío Nights*).

Noches Tapatías was inaugurated under the direction of Sauza's publicity agents Ferrer and Salvador de Aguinaga in 1952 as a radio program. It became a weekly television show in 1956 and was on the air until 1980.[67] The program showcased the music, poetry, and culture of an idealized rural Jalisco. Interspersed between the performances of almost every ranchero music star Mexico has ever produced, Sauza aired ads for his tequila. Like his other publicity, *Noches Tapatías* promoted tequila and the rural culture of Jalisco as the essence of a Hispanic (read: not Indian) national identity.[68]

As noted above, neither Sauza nor Ferrer invented this mythologized image of Mexicanidad. They borrowed it from a generation of Hispanophile writers, poets, moviemakers, and politicians that came of age in the 1930s and 1940s. These cultural power brokers, reacting to the *mestizaje* (miscegenation) and indigenista ideologies, promoted the population of the state of Jalisco in general, and the population of Los Altos de Jalisco in the northeast part of Jalisco, in particular, as the living, untainted repository of Spanish racial genes and cultural memes. According to the highly selective narrative of these intellectuals, *Alteños*, as the people of Los Altos are known, were an aristocratic people who, from their redoubt in the highlands of Jalisco, had steadfastly refused to miscegenate with the indigenous population below.[69] *Hispanistas* (proponents of *hispanismo*, ideology favoring Spanish heritage over native culture) argued that this act of racial and cultural pride had allowed the Alteño gene pool and cultural practices to remain untainted by the syncretic cultural formations and physical abominations that were common elsewhere in Mexico. Alteño women were white-skinned beauties (they have the reputation of being the most beautiful women in Mexico) whose spiritual devotion to the Catholic Church and the domestic space protected them from the corrupting influence of North American culture. They kept their hair long, they did not smoke or drink, and they embodied traditional Spanish/Catholic culture. Alteño men were equally light skinned. They were a breed of machos who, when not drinking tequila, riding horses, or singing mariachi music, were out defending their form of nonsyncretic Catholicism (the religiously motivated Cristero Rebellion of 1926–1929 and the right-wing, fascist Sinarquista movement of the 1940s were particularly violent and widespread in the region) and/or the sacred rights of private property against the supposedly atheistic and communistic maneuverings of Mexico's revolutionary regimes.[70]

So renowned had Alteños become—their image was the raw material for the famous ranchero movies of the golden age of Mexican cinema (1936–1957)[71]—that by the late 1950s the philosopher and former Secretary of Public Education José Vasconcelos was able to confidently anoint them as "the best racial contingent that our country has. [They] are of pure Spanish blood."[72] By the late 1950s when Vasconcelos penned that tribute to Alteños, he was a discredited intellectual who had publicly flirted with Nazism and white supremacist theories during World War II. Sauza's hispanismo was not the virulently anti-Indian strain that Vasconcelos promulgated in his later writings and was the hallmark of social Catholic movements in the three decades after the end of the revolution.[73] Nonetheless, Sauza's tequila discourse was similar to these ideologies in two significant ways.

First, like all hispanista ideologies, whether embedded in a conservative Catholic political movement, ranchero movies, or mariachi songs, Sauza's advertising initiated a racially freighted engagement with everyday Mexicans about the meaning of community. All of these discussions took place in a historical context where the moorings for what it had traditionally meant to be part of a community in Mexico (rural, religious, small-scale, extended family) were being redefined by urbanization, industrialization, mass consumerism, and immigration. In this context of flux, the Cristeros and the Sinarquistas had promised Mexicans willing to fight and die for their beliefs a return to the Hispanic Catholic theocracy of an imagined colonial world that never was.[74] Sauza, on the other hand, used mass media to promise his compatriots that drinking tequila would help create a transnational Mexican community that had an idealized rural Hispanic world as its historical and cultural reference point. His was the modern expression of the idea that significant liquids can nurture and excite certain individual qualities and that these qualities, when generalized, can serve as the basis for larger (idealized) conglomerations of individuals: cultures, races, religions, genders, and/or nations. The conflation of tequila with nation (indeed, in Sauza's discourse, tequila was a synecdoche for Mexico) was expressed in ads that promised that Tequila Sauza was "a little bit of Mexico" that should be enjoyed "on both sides of the border."[75]

In the past the promise of this community had conjured images of degeneration, filth, and smell that essentially put Mexicans and their vital fluids (water, pulque, blood, tequila) on the wrong side of a divide created and maintained by disgust. What Francisco Javier Sauza promised was a historic redemption, a cleansing, destined to right the historical wrongs perpetuated by past elites (foreign and domestic) whose preference for all things foreign had unfairly given Mexicans and their tequila (their blood, their water) a vulgar reputation around the world. In the early 1960s this promise was distilled into an advertising campaign that featured some of

Europe's most recognizable national icons bowing to bottles and shot glasses of Sauza tequila. One featured the leaning tower of Pisa with the slogan, "Italy also bows for Tequila Sauza."[76]

This message, and the magical logic it was based on, remained central to Sauza advertising throughout the 1960s and received its most polished and historically significant expression in a series of print and television ads that appeared in 1969 and featured the iconic French actor Maurice Chevalier.[77] Chevalier is instructed by director's notes to romance his glass of tequila:

—Zoom Back: We see Maurice Chevalier serving himself tequila with a happy and mischievous expression.

—He says his lines, half sung half spoken, and lifts his glass: "*C'est si bon . . . !*" [It is good . . . !]

—He places on hand on the glass and the other on the bottle, almost as if he were dancing: "*Si bon . . . !*" [It is good . . . !]

—He takes the glass and with it nearly touching his lips he speaks: "Si bon . . . !"

—Having finished the glass of tequila we see him lick his lips and put on his classic straw hat as if readying himself to leave: "Haaa . . . !"

—The announcer: "According to Murice [*sic*] Chevalier, Tequila Sauza is one of the finer things in the world . . . it gives flavor to one's life!"[78]

This was the romantic interlude that three generations of Sauzas, and many of Mexico's Europhile elite, had been waiting almost a century to consummate. After years of foreigners expressing open disdain for all manner of Mexican fluids, the image of a Frenchman sipping the nectar of the Mexican countryside to such an ecstatic conclusion was indeed one of the finer things in the world.

Notes

1. Alberto Ruy-Sánchez Lacy, "In the Shadow of Tequila," in *Artes de México, El Tequila: Arte Tradicional de México* (Mexico City: Artes de México y del Mundo, 1994), 81.

2. The phrase "tequila discourse" is a play on Jeffrey M. Pilcher's "Tortilla Discourse." See Pilcher, chapter 4, "The Tortilla Discourse: Nutrition and Nation Building," in *¡Que vivan los tamales! Food and the Making of Mexican Identity* (Albuquerque: University of New Mexico Press, 1998).

3. Biographical information available in Gabriel Agraz García de Alba, *Historia de la industria Tequila Sauza: Tres generaciones y una tradición* (Guadalajara: Departamento de Investigaciones Históricas de Tequila Sauza de Jalisco, 1963).

4. On the politics and history of what mezcal can be called *tequila*, see Lucie Leclert, "Who Benefits from the 'Denominación de Origen' Tequila?" (MA thesis, Wageningen University, 2007).

5. The transition from artisanal to industrial production in Tequila roughly corresponds with the shift of nomenclature from *mezcal* or *vino de mezcal* to *tequila*.

6. Agraz, *Historia*, 45.

7. Ibid., 30.

8. "Noventa años de historia de Tequila Sauza: Tres Generaciones y una Tradición," 1963, Archivo Personal de Francisco Javier Sauza (hereafter APFJS), Biblioteca Eladio Sauza—an advertisement produced in 1963 to commemorate the ninetieth anniversary of the company. The information it contained was based on Agraz's book *Historia*.

9. Agraz, *Historia*, 39.

10. Ibid., 45–46; Rogelio Luna Zamora, *La historia del tequila, de sus regiones y sus hombres* (Mexico City: Consejo Nacional para la Cultura y las Artes [hereafter Conaculta], 1991), 84–94.

11. In 1873 the physical plant of La Perseverancia encompassed 2,688 square meters. By 1888 the distillery measured 15,752 square meters. "Noventa años."

12. With the completion of the railroad into Guadalajara in 1888 and its extension to Tequila by 1909, mezcal producers of this region were able to export about a third of their product abroad during the last quarter of the nineteenth century: 80 percent to the United States, 12 percent to Central and South America, and 8 percent to the United Kingdom. The introduction of the railroad to Guadalajara facilitated its growth, and between 1900 and 1930 it became the largest market for tequila. Luna Zamora, *La historia del tequila*, 65, 81–82; Enrique Martínez Limón, *Tequila: The Spirit of Mexico* (Mexico City: Revimundo, 1988), 74; George Sánchez, *Becoming Mexican American: Ethnicity, Culture, and Identity in Chicano Los Angeles, 1900–1945* (Oxford: Oxford University Press, 1993), 43.

13. Agraz, *Historia*, 44, 49–51, 54–57.

14. Nancy Leys Stepan calls this ambiguous embrace of modernity and the social reform aimed at making Mexico modern a form of "constructive miscegenation." Stepan, *"The Hour of Eugenics": Race, Gender, and Nation in Latin America* (Ithaca, NY: Cornell University Press, 1991), 147.

15. Mesoamericans used the fibrous leaves of the maguey to make paper, clothes, sandals, and roofing materials. They also used the thorns at the tip of the leaves as pins, sewing needles, and nails. Inga Clendinnen, *Aztecs* (Cambridge: Cambridge University Press, 1991), 48–51; William B. Taylor, *Drinking, Homicide, and Rebellion in Colonial Mexican Villages* (Stanford, CA: Stanford University Press, 1979), 28–72; Raúl Guerrero Guerrero, *El Pulque* (Mexico City: Editorial Joaquín Mortiz-Instituto Nacional de Antropología e Historia, 1985); José Jesús Hernández Palomo, *La renta del pulque en Nueva España, 1663–1810* (Seville: Escuela de Estudios Hispano-Americanos de Sevilla, 1979), 1–13.

16. Sonia Corcuera de Mancera, "Luna Aturdida: El Pulque, su Uso y Abuso," in *Artes de México, Maguey* (Mexico City: Artes de México y del Mundo, 2000), 56.

17. Taylor, *Drinking, Homicide*, 40–42.

18. "Their wine, before they ferment it with certain roots which they add to it, is clear and sweet like honey and water. After it is fermented it becomes somewhat thick and has a bad odor, and those who get drunk smell even worse. . . . It was pitiable to see men created in the image of God become worse than brute beasts; and worse still, they did not confine themselves to that one sin, but committed many others, striking, wounding, and even killing one another, though they might be friends and close relatives." Toribio de Benavente Motolinía, *History of the Indians of New Spain* (Berkeley, CA: Cortés Society, 1950), 45.

19. Fear of pulque's power to introduce political disorder and racial contagion was part of an intricate web of signification and magical thinking that informed the well-known elite fears of miscegenation and their less known fear that the breast milk of the mostly *mulata* wet nurses would transmit undesirable racial characteristics to their progeny. See Ilona Katzew, *Casta Paintings: Images of Race in Eighteenth-Century Mexico* (New Haven, CT: Yale University Press, 2004), 113; María Elena Martínez, *Geneological Fictions: Limpieza de Sangre, Religion, and Gender in Colonial Mexico* (Stanford, CA: Stanford University Press, 2008).

20. Alexandra Minna Stern, "Buildings, Boundaries, and Blood: Medicalization and Nation-Building on the US-Mexico Border, 1910–1930," *Hispanic American Historical Review* 79 (1999), 41–81; Stern, "Secrets Under the Skin: New Historical Perspectives on Disease, Deviation, and Citizenship. A Review Article," *Society for Comparative Study of Society and History* 41, no. 3 (1999), 589–96.

21. W. E. Carson, *Mexico: The Wonderland of the South* (New York: Macmillan, 1909), 104.

22. Gilbert Haven, *Our Next Door Neighbor: A Winter in Mexico* (New York: Harper and Brothers, 1875), 81–82.

23. Ibid., 135–36.

24. Cited in Henry J. Bruman, *Alcohol in Ancient Mexico* (Salt Lake City: University of Utah Press, 2000), 71.

25. On viscosity and its disgust-inducing properties, see William Ian Miller, *The Anatomy of Disgust* (Cambridge, MA: Harvard University Press, 1997), 60–66.

26. Michael Johns, *The City of Mexico in the Age of Díaz* (Austin: University of Texas Press, 1997), 17–31.

27. George Orwell understood the importance of smell in creating rifts between classes in Britain: "[The] real secret of class distinctions in the West—the real reason why a European of bourgeois upbringing, even when he calls himself a Communist, cannot without a hard effort think of a working man as his equal, it is summed up in four frightful words which people nowadays are chary of uttering, but which were bandied about quite freely in my childhood. These words were: *The lower class smell*." *The Road to Wigan Pier*, qtd. in Miller, *Anatomy of Disgust*, 240. See also Mauricio Tenorio-Trillo, *Mexico at the World's Fairs: Crafting a Modern Nation* (Berkeley: University of California Press, 1996), 118. In the same vein, Stepan in *"The Hour of Eugenics"* notes: "The fantasies of human transmutation remind us that eugenics was above all an aesthetic-biological movement concerned with beauty and ugliness, purity and contamination, as represented by race" (135).

28. Miller, *Anatomy of Disgust*, 251. New research on the social function of disgust seems to indicate that Miller is correct. See Dan Jones, "Moral Psychology. The Depths of Disgust," *Nature* 447 (2007), 768–71.

29. The very fact that pulque would have spoiled after a couple of days, hence preventing its presentation in the World's Fair in Chicago, highlighted the cosmopolitan nature of mezcal.

30. Alan Knight, "Racism, Revolution, and *Indigenismo*: Mexico, 1910–1940," in *The Idea of Race in Latin America, 1870–1940*, ed. Richard Graham (Austin: University of Texas Press, 1990), 71–85; Robert M. Buffington and William E. French, "The Culture of Modernity," in *The Oxford History of Mexico*, ed. Michael C. Meyer and William H. Beezley (Oxford: Oxford University Press, 2000), 397–432; Pilcher, *¡Que vivan los tamales!*, 77–97.

31. Guido Marx, "Whiskies, etc.," in *Report of the Committee on Awards of the World's Columbian Commission: Special Reports upon Special Subjects or Groups*, vol. 2 (Washington, DC: Government Printing Office, 1901), 1013.

32. Tenorio-Trillo, *Mexico at the World's Fairs*, 156.

33. According to Luna Zamora, this crisis was caused by a combination of factors: Mexico's transition from a silver to a gold standard in 1905, the rampant adulteration of mezcal with other cheaper alcohols and water, and overproduction. Luna Zamora, *La historia del tequila*, 118–21, 129.

34. Agraz, *Historia*, 68–69.

35. Luna Zamora, *La historia del tequila*, 129, 130–53, 170 chart 27.

36. Mariano Azuela immortalized these men and their love of tequila in his serialized novel, *Los de Abajo* (Mexico City: Fondo de Cultura Económica, 1986): "Men stained with dirt, smoke and sweat, of matted beards and tangled hair. . . . Instead of Champagne that shimmers in bubbles under the fading light of candles, Demetrio Macias prefers the clear tequila of Jalisco" (74).

37. María Áurea Toxqui Garay, "'El Recreo de los Amigos': Mexico City's Pulquerías During the Liberal Republic (1856–1911)" (PhD diss., University of Arizona, 2008).

38. Katherine E. Bliss, "For the Health of the Nation: Gender and the Cultural Politics of Social Hygiene in Revolutionary Mexico," in *The Eagle and the Virgin: Nation and Cultural Revolution in Mexico, 1920–1940*, ed. Mary Kay Vaughan and Stephen E. Lewis (Durham, NC: Duke University Press, 2006), 196–218; Patience A. Schell, "Nationalizing Children Through Schools and Hygiene: Porfirian and Revolutionary Mexico City," *The Americas* 60, no. 4 (2004), 559–87.

39. Guerrero, *El Pulque*, 3.

40. Ernest Gruening, *Mexico and Its Heritage* (New York: Appleton-Century, 1936), 538.

41. Rodolfo Fernández and Daria Deraga, "El uso de material fecal en la fermentación alcohólica," *Diario de Campo* 89 (2006), 80–85; Rubén Hernández, "Que Siga la Tradición Pulquera," *Reforma*, September 18, 2003; Mario Ramírez Rancaño, *Ignacio Torres Adalid y la Industria Pulquera* (Mexico City: Instituto de Investigaciones Sociales, Universidad Nacional Autónoma de México, 2000).

42. Indeed, all the tropes that the beer companies trotted out in the 1920s had been previously used by the defenders of pulque since the colonial period and more recently by mezcal's partisans in the late nineteenth century. See Lázaro Pérez, *Estudio sobre el maguey llamado mezcal en el estado de Jalisco* (Guadalajara: Imprenta Ancira, 1887).

43. Ronald Takaki, *Iron Cages: Race and Culture in 19th Century America* (Oxford: Oxford University Press, 2000).

44. "Tequila Sauza, What It Is," December 14, 1933, APFJS.

45. Marie Sarita Gaytán, "Drinking the Nation and Making Masculinity: Tequila, Pancho Villa and the US Media," in *Toward a Sociology of the Trace, ed.* Herman Gray and Macarena Gómez-Barris (Minneapolis: University of Minnesota Press, 2010), 207–33.

46. Francisco de Jesús Aceves González, "Génesis de la Radiodifusión Jalisciense estudio aproximativo," *Comunicación y Sociedad* 4/5 (1989), 58–96.

47. Wolfgang Schivelbusch, *Tastes of Paradise: A Social History of Spices, Stimulants, and Intoxicants* (New York: Vintage Books, 1993), 39, 15–84.

48. Ibid., *Tastes of Paradise*, 85–95.

49. "Propaganda 'Tequila Sauza' Textos de Benjamín D. Castillo," August 1936, APFJS. Up until recently, tequileros produced three types of tequila: Blanco which is bottled right after distillation, Reposado which is aged a minimum of two months before being bottled, and Añejo which is bottled after a minimum of one year of aging.

50. "Como una mujer honrada, 'Tequila Sauza,' se impone por su propia pureza" ("Like an Honorable Woman, 'Tequila Sauza' prevails because of its purity"). "When we asked that charming woman who won in a beauty contest what kind of cream she used to keep her complexion so fresh and smooth, she responded without hesitation: *Crema Sauza,* the best of creams, a gift to my palate and [it] gives my cheeks the smoothness of fresh rose pedals." Rosy cheeks were a sign not only of good health but also of whiteness. "Propaganda 'Tequila Sauza' Textos de Benjamín D. Castillo," August 1936, APFJS.

51. "El Tequila Sauza . . . ha venido a convertirse por su calidad de pureza y exquisito bouquet, en la sensación mundial 1936!," 1936, APFJS.

52. Kelley R. Swarthout, *"Assimilating the Primitive": Parallel Dialogues on Racial Miscegenation in Revolutionary Mexico* (New York: Peter Lang, 2004).

53. Helen Delpar, *The Enormous Vogue of Things Mexican: Cultural Relations Between the United States and Mexico, 1920–1935* (Tuscaloosa: University of Alabama Press, 1992); Mariana Torgovnick, *Gone Primitive: Savage Intellects, Modern Lives* (Chicago: University of Chicago Press, 1990); Roger Bartra, "Paradise Subverted: The Invention of the Mexican Character," in *Primitivism and Identity in Latin America: Essays on Art, Literature, and Culture,* ed. Erik Camayd Freixas and José Eduardo Gonzaléz (Tucson: University of Arizona Press, 2000), 3–22.

54. Advertisement text circa 1933, APFJS.

55. "Radiodifusora Comercial X.E.D. Textos de Tequila Sauza," circa 1933, APFJS.

56. "I was young playboy, but when my father died 20 years ago I took over and modernized it all. Others have followed us in modernization." Francisco Javier Sauza, qtd. in Frank Meyer, "South of Border They Brew Away," *Miami Beach Daily News,* May 13, 1968.

57. Agraz, *Historia,* 89–91; Nancy Cleeland, "A Bottle Full of Fire," *San Diego Reader,* February 12, 1987, www.sandiegoreader.com/news/1987/feb/12/bottle-full-fire/.

58. Cleeland, "A Bottle Full of Fire."

59. See letters written to Louie Welch, Mayor of Houston, 1969; Enrique (Kika) de

la Garza, Congressman, 15th District, Texas, 1970; John Connally, Secretary of the Treasury, 1970, APFJS.

60. Letter to Antonio Armendáriz, Mexican ambassador to England, October 3, 1963, APFJS.

61. Letter to *Business Week*, February 13, 1968, APFJS.

62. *Tapatío* is the demonym for people and things from Guadalajara, the capital of the state of Jalisco.

63. Ronstadt was father of future rock star Linda Ronstadt. In 1969 Sauza was awarded the International Goodwill Award by the Tucson Trade Bureau. *Tucson Trade Bureau Bulletin*, September 5, 1969, APFJS.

64. Sauza refers to the Mayahuel as the "Goddess of Mezcal Mayahuel." Text of speech given by F. J. Sauza to the City Council of the City of Victoria, British Columbia, n.d. (circa 1972), APFJS.

65. Ranchero movies wove together comedy, popular music (mostly mariachi), and idyllic settings.

66. The ads usually made comparisons such as "Two great names! Torero: Capetillo. Tequila: Sauza. Both are from Jalisco." Manuel Capetillo (1926–2009), a famous Mexican bullfighter, was born in Ixtlahuacán de los Membrillos, Jalisco. "Two Great Names," circa 1962, APFJS.

67. C. Manuel García Gutiérrez, *Memoria Gráfica de Noches Tapatías* (Guadalajara: Tequila Sauza, 1983).

68. This connection was intentional: "Don Francisco Javier Sauza conceived of [*Noches Tapatías*] as a publicity campaign in which the national values, *la mexicanidad*, beauty and color or our *jirones patrios* [patriotic emblems] were exalted ... a publicity campaign that had to be a spontaneous song from the Mexican province [represented by Jalisco] to all the nation." Ibid., 19.

69. Among the most prominent of these intellectuals were José Vasconcelos, Agustín Yáñez, Antonio Gómez Robledo, and José López-Portillo y Weber.

70. Alteños were thought to eschew the ejido in preference of their small, homestead-like ranchos. This made them the darlings of Mexican conservatives, who opposed land redistribution, especially during the Cárdenas presidency. José Orozco, "*Esos Altos de Jalisco*: Immigration and the Idea of Alteño Exceptionalism, 1926–1952" (PhD diss., Harvard University, 1998); Olga Nájera-Ramírez, "Engendering Nationalism: Identity, Discourse, and the Mexican Charro," *Anthropological Quarterly* 67, no. 1 (1994), 1–14.

71. Carl J. Mora, *Mexican Cinema: Reflections of a Society, 1896–1988* (Berkeley: University of California Press, 1989); Joanne Hershfield and David Maciel, *Mexico's Cinema: A Century of Film and Filmmakers* (Wilmington, DE: Scholarly Resources, 1999).

72. José Vasconcelos, *La Flama* (Mexico City: Compañia Editorial Continental, 1959), 19; Orozco, "*Esos Altos de Jalisco*."

73. On social Catholicism, see Manuel Ceballos Ramírez, *El catolicismo social: un tercero en discordia*, Rerum Novarum, "*la cuestión social*" y *la mobilización de los católicos mexicanos (1891–1911)* (Mexico City: El Colegio de México, 1991).

74. On the Sinarquista movement, see Pablo Serrano Álvarez, *La batalla del espíritu: El movimiento sinarquista en el Bajío (1932–1951)*, Colección Regiones 2

(Mexico City: Conaculta, 1992); Jean Meyer, *El sinarquismo: un fascismo mexicano? 1937–1947* (Mexico City: Joaquín Mortiz, 1979).

75. "A little bit of Mexico in each bottle," ad, April 1958, APFJS.

76. "Italia también se inclina por Tequila Sauza," April 1964, APFJS. The word *inclina* is used to mean both "to bow" and "to favor."

77. Wolfgang Schivelbusch in *Tastes of Paradise* explains this logic in the following manner: "What makes drinking more important than eating is the fact that here the individual life or *soul* of a thing is being directly assimilated. In magical thinking every fluid symbolizes blood, and the blood or vital fluid of an animal or a plant [or a nation] *is* its soul" (168–69).

78. "C'est si bon!" director's notes, April 14, 1969, APFJS.

CHAPTER NINE

Essence and Identity

Transformations in Argentine Wine, 1880–2010

Steve Stein

A driving force for the development of business strategies for wine industries worldwide has been the assessment and targeting of the consumer market. In the case of Argentina, consumers and their tastes have changed substantially over the history of the industry from its inception in the 1880s. That history encloses three watershed periods, each with its own distinctive consumer market. In the first era, from the 1890s through the 1920s, an artisan industry grew to become the fifth largest in the world. The most visible feature of this rapid expansion was the appearance of virtual wine factories that turned out undifferentiated products exclusively for the domestic market, made up of the enormous numbers of Southern European immigrants that had begun to arrive in the country during the latter decades of the nineteenth century. The "wine culture" of this group regarded the beverage as essentially a staple, part of the daily meal; top priorities were easy access and low price. The second watershed period comprises the 1950s through the 1970s, when Argentina's major cities, especially the capital, Buenos Aires, experienced massive population growth fueled largely by internal migration from the provinces. The market continued to be exclusively national, and abundance and price continued to be wine culture priorities. Given the lack of consumer demand for diversity or quality, the industry pursued a "producer-centered" model that sought above all to maximize volume and minimize cost. The result was unremarkable and often palpably distasteful wines.

It took one hundred years and a precipitous drop in per capita domestic consumption for fundamental transformations of productive and commercial structures to be set in motion. They were part of a veritable "wine revolution" beginning in the 1990s that for the first time made quality a fundamental goal. Two cornerstones of the revolution were changes in the makeup of the market—no longer entirely national but, rather, increasingly international—and in the wine preferences of its consumers. The search for enjoyable tastes and the identification of wine with pleasurable and often special moments became priorities. Winemakers became aware that they needed to make their decisions based on a consumer-centered model if they expected to compete successfully for these changing and increasingly demanding markets. As a result, Argentina's wines have undergone a remarkable upswing in quality. Buttressed by international acclaim, they have finally become a source of pride and a positive component of national identity.

My analysis of each period begins with a discussion of the emergence and makeup of the core consumer market and an exploration of the distinctive meanings of wine—or wine cultures—that emerged. I then reproduce descriptions of the aroma and flavor profiles of representative wines, utilizing the writings of contemporaries who tasted them in order to determine the extent to which production decisions responded to consumer preferences or to other considerations. Finally, I undertake content analyses of the images reproduced on labels and in advertising to understand how wineries' perceptions of the wine cultures of consumers guided the creation of identities for their products.

The Founding Years: 1885–1920

The birth of Argentina's modern wine industry has a clearly identifiable date: May 25, 1885. That day marked the opening of the rail line between Mendoza, the principal wine-producing area, and Buenos Aires, the largest market. Wine had been produced in Mendoza since the mid-sixteenth century, but the two months of transport on the backs of mules to the urban centers of consumption entailed a prohibitively high cost, with most ruined on the way. The railroad reduced delivery time to three days.

While the takeoff of the industry might appear to have occurred quite suddenly, in preceding decades the local population and regional authorities were keenly aware of the prospects for growth, as Nancy Hanway shows in chapter 4 of this volume. As a result, by the mid-1870s, Mendoza's provincial government had already begun preparing for the birth of a modern wine industry. These steps included undertaking large irrigation projects to provide the water to create vineyards in Mendoza's virtual desert at the foot of the Andes, the establishment in 1881 of a tax exemption for vineyard plantings, and the institution in the 1890s of high tariff barriers on imported wines that virtually proscribed foreign competition for over a century. As part of the country's concerted effort to attract immigrants as a key building block for modernization—a principle enshrined in the 1853 constitution—Mendoza launched its own recruitment program in 1884 to attract southern Europeans with farming experience.[1]

Most important for the growth of wine production and consumption was precisely the arrival of those immigrant groups, but not so much to Mendoza as to Buenos Aires and Argentina's other large cities. The numbers were impressive. Between 1847 and 1939, the country received approximately seven million immigrants. The great majority came from Italy (three million) and Spain (two million). For the massive wave of people who left Europe for the New World, driven by harsh economic conditions and convulsed politics, Argentina's promise as a relatively peaceful and prosperous country that officially declared the attraction of immigrants to be an imperative (*poblar es gobernar*—to populate is to govern) made it an attractive destination. The demographic impact was undeniable; 60 percent of the population of the capital city and almost 30 percent of the population of the provinces of Buenos Aires, Córdoba, and Santa Fe were immigrants. For the nascent industry, the presence of people with a centuries-old tradition of wine as a fundamental part of life was a true godsend. A look at Argentina's consumption figures shows both the importance of wine for the immigrant consumers and their magnitude as a market. By the second decade of the twentieth century, Argentines of Southern European descent were drinking sixty-two liters per year, and together, Italian and Spanish immigrants consumed 80 percent of all the wine produced in the country.[2]

A list of descriptors from early twentieth-century "tasters" provides insights into the kinds of wines produced in Argentina during the initial period. Among those traits were "elevated alcohol content," "thick," "low acidity," "low tannins," "lack of individuality," "inconsistent," "lots of color but lacking in vibrancy," "cloudy." Taken as a whole, these beverages hardly appear to have had any pretensions to quality.[3] In part, these unenthusiastic characterizations derived from the enormously rapid pace at which the industry grew from infancy to adulthood. As turn-of-the-century wine expert A. N. Galante noted, "The growth of viticulture was so rapid . . . that in no way could oenology keep pace. In addition, given the type and goals of grape production, it was easy to establish wine-making as a manufacturing activity, and with almost assured success."[4] One early wine entrepreneur felt so confident about the potential that he actually suggested building a wine pipeline between Mendoza and Buenos Aires. Hurried growth to "multiply production to extreme limits" in order to reap the benefits of certain success in a market where demand usually outstripped supply tellingly affected the types of wines produced.[5]

Beyond optimistic perceptions of supply and demand, fundamental production decisions dictated the composition of the products. Argentina's wineries were, after all, selling to immigrants from countries where wine was considered a necessary part of the daily diet, an important source of calories, and an excellent substitute for nonpotable water. As authority Francisco Trianes noted, "There is a large population that needs wine and that consumes no less than one liter a day."[6] In quantitative terms, the "necessity measure" for this group is made clear by the fact that after bread and meat, the beverage occupied third place in the family shopping basket. Although they came from countries with well-established wine traditions, for these largely poor, male immigrants of peasant background, taste was not a significant consideration. Rather, their main concern was access to an abundant and, above all, cheap commodity. Three of the common characteristics noted by our tasters—high alcohol, thickness, and heavy color—permitted consumers to stretch their pesos as they stretched their wine through the process of diluting with water. Producers referred to this time-honored practice as "correction" or "straightening out." Wholesale distributors and sales outlets also favored these wines as they could stand a greater injection of water than more refined products.[7]

Two constants in the market of the early twentieth century, its immigrant origins and the demand for abundance and low price, clearly influenced the branding undertaken by wineries to identify themselves and promote their products. The labels affixed to barrels used for shipping wines to Buenos Aires and other major markets represent a key source for names and images. Given the relative absence of bottles as containers, these barrels on the shelves of bars and local markets displayed the faces of each brand to the public.

A label that clearly sought to identify with the origins of immigrant consumers was Bodegas López's El Vasquito (The Little Basque) (see figure 9.1). The label focuses on a male figure in Basque regional dress. As men made up the great majority of the initial waves of immigrants, the choice of gender would appear quite deliberate. His comfortable, straightforward pose helps assure consumers that the wine was genuine and pure as he appeared to be. It is no coincidence that the red and white of the

Figure 9.1. Circa 1910 label for the Bodegas López's El Vasquito, with an immigrant from the Basque region of Spain. (Image provided to the author by Bodegas López)

label and of the drinker's outfit are the traditional colors of the Basque region. And as the man is pictured with the traditional leather *bota* (wineskin) of his homeland, the message is clear: by drinking this wine, immigrants in Argentina could re-create the life of their native land. The label also subtly renders the immigrant's adopted country. Placing El Vasquito within a blue circle and on a background of a blue sky with white clouds, Bodegas López surrounded him with the colors of the Argentine flag, reproducing the nationalist discourse of the period. So, the man on the label, like the many immigrants who made up the consumer market, was firmly situated in his new country, but he could still have a foot in his homeland by drinking these wines that referred, visually at least, to his geographical and cultural origins. Ironically, the people and places portrayed

on this and similar labels targeting immigrants did not necessarily corre-
spond to the birthplaces of the wineries' owners. True, Bodegas López was
founded by a Spanish immigrant, but the family did not originate in the
Basque region; rather, they came from Andalucía.[8]

If the illusion of the homeland was a valued branding identity for the
wineries of this period, so was a testimonial to being modern and efficient.
In early twentieth-century Argentina, the most admired wineries were not
necessarily those that made the finest wines, but rather those that produced the most. These were the modern and well-equipped establishments that closely approximated the "wine factories" pictured on the 1910
barrel label of one of the country's largest, La Rural, founded by the Italian
immigrant Rutini family (see figure 9.2). The label is filled with the
symbols of mass production: imposing factory buildings at its center, a

Figure 9.2. Circa 1910 label for La Rural winery, depicting it as a modern and
efficient factory. (Image provided to the author by Vinos y Bodegas La Rural)

prominent stack belching smoke, workers carting barrels across the yard. The depiction of an uncluttered winery, with only two workers, together with reproductions of the two sides of a gold medal awarded to La Rural by the Argentine Industrial Union at the 1910 Centennial Industrial Exposition matched the widely espoused industrial ideology of the period that touted machines as capable of providing abundance for a better and happier life. Reflecting the drive for modernization current throughout Latin America, La Rural's barrel label highlighted the meanings of modernization for the Argentine wine industry: outfit installations with up-to-date equipment capable of generating efficiencies to achieve standardized and volume production. At the same time, the firm explicitly communicated priorities that fit well with those of Argentina as a nation: *trabajo y perseverancia* (work and perseverance).

Ups and Downs in Wine's Middle Period: 1950–1980

In this next watershed period of development, the wine factory pictured on La Rural's barrel label would become ubiquitous in the country's producing regions. Grape production continued to increase steadily; from 2 percent per year between 1910 and 1930, it accelerated in the 1940s and 1950s, approaching a rate of 3.5 percent. But these numbers paled in comparison to the jump of the next two decades. In 1972–1973 alone, the total amount of land in grape production went up by 10.5 percent, leading to an all-time high in hectares of three hundred fifty thousand in 1977.[9]

In large part, increased production was a response to growing demand from Argentine consumers during this period. In the mid-1940s, per capita consumption stood at fifty-five liters; by 1977 it reached its all-time high of eighty-eight.[10] Buenos Aires's ninety-nine liters per capita placed it roughly equal to Paris and Rome among the world's highest wine-drinking cities. This high level of consumption coincided with the recommendations of a member of the Argentine Wine Association's publication staff, who laid out guidelines for *daily* drinking: for workers, between 0.75 and 1.5 liters; employees and intellectuals, 0.75 liter; all adults, at least 0.5 liter at each meal; and children, according to their age, up to one glass of wine a day.[11]

The expectant urgings of industry spokespersons hardly explain the spike in consumption. In fact, there were multiple factors at work. In the decades following World War II, demographic growth and, in particular, the expansion of Argentina's urban population fueled by migrants from the countryside generated a consumer market that by 1980 had more than doubled in size. Equally or more important, beginning with the populist government of Juan Domingo Perón in 1946, were government policies supporting full employment and a significant redistribution of income that particularly favored lower- and middle-class urban populations. Workers' real wages rose 70 percent in the first three years of the Peronist regime and although later facing ups and downs, remained high for most through mid-1970s. At the same time, the relative price of wine continued to decrease as it had since the 1920s. The result was a serious shortage of wine from the beginning years of the Peronist government, exacerbated by the fact that producers had actually pulled up vines during the 1930s in response to economic hardships of the Depression years. The longtime dean of Argentine enologists, Raúl de la Mota, remembered how the regime, in the person of the first lady, Evita Perón, responded to the shortage by encouraging producers to water their wine in order to increase supply. That Evita herself met with the owners of the country's largest wineries to ensure that all "her workers" had sufficient wine on the table makes clear the importance of the beverage to the populist policies followed by the Peronist and subsequent governments that viewed the availability of low-priced consumer products as a blueprint for controlling politically pivotal urban populations.[12]

By the late 1960s several instances of ups and downs in demand led some to predict the inevitability of market saturation and the possibility of an imminent decline in consumption, but it appeared that industry leaders agreed with the 1973 affirmation by the head of the National Wine Institute's Economy and Development Department that "there are no indications that the post-War growth rate will change."[13] As one expert wrote in 1982, looking back over the previous three decades, the vision of a large and expanding domestic market "set the direction of the nation's wine industry, and the only condition for that production was to make enough wine to keep pace with the growth of consumption."[14]

The clearest and most reverberating expression of this volume obsession was the massive replanting of vineyards with the high-yielding *uva Criolla*, or Mission grape, that began in the 1960s. A century before, government and private efforts had led to the widespread introduction of French varietals, including Malbec, Cabernet Sauvignon, and Semillon, to replace uva Criolla vines originally brought by Spanish missionaries in the colonial period, as Nancy Hanway demonstrates in chapter 4. But now confidence in increasing demand convinced the major decision makers, public and private, that low cost and high production plainly outweighed all other considerations. This approach was reinforced by a series of laws passed in the 1960s that provided huge tax incentives for planting vine-yards and building wineries. Ostensibly intended to encourage agricul-tural production in arid zones on the eastern edge of the traditional vine-yard areas, these laws attracted many new investors with little commitment to, or knowledge of, making quality wine. Existing producers also seized the opportunities presented by these tax breaks to expand their facilities. The result was embodied in the familiar boast of industry leaders old and new, repeated no less than by the Office of the President of the Republic in 1970, that Argentina had become number one in the world in amount of wine produced per hectare of vineyard land, eighty hectoliters on aver-age, compared with forty in other wine-producing countries.[15]

An expanding consumer market and favorable tax laws encouraged mas-sive production of wines that received even harsher criticism than those made a half-century earlier. Given the historical stature of some of the critics, it is worth identifying them along with their evaluations. Nicolás Catena, the leading figure in Argentina's "wine revolution," observed, "*Vino común* [table wine] . . . basically an acidic alcohol mixture . . . The so-called *vinos finos* [fine wines] were super-oxidized where the fruit ended up being zero." Gaudencio Magistocchi, Argentina's most prominent enol-ogist in the 1930s to the 1950s, remarked, "Detestable wines with a taste of very pronounced, very disagreeable, bitter and herbaceous dirt. Almost no fruit." David Stevens, Director of the Masters of Wine Institute, from notes taken from a 1966 visit to Argentine wineries, categorized the wine as "Made for the 'Argentine Taste,' poor in color, little aroma and a flavor dominated by a high level of alcohol and oxidized." And Raúl de la Mota, Argentina's most prominent enologist from 1960 to 2000, had an even lesser opinion: "As one of my colleagues said, 'they're like pigeon dung.'"[16]

Judging by the extraordinarily high levels of per capita consumption, wine drinkers largely ignored these faults. Ultimately, Argentines' tacit ap-proval of poor-quality wines was the consequence of the role they assigned to the beverage. As Alberto Alcalde, Argentina's top agronomist of the pe-riod, put it, "There wasn't anybody who tasted wine. You just drank it."[17] In essence, the so-called "Argentine Taste," whether a characterization of wine drinkers' expectations or a term invented by the industry to affirm the "unique qualities" of their products, had remained constant since the early twentieth century. Whether they were the descendants of the wave of Southern European immigration, urban dwellers from similar origins, or internal migrants from the provinces, for them wine was simply a neces-sary component of daily meals. In this context, consumers fundamentally accepted what the wineries produced. And given the overall sameness of the Argentine wines of the period, as contemporary wine expert Jorge Aldo Perone affirmed: "Anyone who hopes to be more than a simple consumer . . . who would like to be a connoisseur, to know how to choose, buy, discuss, bring to mind, to in some way participate in the broad world of wine, unfortunately finds himself frustrated by the lack of differences." In light of these shortcomings, historian Adolfo Cueto is quite credible when he recalls that "giving a bottle of wine as a gift was an insult."[18]

Faced with the overall paucity of quality and diversity, Argentine consumers did adopt certain strategies. On the purchasing side, as was the case a half-century earlier, price was a major priority both for retailers and for their customers. Antonio Pulenta, the owner of Peñaflor, Argentina's largest winery during much of the period, remarked that shopkeepers preferred his cheaper if less well-known brands, as they invariably sold better. Indeed, one of the attractions of wine in the first place was that it cost significantly less than beer and even nonalcoholic drinks. The other major purchasing criteria were high levels of alcohol and color. To minimize unpleasant aromas and tastes, drinkers habitually added ice and soda water to each glass. The effects of cooling and dilution made them more palatable, and those wines with greatest color and alcohol tolerated maximum watering.[19]

In this context, industry leaders, both longtime winery owners and recent arrivals, implemented a variety of approaches to the market. Initially they devoted themselves to reinforcing the uniformity of expectations in order to obtain maximum profits. In production terms this meant standardizing wines by deliberately disguising any recognizable characteristics attributable to region, varietal, or vintage. In relation to consumers, the industry almost overwhelmingly rejected the concept of a segmented market and made virtually no effort to gauge buyer preferences. In 1967, the Argentine Wine Association's magazine explained that "learning about the tastes of our customers in order to satisfy them . . . is a virgin field." Six years later the same publication reported that nobody about to set up a new winery or make a new wine would consider first studying the market. In short, the industry was virtually engaged in anti-marketing.[20]

Advertising throughout this second period reflected the industry's approach. Typically, ads were bereft of images, simply communicating the availability of their products. Many of those that did include visuals featured photos of their factory-like wineries with accompanying text that touted the mechanized nature of winemaking process. The industrial-looking building that filled a 1963 ad for Bodegas y Viñedos Corces featured its belching smokestacks and the words "Industrial and Commercial." It bore an uncanny resemblance to the winery pictured on the La Rural "Work and Perseverance" barrel label produced fifty years earlier, reiterating the emphasis on size and efficiency. [21]

A decade later, Bodegas y Viñedos Gargantini communicated its identity by placing an image of their factory-like winery, with smokestacks and all, in the center of a wine glass (see figure 9.3). To support the message, they explained profusely the character of their firm, using such terms as *industrialization, modern machines,* and *factory* in the accompanying text, elements that underlined their identity as a producer of wines with the "Argentine Taste."[22]

Notwithstanding the confidence in the boundless growth of the market that accompanied the generalized disregard for consumer preferences, beginning in the late 1960s several prominent firms began to communicate new identities for wines to boost sales. Their pioneering efforts coincided with the rapid growth of mass media and, in particular, the extension of television throughout Argentina. Just as he would be a trailblazer twenty years later in moving the Argentine wine industry to stress quality over quantity, Nicolás Catena, who headed one of the country's largest wineries, in his words "invented the idea of publicity" with his highly successful 1967 television ad for Crespi Seco. As he commented in an interview with the author, "It was actually a red wine to which I added sugar, but I called [it] *seco* (dry) using the term *sec* from Champagne as a marketing ploy." Catena's commercial corresponded to what he called "emotional publicity":

The slogan was, "Beautiful things happen in the family, and many are lived with Crespi Seco." It revolved around a wife announcing to her husband that she is pregnant. In the first spot, the most famous, she calls him on the phone to tell him there will be a third person for dinner, and she puts a pair of booties on the table. Imagine, I did an ad with baby booties and wine! When he gets home and asks her what they should drink, she answers, "What we drink every day," and he pours her a glass of Crespi. It was an ad designed to say that we were good people, people who wanted good things for the whole family and for the baby. When we tested the Crespi spots, men actually cried. And if they didn't cry, we didn't put them on the air. This was so successful that by 1972 I had become the largest advertiser in Argentina, on all the television channels, all the magazines, all the billboards. . . . Obviously when things

Figure 9.3. Ad for Bodegas y Viñedos Gargantini, 1972, showing them as modern and industrialized. (Courtesy of Bodegas Argentina)

went well for me my competitors followed suit, they copied me, and the growth in consumption of the '70s was basically the result of that publicity, and not only for me.[23]

This path-breaking ad also emphasizes that Crespi Seco is a regular table wine, as the voiceover states twice, "Your everyday wine." The publicity was a novelty, but not the wine.

The remarkable success of these initial forays into mass media advertising encouraged Catena to contact a North American company to research the consumer market, resulting in the identification of four distinct market segments. The two most important were people for whom family was the top priority (within that cluster, he recalls, nearly half were of Italian origin); the other was a group he refers to as the "romantic segment." Catena's description of this group is intriguing:

> For this segment, the woman was very important in the decision to buy wine. Although the woman did it to satisfy the man, she made the decision. So we invented a brand called Casa de Troya, which was for the romantics, and all the television spots were fairy tales. The first spot was a story that took place in an inn, Casa de Troya, which was located in Spain in a small village where sick people were taken to be cured by drinking wine. In the first picture we cured a mute girl.[24]

The other two market segments were "the social climbers and the anarchists—anti-system, anti-everything—who today would be environmentalists or anti-globalists." Deemed smaller than the family and romance groups, Catena nevertheless included them in his marketing plan. He created a brand specific to each one: Algarbes for the *arrivistes*; and (the gaucho) Facundo for the "anti" category. The Algarbes ad portrayed a man, dressed in a tuxedo, arriving at a luxurious mansion where a beautiful young woman is climbing out of the swimming pool. They sit down together and drink a bottle of Algarbes. As Catena explained it, "With this ad we transformed a common table wine into an absolutely respectable drink." For Facundo: "We used the image of the famous gaucho because he was a symbol of social and political rectitude and of success."[25]

As Catena noted, the effectiveness of his strategy encouraged his competitors to follow suit; one of the first was Bodegas y Viñedos Peñaflor, which launched a campaign to link their wine to the life of the capital city, home of the largest number of consumers. In a 1969 ad, a bottle of Peñaflor Tinto (red wine) rises over Buenos Aires's most recognizable square (see figure 9.4). With a backdrop of imposing buildings and buzzing traffic, the wine becomes a modern symbol in a modern metropolis. At the same time, it dominates the city's most famous monument, the Obelisk, forging an intimate relationship with an icon of the urban landscape. For its part, the text takes pains to establish the wine's urban identity. "The taste of Buenos Aires. On its streets, in its people, in its songs, Buenos Aires shows its spirit. In the goodness of its wine, Buenos Aires shows its preference: Peñaflor Tinto, consistent quality."[26]

Figure 9.4. Ad for Peñaflor Tinto, 1969, showing the bottle in the modern setting of Buenos Aires. (Courtesy of Bodegas Argentina)

Peñaflor recognized that city life was not an unadulterated value for urban consumers. By the 1970s, a large proportion of the capital's population was made up of the unabated wave of provincial migrants that had begun arriving in the 1930s. While for this group the attraction of the modern elements of Buenos Aires life had figured prominently in the decision to move, many remained nostalgic about what they left behind. So the same winery that had identified its Peñaflor Tinto with the novel experiences of the city stressed the memories of provincial life in its ads for another of its products, Peñaflor Rosado. The *"vino de mi pueblo"* (wine of my hometown) campaign represented an updated version of the immigrant theme on early barrel labels (see figure 9.5). It combined images and text that appealed directly to those who had recently arrived in the country's large cities, much as José Orozco shows in chapter 8 for the Tequila Sauza ads in the 1980s. The imagery focused on the migrants' present circumstances by using a classic urban neighborhood scene as a backdrop to a food-laden table dominated by a nearly three-dimensional image of its *vino de mesa rosado* (rosé table wine). The text makes clear references to the past, evoking romanticized features of life *before* the big city.

> Everything is marvelous in my hometown, everything makes me happy and sad: the character of the old walls and the front doors of wood. . . . The land, the grass, the plants, the flowers, the streets and the church, the market, the plaza, the nights, the days, the afternoons with their siesta. . . . The people of my hometown are very good, everything is good, even the stones. . . . But the wine, the wine of my hometown is the most beautiful thing of all.

The parallels with El Vasquito barrel labels of the first period are patently clear. While the people sitting at the table are enjoying a meal in the modern city, the wine—in this case, Peñaflor Rosado—speaks to their nostalgia as it transports them back to their place of birth in the countryside.[27]

Beginning in the late 1960s, the proliferation of ads that featured role models and evoked ways of life were part of wineries' growing realization that constructing a different kind of relationship with their consumers could lead to greater sales and market share. In that vein, a 1967 article in the industry's trade magazine *Vinos y viñas* urged industry leaders to "create or publicize the image of your firms . . . real communication is needed between productive enterprises and that group of people called consumers . . . accentuate the special characteristics or personalize the product. . . . A common wine [*vino común*] becomes less common."[28] What is clear from

el vino de mi pueblo

Todo es maravilloso en mi pueblo,
todo me da alegría y tristeza:
el sabor de los viejos muros,
los portones de madera.

Pero el vino, el vino de mi pueblo,
el vino de mi pueblo
es la cosa más bella.

La tierra, la hierba, las plantas,
las flores, las calles y la iglesia,
la feria, la plaza, las noches, los días,
las tardes con su siesta.

Pero el vino, el vino de mi pueblo,
el vino de mi pueblo
es la cosa más bella.

La gente en mi pueblo es muy buena,
todo es bueno hasta las piedras:
el color, el color de las cosas nuevas
y también la vieja escuela.

Pero el vino, el vino de mi pueblo,
el vino de mi pueblo
es la cosa más bella.

Figure 9.5. Ad for Peñaflor Rosado, 1971, allowing the viewer to reminisce about their hometown. (Courtesy of Bodegas Argentina)

the Catena and Peñaflor ads, however, is that wine taste was yet to be one of the "accentuated characteristics." These and similar ads, nevertheless, expanded significantly on those earlier efforts that established identity by highlighting immigrants and factories; now, by featuring expectant parents or romantic couples or gauchos, they reproduced broad social values to establish a new meaning and place for wine in the life of the consumer.

If during these years the persistent decline in the quality of Argentine wine marked a step backward for the industry, the eventual recognition of the need to concoct/communicate the individual qualities of their products to differentiated consumer segments heralded a step forward. The industry's changing vision of consumers, even in the boom years, and their resulting publicity campaigns may actually have begun to sow the seeds of a new wine culture. Certainly in subsequent decades, for producers and consumers alike, the beverage came to take on a very different meaning than it had previously, and that meaning would constitute a central feature of Argentina's ongoing "wine revolution."

The Wine Revolution: 1990–

Despite increased sales during the 1970s, at the end of the decade growing numbers of observers began to warn that the market was reaching a saturation point. And indeed, in the following twenty years the industry experienced the worst crisis in its history, marked by a two-thirds decline in consumption. While it is clear that some of Argentina's producers knew they were in trouble, few foresaw the severity of the impending crisis. In the 1980s a staggering number of wineries would go bankrupt, many would be abandoned, and vast acres of vineyards would be pulled up to make room for other projects, particularly urban and suburban development. Wine consumption was suffering from a severe economic recession that cut deeply into the purchasing power of the working- and middle-class populations that had formed the core of the domestic market. Simultaneously, alternative beverages, specifically beer and soft drinks like Coca-Cola and 7Up, grew rapidly in popularity. It is very possible that the success of these alternative beverages originated, in part, from the gap between the rising expectations of consumers exposed to the mounting number of effective wine ads and the reality of being limited to altogether low-quality products. Whatever the cause, Argentine winemakers understood that future growth and development would not be possible without profound and fundamental changes. The first would be to seek new prospects beyond the protected domestic market that had been their sole concern for a century. To achieve that objective, producers would have to concentrate on making wines of sufficient quality to compete internationally, as well as in a changing domestic market. Guiding the whole process was the realization that the Argentine industry needed to change from its traditional goal of low-cost mass production to a focus on products that would appeal to consumers' tastes.

Once again, Nicolás Catena, whose media campaigns had made his Bodegas Esmeralda into one of the country's largest and most profitable producers, played a leadership role by redirecting his enterprise to the production of internationally competitive wines. Others soon followed suit, contributing to what became known as the "reconversion" of the Argentine wine industry. The process involved equipping wineries with the most up-to-date fermentation tanks and presses, importing oak barrels for aging—for the first time in over fifty years—and hiring top experts from the United States and Europe to help upgrade enological practices. While the initial thrust of advances in technology and professional competence focused largely on the winery, it quickly became clear that quality grapes were crucial for quality wines. By the mid-1990s the perception of Malbec's quality and potential had become broadly accepted, and the upgrading of vines in general became a fundamental priority. The push to replace uva Criolla with premium grape vines is borne out by the numbers. Malbec, which had remained at the 1984 level of ten thousand hectares into the early 1990s, rose 250 percent in extension by 2005. The growth of other fine varieties, including Cabernet Sauvignon, Syrah, Merlot, and Chardonnay, was even more dramatic, jumping up to seven or eight times in acreage. Overall, grapes with high enological value increased from approximately 20 percent of plantings in 1990 to 41 percent in 2001 and to 67 percent by 2007.[29]

Argentina's "revolutionized" wines stand in stark contrast to their predecessors, as Master of Wine Jancis Robinson makes clear: "It is difficult to exaggerate how much Argentine wines have changed in the past few years, wonderfully rich, sumptuous, voluptuous,"[30] characteristics that contrast dramatically to the "alcoholic," "thick," and "cloudy" wines of the foundation period and the "insipid," "dirty," "pigeon dung" products of the massive growth years. The appealing attributes assigned by Robinson to Argentina's new wines are echoed in the appraisals of the world's most prestigious critics. Robert Parker said: "Rich, intense and layered, bordering on opulent, pure and elegant, superb concentration and focus, impeccable balance, terrific depth, panache, complexity and unbridled deliciousness." The *Wine Spectator* wrote: "Powerfully rendered, opulent, lush, impressive depth and range, dense and layered, rich, ripe racy, full-throttle reds, remarkably supple, vivid, impressive precision and balance, exotic." And the *Wine Enthusiast* stated: "Huge and show finesse, mile-long finish is awesome, big, bold, rich, stout and smooth, mouth feel is fabulous, lush and giant, pure as can be, smooth as silk, lofty and rich, sexy."[31]

Just as their wines underwent dramatic changes, the industry's revolution prompted a fundamental change in the meanings of modernity. During its first century of development, modernity translated into a producer-centered model where decisions about the structuring and equipping of wineries were made with an eye to controlling costs and increasing volume. The result was undifferentiated, one-dimensional wine, but a beverage that fit with the expectations of the market. Responding to the downturn of the 1980s, winemakers became increasingly consumer-centric and began to prioritize the production of complex, multilayered wines. With upgrading of quality as the goal, modernity took on a whole new meaning. It now centered on the acquisition of cutting-edge technology and know-how to produce a diversity of distinctive wines capable of appealing to segmented markets of discriminating consumers.

Beginning in the 1990s leading executives increasingly identified the production of quality for export as the key to salvation. The success of their strategy soon became evident. The Argentina that twenty years earlier sold virtually no wine abroad quickly rose to seventh place among exporting countries. International sales took off decisively after 2001 when the combination of an undervalued peso and low and declining land and labor costs, the result of a severe economic crisis, made Argentine wines almost overnight international leaders in price/quality ratio. Sales to the United States experienced the greatest expansion, with annual growth exceeding 30 percent in most years, eventually making up one-third of all exports. Malbec became the star of this impressive export boom. Its 60 percent jump in 2009 made it the fastest growing varietal in the US market.[32]

Notwithstanding these dramatic successes, the recent emphasis on exports tends to obscure an important reality: Argentina's domestic market has continued to occupy a vital position in the calculations of the country's wineries. At eighth place, Argentina remains one of the world's largest wine-consuming countries. Even with its twenty-year decrease, bottoming out at twenty-nine liters per capita in 2005, the Argentines still drink some 80 percent of national output.[33]

A distinct shift in the preferences of Argentine wine drinkers over the past decade has actually reinforced production changes originally triggered by export initiatives. As overall consumers moved away from wine toward beer and soft drinks, wealthier and middle-class Argentines, many of whom spent their country's strong national currency in the 1990s on international travel, began to learn about and insist on "distinctive" wines that tasted "as good as" those they tried abroad. They have populated the proliferating wine clubs, fairs, and appreciation courses (estimated to have over ten thousand students as early as 2003). They are the readers of a mounting number of glossy magazines dedicated to the presentation and discussion of fine wines. A particularly clear indicator of this new interest in seeking and understanding quality has been the growth of shops dedicated exclusively to the sale of wine and other alcoholic beverages. With employees trained to respond to customers' queries, carefully designed displays of superpremium and often hard-to-find boutique bottlings and specially conditioned storage areas, these *vinotecas* (wine shops) have become ubiquitous in Argentina's major cities. Their appearance is particularly notable given that, prior to the late 1990s, it was almost impossible to find anything approaching a wine shop, even in the nation's capital. Until the turn of the century, major commercial outlets had continued to be corner grocery stores and some supermarkets.[34]

The wine culture of growing numbers of Argentine consumers has undergone a profound change, merging with worldwide tendencies where the beverage has ceased to be a staple placed on the table next to the rest of the daily meal and instead has become an integral element of a more expansive lifestyle. As French wine-marketing guru Michel Bourqui declared on a consulting trip to Argentina in 2000, "Before you worked for a wine drinking market. Today you have to take aim at a market that looks for pleasure."[35]

This fundamental change in wine culture, perhaps begun by the increased expectations generated by the publicity campaigns of the 1970s, was decisively influenced by the increased presence of export-driven superior wines. While the change was led by the wealthier sectors of the market, lower-income consumers also began to be more discriminating in their purchasing decisions, shifting away from the traditional view of wine as a simple commodity. Just like their wealthier compatriots, they began buying into the new wine culture that highlighted taste and lifestyle concerns. And fortunately for this group, the quality jump was not just limited to the premium segment. The application of new technologies and the replanting of vineyards affected the industry as a whole; even lower-end producers strived to improve their products as they responded to an ever more selective public that at all levels began opting for better wines.

Faced with consumers who no longer accepted wine as a simple commodity but, rather, appreciated it as an experience, Argentina's wineries sought to transform their identities and those of their products. This is most clearly reflected in their expanding use of publicity that featured a whole new series of attributes. A 2005 Catena ad for its moderately priced Alamos bottling, published in a widely circulated domestic wine magazine, boldly proclaimed the brand's international success, declaring that the prestigious British publication *Decanter* had rated it among the fifty best wines in the world. Images of *Decanter*'s cover and the pages referring to Alamos dominate the ad. The message for domestic consumers is clear: when purchasing an Argentine wine, you can be sure you will be pleased if you select one that has achieved international stature.[36] Argentine consumers' affinity for foreign recognition mirrors that of their Mexican counterparts in the 1980s, as José Orozco shows in chapter 8.

The Catena ad marked a novel approach to the market, providing concrete details to guide consumers' purchasing decisions. While the 1910 La Rural label had made an implicit reference to the contents in the barrel by symbolizing a reliable and abundant beverage, "informational" ads in the 2000s have gone much further to emphasize specific wine components such as *terroir*, grape varietal, and production methods. These ads demonstrate the degree to which Argentine consumers had, by the early 2000s, begun to seek identifiable characteristics in their wines. A prime example is Finca Flichman's stress on the importance of terroir in its ad declaring that the Tupungato and Barrancas wines, shown on a dramatic black-and-white background of the snow-covered Andes, "Carry the land in their soul" (see figure 9.6). Picturing the Andes has been a persistent element for establishing a clear sense of place in Argentine wine ads, but Finca Flichman went beyond the simple assertion of terroir to explain that the distinctive qualities of each of its new site-specific wines was the product of "different land, different water, different climate and different men." The winery heightened its emphasis on the individuality of terroir by placing distinguishing photos on the labels of each of these individual products. The proliferation of informational ads reveals that wineries realized the need to adapt the content of their ads to changing market expectations. If Argentine drinkers prized complete information on what to expect from their wine, these ads certainly provided it.[37]

Consumers seeking hard facts to decide which wine to drink constituted only one component of what Catena correctly saw as a segmented market, a market that would become infinitely more diverse in the decades following his initial study. While information-filled ads like Flichman's have become matter-of-course, ads that made virtually no reference to the concrete characteristics of the liquid in the bottle became even more commonplace. As in the earlier ads of Catena and Peñaflor, references to the ideal—whether lifestyles, role models, or relationships—represent the most pronounced pattern. Familia Zuccardi's 2003 ad placed its bottle and tiny labels in a secondary position in relation to the classy footwear that dominates the page (see figure 9.7). The caption of the main picture reads "Detalles" (Details), and the consumer is informed that "small details say a lot about you." Buying, drinking, and serving Zuccardi's wines

Figure 9.6. Ad for Tupungato and Barrancas wines, 2003, appealing to Argentine consumers' need for information about terroir and other features. (Courtesy of *Master Wine*)

set consumers apart, establishing their elevated place in the world. Notably, the bottlings pictured here were not top-of-the-line products but came from the winery's middle range, thereby offering the patina of elite status to purchasers from broader segments of the consumer market.[38]

Depicting a scene of secure elegance, class, and style, Norton's 1997 ad for its top-of-the-line Perdriel offered a number of rewards (see figure 9.8). In the foreground, an expensive gold watch rests on a cherished book, denoting inherited style. The highlighted female form of the curved bottle suggests sensuality in the wine experience. The hunting dog passes its loyalty to the adjoining bottle. And by presenting a minimally detailed couple

Figure 9.7. Ad for Familia Zuccardi for middle-of-the-line wines that allowed consumers to feel elite, 2003. (Courtesy of *Joy de los Placeres: la revista latina de vinos y gastronomía*)

Figure 9.8. Ad for Norton Perdriel wine, 1997, offering consumers "the best in life," including wealth, status, and romance. (Courtesy of Bodega Norton)

in the background, shown only in silhouette, Perdriel offers anyone the possibility to be them, despite the fact that the relatively high cost of the wine suggests that it was clearly targeting the elite segment. Its price notwithstanding, the ad's text reflected the broad contours of Argentina's new wine culture, affirming that the beverage is no longer a simple commodity but "the best thing in life," giving so much enjoyment that it makes "every moment unforgettable."[39]

Irrespective of price, the wines featured in the Zuccardi and Norton ads served to affirm the elevated class identities of their consumers, a process that could not occur as long as the beverage was considered a mere staple. With the transformation of the image as well as the substance of Argentine wine, for the first time it became an article of pride, a far cry from something one would not dare give as a gift. Encouraged by its new status, consumers enrolled in classes or read specialized magazines, not only to increase their knowledge and appreciation but also to raise their place in society by ensuring that they made the "right choices" when purchasing, serving, or discussing wine. Moreover, as Argentine exports increasingly pervaded the shelves of wine shops and supermarkets in the United States and Europe, foreign consumers came to identify Argentina with quality wine, leading finally to its emergence within Argentina as a highly positive symbol of national identity.

Although not based on any quantitative measuring of the most frequent themes in Argentine winery publicity, the relationship between wine and pleasure enunciated in the Perdriel ad has clearly become an increasingly important goal. Indicative of this trend is the prevalence of ads that connect wine with relations between the sexes. Two recurrent components in "relationship portrayal," a common advertising theme, are *eros*, which stresses the erotic, and *agape*, which highlights the romantic ideal of selfless love. A 2003 Navarro Correas ad straightforwardly portrays the eros side (see figure 9.9). While there is a good deal of text at the bottom enumerating the wines of their Colección Privada (Private Collection), plus a description of how they were made, all attention is focused on the dominant, self-absorbed macho figure basking in the rapt gaze of an ardent female. Is there any question about which brand of wine he should be drinking, as the last sentence in the text states, "to enjoy the good moments of life"?[40]

In the same year Pacheco Pereda published an ad for its Malbec, which for the most part presented images depicting the agape relationship but also contained some elements of the eros side. The ad is divided into two

Figure 9.9. Ad for Navarro Correas wines, 2003, which promise to allow drinkers "to enjoy the good moments of life," like time with a beautiful woman. (Courtesy of *Joy de los Placeres: la revista latina de vinos y gastronomía*)

planes, "Day" on top, and "Night" on the bottom. The day section, with its vineyard, a sepia-toned, timeless image of a worker carrying fruit for the harvest and the eventual bottled product, depicts the conversion of grapes into wine. The text refers to the wholesome elements of "plenty" and "nature." If the day is about work, the night is about pleasure. In "night" a couple looks lovingly into each other's eyes, with expressions and body language that seem to represent a pure and romantic relationship. But the text speaks of "satisfaction," and the sensual depiction of the glass of red wine, with its angle, color, and texture, suggests this can be achieved on many levels through Pacheco Pereda.[41]

While sexual innuendo has been an important feature of innumerable ads, images and texts have undergone something of an evolution. In 1997 Bodegas Suter launched its Suter Rojo with an intense, blood red label that communicated a kind of oriental exoticism; the intention was "to modernize the product by employing the new methods of wine marketing in Argentina."[42] Six years later when driving by the winery, located at the entrance to the wine-producing town of San Rafael in Mendoza Province, I was confronted with an updated representation of Suter Rojo, this time on an enormous billboard (see figure 9.10). The label and the bottle had

Figure 9.10. August 2003 billboard ad for Suter Rojo, utilizing an "exotic"-looking woman to demonstrate that sensuality and elegance are within reach of the consumer. (Photograph by the author)

not changed from 1997, but in 2003 they were dominated by an exotic and seductive, partially clad woman urging: "Let yourself be captivated by the sensuality of Rojo." Her lean, inviting body and Moorish eyes are a far cry from the domesticated housewife of Catena's groundbreaking Crespi Seco ad aired some forty years earlier. The elegance of her pose perhaps was meant to match the elegance of Suter Rojo. But hers (and the wine's) is an attainable elegance, just as her engaging gaze and the implicit offering of her partially covered breast shows that she and Suter Rojo are within reach. Both are available objects of desire.

Conclusion

Argentina's wine, its consumers and their drinking cultures, and the linkage between producers and the market underwent significant changes over the course of the last century and a half. For the first hundred years, the changes were relatively modest. Consumers viewed wine as a daily staple, demanding little in terms of quality or diversity. Producers prized high volume and low price to maximize competitiveness. Their limited efforts to connect to consumers ranged from lionizing the industrial efficiency of their installations to fashioning associations between their wines and the assumed origins of customers.

The decade of the 1980s marked a watershed for nearly every facet of the Argentine wine industry. Stimulated in part by the wineries' own advertising campaigns in the previous decade, the culture of Argentine consumers began to undergo changes as dramatic as the wines in their bottles. The elements of pleasure and lifestyle became more and more decisive, paralleling the expectations of the increasing numbers of international consumers of Argentine wines. For their part, the country's wineries not only began turning out products that could appeal to desires of domestic as well as international consumers but also increasingly tailored their public images to communicate that appeal. In all its facets, the Argentine wine industry had truly experienced a revolution.

Notes

University of Miami Professor Tom López provided invaluable insights on the analysis of the images and expert help in reproducing several of the photographs that accompany the text.

238 • *Steve Stein*

1. On the antecedents of the Mendoza wine industry, see Ana María Mateu, "Mendoza entre el orden y el progreso 1880–1918," in *Mendoza, a través de su historia*, ed. Arturo Roig, Pablo Lacoste, and María Satlari (Mendoza, Argentina: Editorial Caviar Bleu, 2004), chap. 7.

2. On immigration trends, see Pablo Lacoste, *El vino del inmigrante: Los inmigrantes europeos y la industria vitivinícola argentina* (Mendoza, Argentina: Universidad del Congreso, 2003), esp. 32–33. Similarly, by 1895, 83 percent of Mendoza wineries were owned by immigrants. See Mateu, "Mendoza entre el orden y el progreso," 6. Figures on wine consumption are found in Alejandro E. Bunge, *Informe del Ingeniero Alejandro Bunge sobre el problema vitivinícola* (Buenos Aires: Compañía Impresora Argentina, 1929), 128.

3. Pedro Arata, *Investigación vinícola: Informes presentados al Ministro de Agricultura por la Comisión Nacional* (Buenos Aires: Talleres de la Oficina Meteorológica, 1903), 90, 136.

4. A. N. Galante, *La industria vitivinícola Argentina* (Buenos Aires: Talleres S. Ostwald, 1900), 94.

5. Manuel Lemos, *Algunos apuntes sobre la cuestión vitivinícola en Mendoza: Orientaciones necesarias* (Mendoza, Argentina: Gutenberg, 1922), 52. Information on the wine pipeline was found in William J. Fleming, "Regional Development and Transportation in Argentina: Mendoza and the Gran Oeste Argentino Railroad, 1914" (PhD diss., Indiana University, 1976), 53.

6. Francisco Trianes, *La viña bajo la tormenta* (Buenos Aires: Librería y editorial El Ateneo, 1938), 140.

7. Santiago E. Bottaro, "La industria vitivinícola entre nosotros" (thesis, Universidad de Buenos Aires, Facultad de Ciencias Económicas, 1917). The information on wine's importance as a consumer good comes from Bunge, *Informe*, 8.

8. An excellent discussion on wine branding in this period is contained in Lacoste, *Vino del inmigrante*, esp. 173–76, 267, 316–25.

9. Daniel Aspiazu and Eduardo Basualdo, *El complejo vitivinícola argentino en los noventa: Potencialidades y restricciones* (Buenos Aires: Centro de Estudios y Promoción Agraria [hereafter CEPA], 2000), 8.

10. Instituto Nacional de Vitivinicultura, "Consumo de mercado interno," http://www.inv.gov.ar/est_consumo.php, accessed July 8, 2010.

11. José Ernesto Riveros, "El vino, sus propiedades y su consumo," *Vinos, viñas y frutas*, May 1954, 531.

12. Raúl de la Mota, interview with the author, Mendoza, Argentina, August 2004. Information on real wages is from Gilbert W. Merkx, "Sectoral Clashes and Political Change: The Argentine Experience," *Latin American Research Review* 4, no. 3 (1969), 96.

13. Mario Domingo Rodríguez, "El 'Gran Buenos Aires,' extraordinario consumidor de vino," in *Anuario vitivinícola Argentino*, ed. Asociación Vitivinícola de Argentina (Buenos Aires: Editorial La Empresa Agropecuaria, 1973), 38–40.

14. Aldo Biondolillo, "Exportaciones vitivinícolas argentinas," in *Crisis vitivinícola: Estudios y propuestas para su solución*, ed. Eduardo Díaz Araujo et al. (Mendoza, Argentina: Universidad de Mendoza, Editorial Idearium, 1982), 129.

15. Argentina Secretaría General, *Vitivinicultura* (Buenos Aires: Secretaría General de Argentina, 1970), 16–17. For a brief but enlightening analysis of the vineyard

replanting, see Polly Maclaine Pont and Hernán Thomas, "How the Vineyard Came to Matter: Grape Quality, the Meaning of Grapevines and Technological Change in Mendoza's Wine Production," *Universum* 22, no. 1 (2007), 218–34. On the content of the laws, see Ricardo Augusto Podestá, "Intervención del Estado," in Díaz Araujo, *Crisis vitivinícola*, 64–65.

16. Nicolás Catena, interview with the author, Mendoza, Argentina, June 2005; Raúl de la Mota, interview with the author, Mendoza, Argentina, August 2003; David Stevens, interview with the author, telephone interview from Miami, Florida, October 2006; Gaudencio Magistocchi, *Tratado de enología: Técnica adaptada a la vinificación cuyana* (Mendoza, Argentina: Talleres Gráficos J. Peuser, 1934), 708, 831.

17. Alberto Alcalde, interview with the author, Mendoza, Argentina, August 2004.

18. Jorge Aldo Perone, *Identidad o masificación: Una encrucijada en la industria vitivinícola argentina* (Mendoza, Argentina: Universidad Nacional de Cuyo, Facultad de Ciencias Económicas, 1985), 18; Adolfo Cueto, interview with the author, Mendoza, Argentina, August 2003; CEPA, Equipo de Economías Regionales, *La economía vitivinícola en la década del 70* (Buenos Aires: CEPA, 1984), 11–12.

19. Augusto Pulenta, interview with the author, Mendoza, Argentina, June 2005. Information on wine pricing was obtained from Centro de Estudios y Promoción Agraria, *La economía vitivinícola*.

20. *Vinos y viñas*, July–August 1967, 658; José de Lamo, "Investigación de mercado, clave del éxito," *Vinos y viñas*, July 1973, 4.

21. *Vinos y viñas*, March 1963, 34.

22. Asociación Vitivinícola Argentina, *Anuario vitivinícola argentino, the Argentine wine-growing yearbook* (Buenos Aires: Editorial La Empresa Agropecuaria, 1972), 48.

23. Nicolás Catena, interview with author, Mendoza, Argentina, June 2005. The spot can be viewed at http://www.youtube.com/watch?v=loKMwfyoLxI, July 9, 2010.

24. Catena interview. One of the Casa de Troya spots can be viewed at http://www.youtube.com/watch?v=Rkrd2KZuRYM. July 9, 2010. A similarly romantic ad from the period for a Mil Rosas may be viewed at http://www.youtube.com/watch?v=QVJZsTEHG90, July 9, 2010.

25. Catena interview. *Facundo* refers to one of Argentina's legendary gaucho figures, Juan Facundo Quiroga, the so-called *Tigre de los Llanos* (Tiger of the Plains), who led several gaucho armies in successful campaigns in 1820s Argentina.

26. The description of the Sabor Buenos Aires campaign is in *Vinos y viñas*, July 1969, 13. The print ad appeared in *Vinos y viñas*, May 1969, 2.

27. *Vinos y viñas*, June 1971, 5.

28. Jorge J. Melillo, "El diseño y la empresa moderna," in *Vinos y viñas*, July–August 1967, 685.

29. On the increase in premium grape plantings, see Instituto Nacional de Vitivinicultura, "V censo vitícola nacional," http://www.inv.gov.ar/PDF/Estadisticas/RegistroVinedos/registrovinedossuperficie2005, accessed June 11, 2010; Roxana Badaloni, "Nace una nueva gerencia vitícola," *Bodegas y Terruños* 2 (July 1999), 42–45; Gerald A. McDermott, "The Politics of Institutional Renovation and Economic Upgrading: Recombining the Vines That Bind Argentina," *Politics and Society* 35 (2007), 109; Luis A. Fermosel. "Las uvas de primera calidad duplican en hectáreas a las criolla grande y cerezas," *Los Andes* (Mendoza), April 16, 2007. For more information on the reconversion process, see Steve Stein, "New Markets and New Strategies in Argentina's

Wine Revolution," *Economics, Management, and Financial Markets* 5, no. 1 (2010), 64–98.

30. Jancis Robinson, "Argentina Gets More Polish," *Jancis Robinson.com*, October 11, 2008, http://www.jancisrobinson.com/articles/a200810073.html, accessed May 31, 2010.

31. Robert Parker, "Argentina's Greatest Wines," Parker, "2007 mendel unus," *Wine Advocate*, December 31, 2008, http://www.mendel.com.ar/img/prensas/68.pdf; *Businessweek*, May 29, 2008. Other comments by Parker are at: http://www.business week.com/lifestyle/content/may2008/bw20080529_268512.htm; Parker, "2006 mendel unus," *Wine Advocate*, August 31, 2009, http://www.mendel.com.ar/img/prensas/ 53.pdf; and Parker, "Argentina Is the Most Exciting New World Country," *Wines of Argentina*, July 1, 2009, http://www.winesofargentina.org/en/mercados/uk/ver/2009/ 07/01/e-robert-parker-argentina-is-the-most-exciting-new-world-country/; James Molesworth, "More Malbec Please," *Wine Spectator*, December 2008, 105–6. See also: Molesworth, "Malbec Madness," *Wine Spectator*, December 2009, 100; Michael Schachner, "Malbec in the Spotlight," *Wine Enthusiast*, February 9, 2010, http://www .winemag.com/Wine-Enthusiast-Magazine/February-2010/Top-10-Argentine-Malbecs -of-the-Past-Year/.

32. Patricia Ortiz, interview with the author, Miami, Florida, April 2008. On price competitiveness, see David J. Lynch, "Golden Days for Argentine Wine Could Turn Cloudy," *USA Today*, November 16, 2007, http://www.usatoday.com/money/world/ 2007-11-15-argentina-wine_N.htm?csp=34. Recent information on exports is contained in Laura Saieg, "Malbec Consumption Triples," *Winesur*, May 12, 2010, http:// www.winesur.com/top-news/malbec-consumption-triples; *Wines of Argentina*, "Frequently Asked Questions," http://www.winesofargentina.org/en/faq/, accessed June 2, 2010.

33. Instituto Nacional de Vitivinicultura, "Consumo de mercado interno," http:// www.inv.gov.ar/est_consumo.php, accessed July 8, 2010; and *Wines of Argentina*, "Export Stats," http://www.winesofargentina.org/en/estadistica/exportacion/, accessed June 2, 2010.

34. Denise González Eguilior, "Una tendencia que se consolida: Las vinoteras de Buenos Aires apuestan y ganan," *Vinos y viñas*, May 2003, 38–43; ad from *El Conocedor*, Buenos Aires, June 2002, inside front cover and page 1.

35. Qtd. in *Bodegas y terruños* 6, May 2000, 28. Alejandro Luque, the business manager of Salentein, one of the country's fastest growing wineries, offered a perceptive description of the transformed wine culture in Denise González Eguilior, "Las estructuras comerciales se adaptan: Hacia el jardín de la abundancia," *Vinos y viñas*, July 2003, 37. On the shift to quality in domestic consumption, see also Ana María Ruiz and Hernán Vila, "Cambios en la demanda de vinos en el fin del milenio," *IDIA XXI, Revista de información sobre investigación y desarrollo agropecuario* 1 (November 2001), 44; and Hugo Centrángolo et al., *El Negocio de los Vinos Finos en la Argentina* (Buenos Aires: Universidad de Buenos Aires, Facultad de Agronomía, 2002), 62.

36. From *El Conocedor*, June–July 2005, 15.

37. Finca Flichman ad from *Master Wine*, 5, no. 32 (2003), 7.

38. Ad in *Joy de los Placeres: La revista latina de vinos y gastronomía*, January–February 2003, 17.

39. Ad in *Profesional del vino: Revista para el consumidor*, April 1997, 35.

40. Ad in *Joy de los Placeres: La revista latina de vinos y gastronomía*, January–February 2003, 79.

41. Ad in *Master Wine*, 2003, 21.

42. Juan Fosch, "Suter rojo," *Profesional del vino: Revista para el consumidor*, April 1997, 67.

CHAPTER TEN

Of Chicha, Majas, *and* Mingas

Hard Apple Cider and Local Solidarity in Twenty-First-Century Rural Southern Chile

Anton Daughters

Situated just above Patagonia, southern Chile's Región de los Lagos (Lakes Region) is a wild stretch of territory marked by volcanoes, fjords, and cold-weather rainforests. Every summer, neighbors in rural sectors of this lacustrine region band together for a practice that has become a centerpiece of their identity as rural Chileans: the *maja de manzana*. Part work session, part party, the *maja* is, simply stated, the production of hard apple cider — *chicha de manzana*. It is a process that involves the gathering and mashing of apples and, not infrequently, the consumption of large amounts of fermented reserves from the previous year. The practice dates back more than three centuries, combining Native American labor arrangements, local alcohol production techniques, and a fruit imported from Europe in the mid-sixteenth century. Today, with extractive export industries increasingly shaping the regional economic landscape, the maja is one of the few collective gatherings between neighbors that helps maintain the long tradition of labor reciprocity with which these rural Chileans so strongly identify. Indeed, beyond its practical functions, the maja has become an act of solidarity and cultural affirmation in the face of globalization and economic change.

Chicha in Chile

In Chile and throughout Latin America, *chicha* can refer to a variety of fermented drinks derived from grains, roots, fruits, and nuts. Any discussion of chicha, therefore, should begin with an examination of the term itself and the meanings it can convey in different parts of Chile. In northern Chile, *chicha* typically refers to fermented maize, a drink that, as discussed in chapter 1 of this volume, dates back centuries before the arrival of Europeans to the region. This maize variety continues to be popular today throughout Central and South America, particularly in the Andean highlands. Many linguists consider chicha to be a derivative of the word *chichah co-pah*, meaning "maize drink" in the language of the Cuna, a Central American indigenous group. Given the importance of corn as a staple crop prior to contact, as well as this linguistic connection between chicha and maize, there is general consensus that this variety of chicha is, at least historically, the most commonly produced and consumed throughout Latin America.[1]

In Chile's Norte Chico and central regions, however, the term *chicha* is associated less with the ubiquitous maize-based drink than with an alternate variety—fermented grape juice. *Chicha de uva*, a rudimentary, homemade wine sometimes referred to as *vino ordinario* (common wine), dates back to the introduction of grapes and vineyards to central Chile by the first Spanish settlers in the mid-1500s.[2] Although its consumption is generally associated with the Fiestas Patrias—Chile's September 18 independence day celebrations—rural households throughout this north-central portion of the country produce, store, and sell the drink year round.

South of Chile's Bío Bío River, in a section of the country encompassing Concepción, Valdivia, Osorno, Puerto Montt, and the Archipelago of Chiloé, chicha is more commonly associated with yet other varieties of fruits: strawberries, Calafate berries, the fruits of the native molle tree and *murtilla* shrub, and the *piñones* (pine nuts) produced by *Araucaria* trees. As with maize chicha, fermented drinks from these native fruits were widely consumed around the time of contact with Europeans. The Spanish soldier and chronicler Francisco Núñez de Pineda, who traveled the region in the early 1600s, lavished praise on them, calling chicha "the greatest gift" a host could bestow upon a stranger and revealing a penchant for varieties that were "strong, spicy, and well-aged."[3] Writing later that same century, the Jesuit priest and historian Diego de Rosales described chicha as central to the courtesy and hospitality rites of indigenous custom. "They say it is better than wine," he wrote, "and the delight of all gatherings."[4]

Since the seventeenth century, however, the most common form of chicha to emerge in this southern end of Chile is one made of a fruit that, like grapes, was brought to the Americas by Europeans: the apple. As with other Old World fruits found in Chile, apples were introduced to the *valle central*—the fertile swath of land that runs several hundred miles to the north and south of Santiago—by the first Spanish settlers in the mid-sixteenth century. Within a few generations, the fruit was common throughout Chile. Apple trees were growing wild in the south where the cold, damp climate was favorable to dozens of varieties, and cider—both fresh and fermented—had become a significant regional subsistence product that enjoyed modest success as a regional export.[5] When Charles Darwin visited the area in 1834, he commented on the pervasiveness of apple trees and the speed with which they could be grown. He noted admiringly that most apples were particularly well suited for cider: "Not above one in a hundred have any seeds in its core. . . . In three years," he added, "it is possible to have an orchard of large, fruit-bearing trees."[6]

Today, southern Chile is dotted with apple orchards. In the Los Lagos region's Archipelago of Chiloé, where apple trees are particularly abundant, the fruit is ascribed qualities ranging from the medicinal to the supernatural. Some residents believe that placing an apple near the head of an asthmatic child while that child sleeps will, over the course of a month, cure the boy or girl of their ailment. Others swear that dreaming of certain varieties of apples can carry particular consequences: yellow apples portend good health, green apples are a sign of sorrows to come, while apple trees in a dream foretell of a death in the household. Still other residents of the region believe that an apple bundled against a man's chest and hidden from view will help that man win over the woman of his choosing. At the proper moment, explains cultural historian Renato Cárdenas, the man should offer the apple to the woman he is interested in. If she accepts and eats it, "he will be able to conquer her and they will make love with mutual satisfaction."[7]

Local scholars point out that these beliefs, many of which are laced with biblical overtones, are reflective of the centrality the apple has acquired in local lore and custom. This has to do in large part with the fact that apples are the source of what has been the most common drink in the region for the past several centuries: chicha. In a 2005 book on the botany of Chiloé, Cárdenas, a native of the archipelago, and Carolina Villagrán Moraga, a biologist at the University of Chile, wrote that "the apple *is* chicha for Chilotes."[8] This correlation between apples and chicha, as well as the broader cultural significance of both products, is best understood by examining the unique history of the region and the development of the practice of the maja de manzana.

Majas and Mingas

In 2006 I traveled to the Archipelago of Chiloé for a year of anthropological fieldwork. My research, aimed in part at documenting rural livelihoods in the region, gave me a firsthand view of long-standing subsistence practices. Among these was the gathering and mashing of apples: the maja.

The first maja I witnessed took place in Llingua, an island community of about a hundred families located along the eastern side of the Archipelago of Chiloé—geographically speaking, the heart of the Los Lagos region. It was a rare sunny day in Llingua as the Mansilla family gathered in their small orchard with a dozen neighbors and friends. Using long wooden poles cut for the occasion, the men, women, and children in the group spent the morning knocking hundreds of apples off the gnarled but lush trees scattered across their backyard. They used swift, deliberate motions, sometimes crouching for a better angle, then grinning at their success at dislodging hard-to-reach fruit. The apples were collected, tossed in nylon sacks, and stored in a wooden shed for mashing later in the week.

The occasion had a festive feel to it, with food and drink offered by the Mansillas as partial compensation for the help provided by neighbors. Nevertheless, as beneficiaries of the work party, the Mansillas remained indebted to those who had lent their labor that day. They would repay their friends and neighbors with their own sweat and muscle when the need arose. No specific date or task had been set for the anticipated acts of reciprocity; however, a general sense of mutual dependence had been strengthened between the parties, with the weight of indebtedness shifting to the Mansillas.

The labor reciprocity carried out as part of the maja that day was reflective of a work system that had been in place in the region for at least five hundred years. At the time of the arrival of Europeans, the Los Lagos region was occupied by an indigenous group known as the Huilliche. An offshoot of Chile's largest Native American tribe (the Mapuche), the Huilliche were a sedentary, agricultural people who migrated south from what is today south-central Chile several centuries before contact. With a diet consisting largely of fish, shellfish, and potatoes, the group was loosely organized into villages of scattered households.[9] Each household generally oversaw its own plot of land. However, projects that required greater manpower than what a single household could provide—the planting or harvesting of a large potato field or the construction of a dwelling, for example—were carried out by way of a reciprocal labor arrangement common among other indigenous groups in Central and South America: the *minga*. Mingas essentially amounted to labor swapping or labor sharing within communities. Because they were based on relationships of mutual dependence, they had the effect of establishing, and reinforcing over time, a sense of obligation and solidarity among neighbors. Years and generations of such collaboration ultimately strengthened official kinship networks within the group while also creating practical, nonconsanguine ones. Indeed, social networks among the Huilliche were often as much based on reciprocal labor relationships as on familial blood ties.

In many parts of Central and South America, the practice of the minga faded in relevance — in some cases disappeared entirely — with the imposition of Spanish institutions and work patterns beginning in the sixteenth century. However, in southern Chile, particularly the Archipelago of Chiloé, mingas remained central to the subsistence strategies and social structures of communities well into the twentieth century. The reasons for this have to do with the particular combination of circumstances — geographic, political, and economic — that affected the inhabitants of the region.

Colonial Chiloé

By the mid-1500s, Spain had established settlements on the southwestern coast of the continent as far south as Osorno. Most of what is today known as the Los Lagos region was unoccupied by Europeans, settled primarily by Mapuches and Huilliches. That changed in 1567, when Rodrigo de Quiroga, the son-in-law of Chile's appointed governor, launched an expedition aimed at settling the extensive Archipelago of Chiloé about one hundred miles south of Osorno. With the help of local Huilliche bands, Quiroga and his ragtag group of fewer than two hundred civilians and soldiers crossed the two-mile channel separating the continental mainland from Chiloé's largest island. Later that year he established the hamlet of Castro near the center of the archipelago.

The new arrivals had hoped to find gold deposits and to exploit the Indian population for labor. When neither of these prospects materialized (the Huilliche population of the archipelago was far lower than they had anticipated), they found themselves virtually stranded. A hostile *cabildo* (town council) in Santiagó that had opposed the enterprise from the beginning offered little material or moral support, forcing the Spaniards to rely on the natives for survival. As the years progressed, this reliance deepened, leading not just to a carryover of certain Huilliche practices but also to a greater degree of *mestizaje* than in other parts of Chile.[10] By the end of the century, the unique meld of Huilliche and Spanish cultural elements that would give rise to the collective identity of the inhabitants of the region was well in place.

One of the first significant, postcontact developments to affect the archipelago's new residents was a native uprising on the continent in 1598. Inflamed by continued Spanish incursions into their territory, the Mapuche Indians of south-central Chile—ethnic cousins of the Huilliche—expelled or killed all European settlers in a series of well-coordinated, ferocious, and sustained attacks. By 1603, the Mapuche had regained control of a three-hundred-mile swath of territory just north of Chiloé (between Chile's Bío Bío River and the northern boundary of the archipelago), making Castro and the handful of tiny Spanish settlements on the archipelago the only colonial outposts south of the Bío Bío River. Land routes from central Chile to what is today the Los Lagos region were in effect cut off for Spaniards, a circumstance that persisted for nearly two centuries following the Crown's reluctant recognition of Mapuche sovereignty in the 1600s.[11]

Subsequent raids on Castro and other settlements by Dutch pirates in the early 1600s deepened the material poverty of the already marginalized settlers. With few supplies arriving from Santiago and no cash economy, Spaniards came to rely ever more desperately on the practices and subsistence techniques of indigenous peoples. By the late seventeenth century, work arrangements (mingas), patterns of land distribution (smallholdings called *minifundios*), economic exchanges (a barter system known as *trueque*), dialects (Mapudungun), and the very layout of towns and villages bore a greater resemblance to the way of life of the Huilliche than that of the Spanish.[12] Spanish institutions like the *encomienda* (grants of Indian labor to Spanish settlers), the court system, and Catholic missions were successfully established. However, many of them—the encomienda and the secular courts in particular—remained weak, poorly organized, and difficult to maintain because of the poor supply routes and the great distances that existed between Chiloé and larger Spanish settlements to the north.

Two indigenous cultural carryovers in particular—still present on the archipelago today—shaped the social life and broader group identification of rural inhabitants of the region. The reciprocal labor practices known as mingas gave rise to a strong sense of mutual obligation and relative egalitarianism between neighbors. And the structure of land distribution—widespread ownership among families of five- to ten-hectare minifundios (similar to Huilliche household plots)—furthered this sense of egalitarianism and solidarity within communities. These conditions contrasted sharply with those of mainland Chile, where a handful of families owned enormous tracts of land (*latifundios* that sometimes stretched from the Andes to the Pacific Ocean), and the majority of the population worked as landless peasants in an *inquilino-patrón* debt patronage system.

Mingas and minifundios complemented a set of subsistence practices that revolved around fishing, farming, livestock raising, the gathering of ocean foods like shellfish and seaweed, and the production of fermented beverages. With apples as one of the most abundant fruits in the region by the seventeenth century, chicha de manzana emerged as the most common fermented drink in the region, replacing other varieties of chicha—strawberry and Calafate berry—widely consumed on both the archipelago and mainland prior to the arrival of Europeans.[13]

Postcolonial Chiloé

In the early 1800s, Chilote culture was shaken yet again by external political circumstances largely beyond the control of islanders. A succession of events, beginning with the invasion of the Iberian Peninsula by Napoleon Bonaparte in 1807 and the subsequent declarations of independence by provisional governments throughout Spanish America, permanently shifted the political landscape of the continent. Within a few years of the fall of the Crown in Spain, a national junta in Chile had established an independent provisional government. In 1818, Chile's separatist leaders formally declared independence and drew up national boundaries for a new republic that included, without the consent of islanders, the Archipelago of Chiloé.

Residents of Chiloé unequivocally rejected the aims of Chile's separatists. Their reasons were complex. For nearly fifty years, the archipelago had been under the political oversight of the Viceroyalty of Peru, a bastion of royalist support. Likewise, what little trade it carried out was primarily with ships and merchants from Peru, rather than Chile. Beyond these political and economic ties with the viceroyalty, however, Chilotes had long ago developed a sense of disconnect from mainland Chileans. Since the establishment of Castro in 1567, islanders had received little material support from Santiago. Migrations to central Chile were minimal, and direct political contact was virtually nonexistent. The unique meld of Huilliche and Spanish practices found in Chiloé, moreover, along with the fierce self-reliance of islanders, exacerbated the differences Chilotes perceived between themselves and Chileans. In sum, the archipelago's relationship with Chile was minimized over time, while its ties to Peru were strengthened.

Most Chilotes therefore sided with the viceroyalty—and, by extension, Spain—during the Independence Wars. Nearly five thousand of them fought for the royalist cause on the mainland. Several thousand more later took up arms against naval forces sent by the newly formed Republic of Chile to conquer and annex the archipelago in the 1820s. They repelled an attack by Lord Thomas Cochrane—commander of the Chilean separatist fleet—in 1820. Four years later they battled a squadron under the leadership of Chile's new supreme director, Ramón Freire. By 1826, Chiloé was the last remaining royalist stronghold in Spanish America. That same year, Chile undertook a full-scale invasion of the archipelago, forcibly annexing the islands after series of bloody battles. The strong resentments and antagonisms generated during this period of conflict deepened the disconnect Chilotes felt toward mainland Chileans.

The immediate consequence of Chiloé's brief war with Chile was a change in political status. The archipelago went from being an *intendencia* (administrative division) of the Viceroyalty of Peru—a status it never formally relinquished despite the fall of the viceroyalty in 1824—to a *provincia* (province) of Chile. Beyond this political rearrangement, however, everyday life changed little for islanders. Chilotes continued to extract much of what they needed from the archipelago itself, relying on long-standing subsistence practices and reciprocal arrangements. And much like during colonial times, the province remained politically and economically marginalized, largely overlooked by a government in Santiago that lacked a clear incentive to expend significant resources on the region.

Chilote culture by no means became static. New technologies brought to the archipelago in the late nineteenth and early twentieth century altered bit by bit certain aspects of islander life. A boom in forestry exports on the continent in the 1890s increased the availability of machine-cut wood, slowly changing the shape, size, and look of Chilote houses. The construction of a narrow-gauge rail line in 1911 allowed islanders the option of travel by land from Castro, on the eastern side of Chiloé's largest island, to Ancud, on the western side, something hitherto unthinkable given the dense jungle growth of the island's interior. By the 1920s, locally built sailboats had largely replaced *dalcas* (canoes) as the principal means of transportation. The first boat engines were imported in the 1950s, expanding the range of fishermen and creating over time a limited dependence on gasoline. And durable, Japanese-made nylon fishing nets, introduced the following decade, ushered in what was referred to locally as *el milagro de las redes* (the miracle of the nets). Overall, the flow of goods to and from the islands increased over time, easing some of the economic isolation of Chilotes.

Some Chilotes, furthermore, began migrating to the continent in search of jobs. This trend intensified in the mid-twentieth century as transportation to mainland Chile became more affordable. Given the near absence of wage-paying jobs on most parts of the archipelago as late as the 1970s, itinerant work in southern Argentina and the Chilean Patagonia became the principal source of what little cash circulated throughout the islands.

Despite the out-migration and changes in technology, however, the basic rural livelihoods and practices that had long formed the core of Chilote culture remained the same. Communities primarily sustained themselves through the constants of fishing, farming, animal husbandry, and the gathering of shellfish and seaweed, while land ownership in the form of minifundios continued to be widespread. Still largely a cashless society, barter and reciprocity formed the basis of commercial exchanges and work arrangements. Gift-giving sessions by neighbors—*medanes* (an offshoot of precontact Huilliche traditions)—kept particular families afloat when tragedy befell. Communal fish-and-potato feasts, fish-corral projects, and shellfish-gathering sessions—carried out by way of mingas—brought neighbors together on a regular basis, strengthening formal and informal ties within communities. Indeed, the values and sentiments with which rural southern Chileans identified—mutual obligation, solidarity, reciprocity, cultural autonomy—remained the product of long-standing ways of being and doing well into the latter half of the twentieth century.

Chicha Production

Throughout this period, chicha remained central to the subsistence and customs of islanders. Whereas the basic work arrangements for preparing chicha remained constant, the methods of production changed over time and place. Prior to contact with Europeans in the sixteenth century, fruits were mashed either by hand, with *metates* (grinding stones), or by chewing. The juice and pulp was then mixed with some water and allowed to ferment in wooden containers for several weeks. Sometimes this yeast base was added to other fruit juices to speed up the fermentation process.[14]

With the introduction of apples following contact, slightly more elaborate methods for grinding the fruit were developed. The most common involved placing apples in an open-ended trough and then beating the fruit to a pulp with long, wooden poles. The resulting mash was placed in burlap sacks and squeezed by a wooden press to extract more juice, which in turn was stored in wooden barrels for fermentation. Grinding machines became more common in the early 1900s. These generally consisted of a wooden box with a nail-studded cylinder across the center. Apples were poured into the box and crushed by the cylinder, which could be rotated by hand by way of a crank and a system of pulleys. By the late 1900s, small, rudimentary kerosene engines powered some of these machines.

Despite these variations in technology and technique, majas had one important thing in common: as a type of minga, they brought households together for collective, reciprocal labor projects. In so doing, they helped strengthen ties of reciprocity and unofficial kinship networks within communities.

This latter function of the maja became especially important to rural residents of the Los Lagos region when, starting in the 1970s, significant economic changes began sweeping across Chile's south. In 1973, a violent, US-supported coup in Chile overthrew a democratically elected socialist government that had practiced state-led development, protectionism, and redistribution of wealth. Within a few years of the coup, the new military regime, led by General Augusto Pinochet, embarked on an economic policy that encouraged, among other things, the extraction of national resources for export by large national and foreign companies. Rural regions of southern Chile—particularly the Los Lagos region—were rapidly opened up to lumber, fishing, and aquaculture interests, triggering a dramatic shift—one that is still taking place today—in the kinds of livelihoods available to people there.[15]

On the Archipelago of Chiloé, the heart of the Los Lagos region, the changes were particularly dramatic. In the mid-twentieth century, nearly three-quarters of families had been engaged in small-scale fishing, farming, and animal husbandry. By the early 2000s, following an unprecedented burst in growth in the farmed-salmon industry, the majority of residents on the archipelago lived and worked as wage laborers in small industrial cities like Castro, Ancud, and Quellón. Subsistence farming and fishing had been largely replaced by low-paid, unskilled jobs in processing plants, fish food factories, and aquaculture centers.[16] The region had become far more urbanized, and its economy—embedded in a web of international trade and overseas demand for fish—was now subject to the capricious fluctuations of the global market. The self-sufficiency and economic independence that for centuries had characterized rural communities in Chiloé and parts of the mainland had started to break down.

Chicha and Identity

The increased dependence on wage labor, export industries, and a globalized economy that residents of the region underwent in the late twentieth century had consequences that extended beyond just the economics of southern Chile. With young adults on minifundios increasingly gravitating toward cities or nearby aquaculture centers for work, the pool of available labor for reciprocal projects dwindled significantly in rural communities. Moreover, households that did receive assistance from neighbors for farming and other subsistence activities were often asked to pay with cash rather than promises of reciprocity, reinforcing yet more the need for wages and a regular source of income. Over time, families and entire communities were pulled into an emerging cash economy, and the bonds of mutual dependence and reciprocal obligations that had long formed the cornerstone of social relations in the region began to fray. One elderly informant characterized the effects of this change as "a crisis in our identity."[17]

Not all mingas, however, faded in relevance. The maja de manzana, often carried out on weekends when neighbors with wage-paying jobs were available to help, remained strong. To this day it is the most widely practiced form of labor reciprocity in rural communities in Chiloé. It is seasonal, festive in atmosphere, less time consuming than other mingas, and less labor intensive, factors that have contributed to its survival as a cultural practice. Moreover, it yields a product that itself is strongly associated with reciprocity and solidarity among neighbors, a beverage that over time has acquired symbolic cultural value. "More than wine, more than beer, chicha has always been what we drink," explained Armando Bahamonde, a cultural historian from the village of San Juan, in 2006 as he showed me a small apple orchard on his property. "We watch the apple trees grow. We watch the fruits mature. We grind the apples and we store the juice. We follow it every step of the way, from the moment the first stem comes out of the ground. It is ours." Indeed, the drink, he said, once extended to all facets of rural life. "When we had a minga, what did we drink? Chicha. When we went out fishing, what did we drink? Chicha. When we had a party and invited our neighbors, what did we drink? Chicha. It was and still is," he said, "a drink of work and solidarity."[18]

I got a direct sense of Armando's words during a minga I participated in later that year. The setting was the island of Llingua on the eastern flank of the Archipelago of Chiloé.[19] Over the past decades, a favorable combination of circumstances—a solid, preexisting fishing infrastructure, access to local centers of trade, and ongoing practical kinship ties—had allowed residents of this tiny island, unlike much of the rest of the archipelago, to carry on successfully with certain traditional livelihoods and reciprocal labor practices despite the industrialization of the region. On this particular morning in 2006, six neighbors had shown up at the two-hectare field owned by Hugo and Irene Mansilla to help the couple plant potatoes for the season. These neighbors had been beckoned weeks earlier by way of a *súplica*—an informal solicitation for help generally made during a social visit for *once* (afternoon tea) at the person's home.[20] Aristide—Irene's burly and jovial brother—was there, along with her sister, Hugo's brother-in-law, and three other neighbors considered "kin" because of the reciprocal obligations they shared with the Mansillas.

The spring day was mild and cool, a blue ocean stretching out before us. The stillness of the morning was punctuated by the snorting of oxen, the sharp commands from the workers, and the occasional cackle of a rooster in the distance. Mickey, the couple's stubby-legged dog, scampered excitedly around the unplowed side of the field. The rest of us lumbered slowly across the black, overturned earth, backs arched, arms in motion.

No one directed the work since each person knew what to do. Aristide guided a plow pulled by two oxen, his thick arms shaking with the effort of holding the apparatus upright. Irene and her neighbor Leticia placed the potatoes behind him, bobbing up and down rhythmically. Gastón, a short, stocky fisherman from the opposite side of the island, guided the oxen, coaxing the beasts with a mix of soothing clicks and harsh commands that rolled off his tongue in well-rehearsed cadences. Hugo followed the two women, sprinkling fertilizer out of a metal bucket. I lingered behind all of them, swinging a hoe to scoop chunks of sod onto the potato bulbs.

It was a concerted effort, and the work was carried out mostly in silence except for the occasional joke. Every hour or so we stopped for a break and drank chicha out of a red plastic cup that was filled repeatedly and passed around. The buzz from the fermented cider allayed the strain of the work. As the morning progressed, and the chicha settled into our empty bellies, the jokes flew out with increasing ease—a gentle teasing meant to cut everyone down to size. "Your rows are more crooked than *El Pinocho*," Irene quipped to her brother, letting forth a strong laugh.[21] "You need to grab the plow with strength!" she said, knowing full well that he was the strongest person there. I laughed along, though moments later the ribbing was directed at me for wearing jeans that seemed far too clean for a minga.

Just before midday, Irene stole off to her house to make final preparations for lunch. We soon shuffled into the Mansilla kitchen, crowded around the scarred wooden table, and partook of a *cazuela* (chicken stew) that had been simmering since early morning. Once again chicha was passed around, this time in a large glass jug. We poured generous servings into our cups, which, once emptied, were immediately refilled by Irene to ensure that our spirits remained upbeat. An hour later we were back at work, and though our lower backs—mine in particular—were starting to ache, the chicha breaks increased in frequency and duration. The last rows were planted by mid-afternoon, at which point we filed back into the kitchen, and the chicha rounds continued.

During this and other mingas, chicha—more than just a drink—fulfilled several functions. As a mild intoxicant it took the edge off the strain of work. It satiated our thirst, staved our appetite, and eased our mood, helping create a more festive and lighthearted atmosphere throughout the day. The barbs and mild insults thrown back and forth that morning were not meant to alienate or demean—quite the opposite: they were meant to strengthen the sense of belonging to the group, of being part of a common work project, of participation in a collective effort between equals. In the following weeks, Irene and Hugo Mansilla would be called upon to help Aristide, Leticia, and others sow their own potato fields; they would likewise be subject to chicha-induced ribbing, coded reminders of a friendship and camaraderie born of reciprocal obligations.

The chicha also symbolized something more. As later described to me by Chilote historian Renato Cárdenas, it stood for—and was quite consciously regarded as representing—"the solidarity of the occasion." While in the field, everyone drank from a single cup that was passed around in almost ritual fashion. "Just like with *mate* [a regional tea]," Cárdenas explained, "the act of drinking is a communal one in which the cup is shared. No one is granted special privileges; everyone draws from a common source."[22]

Reciprocity versus Wage Labor

The neighbors who gathered at the Mansilla plot on that day had been helping each other for decades, repaying a debt of obligation that had been incurred between families over many generations. The assistance they provided each other was vital to their subsistence; none of them could survive exclusively from the cash flow they received from fishing, the cultivation of seaweed, and the sales of vegetables at the local market. In this regard, their mutual dependence was born not of altruism, idealism, or even good intentions, but rather of necessity. Nevertheless, over the years, this dependence had generated a powerful sense of trust, reliance, and camaraderie—in sum, a bond of solidarity—among the families. Each household knew that it could count on the other in times of need, call upon a neighbor at a moment's notice, and draw from a tradition of obligation and duty that stretched back generations.

As dramatic economic changes have swept across the archipelago during their lifetime, and livelihoods have become increasingly pegged to wage-paying jobs rather than collective work arrangements, this bond of mutual obligation and solidarity between households has become endangered. The reasons have to do in part with a fundamental difference between work relationships in a *cash*-based society and work relationships in a *reciprocity*-based society. When cash (or any form of money, for that matter) is introduced, labor can be compensated immediately with a payment. Any obligations or debts between the parties, therefore, are formally severed. Services have been rendered and paid for. No one owes anyone anything. Reciprocal work arrangements, by contrast, are rarely compensated immediately. They incur, instead, a debt of obligation that is repaid by a corresponding act of labor at some indefinite point in the future. Relationships are therefore perpetuated through debts that are carried over from one act of labor to another. When these reciprocal work exchanges take place repeatedly, over extended periods of time, and with the same individuals, they establish a permanent sense of obligation between the parties, a mutual understanding that they are responsible for one another.[23]

This important distinction was explained to me by Hugo Mansilla one night during the early stages of my fieldwork. He said that he had deliberately refused work at a nearby salmon farm years earlier, since "a person there works only for himself and his family." The wage-paying job would have pulled him out of a network of labor reciprocity and isolated him from the community. "I would still know my neighbors, but it would not be the same. I would owe them nothing and they would owe me nothing."[24]

Hugo Mansilla and other residents of Llingua have been able to maintain this tradition of reciprocity despite the industrialization of much of the rest of the archipelago. Easy access to centers of trade, a solid fishing infrastructure built up in the late twentieth century, and the availability of arable land have been factors contributing to Llingua's success at viably maintaining the minga. Full-time wage labor has been rejected by most of the tiny island's residents precisely because it is disruptive to a long-standing reciprocal labor system that continues to serve them well and that speaks to their collective identity as Chilotes.

Other communities in Chiloé and the Los Lagos region—places where arable land is scarcer, fishing less viable, and the range of subsistence live-lihoods narrower—have been pulled more abruptly into the new cash-based economy. In these communities, mingas for everyday subsistence crops like potatoes, as practiced regularly on Llingua, are rare. However, majas—the reciprocal-work parties aimed specifically at chicha produc-tion—are still common, largely because they are carried out seasonally and on the weekends. Like the potato-farming mingas of Llingua, these majas have become, in a globalized Chiloé, the glue that holds together reciprocal networks of old.

In late summer 2006, I attended majas in the towns of San Juan, Calen, and Achao, as well as on the island of Llingua. Some of these involved a single family and a few neighbors; others were organized as town festivals celebrating an aspect of Chilote heritage. All of them, formally or infor-mally, revolved around themes of solidarity, history, and identity, concepts that often seem abstract and academic in the United States but commonly form the basis of conversations in places like Chiloé and the Los Lagos region, where ordinary people grapple with rapid culture change on a daily basis. The majas, on these occasions, served a practical function: a means of maintaining reciprocal networks within the community—how-ever frayed and weakened these may have been—as well as an opportunity to produce one of the most popular drinks in the region. They also served a symbolic function: an affirmation of the values of solidarity and mutual obligation in the face of an economic system that championed individual ambition over collective enterprise. Stated differently, they were, to many of the Chilotes who took part in them, bastions of solidarity.

Armando Bahamonde, municipal official and cultural historian, was most explicit in explaining the maja to me. Born in Chiloé in the late 1950s and raised in a rural community on the Isla Grande, Armando had been witness to countless mingas. On a cool March afternoon in 2006, he hosted yet another at his home in San Juan.[25] Several neighbors were there to assist Armando, his wife, and two of his sons. Using a wooden grinding machine built at a nearby town, they ground several sacks of green apples picked from Armando's orchard earlier in the season. The lumpy mush was packed into large baskets made of *fibra vegetal* ("vegetable fiber" or wild grass), which in turn were placed under a wooden press. Armando's sons slowly rotated the broad handle of the press, squeezing the baskets and extracting a pure apple nectar into a bucket.

As they worked, they drank chicha that had been sitting in a barrel on their property for nearly twelve months. The cider was well fermented at that stage, offering a sharp bite and a reminder of why they were there. As with the potato-planting minga on Llingua, the chicha added a festive element to the gathering. The labor, however, was far less strenuous, and many of those present did little else than drink chicha and socialize.

The gathering, nevertheless, carried meaning that extended beyond what could readily be seen and heard. In an interview conducted weeks later, Armando discussed the tenuous state of reciprocal labor networks in San Juan and the slow attrition of neighbors to wage-paying jobs at nearby processing plants and salmon farms. What had once been robust gatherings held every few weeks had dwindled to two or three neighbors meeting annually in his backyard. He wondered aloud how much longer such practices would last. At the same time, he passionately argued that it was vital to carry on the tradition, even if it was with less frequency and fewer participants. Chiloé was at a crossroads, he explained. "I believe that the minga is central to who we are as Chilotes," he said. "We can survive without it. But if it disappears, but we will be different, and something of our identity will have been lost."[26]

Concluding Remarks

Altogether, every aspect of chicha—the fruit from which it is made, the reciprocal arrangements involved in its production, the occasions in which it is consumed, and the act of consumption itself—stand for core elements in the collective identity of rural residents of southern Chile. The apple, common in the region for nearly four hundred years, carries supernatural significance, portending a variety of fates ranging from good health to healthy sex to death. The maja de manzana, a derivation of Huilliche reciprocal traditions, stands as one of the few mingas still widely practiced in the new cash-based economy of rural southern Chile, helping maintain not just long-standing ties of reciprocity between certain rural households but also the sense of solidarity with which these Chileans identify. And the consumption of chicha, especially common during festivities and mingas, remains an act that, from the point of view of the participants, is filled with cultural and historical significance. These connections between chicha and majas, on the one hand, and collective identity, on the other, are not

just vaguely imagined; rather, they are consciously stated and often deliberately acted on, making chicha and chicha production elements of explicit symbolic value throughout rural sectors of the Los Lagos region.

Notes

1. Oriana B. Pardo, "Las chichas en el Chile precolombiano," *Chloris chilensis: revista chilena de flora y vegetación* 7, no. 2 (2004), http://www.chlorischile.cl/chichas/chichas.htm.
2. Claudio Gay, *Historia física y política de Chile*, vol. 5, *Agricultura* (Santiago, Chile: Instituto de Capacitación e Investigación en Reforma Agraria, 1973).
3. Francisco Núñez de Pineda y Bascuñan, *Cautiverio feliz y razón individual de las guerras dilatadas del reino de Chile* (Santiago, Chile: Editorial Universitaria, 1973), 55.
4. Diego de Rosales, *Historia general del reino de Chile, flandes indiano* (Santiago, Chile: Editorial Andrés Bello, 1989), 1378.
5. Gay, *Historia física*.
6. Richard Keynes, *Charles Darwin's Zoology Notes and Specimen Lists from the H.M.S. Beagle* (Cambridge: Cambridge University Press, 2000), 237.
7. Renato Cárdenas Álvarez and Carolina Villagrán Moraga, *Chiloé, botánica de la cotidianidad* (Santiago, Chile: Gráfica Lascar 2005), 226.
8. Ibid., 225. *Chilotes* refers to residents of Chiloé.
9. José Bengoa, *Historia de los antiguos Mapuches del sur* (Santiago, Chile: Catalonia, 2003); Renato Cárdenas Álvarez, Dante Montiel Vera, and Catherine Grace Hall, *Los chonos y veliche de Chiloé* (Santiago, Chile: Ediciones Olimpho, 1991).
10. Paola P. Rocco et al., "Composición genética de la población chilena," *Revista médica de Chile* 130, no. 2 (2002), 125–31.
11. Simon Collier and William F. Sater, *A History of Chile, 1808–2002*, 2nd ed. (Cambridge: Cambridge University Press, 2004).
12. Rodolfo Urbina Burgos, *Población indígena, encomienda, y tributo en Chiloé, 1567–1813* (Valparaíso, Chile: Universidad Católica de Valparaíso, 2004); David J. Weber, *Bárbaros: Spaniards and Their Savages in the Age of Enlightenment* (New Haven, CT: Yale University Press, 2005).
13. Pardo, *Las chichas*.
14. Ibid.
15. Peter Winn, ed., *Victims of the Chilean Miracle: Workers and Neoliberalism in the Pinochet Era, 1973–2002* (Durham, NC: Duke University Press, 2004).
16. Rachel Schurman, "Shuckers, Sorters, Headers, and Gutters: Labor in the Fisheries Sector," in *Victims of the Chilean Miracle*, ed. Peter Winn (Durham, NC: Duke University Press, 2004), 298–336.
17. Armando Bahamonde, interview with the author, San Juan, Chiloé, Chile, August 13, 2006.
18. Ibid.
19. Descriptions taken from the author's field notes, Llingua, Chile, September 12, 2006.

20. The *once* is an evening snack, generally involving tea, coffee, or *mate* and light food. The origin of the term is unclear, though generally it is believed to be drawn from the concept of the mid-morning meal common in England and Spain's Basque region (*once* means "eleven" in Spanish).

21. "El Pinocho" in this case is a reference to Augusto Pinochet, the military general who ruled Chile from 1973 to 1990.

22. Renato Cárdenas Álvarez Castro, interview with the author, Calen, Archipelago of Chiloé, Chile, November 11, 2006.

23. See David Graeber's *Debt: The First 5,000 Years* (Brooklyn, NY: Melville House Printing, 2011) for an excellent and accessible overview of how this dynamic has played out in human history and human relations over the past millennia.

24. Hugo Mansilla, interview with the author, Llingua, Chile, September 8, 2006.

25. March, in the Southern Hemisphere, is late summer.

26. Armando Bahamonde, interview with the author, San Juan, Chiloé, Chile, June 16, 2006.

Glossary

aguardente (*de cana*)   Literally "burning water," this Brazilian rum is distilled from sugarcane.

aguardiente   Like *aguardente*, this is the Spanish spelling of "burning water." The sugarcane-distilled rum is common in many places, including Mexico, Cuba, and Colombia.

alcabala   Customs duty.

alcalde   A word with multiple meanings—it could refer to a minister of a religious confraternity, a civil magistrate, or a town mayor.

bodega   Winery.

bota   Wineskin.

cabildo   A town council in colonial Spanish America.

caboco/caboclo   Terms used in colonial Brazil to refer to acculturated indigenous peoples, or to those of mixed European and native heritage.

cabras   A racially mixed social group in Brazil.

cachaça   Originally, during the colonial period in Brazil, this term referred to the foam that arose from the cauldrons when sugarcane was boiled into a broth at the beginning of the process of sugar production. Since then, it has come to mean a distilled drink produced from sugarcane.

cachaceiros   Drinkers of *cachaça*.

casillas   Tent-like stalls or taverns that sell pulque.

castas   A term generically referring to people of racially mixed heritage. It was common during the colonial era of roughly the sixteenth through the early nineteenth century.

caudillos Provincial military authorities who dominated Latin American politics in the nineteenth century. The rule by these figures is called *caudillismo*.

cauim A beverage made from fermented manioc, corn, fruits, or vegetables in Brazil.

cerveceros Producers of *cerveza*, beer.

charape A Mexican fermented beverage, often associated with indigenous peoples, made from barley or pineapple and sugarcane molasses.

charros Cowboys and rodeo riders who come from Jalisco, Mexico, and other nearby states.

chicha A beverage made from fermented maize, yucca, peanuts, or other ingredients in the Andean region. In Guatemala it was also made from maize or fruit. The drink is much like beer.

chicha de manzana A hard apple cider found in Chile.

chicha de uva A homemade grape wine made in Chile, it is frequently referred as *vino ordinario*, or common wine.

chilmoleras Women who make different dishes, among them *mole*, a Mexican sauce made from a variety of ingredients.

conquistadores The term for the European conquerors who defeated Amerindians and paved the way for the new colonies in the Americas.

criollos People of European descent born in the Americas. The term was mostly used before Latin American colonies received their independence in the early nineteenth century. After independence, its meaning changed to refer to people of Spanish heritage.

don/doña Honorific titles given to men and women with status.

ejidos Communally owned properties that were granted to Mexican peasants during the Revolution of 1910–1940.

enchiladera Female enchilada maker.

ex-votos Devotional art, typically painted by an academically untrained artist on a piece of wood or tin, thanking a religious figure for a miracle performed in the commissioner's life.

fazendeiros Owners of large agricultural estates, called *fazendas*, in Brazil.

fincas Large landed estates in Guatemala.

fondas Small eateries that often sold pulque.

frucanga An alternate name for *hidromiel*; a fermented mix of water and honey with some kind of fruit such as pineapple, orange, or lime common in Cuba.

garapa/grappe/grippo/guarapo   The Portuguese, French, English, and Spanish words for a type of sugarcane wine popular during the colonial period in Brazil and the Caribbean.

gaucho   Cowboy of the South American plains.

Guardia Nacional   The National Police of Guatemala.

guaro   The Guatemalan name for moonshine.

guiñapo   A pre-Hispanic term from the Andes used for alcoholic beverages.

hacendado   The owner of an *hacienda*.

haciendas   Large agricultural estates found throughout much of Spanish-speaking Latin America.

hidromiel   An alternate name for *frucanga*.

hispanismo   A doctrine that promotes Latin Americans' Hispanic identity over their indigenous or African ones. This embracing of Spanish culture came to prominence after World War II.

indígenas   Indigenous peoples.

indigenismo   A doctrine celebrating Latin Americans' indigenous heritage. Although this ideology was associated with the rise of nationalism and populism in the first half of the twentieth century, even its proponents, *indigenistas*, were not exempt from racism. They often praised the idea of the native past and ignored the plight of current indigenous people.

indigenista   A supporter of *indigenismo*.

indio/a   A native person, either male or female.

inquilino-patrón   A debt-patronage system binding together a renter (*inquilino*) and the landlord (*patrón*) in Chile (although similar systems existed across the region). The system often left the inquilino in debt for a lifetime.

jefe político   Term with different meanings, such as political boss and governor.

jeribita/geribita   An early colonial word used for *cachaça*.

jornaleros   Day laborers.

keros   Drinking cups used by pre-Hispanic Andean peoples to cement social relationships.

kusa   A pre-Hispanic term from the Andes used for alcoholic beverages.

k'uxa   A Maya Guatemalan homemade brew derived from sugarcane.

ladinos   A term for Spanish-speaking natives or people of non-native descent.

latifundios   Large landholdings that are part of a larger Latin American pattern of the coexistence of a few immense estates that often contain unused land and many plots that are too small to be economically viable.

maja de manzana   A festive, communal work session dedicated to producing *chicha de manzana*.

mamakona   "Chosen" women who labored for the Incan state; their labor might include brewing *chicha*.

mestizaje   The process of racial mixing that has characterized Latin America since the conquest.

mestizo/a   A term used especially in Mexico to refer to the racial mixture consisting of European and native ancestry.

metate   A large stone mortar and pestle used to grind corn for tortillas or fruits for alcoholic production.

mezcal   A distilled Mexican drink with a chemical composition similar to tequila.

mezcaleros   Producers of mezcal.

milpas   Communally held fields or small, personal plots of land.

mingas   Labor-sharing arrangements within Chilean rural communities.

minifundios   Small landholdings of a few hectares. They are part of a larger Latin American pattern of the coexistence of a few incredibly large estates that often contain unused land (*latifundios*), and many smaller ones, some of which are too tiny to be economically viable.

molle   A fruit native to the Andes that *chicha* is often made from.

mulato/a   A person of mixed European and African heritage.

muñeca   A piece of feces wrapped in cloth that resembles a rag doll. It was occasionally used to speed up the fermentation process of pulque, which contributed to the drink's unsanitary reputation.

negro   Literally "black," it is a common term in both Spanish and Portuguese used to refer to people of pure African ancestry.

poblar es gobernar   A phrase meaning "to populate is to govern," this nineteenth-century ideology drove many politicians, including those in Argentina, to promote immigration, especially from Europe.

pulque   Beverage made from the fermented sap of the maguey, or agave, plant. This beverage comes from central Mexico.

pulquería   A tavern selling pulque.

pulqueros   Producers of pulque.

¡Salud! "Cheers!" in Spanish.

sambumbía An alternate spelling of *zambumbía.*

Saúde! "Cheers!" in Portuguese.

soltero/a Single man or woman.

taberna Tavern.

tepache A drink made by adding sugar, pineapple, and some *aguardiente* to pulque.

tequileros Makers of tequila.

terroir Literally "provenance," this French word refers to how the place in which wine grapes are grown affects the characteristics of the wine.

teshuino/tesgüino A fermented beverage made from corn in the Sierra Madre region of Mexico. It is a sacred beverage to the Tarahumara people.

trueque A barter system.

uva Criolla The Mission grape, originally brought to Argentina in the sixteenth century by Spanish friars.

vino común/vino de mesa Table wine.

vinos finos Fine wines.

vinotecas Wine shops.

vino tinto Red wine.

zambumbía A drink made by African slaves and free men in Cuba using fermented molasses, water, sugarcane juice, and sometimes fruit. An alternate spelling is *sambumbía.*

Bibliography

Archives and Libraries

Argentina

Colección Privada de las Bodegas López
Colección Privada de Vinos y Bodegas La Rural

Guatemala

Archivo General de Centro América, Guatemala City
Archivo Municipal de Patzicía, Chimaltenango
Dirección General de Estadística de Guatemala, Guatemala City

Mexico

Archivo General de la Nación, Mexico City
Archivo Histórico de la Secretaría de Educación Pública, Mexico City
Archivo Histórico del Ayuntamiento de Pátzcuaro, Michoacán
Archivo Histórico del Distrito Federal, Mexico City
Archivo Histórico del Estado de Sonora, Hermosillo
Archivo Histórico de Salubridad y Social Asistencia, Mexico City
Biblioteca del Colegio de Sonora, Hermosillo
Biblioteca Eladio Sauza, Tequila, Jalisco
Fideicomiso Archivos Plutarco Elías Calles y Fernando Torreblanca, Mexico City
Hemeroteca Nacional, Universidad Nacional Autónoma de México, Mexico City

United States

Regenstein Library, University of Chicago, Chicago, Illinois

Magazines and Newspapers

Argentina

Bodegas y terruños, Buenos Aires
El Conocedor, Buenos Aires
El Profesional del vino: Revista para el consumidor, Buenos Aires
Joy de los Placeres: La revista latina de vinos y gastronomía, Buenos Aires
Los Andes, Mendoza
Master Wine, Buenos Aires
Vinos, viñas y frutas, Buenos Aires
Vinos y viñas, Buenos Aires

Guatemala

Diario de Centro América. Periódico Oficial, Guatemala City
El Imparcial, Guatemala City
La Gaceta: Revista de Policía y Variedades, Guatemala City
La República

Mexico

Diario del Hogar, Mexico City
El Maestro Rural, Mexico City
El Nacional, Mexico City
El Observador, Hermosillo, Sonora
El Pitic, Hermosillo, Sonora
El Radical, Mexico City
El Universal, Mexico City
Monitor Republicano, Mexico City
Orientación, Hermosillo, Sonora
Reforma, Mexico City

United States

Miami Beach Daily News, Miami
Wine Spectator, New York City
USA Today

Published Primary Sources

Aires de Casal, Manuel. *Corografía Brasílica ou Relação Histórico-Geográfica do Reino do Brasil*. Belo Horizonte/São Paulo: Itatiaia/Editora da Universidade de São Paulo (hereafter Edusp), 1976 [1817].

Almonte, Juan Nepomuceno. *Guía de forasteros y repertorio de conocimientos útiles*. Mexico City: Imprenta de Ignacio Cumplido, 1852.

Anais da Biblioteca Nacional, vol. 37. Rio de Janeiro: Biblioteca Nacional, 1915.

Antonil, André João. *Cultura e Opulência do Brasil*. São Paulo: Companhia Editora Nacional, 1967 [1711].

Arata, Pedro. *Investigación Vinícola: Informes presentados al Ministro de Agricultura por la Comisión Nacional*. Buenos Aires: Talleres de la Oficina Meteorológica, 1903.

Argentina, Secretaría General. *Vitivinicultura*. Buenos Aires: Secretaría General de Argentina, 1970.

[Arquivo do Estado de São Paulo.] *Inventários e testamentos*, vol. 3, *1603–1648*. São Paulo: Publicação Oficial do Arquivo do Estado de São Paulo, 1920.

Asociación Vitivinícola Argentina. *Anuario vitivinícola argentino, the Argentine wine-growing yearbook*. Buenos Aires: Editorial La Empresa Agropecuaria, 1972.

Asturias, Miguel Angel. *Sociología Guatemalteca: El problema social del indio*. Translated by Maureen Ahern. Tempe: Arizona State University, 1977 [1923].

Bottaro, Santiago E. "La industria vitivinícola entre nosotros." Thesis, Universidad de Buenos Aires, Facultad de Ciencias Económicas, 1917.

Brandão, Ambrósio Fernandes. *Diálogos das Grandezas do Brasil*. Recife: Fundação Joaquim Nabuco/Editora Massangana, 1997 [1930].

Bueno, João Ferreira de Oliveira. "Simples narração da viagem que fez ao Rio Paraná o thesoureiro-mór da Sé d'esta cidade de S. Paulo . . ." *Revista do Instituto Historico e Geographico do Brazil* 1, no. 3 (1839): 139–50.

Bunge, Alejandro E. *Informe del Ingeniero Alejandro Bunge sobre el problema vitivinícola*. Buenos Aires: Compañía Impresora Argentina, 1929.

Burkitt, Robert. "Explorations in the Highlands of Western Guatemala." *Museum Journal (University of Pennsylvania)* 21, no. 1 (1930): 41–72.

Calderón de la Barca, Madame [Frances Erskine]. *Life in Mexico During a Residence of Two Years in That Country*. New York: E.P. Dutton, 1954.

Caro, Brígido. *Plutarco Elías Calles: dictador bolsheviqui de México. Episodios de la Revolución Mexicana, desde 1910 hasta 1924*. Los Angeles, CA: Talleres Linotipográficos de "El Heraldo de México," 1924.

Carson, W. E. *Mexico: The Wonderland of the South*. New York: Macmillan, 1909.

Cobo, Bernabé. *History of the Inca Empire: An Account of the Indians' Customs and Their Origin Together with a Treatise on Inca Legends, History, and Social Institutions*. Translated and edited by Roland Hamilton. Austin: University of Texas Press, 1979 [1653].

Código Civil de la República de Guatemala, Libro Primero del año 1927. Guatemala City: Tipografía Nacional, 1927.

Condamine, Charles-Marie de la. *Viagem pelo Amazonas—1735–1745*. Rio de Janeiro/São Paulo: Nova Fronteira, 1992 [1745].

Congreso Constituyente de 1857. *Constitución federal de los Estados Unidos Mexicanos sancionada y jurada por el congreso general constituyente el día 5 de febrero de 1857*, http://www.agn.gob.mx/constitucion1857/constitucion1857.html, accessed June 30, 2012.

Congreso Constituyente 1916–1917: *Diario de Debates*. vol. 2. Mexico City: Instituto Nacional de Estudios Históricos de la Revolución Mexicana, 1985.

[Consejo de Indias]. *Recopilación de leyes de los reinos de las Indias*. Facsimile. Mexico City: Librería de Miguel Ángel Porrúa, 1987 [1681].

D'Evreux, Yves. *Viagem ao norte do Brasil feita nos anos de 1613 a 1614*. São Paulo: Siciliano, 2002 [1864].

Daniel, João. *Tesouro Descoberto no Máximo Rio Amazonas*, vol 2. Rio de Janeiro: Contraponto, 2004 [1820].

Dirección General de Estadística. *Censo de la república levantado el 28 de agosto de 1921*. 4o Censo, Parte II. Guatemala City: Talleres Gutenberg, 1926.

Documentos Históricos da Biblioteca Nacional, vol. 16, *Patentes, Provisões e Alvarás, 1631–1637*. Rio de Janeiro: Biblioteca Nacional, 1930.

Documentos Históricos da Biblioteca Nacional, vol. 32, *Provisões, Patentes, Alvarás, Mandados, 1651–1693*. Rio de Janeiro: Biblioteca Nacional, 1936.

Documentos Históricos da Biblioteca Nacional, vol. 53, *Provisões, 1717–1718—Portarias, 1711–1715*. Rio de Janeiro: Biblioteca Nacional, 1941.

Documentos Históricos do Arquivo Municipal, vol. 2, *Atas da Câmara, 1641–1649*. Salvador: Prefeitura do Município de Salvador, 1949.

Documentos Históricos do Arquivo Municipal, vol. 3, *Atas da Câmara, 1649–1659*. Salvador: Prefeitura do Município de Salvador, 1949.

Documentos Interessantes para a História e Costumes de São Paulo, vol. 22. São Paulo: Typographia da Companhia Industrial de São Paulo, 1896.

Dollero, Adolfo. *México al día. Impresiones y notas de viaje*. Paris: Librería de la vda. de C. Bouret, 1911.

Dunlop, Robert Glasgow. *Travels in Central America, Being a Journal of Nearly Three Years' Residence in the Country. Together with a Sketch of the Republic, and an Account of Its Climate, Productions, Commerce, Etc*. London: Longman, Brown, Green, and Longmans, 1847.

García Granados, Jorge. *Evolución sociológica de Guatemala / Ensayo sobre el gobierno del Dr. Mariano Gálvez*. Guatemala: Sánchez and de Guise, 1927.

Génin, Auguste. *Notes sur le Mexique*. Mexico City: Imprenta Lacaud, 1910.

Gruening, Ernest. *Mexico and Its Heritage*. New York: Appleton-Century, 1936.

Haefkens, Jacobo. *Viaje a Guatemala y Centroamerica*. Edited by Francis Gall. Translated by Theodora J. M. van Lottum. Guatemala: Editorial Universitaria, 1969.

Haven, Gilbert. *Our Next Door Neighbor: A Winter in Mexico*. New York: Harper and Brothers, 1875.

Hernández de León, Federico. *Viajes presidenciales: breves relatos de algunas expediciones administrativas del General D. Jorge Ubico, presidente de la República*, vol. 2. Guatemala: Tipografía Nacional, 1940.

Huerta, Adolfo de la. *Memorias de Don Adolfo de la Huerta: Según su propio dictado*. Transcribed by Roberto Guzmán Esparza. Hermosillo, Mexico: Gobierno del Estado de Sonora, 1957.

Juárez Muñoz, J. Fernando. *El indio Guatemalteco: Ensayo de sociología nacionalista.* Guatemala City: Tipografía Latina, 1931.

Lemos, Manuel. *Algunos apuntes sobre la cuestión vitivinícola en Mendoza: Orientaciones necesarias.* Mendoza, Argentina: Gutenberg, 1922.

Lincoln, Jackson Steward. "An Ethnographic Study of the Ixil Indians of the Guatemalan Highlands." Microfilm Collection of Manuscripts on Middle American Cultural Anthropology, University of Chicago, no. 1, 1945.

López Lara, Ramón. *El Obispado de Michoacán en el Siglo XVIII: Informe Inédito de Beneficios, Pueblos y Lagunas.* Morelia, Mexico: Fimax Publicistas, 1973.

Magistocchi, Gaudencio. *Tratado de enología: Técnica adaptada a la vinificación cuyana.* Mendoza, Argentina: Talleres Gráficos J. Peuser, 1934.

Marcgrave, Jorge. *História Natural do Brasil.* São Paulo: Imprensa Oficial, 1942 [1648].

Marx, Guido. "Whiskies, etc." In *Report of the Committee on Awards of the World's Columbian Commission: Special Reports upon Special Subjects or Groups,* vol. 2. Washington, DC: Government Printing Office, 1901.

Mello, José Antônio Gonsalves de, ed. *Fontes para a História do Brasil Holandê,* vol. 1, *A Economia Açucareira.* Recife: Compahnia Editora de Pernambuco, 2004.

Mello e Souza, Marina de. *Reis Negros no Brasil Escravista: História da Festa de Coroação de Rei Congo.* Belo Horizonte: Editora Universidade Federal de Minas Gerais, 2002.

Memoria de la Secretaría Hacienda y Crédito Público, vol. 1, *23 de febrero de 1913 a 15 de abril de 1917.* Mexico City: Talleres Gráficos de la Nación, 1952.

Memoria de la Secretaría Hacienda y Crédito Público, vol. 3, *16 de abril de 1917 a 21 de mayo de 1920.* Mexico City: Talleres Gráficos de la Nación, 1959.

Motolinía, Toribio de Benavente. *History of the Indians of New Spain.* Translated and edited by Elizabeth Andros Foster. Berkeley: Cortés Society, 1950.

Moussy, Martin de. *La Confederation Argentine a l'Exposition Universelle de 1867 a Paris: Notice Statistique Generale et Catalogue.* Paris: Bouchard-Huzard, 1867.

Nieuhof, Johan. *Memorável Viagem Marítima e Terrestre ao Brasil.* Belo Horizonte/São Paulo: Itatiaia/Edusp, 1981 [1682].

Payno, Manuel. *Los bandidos de Río Frío,* 16th ed. Mexico City: Porrúa, 1996 [1891].

———. *Memoria del maguey mexicano y sus diversos productos,* Mexico City: A. Boix, 1864.

Paz, José. *En defensa del pulque: 668,677 viven de la industria pulquera: el medio de vida de estos proletarios debe respetarse.* Mexico City: n.p., 1935.

Paz, Teodoro O. *Guaymas de Ayer.* N.l.: n.p., n.d. (manuscript in possession of the Biblioteca del Colegio de Sonora).

Pérez, Lázaro. *Estudio sobre el maguey llamado mezcal en el estado de Jalisco.* Guadalajara, Mexico: Imprenta Ancira, 1887.

Policía Nacional de Guatemala. *Memoria de la Dirección General de la Policía Nacional, presentada al Ministro de Gobernación y Justicia.* Guatemala City: Tipografía Nacional, 1899–1944.

Prieto, Guillermo. *Memorias de mis tiempos. Obras Completas de Guillermo Prieto,* vol. 1. Mexico City: Consejo Nacional para la Cultura y las Artes (hereafter Conaculta), 1992.

Pyrard de Laval, François. *Viagem de Francisco Pyrard, de Laval: contendo a noticia de sua navegação às Indias Orientaes, ilhas de Maldiva, Maluco, e ao Brazil, e os differentes casos, que lhe aconteceram na mesma viagem nos dez annos que andou nestes paizes: (1601 a 1611) com a descripção exacta dos costumes, leis, usos, policia, e governo: do trato e commercio, que nelles há; dos animaes, arvores, fructas, e outras singularidades, que alli se encontram*, vol. 2. Nova Goa: Imprensa Nacional, 1862.

Representación al Exmo. Sr. Presidente de la República por los hacendados de los Llanos de Apan y tratantes en el ramo de pulques, para que se suspenda la ley sobre aumento de fondos municipales. Mexico City: Establecimiento Tipográfico de Andrés Boix, 1857.

Rodrigues do Prado, Francisco. "Historia dos Indios Cavalleiros ou da Nação Guay-curu." *Revista do Instituto Historico e Geographico do Brazil 1*, no. 1 (1839 [1793]): 21–44.

Rodríguez, Mario Domingo. "El 'Gran Buenos Aires,' extraordinario consumidor de vino." In *Anuario vitivinícola Argentina*. Edited by Asociación Vitivinícola Argentina, 38–40. Buenos Aires: Editorial la Empresa Agropecuaria, 1973.

Sahagún, Bernardino de. *Florentine Codex* or *Historia General de las Cosas de la Nueva España*. Mexico City: Editorial Nueva España, 1946.

Salvador, Vicente do. *História do Brasil, 1500–1627*. São Paulo/Brasília: Melhoramentos/ Instituto Nacional do Livro, 1975 [1627].

Sarmiento, Domingo Faustino. *Obras Completas*. 51 vols. Buenos Aires: Mariano Moreno, 1899.

———. *Recuerdos de provincia*. Buenos Aires: Editorial de Belgrano, 1981.

———. *Recollections of a Provincial Past*. Translated by Elizabeth Garrels and Asa Zatz. London: Oxford University Press, 2005.

Spix, Johann B. von, and Carl F. von Martius. *Viagem pelo Brasil—1817–1820*. São Paulo: Melhoramentos/Instituto Histórico e Geográfico Brasileiro/Imprensa Nacional, 1976 [1828–1829].

Stephens, John. *Incidents of Travel in Central America, Chiapas, and Yucatán*, vol. 2. New York: Dover, 1969 [1841].

Tempsky, G. F. von. *Mitla: A Narrative of Incidents and Personal Adventures on Journey in Mexico, Guatemala, and Salvador in the Years 1853 to 1855*. London: Longman, Brown, Green, Longmans, and Roberts, 1858.

Trianes, Francisco. *La viña bajo la tormenta*. Buenos Aires: Librería y editorial El Ateneo, 1938.

Trujillo, Diego de. *Una relación inédita de la conquista: la Crónica de Diego de Trujillo*. Edited by Raúl Porras Barrenecha. Lima: Instituto de Raúl Porras Barrenecha, 1948 [1571].

Vasconcelos, José. *La Flama*. Mexico City: Compañía Editorial Continental, 1959.

Vetancurt, Agustín de. *Teatro Mexicano*. Facsimile. Mexico City: Editorial Porrúa, 1971 [1697].

Vieira, Antônio. *Cartas do Brasil, 1626–1697—Estado do Brasil e Estado do Maranhão e Grã Pará*. São Paulo: Hedra, 2003.

Yupanqui, Diego de Castro [Titu Cusi]. *Titu Cusi, a 16th Century Account of the Conquest: Instrucción del Inga Don Diego de Castro Titu Cusi Yupanqui para el muy ilustre Señor el Licenciado Lope García del Castro.* Edited and translated by Nicole Delia Legnani. Cambridge, MA: Harvard University Press, 2005 [1570].

Secondary Sources

Aceves González, Francisco de Jesús. "Génesis de la Radiodifusión Jalisciense estudio aproximativo." *Comunicación y Sociedad* 4/5 (1989): 58–96.

Adams, Walter Randolph. "Guatemala." In *International Handbook on Alcohol and Culture.* Edited by Dwight B. Heath, 99–109. Westport, CT: Greenwood Press, 1995.

Adelman, Jeremy. *Sovereignty and Revolution in the Iberian Atlantic.* Princeton, NJ: Princeton University Press, 2006.

Agraz García de Alba, Gabriel. *Historia de la industria Tequila Sauza: Tres generaciones y una tradición.* Guadalajara, Mexico: Departmento de Investigaciones Históricas de Tequila Sauza de Jalisco, 1963.

Alencastro, Luiz Felipe de. *O Trato dos Viventes: Formação do Brasil no Atlântico Sul—Séculos XVI e XVII.* São Paulo: Compahnia das Letras, 2000.

Algranti, Leila M. "Aguardente de cana e outras aguardentes: por uma história da produção e do consumo de licores na América portuguesa." In *Álcool e drogas na história do Brasil.* Edited by Renato P. Venâncio and Henrique Carneiro, 71–92. São Paulo/Belo Horizonte: Alameda/Editora Pontifícia Universidade Católica de Minas Gerais (hereafter PUC Minas), 2005.

Allen, Catherine J. *The Hold Life Has: Coca and Cultural Identity in an Andean Community.* 2nd ed. Washington, DC: Smithsonian Institution Press, 2002.

Almeida, Rita Heloísa de, ed. *O Diretório dos Índios: Um projeto de "civilização" no Brasil do século XVIII.* Brasília: Editora Universidade de Brasília, 1997.

Althouse, Aaron P. "Contested Mestizos, Alleged Mulattos: Racial Identity and Caste Hierarchy in Eighteenth Century Pátzcuaro, Mexico." *The Americas* 62, no. 2 (2005): 151–75.

Amoroso, Marta R., and Nádia Farage, eds. *Relatos da Fronteira Amazônica no Século XVIII. Documentos de Henrique João Wilkens e Alexandre Rodrigues Ferreira.* São Paulo: Núcleo de História Indígena e do Indigenismo/Universidade de São Paulo/ Fundação de Amparo à Pesquisa do Estado de São Paulo (hereafter FAPESP), 1994.

Andermann, Jens. "Tournaments of Value: Argentina and Brazil in the Age of Exhibitions." *Journal of Material Culture* 14, no. 3 (2009): 333–63.

Anderson, Karen. "Tiwanaku Influence on Local Drinking Patterns in Cochabamba, Bolivia." In *Drink, Power, and Society in the Andes.* Edited by Justin Jennings and Brenda Bowser, 167–99. Gainesville: University Press of Florida, 2009.

Andreas, Peter. *Smuggler Nation: How Illicit Trade Made America.* New York: Oxford University Press, 2013.

Aquino, Francisco, et al. "Amino Acids Profile of Sugar Cane Spirit (Cachaça), Rum, and Whisky." *Food Chemistry* 108 (2008): 784–93.

Arrom, Silvia Marina. *The Women of Mexico City, 1790–1850.* Stanford, CA: Stanford University Press, 1985.

Aspiazu, Daniel, and Eduardo Basualdo. *El complejo vitivinícola argentino en los noventa: Potencialidades y restricciones.* Buenos Aires: Centro de Estudios y Promoción Agraria (hereafter CEPA), 2000.

Azevedo, Thales de. *Povoamento da Cidade do Salvador.* Salvador: Itapuã, 1969 [1949].

Azuela, Mariano. *Los de abajo.* Mexico City: Fondo de Cultura Económica (hereafter FCE), 1986.

Babb, Florence E. *Between Field and Cooking Pot. The Political Economy of Marketwomen in Peru.* Austin: University of Texas Press, 1989.

Bajwa, Uttam. "Immigrant Family Firms in the Mendoza Wine Industry, 1884–1914." PhD diss., Johns Hopkins University, 2012.

Bantjes, Adrian A. *As If Jesus Walked on Earth: Cardenismo, Sonora, and the Mexican Revolution.* Wilmington, DE: Scholarly Resources (hereafter SR) Books, 1998.

———. "Saints, Sinners, and State Formation: Local Religion and Cultural Revolution in Mexico." In *The Eagle and the Virgin: Nation and Cultural Revolution in Mexico, 1920–1940.* Edited by Mary Kay Vaughan and Stephen E. Lewis, 137–56. Durham, NC: Duke University Press, 2006.

Bartra, Roger. "Paradise Subverted: The Invention of the Mexican Character." In *Primitivism and Identity in Latin America: Essays on Art, Literature, and Culture.* Edited by Erik Camayd Freixas and José Eduardo Gonzaléz, 3–22. Tucson: University of Arizona Press, 2000.

Batres Jáuregui, Antonio. *Los indios: Su historia y su civilización.* Guatemala City: Tipografía La Unión, 1894.

Beezley, William H. "La senda del Malbec: la cepa emblemática de Argentina." *Revista Universum* 20, no. 2 (2005): 288–97.

Bellingeri, Marco. *Las haciendas en México. El caso de San Antonio Tochatlaco.* Mexico City: Secretaría de Educación Pública/Instituto Nacional de Antropología e Historia (hereafter INAH), 1980.

Bengoa, José. *Historia de los antiguos Mapuches del sur.* Santiago, Chile: Catalonia, 2003.

Benjamin, Thomas. "Rebuilding the Nation." In *The Oxford History of Mexico.* Edited by Michael C. Meyer and William H. Beezley, 438–70. Oxford: Oxford University Press, 2000.

Biondolillo, Aldo. "Exportaciones vitivinícolas argentinas." In *Crisis vitivinícola: Estudios y propuestas para su solución.* Edited by Eduardo Díaz Araujo et al., 129–39. Mendoza, Argentina: Universidad de Mendoza/Editorial Idearium, 1982.

Bliss, Katherine E. "For the Health of the Nation: Gender and the Cultural Politics of Social Hygiene in Revolutionary Mexico." In *The Eagle and the Virgin: Nation and Cultural Revolution in Mexico, 1920–1940.* Edited by Mary Kay Vaughan and Stephen E. Lewis, 196–218. Durham, NC: Duke University Press, 2006.

Bliss, Katherine Elaine. *Compromised Positions: Prostitution, Public Health, and Gender Politics in Revolutionary Mexico City.* University Park: Pennsylvania State University Press, 2001.

Bórmida, Eliana. "Patrimonio de la industria del vino en Mendoza." Paper presented at Jornadas de Trabajo Patrimonio industrial. Fuerza y riqueza del trabajo colectivo of the Centro Internacional para la Conservación del Patrimonio, Buenos Aires, Argentina, July 1–2, 2003.

Bouret, Daniela. "El consumo de vinos en el Uruguay del novecientos. El desarrollo de la industria vitivinícola vrs. campañas antialcoholistas." *Boletín Americanista* 59 (2009): 155–76.

Boyer, Christopher R. *Becoming Campesinos: Politics, Identity, and Agrarian Struggle in Postrevolutionary Michoacán, 1920–1935*. Stanford, CA: Stanford University Press, 2003.

Bray, Tamara L. "Inka Pottery as Culinary Equipment: Food, Feasting, and Gender in Imperial Design." *Latin American Antiquity* 14 (2003): 3–28.

Brennan, Thomas E. *Burgundy to Champagne: The Wine Trade in Early Modern France*. Baltimore, MD: Johns Hopkins University Press, 1997.

Brito Rodríguez, Félix. "La cultura política en el Sinaloa posrevolucionario: elecciones, alcohol, y violencia." Paper presented at the thirtieth Simposio de Historia y Antropología de Sonora, Hermosillo, Mexico, February 25, 2005.

Browman, David. "Political Institutional Factors Contributing to the Integration of the Tiwanaku State." In *Emergence and Change in Early Urban Societies*. Edited by Linda Manzanilla, 229–43. New York: Plenum, 1997.

Bruera, Matías. *La Argentina fermentada: vino, alimentación y cultura*. Buenos Aires: Paidós, 2006.

Bruman, Henry J. *Alcohol in Ancient Mexico*. Salt Lake City: University of Utah Press, 2000.

Buffington, Robert. "Prohibition in the Borderlands: National Government-Border Community Relations." *Pacific Historical Review* 63, no. 1 (1994): 19–38.

Buffington, Robert M., and William E. French. "The Culture of Modernity." In *The Oxford History of Mexico*. Edited by Michael C. Meyer and William H. Beezley, 397–432. Oxford: Oxford University Press, 2000.

Bunzel, Ruth. "The Role of Alcoholism in Two Central American Cultures." *Psychiatry* 3 (1940): 361–87.

———. *Chichicastenango: A Guatemalan Village*. Seattle: University of Washington Press, 1959.

Burger, Richard L., and Nikolaas J. Van Der Merwe. "Maize and the Origins of Highland Chavín Civilization: An Isotopic Perspective." *American Anthropologist* 92 (1990): 85–95.

Burkhart, Louise M. "Mexica Women on the Home Front. Housework and Religion in Aztec Mexico." In *Indian Women of Early Mexico*. Edited by Susan Schroeder et al. 25–54. Norman: University of Oklahoma Press, 1997.

Calvo Isaza, Óscar Iván, and Marta Saade Granados. *La ciudad en cuarentena: Chicha, patología social y profilaxis*. Bogotá: Ministerio de Cultura, 2002.

Câmara Cascudo, Luís da. *Dicionário do Folclore Brasileiro*. São Paulo: Global, 2000.

———. *Prelúdio da Cachaça: etnologia, história e sociologia da aguardente no Brasil*. Belo Horizonte: Itatiaia, 1986 [1968].

Campos, Isaac. *Home Grown: Marijuana and the Origin of Mexico's War on Drugs*. Chapel Hill: University of North Carolina Press, 2012.

Cárdenas Álvarez, Renato, and Carolina Villagrán Moraga. *Chiloé, botánica de la cotidianidad*. Santiago, Chile: Gráfica Lascar, 2005.

Cárdenas Álvarez, Renato, Dante Montiel Vera, and Catherine Grace Hall. *Los chonos y veliche de Chiloé*. Santiago, Chile: Ediciones Olimpho, 1991.

Cardoso, Daniel, et al. "Comparison between Cachaça and Rum Using Pattern Recognition Methods." *Journal of Agricultural and Food Chemistry* 52 (2004): 3429–33.

Carey, Elaine. "'Selling Is More of a Habit Than Using.' Narcotraficante Lola la Chata and Her Threat to Civilization, 1930–1960." *Journal of Women's History* 21, no. 2 (2009): 62–89.

Carey, Elaine, and Andrae M. Marak, eds. *Smugglers, Brothels, and Twine: Historical Perspectives on Contraband and Vice in North America's Borderlands.* Tucson: University of Arizona Press, 2011.

Carey, David, Jr. *Our Elders Teach Us: Maya-Kaqchikel Historical Perspectives. Xkib'ij kan qate' qatata'.* Tuscaloosa: University of Alabama Press, 2001.

———. "'Hard Working, Orderly Little Women.' Mayan Vendors and Marketplace Struggles in Early-Twentieth-Century Guatemala." *Ethnohistory* 55, no. 4 (2008): 579–607.

———. "Maya Soldier-Citizens: Ethnic Pride in the Guatemalan Military, 1925–1945." In *Military Struggle and Identity Formation in Latin America: Race, Nation, and Community During the Liberal Period.* Edited by Nicola Foote and René D. Harder Horst, 136–56. Gainesville: University Press of Florida, 2010.

———, ed. *Distilling the Influence of Alcohol: Aguardiente in Guatemalan History.* Gainesville: University Press of Florida, 2012.

———. "Distilling Perceptions of Crime: Mayan Moonshiners and the State, 1898–1944." In *Distilling the Influence of Alcohol: Aguardiente in Guatemalan History.* Edited by David Carey Jr., 120–56. Gainesville: University Press of Florida, 2012.

———. *I Ask for Justice: Maya Women, Dictators, and Crime in Guatemala, 1898–1944.* Austin: University of Texas Press, 2013.

Carey, David, Jr., and Gabriela E. Torres. "Precursors to Femicide: Guatemalan Women in a Vortex of Violence." *Latin American Research Review* 45, no. 3 (2010): 142–64.

Carneiro, Henrique. *Pequena Enciclopédia da História das Drogas e Bebidas.* Rio de Janeiro: Campus/Elsevier, 2005.

Cassman, Vicki, Larry Carmell, and Eliana Belmonte. "Coca as Symbol and Labor Enhancer in the Andes. A Historical Overview." In *Drugs, Labor, and Colonial Expansion.* Edited by William Jankowiak and Daniel Bradburd, 149–58. New York: Routledge, 2003.

Caulfield, Sueann. "Getting into Trouble: Dishonest Women, Modern Girls, and Women-Men in the Conceptual Language of 'Vida Policial,' 1925–1927." *Signs: Journal of Women in Culture and Society* 19, no. 1 (Autumn 1993): 146–76.

Caulfield, Sueann, Sarah C. Chambers, and Lara Putnam, eds. *Honor, Status, and Law in Modern Latin America.* Durham, NC: Duke University Press, 2005.

Cavero Carrasco, Ranulfo. *Maíz, chicha y religiosidad andina.* Ayacucho, Peru: Universidad Nacional de San Cristóbal de Huamanga, 1986.

Ceballos Ramírez, Manuel. *El catolicismo social: un tercero en discordia*, Rerum Novarum, *"la cuestión social" y la movilización de los católicos mexicanos (1891–1911).* Mexico City: El Colegio de México (hereafter Colmex), 1991.

Centrángolo, Hugo, Sandra Fernández, Javier Quagliano, Vera Selenay, Natalia Muratore, and Francisco Lettieri. *El Negocio de los Vinos Finos en la Argentina.* Buenos Aires: Universidad de Buenos Aires, Facultad de Agronomía, 2002.

Centro de Estudios y Promoción Agraria, Equipo de Economías Regionales. *La economía vitivinícola en la década del 70.* Buenos Aires: CEPA, 1984.

Chambers, Sarah C. *From Subjects to Citizens: Honor, Gender, and Politics in Arequipa, Peru 1780–1854.* University Park: Pennsylvania State University Press, 1999.

———. "Private Crimes, Public Order: Honor, Gender, and the Law in Early Republican Peru." In *Honor, Status and Law in Modern Latin America.* Edited by Sueann Caulfield, Sarah C. Chambers, and Lara Putnam, 27–49. Durham, NC: Duke University Press, 2005.

Chomsky, Aviva. *West Indian Workers and the United Fruit Company in Costa Rica, 1870–1940.* Baton Rouge: Louisiana State University Press, 1996.

Christiansen, Tanja. *Disobedience, Slander, Seduction, and Assault: Women and Men in Cajamarca, Peru, 1862–1900.* Austin: University of Texas Press, 2004.

Chuchiak, John F. "'It Is Their Drinking That Hinders Them': Balché and the Use of Ritual Intoxicants Among the Colonial Yucatec Maya, 1550–1780." *Estudios de Cultura Maya* 24 (Fall 2003): 1–43.

Clendinnen, Inga. *Aztecs.* Cambridge: Cambridge University Press, 1991.

Colby, Benjamin, and Pierre L. Van de Berghe. *Ixil Country: A Plural Society in Highland Guatemala.* Berkeley: University of California Press, 1969.

Collier, Simon, and William F. Sater. *A History of Chile, 1808–2002.* 2nd ed. Cambridge: Cambridge University Press, 2004.

Contreras, Daniel A. "A Mito-Style Structure at Chavín de Huántar: Dating and Implications." *Latin American Antiquity* 21 (2010): 3–21.

Cook, Anita G., and Mary Glowacki. "Pots, Politics, and Power: Huari Ceramic Assemblages and Imperial Administration." In *The Archaeology and Politics of Food and Feasting in Early States and Empires.* Edited by Tamara L. Bray, 173–202. New York: Kluwer Academic/Plenum, 2003.

Corcuera de Mancera, Sonia. *Entre gula y templanza. Un aspecto de la historia mexicana.* 3rd ed. Mexico City: FCE, 1990.

———. *El fraile, el indio y el pulque. Evangelización y embriaguez en la Nueva España (1523–1548).* Mexico City: FCE, 1991.

———. "Luna aturdida: El pulque, su uso y abuso." In *Artes de México, Maguey.* Mexico City: Artes de México y del Mundo, 2000.

Cordy-Collins, Alana. "Chavín Art: Its Shamanic/Hallucinogenic Origins." In *Pre-Columbian Art History.* Edited by Alana Cordy-Collins and Jean Stern, 353–62. Palo Alto, CA: Peek Publications, 1977.

Coria López, Luis Alberto. "El siglo anterior al boom vitivinícola mendocino (1780/1883)." *Revista Universum* 21 (2006): 100–24.

Cornejo Murrieta, Gerardo, ed. *Historia general de Sonora,* vol. 5, *1929–1984.* Hermosillo, Mexico: Gobierno del Estado de Sonora, 1985.

Costa, Wilma Peres. "Do domínio à nação: os impasses da fiscalidade no processo de independência." In *Brasil: Formação do Estado e da Nação.* Edited by István Jancsó, 149–55. São Paulo: Editora Humanismo, Ciência e Tecnologia (hereafter Hucitec)/Editora Unijuí/FAPESP, 2003.

Costa e Silva, Alberto da. *A Manilha e o Libambo: A África e a escravidão de 1500 a 1700.* Rio de Janeiro: Nova Fronteira-Fundação Biblioteca Nacional, 2002.

Courtwright, David T. *Forces of Habit: Drugs and the Making of the Modern World.* Cambridge, MA: Harvard University Press, 2001.

Couturier, Edith. "Women in a Noble Family: The Mexican Counts of Regla, 1750–1830." In *Latin American Women: Historical Perspectives*. Edited by Asunción Lavrín, 129–49. Westport, CT: Greenwood Press, 1978.

———. "Micaela Angela Carrillo: Widow and Pulque Dealer." In *Struggle and Survival in Colonial America*. Edited by Gary B. Nash and David G. Sweet, 362–75. Berkeley: University of California Press, 1980.

Cummins, Thomas B. F. *Toasts with the Inca: Andean Abstraction and Colonial Images on Quero Vessels*. Ann Arbor: University of Michigan Press, 2002.

Curto, José C. "Alcohol and Slaves: The Luso-Brazilian Alcohol Commerce at Mpinda, Luanda, and Benguela During the Atlantic Slave Trade c. 1480–1830 and Its Impact." PhD diss., University of California at Los Angeles, 1996.

———. *Álcool e Escravos: O comércio luso-brasileiro de álcool em Mpinda, Luanda e Benguela durante o tráfico atlântico de escravos (c. 1480–1830) e seu impacto nas sociedades da África Central Ocidental*. Lisboa: Vulgata, 2002.

———. *Enslaving Spirits: The Portuguese-Brazilian Alcohol Trade at Luanda and Its Hinterland, c. 1550–1830*. Leiden: Brill, 2004.

Cutler, Hugh C., and Martín Cárdenas. "Chicha, a Native South American Beer." *Botanical Museum Leaflets* 13, no. 3 (Harvard University, 1947): 33–60.

D'Altroy, Terence N. "From Autonomous to Imperial Rule." In *Empire and Domestic Economy*. Edited by Terence N. D'Altroy and Christine A. Hastorf, 325–39. New York: Kluwer Academic/Plenum, 2001.

———. *The Incas*. Malden, MA: Blackwell, 2002.

———, eds. *Empire and Domestic Economy*. New York: Kluwer Academic/Plenum, 2001.

Dawson, Alexander S. *Indian and Nation in Revolutionary Mexico*. Tucson: University of Arizona Press, 2004.

Deans-Smith, Susan. "The Working Poor and the Eighteenth-Century Colonial State." In *Rituals of Rule, Rituals of Resistance: Public Celebrations and Popular Culture in Mexico*. Edited by William H. Beezley, Cheryl English Martin, and William E. French, 47–75. Wilmington, DE: SR Books, 1994.

DeFelice, John. *Roman Hospitality. The Professional Women of Pompeii*. Warren Center, PA: Shangri-La Publications, 2001.

DeLeonardis, Lisa, and George F. Lau. "Life, Death, and Ancestors." In *Andean Archaeology*. Edited by Helaine Silverman, 77–115. Malden: Blackwell, 2004.

Delpar, Helen. *The Enormous Vogue of Things Mexican: Cultural Relations Between the United States and Mexico, 1920–1935*. Tuscaloosa: University of Alabama Press, 1992.

Dietler, Michael. "Alcohol: Anthropological/Archaeological Perspectives." *Annual Review of Anthropology* 35 (2006): 229–49.

———. "Theorizing the Past: Rituals of Consumption, Commensal Politics, and Power in African Contexts." In *Feasts: Archaeological and Ethnographic Perspectives on Food, Politics, and Power*. Edited by Michael Dietler and Brian Hayden, 65–114. Washington, DC: Smithsonian Institution Press, 2001.

Dosal, Paul. *Power in Transition: The Rise of Guatemala's Industrial Oligarchy, 1871–1994*. Wesport, CT: Praeger, 1995.

Douglas, Mary. *Constructive Drinking: Perspectives on Drink from Anthropology*. New York: Cambridge University Press, 1987.

Druc, Isabelle C. *Ceramic Production and Distribution in the Chavín Sphere of Influence*. New York: Oxford University Press, 1998.

Dudley, Robert. "Fermenting Fruit and the Historical Ecology of Ethanol Ingestion: Is Alcoholism in Modern Humans an Evolutionary Hangover?" *Addiction* 97 (2002): 318–88.

Dunn, Alvis E. "Aguardiente and Identity: The Holy Week Riot of 1786 in Quetzaltenango, Guatemala." PhD diss., University of North Carolina at Chapel Hill, 1999.

———. "'A Sponge Soaking Up All the Money': Alcohol, Taverns, *Vinaterías*, and the Bourbon Reforms in Mid-Eighteenth Century Santiago de los Caballeros." In *Distilling the Influence of Alcohol: Aguardiente in Guatemalan History*. Edited by David Carey Jr., 71–95. Gainesville: University Press of Florida, 2012.

Eber, Christine. *Women and Alcohol in a Highland Maya Town: Water of Hope, Water of Sorrow*. Austin: University of Texas Press, 1995.

———. "'Take My Water': Liberation Through Prohibition in San Pedro Chenalhó, Chiapas, Mexico." *Social Science and Medicine* 53 (2001): 251–62.

Ericastilla, Ana Carla, and Liseth Jiménez. "Las clandestinistas de aguardiente en Guatemala a fines del siglo XIX." In *Mujeres, género e historia en América Central durante los siglos XVIII, XIX, XX*. Edited by Eugenia Rodríguez Sáenz, 13–24. San José, Costa Rica: United Nations Development Fund for Women (UNIFEM)/Burlington, VT: Plumsock Mesoamerican Studies, 2002.

Fallaw, Ben. *Cárdenas Compromised: The Failure of Reform in Postrevolutionary Yucatán*. Durham, NC: Duke University Press, 2001.

———. "Dry Law, Wet Politics: Drinking and Prohibition in Post-Revolutionary Yucatán, 1915–1935." *Latin American Research Review* 37, no. 2 (2001): 37–64.

Farnsworth-Alvear, Ann. *Dulcinea in the Factory. Myths, Morals, Men, and Women in Colombia's Industrial Experiment, 1905–1960*. Durham, NC: Duke University Press, 2000.

Fernandes, João Azevedo. "Cauinagens e bebedeiras: os índios e o álcool na história do Brasil." *Revista Anthropológicas* 13, no. 2 (2002): 39–59.

———. *De Cunhã a Mameluca: A Mulher Tupinambá e o Nascimento do Brasil*. João Pessoa, Brasil: Editora Universidade Federal da Paraíba (hereafter UFPB), 2003.

———. "Cachaça, a rainha do Sul." *Revista Atlântica de Cultura Ibero-Americana* 2 (2005): 84–87.

———. "Feast and Sin: Catholic Missionaries and Native Celebrations in Early Colonial Brazil." *Social History of Alcohol and Drugs* 23, no. 2 (2009): 111–27.

———. *Selvagens Bebedeiras: Álcool, Embriaguez e Contatos Culturais no Brasil Colonial (Séculos XVI–XVII)*. São Paulo: Alameda, 2011.

Fernández, Rodolfo, and Daria Deraga. "El uso de material fecal en la fermentación alcohólica." *Diario de Campo* 89 (2006), 80–85.

Fernández-Aceves, María Teresa. "Once We Were Corn Grinders. Women and Labor in the Tortilla Industry of Guadalajara, 1920–1940." *International Labor and Working-Class History* 63 (2003): 81–101.

Fernández Labbé, Marcos. "Las comunidades de la sobriedad: la instalación de zonas secas como método de control del beber inmoderado en Chile, 1910–1930." *Scripta Nova: Revista Electrónica de Geografía y Ciencias Sociales* 9, no. 194 (August 2005): 59.

Ferreira Ribeiro, Ricardo. "Tortuosas raízes medicinais: as mágicas origens da farmacopéia popular brasileira e sua trajetória pelo mundo." In *Álcool e drogas na história do Brasil*. Edited by Renato P. Venâncio and Henrique Carneiro, 155–84. São Paulo/Belo Horizonte: Alameda/Editora PUC Minas, 2005.

Ferreira, Roquinaldo. "Dinâmica do comércio intracolonial: Geribitas, panos asiáticos e guerra no tráfico angolano de escravos (século XVIII)." In *O Antigo Regime nos Trópicos: A Dinâmica Imperial Portuguesa*. Edited by João Fragoso, Maria F. B. Bicalho, and Maria de Fátima S. Gouvêa, 339–78. Rio de Janeiro: Civilização Brasileira, 2001.

Figueiredo, Luciano. *Rebeliões no Brasil Colônia*. Rio de Janeiro: Jorge Zahar Editor, 2005.

Figueiredo, Luciano Rodrigues, and Renato Pinto Venâncio. "Águas Ardentes: o nascimento da cachaça." In *Cachaça: alquimia brasileira*. Edited by Luciano Figueiredo, Heloisa Faria et al., 12–57. Rio de Janeiro: Design, 2005.

Finucane, Brian C. "Maize and Sociopolitical Complexity in the Ayacucho Valley, Peru." *Current Anthropology* 50 (2009): 535–45.

Fleming, William J. "Regional Development and Transportation in Argentina: Mendoza and the Gran Oeste Argentino Railroad, 1885–1914." PhD diss., Indiana University, 1976.

Foucault, Michel. *Discipline and Punish: The Birth of the Prison*. Translated by Alan Sheridan. New York: Pantheon Books, 1977.

Fowler-Salamini, Heather. "Gender, Work, and Working-Class Women's Culture in Veracruz Coffee Export Industry, 1920–1945." *International Labor and Working-Class History* 63 (2003): 102–21.

Fowler-Salamini, Heather, and Mary Kay Vaughan, eds. *Women of the Mexican Countryside, 1850–1990*. Tucson: University of Arizona Press, 1994.

Francois, Marie Eileen. *A Culture of Everyday Credit: Housekeeping, Pawnbroking, and Governance in Mexico City*. Lincoln: University of Nebraska Press, 2006.

French, John D., and Daniel James, eds. *The Gendered Worlds of Latin American Women Workers*. Durham, NC: Duke University Press, 1997.

———. "Squaring the Circle: Women's Factory Labor, Gender Ideology, and Necessity." In *The Gendered Worlds of Latin American Women Workers*. Edited by John D. French and Daniel James, 1–30. Durham, NC: Duke University Press, 1997.

French, William E. *A Peaceful and Working People: Manners, Morals, and Class Formation in Northern Mexico*. Albuquerque: University of New Mexico Press, 1996.

French, William E., and Katherine Elaine Bliss, eds. *Gender, Sexuality, and Power in Latin America Since Independence*. Lanham, MD: Rowman and Littlefield, 2007.

Galante, A. N. *La industria vitivinícola Argentina*. Buenos Aires: Talleres S. Ostwald, 1900.

García Gutiérrez, C. Manuel. *Memoria Gráfica de Noches Tapatías*. Guadalajara, Mexico: Tequila Sauza, 1983.

García Rodríguez, Mercedes. "El aguardiente de caña y otras bebidas en la Cuba Colonial." Unpublished manuscript, 2010.

———. *Entre haciendas y plantaciones. Los orígenes azucareros de La Habana*. Havana: Ciencias Sociales, 2007.

Garrard-Burnett, Virginia. "Indians Are Drunks, Drunks Are Indians: Alcohol and

Indigenismo in Guatemala, 1890–1940." *Bulletin of Latin American Research* 19, no. 3 (2000): 341–56.

———. "Drunk as Lords: Community Drunkenness and Control in Guatemala." In *Distilling the Influence of Alcohol: Guatemala and* Aguardiente *Since Late Colonial Times*. Edited by David Carey Jr., 157–79. Gainesville: University Press of Florida, 2012.

Garza, James Alex. *The Imagined Underworld: Sex, Crime, and Vice in Porfirian Mexico City*. Lincoln: University of Nebraska Press, 2007.

Gauderman, Kimberly. *Women's Lives in Colonial Quito. Gender, Law, and Economy in Spanish America*. Austin: University of Texas Press, 2003.

Gay, Claudio. *Historia física y política de Chile*, vol. 5, *Agricultura*. Santiago, Chile: Instituto de Capacitación e Investigación en Reforma Agraria, 1973.

Gayford, J. J. "Battered Wives." In *International Perspectives on Family Violence*. Edited by Richard J. Gelles and Flaire Pedrick Cornell. Lexington, MA: Lexington Books, 1983.

Gaytán, Marie Sarita. "Drinking the Nation and Making Masculinity: Tequila, Pancho Villa and the U.S. Media." In *Toward a Sociology of the Trace*. Edited by Herman Gray and Macarena Gómez-Barris, 207–33. Minneapolis: University of Minnesota Press, 2010.

Gerbi, Antonello. *O Novo Mundo: história de uma polêmica — 1750–1900*. São Paulo: Companhia das Letras, 1996.

Gero, Joan M. "Pottery, Power, and . . . Parties!" *Archaeology* 43 (1990): 52–56.

———. "Feasts and Females: Gender Ideology and Political Meals in the Andes." *Norwegian Archaeological Review* 25 (1992): 15–30.

Gibson, Charles. *The Aztecs Under Spanish Rule: A History of the Indians of the Valley of Mexico, 1519–1810*. Stanford, CA: Stanford University Press, 1964.

Goldstein, David J., and Robin Christine Coleman. "*Schinus molle* L. (Anacardiaceae) Chicha Production in the Central Andes." *Economic Botany* 58 (2004): 523–29.

Goldstein, David J., Robin C. Coleman Goldstein, and Patrick R. Williams. "You Are What You Drink: A Sociocultural Reconstruction of Pre-Hispanic Fermented Beverage Use at Cerro Baúl, Moquegua, Peru." In *Drink, Power, and Society in the Andes*. Edited by Justin Jennings and Brenda Bowser, 133–66. Gainesville: University Press of Florida, 2009.

Goldstein, Paul. "From Stew-Eaters to Maize-Drinkers: The Chicha Economy and the Tiwanaku Expansion." In *The Archaeology and Politics of Food and Feasting in Early States and Empires*. Edited by Tamara L. Bray, 143–72. New York: Kluwer Academic/Plenum, 2003.

———. *Andean Diaspora: The Tiwanaku Colonies and the Origins of South American Empire*. Gainesville: University Press of Florida, 2005.

Gonçalves, Marco Antônio. *O Mundo Inacabado: Ação e Criação em uma Cosmologia Amazônica. Etnografia Pirahã*. Rio de Janeiro: Editora Universidade Federal do Rio de Janeiro, 2001.

Gootenberg, Paul. *Andean Cocaine. The Making of a Global Drug*. Chapel Hill: University of North Carolina Press, 2008.

Gose, Peter. *Invaders as Ancestors: On the Intercultural Making and Unmaking of Spanish Colonialism in the Andes*. Toronto: University of Toronto Press, 2008.

Gotkowitz, Laura. "Trading Insults: Honor, Violence, and the Gendered Culture of Commerce in Cochabamba, Bolivia." *Hispanic American Historical Review* 83, no. 1 (2003): 83–118.

Graeber, David. *Debt: The First 5,000 Years.* Brooklyn, NY: Melville House Printing, 2011.

Grandin, Greg. *The Blood of Guatemala: A History of Race and Nation.* Durham, NC: Duke University Press, 2000.

Gravatá, Carlos Eduardo S. *Almanaque da Cachaça,* Belo Horizonte: Formato, 1990.

Guedea, Virginia. "México en 1812: Control político y bebidas prohibidas." *Estudios de historia moderna y contemporánea de México* 8 (1980): 23–64.

Guerrero Guerrero, Raúl. *El Pulque.* Mexico City: Editorial Joaquín Mortiz-INAH, 1985.

Hames, Gina. "Honor, Alcohol, and Sexuality: Women and the Creation of Ethnic Identity in Bolivia, 1870–1930." PhD diss., Carnegie Mellon University, 1996.

———. "Maize-Beer, Gossip, and Slander: Female Tavern Proprietors and Urban, Ethnic Cultural Elaboration in Bolivia, 1870–1930." *Journal of Social History* 37, no. 2 (2003): 351–64.

———. *Alcohol in World History.* New York: Routledge, 2012.

Hamilton, Nora. *The Limits of State Autonomy: Post-Revolutionary Mexico.* Princeton, NJ: Princeton University Press, 1982.

Hanawalt, Barbara A. "The Host, the Law, and the Ambiguous Space of Medieval London Taverns." In *Medieval Crime and Social Control.* Edited by Barbara A. Hanawalt and David Wallace, 204–23. Minneapolis: University of Minnesota Press, 1999.

Hanway, Nancy. *Embodying Argentina: Body, Space and Nation in 19th Century Narratives.* Jefferson, NC: McFarland, 2003.

Harris, Olivia. "Complementaridad y conflicto: Una vision andina del hombre y la mujer." *Allpanchis* 25, no. 21 (1985): 17–42.

Hastorf, Christine A. "The Effect of the Inka State on Sausa Agricultural Production and Crop Consumption." *American Antiquity* 55 (1990): 262–90.

———. "Gender, Space, and Food in Prehistory." In *Engendering Archaeology: Women and Prehistory.* Edited by Joan M. Gero and Margaret W. Conkey, 132–59. Cambridge: Blackwell, 1991.

———. *Agriculture and the Onset of Political Inequality before the Inka.* Cambridge: Cambridge University Press, 1993.

———. "Agricultural Production and Consumption." In *Empire and Domestic Economy.* Edited by Terence N. D'Altroy and Christine A. Hastorf, 155–78. New York: Kluwer Academic/Plenum, 2001.

———. "The Xauxa Andean Life." In *Empire and Domestic Economy.* Edited by Terence N. D'Altroy and Christine A. Hastorf, 315–24. New York: Kluwer Academic/Plenum, 2001.

Hastorf, Christine A., and Sissel Johannessen. "Pre-Hispanic Political Change and the Role of Maize in the Central Andes of Peru." *American Anthropologist* 95 (1993): 115–38.

Hastorf, Christine A., William T. Whitehead, Maria C. Bruno, and Melanie Wright. "The Movements of Maize into Middle Horizon Tiwanaku, Bolivia." In *Histories of Maize: Multidisciplinary Approaches to the Prehistory, Linguistics, Biogeography,*

Domestication and Evolution of Maize. Edited by John Staller, John Tykot, and Bruce Benz, 429–48. Amsterdam: Elsevier Academic Press, 2006.

Hayashida, Frances. "Chicha Histories: Pre-Hispanic Brewing in the Andes and the Use of Ethnographic and Historic Analogues." In *Drink, Power, and Society in the Andes*. Edited by Justin Jennings and Brenda Bowser, 232–56. Gainesville: University Press of Florida, 2009.

Hayden, Brian. "Fabulous Feasts: A Prolegomenon to the Importance of Feasting." In *Feasts: Archaeological and Ethnographic Perspectives on Food, Politics, and Power*. Edited by Michael Dietler and Brian Hayden, 23–64. Washington, DC: Smithsonian Institution Press, 2001.

Heath, Dwight B. "Anthropological Perspectives on Alcohol: An Historical Review." In *Cross-Cultural Approaches to the Study of Alcohol: An Interdisciplinary Perspective*. Edited by Michael W. Everett, Jack O. Waddell, and Dwight B. Heath, 41–101. The Hague: Mouton, 1976.

Hemming, John. *The Conquest of the Incas*. New York: Harcourt Brace Jovanovich, 1970.

———. *Red Gold: The Conquest of Brazilian Indians*. Chatham, Canada: Papermac, 1995.

Hernández Palomo, José Jesús. *La renta del pulque en Nueva España, 1663–1810*. Seville: Escuela de Estudios Hispano-Americanos de Sevilla, 1979.

Hershfield, Joanne, and David Maciel. *Mexico's Cinema: A Century of Film and Filmmakers*. Wilmington, DE: SR Books, 1999.

Holler, Jacqueline. "Conquered Spaces, Colonial Skirmishes: Spatial Contestation in Sixteenth-Century Mexico City." *Radical History Review* 99 (2007): 107–20.

Houaiss, Antônio, Mauro Villar, and Francisco Manuel de Mello Franco, eds. *Dicionário Houaiss da Língua Portuguesa*, CD-ROM. Rio de Janeiro: Editora Objetiva, 2009.

Isbell, William H. "Wari and Tiwanaku: International Identities in the Central Andean Middle Horizon." In *Handbook of South American Archaeology*. Edited by Helaine Silverman and William H. Isbell, 731–59. New York: Springer, 2008.

Jacobsen, Nils, and Cristóbal Aljovín de Losada, eds. *Political Culture in the Andes, 1750–1950*, Durham, NC: Duke University Press, 2005.

Jankowiak, William, and Daniel Bradburd, eds. *Drugs, Labor, and Colonial Expansion*. Tucson: University of Arizona Press, 2003.

Janusek, John Wayne. *Ancient Tiwanaku*. New York: Cambridge University Press, 2008.

Janusek, John Wayne, and Deborah E. Blom. "Identifying Tiwanaku Urban Populations: Style, Identity, and Ceremony in Andean Cities." In *Urbanism in the Preindustrial World: Cross-Cultural Approaches*. Edited by Glen R. Storey, 233–51. Tuscaloosa: University of Alabama Press, 2006.

Jennings, Justin. "La Chichera y el Patrón: Chicha and the Energetics of Feasting in the Prehistoric Andes." In *Foundations of Power in the Prehispanic Andes*. Edited by Christina A. Conlee, Dennis Ogburn, and Kevin Vaughn, 241–59. Arlington, VA: American Anthropological Association, 2005.

———, ed. *Beyond Wari Walls: Regional Perspectives on Middle Horizon Peru*. Albuquerque: University of New Mexico Press, 2010.

Jennings, Justin, and Brenda Bowser, eds. *Drink, Power, and Society in the Andes*. Gainesville: University Press of Florida, 2009.

Jennings, Justin, and Melissa Chatfield. "Pots, Brewers, and Hosts: Women's Power and the Limits of Central Andean Feasting." In *Drink, Power, and Society in the Andes*. Edited by Justin Jennings and Brenda Bowser, 200–31. Gainesville: University Press of Florida, 2009.

Jiménez, Christina M. "From the Lettered City to the Sellers' City: Vendor Politics and Public Space in Urban Mexico, 1880–1926." In *The Spaces of the Modern City. Imaginaries, Politics, and Everyday Life*. Edited by Gyan Prakash and Kevin M. Kruse, 214–46. Princeton, NJ: Princeton University Press, 2008.

Johns, Michael. *The City of Mexico in the Age of Díaz*. Austin: University of Texas Press, 1997.

Johnson, Lyman L. "Dangerous Words, Provocative Gestures, and Violent Acts: The Disputed Hierarchies of Plebian Life in Colonial Buenos Aires." In *The Faces of Honor: Sex, Shame, and Violence in Colonial Latin America*. Edited by Lyman Johnson and Sonya Lipsett-Rivera, 127–51. Albuquerque: University of New Mexico Press, 1998.

Jones, Dan. "Moral Psychology. The Depths of Disgust." *Nature* 447 (June 14, 2007): 768–71.

Joseph, Gilbert M., and Daniel Nugent, eds. *Everyday Forms of State Formation: Revolution and the Negotiation of Rule in Modern Mexico*. Durham, NC: Duke University Press, 1994.

———. "Popular Culture and State Formation in Revolutionary Mexico." In *Everyday Forms of State Formation: Revolution and the Negotiation of Rule in Modern Mexico*. Edited by Gilbert M. Joseph and Daniel Nugent, 3–23. Durham, NC: Duke University Press, 1994.

Julien, Catherine J. *Condesuyo: The Political Division of Territory Under Inka and Spanish Rule*. Bonner Amerikanistische Studien 19. Bonn, Germany: Seminar für Völkerkunde, Universität Bonn, 1991.

Karasch, Mary C. *A vida dos escravos no Rio de Janeiro, 1808–1850*. São Paulo: Companhia das Letras, 2000.

Katra, William H. "Rereading *Viajes*: Race, Identity and National Destiny." In *Sarmiento: Author of a Nation*. Edited by Tulio Halperín Donghi et al., 73–100. Berkeley: University of California Press, 1994.

Katzew, Ilona. *Casta Paintings: Images of Race in Eighteenth-Century Mexico*. New Haven, CT: Yale University Press, 2004.

Kellogg, Susan. *Weaving the Past. A History of Latin America's Indigenous Women from the Prehispanic Period to the Present*. New York: Oxford University Press, 2005.

Keremetsis, Dawn. "Del metate al molino. La mujer mexicana de 1910–1940." *Historia Mexicana* 33, no. 2 (1983): 285–302.

Keynes, Richard. *Charles Darwin's Zoology Notes and Specimen Lists from the H.M.S. Beagle*. Cambridge: Cambridge University Press, 2000.

Kicza, John. "The Pulque Trade of Late Colonial Mexico City." *The Americas* 37, no. 2 (1980): 193–221.

———. *Colonial Entrepreneurs, Families and Business in Bourbon Mexico City*. Albuquerque: University of New Mexico Press, 1983.

Kirkby, Diane. *Barmaids. A History of Women's Work in Pubs*. Cambridge: Cambridge University Press, 1997.

Klubock, Thomas Miller. "Working-Class Masculinity, Middle-Class Morality, and Labor Politics in the Chilean Mines." *Journal of Social History* 30, no. 2 (1996): 435–63.

Knight, Alan. "Racism, Revolution, and *Indigenismo*: Mexico, 1910–1940." In *The Idea of Race in Latin America, 1870–1940*. Edited by Richard Graham, 71–85. Austin: University of Texas Press, 1990.

———. "Revolutionary Project, Recalcitrant People: Mexico, 1910–1940." In *The Revolutionary Process in Mexico: Essays on Political and Social Change, 1880–1940*. Edited by Jaime E. Rodríguez O., 227–64. Los Angeles: University of California Press, 1990.

———. "Popular Culture and the Revolutionary State in Mexico, 1910–1940." *Hispanic American Historical Review* 74, no. 3 (1994): 393–444.

Knobloch, Patricia J. "Wari Ritual Power at Conchopata: An Interpretation of Anadenanthera colubrina Iconography." *Latin American Antiquity* 11 (2000): 387–402.

Lacoste, Pablo. *El vino del inmigrante: Los inmigrantes europeos y la industria vitivinícola argentina*. Mendoza, Argentina: Universidad del Congreso/ Consejo Empresario Mendocino, 2003.

———. "Viticultura y Política Internacional: El intento de reincorporar a Mendoza y San Juan a Chile (1820–1835)." *Historia* 39, no. 1 (2006): 155–76.

———. "Wine and Women: Grape Growers and *Pulperas* in Mendoza, 1561–1852." *Hispanic American Historical Review* 88, no. 3 (2008): 361–91.

LaFarge, Oliver. *Santa Eulalia: The Religion of a Cuchumatán Indian Town*. Chicago: University of Chicago Press, 1947.

Larsen, Clark Spencer. *Bioarchaeology*. Cambridge: Cambridge University Press, 2000.

Lau, George F. "Feasting and Ancestor Veneration at Chinchawas, North Highlands of Ancash, Peru." *Latin American Antiquity* 13 (2002): 279–304.

———. "The Recuay Culture of Peru's North-Central Highlands: A Reappraisal of Chronology and Its Implications." *Journal of Field Archaeology* 29 (2004): 177–202.

———. "House Forms and Recuay Culture: Residential Compounds at Yayno (Ancash, Peru), a Fortified Hilltop Town, AD 400–800." *Journal of Anthropological Archaeology* 29 (2010): 327–51.

Lear, John. *Workers, Neighbors, and Citizens. The Revolution in Mexico City*. Lincoln: University of Nebraska Press, 2001.

Leclert, Lucie. "Who Benefits from the 'Denominación de Origen' Tequila?" MA thesis, Wageningen University, 2007.

León, Rafo. *Chicha peruana, una bebida, una cultura*. Lima, Peru: Universidad de San Martín de Porres, 2008.

Lewis, Stephen E. "La guerra del posh, 1951–1954: Un conflicto decisivo entre el Instituto Nacional Indigenista, el monopolio del alcohol y el gobierno del estado de Chiapas." *Mesoamerica* 46 (2004): 111–34.

———. *The Ambivalent Revolution: Forging State and Nation in Chiapas, 1910–1945*. Albuquerque: University of New Mexico Press, 2005.

———. "Mexico's National Indigenist Institute and the Negotiation of Applied Anthropology in Highland Chiapas, 1951–1954." *Ethnohistory* 55, no. 4 (Fall 2008): 609–32.

Lima, Oswaldo Gonçalves de. *El maguey y el pulque en los códices mexicanos*. Mexico City: FCE, 1956.

Lima, Tânia Stolze. *Um peixe olhou para mim: O povo Yudjá e a perspectiva*. São Paulo/Rio de Janeiro: Editora Universidade Estadual Paulista, Instituto Socioambiental, Núcleo de Transformações Indígenas, 2005.

Little, Walter E. "A Visual Political Economy of Maya Representations in Guatemala, 1931–1944." *Ethnohistory* 55, no. 4 (Fall 2008): 633–63.

Loyola Montemayor, Elías. *La industria del pulque*. Mexico City: Departamento de Investigaciones Industriales del Banco de México, 1956.

Luna Zamora, Rogelio. *La historia del tequila, de sus regiones y sus hombres*. Mexico City: Conaculta, 1991.

Macazaga Ramírez de Arellano, Carlos. *Las calaveras vivientes de José Guadalupe Posada*. Mexico City: Editorial Cosmos, 1976.

MacLachlan, Colin M. *Criminal Justice in Eighteenth Century Mexico: A Study of the Tribunal of the Acordada*. Berkeley: University of California Press, 1974.

Mancall, Peter C. *Deadly Medicine: Indians and Alcohol in Early America*. Ithaca, NY: Cornell University Press, 1995.

Mangan, Jane E. *Trading Roles: Gender, Ethnicity, and the Urban Economy in Colonial Potosí*. Durham, NC: Duke University Press, 2005.

Marak, Andrae M. "Portes Gil's Anti-Alcohol Campaign in Ciudad Juárez, 1929–1934." Paper presented at the annual meeting of the American Historical Association, New York, 2009.

Marques, Teresa Cristina de Novaes. "Beer and Sugar-Cane Spirit Under Temperance in Brazil, in the Beginning of the 20th Century." Paper presented at the Alcohol in the Making of the Atlantic World: Historical and Contemporary Perspectives international workshop, York University, Toronto, 2007.

Martin, A. Lynn. *Alcohol, Sex, and Gender in Late Medieval and Early Modern Europe*. New York: Palgrave, 2001.

Martin, Cheryl English. *Governance and Society in Colonial Mexico: Chihuahua in the Eighteenth Century*. Stanford, CA: Stanford University Press, 1996.

Martínez, María Elena. *Geneological Fictions: Limpieza de Sangre, Religion, and Gender in Colonial Mexico*. Stanford, CA: Stanford University Press, 2008.

Martínez Assad, Carlos. *El laboratorio de la revolución: el Tabasco garridista*. Mexico City: Siglo Veintiuno Editores, 1979.

Martínez Limón, Enrique. *Tequila: The Spirit of Mexico*. Mexico City: Revimundo, 1988.

Martínez-Vergne, Teresita. *Nation and Citizen in the Dominican Republic, 1880–1916*. Chapel Hill: University of North Carolina Press, 2005.

Martiré, Eduardo. *Las Audiencias y la Administración de Justicia en las Indias*. Madrid: Ediciones Universidad Autónoma de Madrid, 2005.

Mateu, Ana María. "Mendoza entre el orden y el progreso 1880–1918." In *Mendoza, a través de su historia*. Edited by Arturo Roig, Pablo Lacoste, and María Satlari, chap. 7. Mendoza, Argentina: Editorial Caviar Bleu, 2004.

Mateu, Ana, and Hugo Ocaña. "Una mirada empresarial a la historia de la vitivinicultura mendocina (1881–1936)." *Boletín Americanista* 59 (2009): 47–67.

Mateu, Ana María, and Steve Stein. "Diálogos entre sordos, los pragmáticos y los técnicos en la época inicial de la industria vitivinícola argentina." *Historia agraria: Revista de agricultura e historia rural* 39 (2006): 267–92.

————, eds. *El vino y sus revoluciones: Una antología histórica sobre el desarrollo de la industria vitivinícola argentina.* Mendoza, Argentina: Editorial de la Universidad Nacional de Cuyo, 2008.

Mauro, Frédéric. *Portugal, o Brasil e o Atlântico, 1570–1670*, vol. 2. Lisbon: Editorial Estampa, 1988.

Mauss, Marcel. *The Gift: The Form and Reason for Exchange in Archaic Societies.* Translated by W. D. Hall. New York: W. W. Norton, 1990.

McCreery, David. *Rural Guatemala 1760–1940.* Stanford, CA: Stanford University Press, 1994.

McDermott, Gerald A. "The Politics of Institutional Renovation and Economic Upgrading: Recombining the Vines That Bind Argentina." *Politics and Society* 35 (2007): 103–44.

McGovern, Patrick E. *Uncorking the Past: The Quest for Wine, Beer, and Other Alcoholic Beverages.* Berkeley: University of California Press, 2009.

McPherson, Alan. "More Notes from a Cockfight: Resistance Through Gambling in *La Española* during US Occupations." Paper presented at the annual meeting of the Rocky Mountain Council on Latin American Studies, Santa Fe, NM, 2011.

Meacham, Sarah Hand. *Every Home a Distillery. Alcohol, Gender, and Technology in the Colonial Chesapeake.* Baltimore, MD: Johns Hopkins University Press, 2009.

Medeiros, Maria do Céu. *Igreja e Dominação no Brasil Escravista: O caso dos Oratorianos de Pernambuco, 1659–1830.* João Pessoa, Brasil: Centro de Ciências Humanas, Letras e Artes-UFPB/Idéia, 1993.

Mello, José Antônio Gonsalves de. *Restauradores de Pernambuco: Biografias de figuras do século XVII que defenderam e consolidaram a unidade brasileira.* Recife, Brazil: Imprensa Universitária, 1967.

Mendelson, E. Michael. "Religion and World-View in Santiago Atitlán." PhD diss., University of Chicago, 1956.

Merkx, Gilbert W. "Sectoral Clashes and Political Change: The Argentine Experience." *Latin American Research Review* 4, no. 3 (1969), 89–114.

Meuwese, Marcus P. "'For the Peace and Well-Being of the Country': Intercultural Mediators and Dutch-Indian Relations in New Netherland and Dutch Brazil, 1600–1664." PhD diss., University of Notre Dame, 2003.

Meyer, Jean. *El sinarquismo: un fascismo mexicano? 1937–1947.* Mexico City: Joaquín Mortiz, 1979.

————. "An Idea of Mexico: Catholics in the Revolution." In *The Eagle and the Virgin: Nation and Cultural Revolution in Mexico, 1920–1940.* Edited by Mary Kay Vaughan and Stephen E. Lewis, 281–96. Durham, NC: Duke University Press, 2006.

Meyer, Michael C., and William H. Beezley, eds. *The Oxford History of Mexico.* Oxford: Oxford University Press, 2000.

Miller, Joseph C. *Way of Death: Merchant Capitalism and the Angolan Slave Trade, 1730–1830.* Madison: University of Wisconsin Press, 1988.

Miller, William Ian. *The Anatomy of Disgust.* Cambridge, MA: Harvard University Press, 1997.

Mitchell, Stephanie. "Por la liberación de la mujer: Women and the Anti-Alcohol Campaign." In *The Women's Revolution in Mexico, 1910–1953.* Edited by Stephanie Mitchell and Patience A. Schell, 173–85. Wilmington, DE: Rowman and Littlefield, 2007.

Mitchell, Tim. *Intoxicated Identities: Alcohol's Power in Mexican History and Culture.* New York: Routledge, 2004.

Moore, Jerry. "Pre-Hispanic Beer in Coastal Peru: Technology and Social Context of Prehistoric Production." *American Anthropologist* 91 (1989): 682–95.

Mora, Carl J. *Mexican Cinema: Reflections of a Society, 1896–1988.* Berkeley: University of California Press, 1989.

Morris, Craig. "Maize Beer in the Economics, Politics, and Religion of the Inca Empire." In *Fermented Food Beverages in Nutrition.* Edited by Clifford F. Gastineau, William J. Darby, and Thomas B. Turner, 21–34. New York: Academic Press, 1979.

———. "The Infrastructure of Inka Control in the Peruvian Central Highlands." In *The Inca and Aztec States, 1400–1800: Anthropology and History.* Edited by George A. Collier, Renato I. Rosaldo, and John D. Wirth, 153–71. New York: Academic Press, 1982.

Moseley, Michael E., Donna J. Nash, Patrick Ryan Williams, Susan D. deFrance, Anna Miranda, and Mario Ruales. "Burning Down the Brewery: Establishing and Evacuating an Ancient Imperial Colony at Cerro Baúl, Peru." *Proceedings of the National Academy of Sciences of the United States of America* 102 (2005): 17264–71.

Murra, John V. "Rite and Crop in the Inca State." In *Culture in History: Essays in Honor of Paul Radin.* Edited by Stanley Diamon, 393–407. New York: Columbia University Press, 1960.

Nájera-Ramírez, Olga. "Engendering Nationalism: Identity, Discourse, and the Mexican Charro." *Anthropological Quarterly* 67, no. 1 (1994): 1–14.

Nash, Donna J. "The Archaeology of Space: Places of Power in the Wari Empire." PhD diss., University of Florida, 2002.

Nash, Donna J., and Patrick Ryan Williams. "Architecture and Power on the Wari-Tiwanaku Frontier." In *Foundations of Power in the Prehispanic Andes.* Edited by Christina A. Conlee, Dennis Ogburn, and Kevin Vaughn, 151–74. Arlington, VA: American Anthropological Association, 2005.

Novo, Salvador. *Cocina Mexicana. Historia gastronómica de la Ciudad de México.* Mexico City: Pórtico de la Ciudad de México–Estudio Salvador Novo, 1993.

Núñez de Pineda y Bascuñan, Francisco. *Cautiverio feliz y razón individual de las guerras dilatadas del reino de Chile.* Santiago, Chile: Editorial Universitaria, 1973.

Oakland, Amy S. "Tiwanaku Textile Style from the South Central Andes, Bolivia and North Chile." PhD diss., University of Texas, 1986.

O'Connor, Erin. "Helpless Children or Undeserving Patriarchs? Gender Ideologies, the State, and Indian Men in Late Nineteenth Century Ecuador." In *Highland Indians and the State in Modern Ecuador.* Edited by A. Kim Clark and Marc Becker, 56–72. Pittsburgh: University of Pittsburgh Press, 2007.

Olcott, Jocelyn. *Revolutionary Women in Postrevolutionary Mexico.* Durham, NC: Duke University Press, 2005.

Olcott, Jocelyn, Mary Kay Vaughan, and Gabriela Cano. *Sex in Revolution. Gender, Politics, and Power in Modern Mexico.* Durham, NC: Duke University Press, 2006.

Opie, Frederick Douglass. "Adios Jim Crow: Afro-North American Workers and the Guatemalan Railroad Workers' League, 1884–1921." PhD diss., Syracuse University, 1999.

———. "Alcohol and Lowdown Culture in Caribbean Guatemala and Honduras, 1898–1920." In *Distilling the Influence of Alcohol: Aguardiente in Guatemalan History*. Edited by David Carey Jr., 96–119. Gainesville: University Press of Florida, 2012.

Orozco, José. "*Esos Altos de Jalisco*: Immigration and the Idea of Alteño Exceptionalism, 1926–1952." PhD diss., Harvard University, 1998.

Owensby, Brian. *Empire of Law and Indian Justice in Colonial Mexico*. Stanford, CA: Stanford University Press, 2008.

Palacios, Guillermo. *La pluma y el arado: Los intelectuales pedagogos y la construcción sociocultural del "problema campesino" en México, 1932–1934*. Mexico City: Colmex, 1999.

Pardo, Oriana B. "Las chichas en el Chile precolombiano." *Chloris chilensis: revista chilena de flora y vegetación* 7, no. 2 (2004), http://www.chlorischile.cl/chichas/chichas.htm.

Penry, S. Elizabeth. "The Rey Común: Indigenous Political Discourse in Eighteenth-Century Alto Perú." In *The Collective and the Public in Latin America: Cultural Identities and Political Order*. Edited by Luis Roniger and Tamar Herzog, 219–37. Brighton, UK: Sussex Academic Press, 2000.

Perone, Jorge Aldo. *Identidad o masificación: Una encrucijada en la industria vitivinícola argentina*. Mendoza, Argentina: Universidad Nacional de Cuyo, Facultad de Ciencias Económicas, 1985.

Piccato, Pablo. "'El Paso de Venus por el disco del Sol': Criminality and Alcoholism in the Late Porfiriato." *Mexican Studies/Estudios Mexicanos* 11, no. 2 (1995): 203–41.

———. "Urbanistas, Ambulantes, and Mendigos: The Dispute for Urban Space in Mexico City, 1890–1930." In *Reconstructing Criminality in Latin America*. Edited by Carlos A. Aguirre and Robert Buffington, 113–48. Wilmington, DE: SR Books, 2000.

———. *City of Suspects: Crime in Mexico City, 1900–1931*. Durham, NC: Duke University Press, 2001.

———. *The Tyranny of Public Opinion: Honor in the Construction of the Mexican Public Sphere*. Durham, NC: Duke University Press, 2010.

Pierce, Gretchen Kristine. "Sobering the Revolution: Mexico's Anti-Alcohol Campaigns and the Process of State-Building, 1910–1940." PhD diss., University of Arizona, 2008.

Pierce, Gretchen. "Parades, Epistles and Prohibitive Legislation: Mexico's National Anti-Alcohol Campaign and the Process of State-Building, 1934–1940." *Social History of Alcohol and Drugs* 23, no. 2 (2009): 151–80.

———. "Fighting Bacteria, the Bible, and the Bottle: Projects to Create New Men, Women, and Children, 1910–1940." In *A Companion to Mexican History and Culture*. Edited by William H. Beezley, 505–17. London: Wiley-Blackwell, 2011.

Pilcher, Jeffrey M. "Tamales or Timbales: Cuisine and the Formation of Mexican National Identity, 1821–1911." *The Americas* 53, no. 2 (1996): 193–216.

———. *¡Que vivan los tamales! Food and the Making of Mexican Identity*. Albuquerque: University of New Mexico Press, 1998.

Podestá, Ricardo Augusto. "Intervención del Estado." In *Crisis vitivinícola: Estudios y propuestas para su solución*. Edited by Eduardo Díaz Araujo et al., 56–72. Mendoza, Argentina: Universidad de Mendoza, Editorial Idearium, 1982.

Pont, Polly Maclaine, and Hernán Thomas. "How the Vineyard Came to Matter: Grape Quality, the Meaning of Grapevines and Technological Change in Mendoza's Wine Production." *Universum* 22, no. 1 (2007): 218–34.

Porter, Susie S. *Working Women in Mexico City: Public Discourses and Material Conditions, 1879–1931*. Tucson: University of Arizona Press, 2003.

Premat, Estela del Carmen. "La Bodega Mendocina en los siglos XVII y XVIII." *Revista Universum* 22, no. 1 (2007): 118–35.

Premo, Bianca. "From the Pockets of Women: The Gendering of the Mita, Migration, and Tribute in Colonial Chuchuito, Peru." *The Americas* 57, no. 1 (2000): 63–94.

Quintero, Gilbert. "Making the Indian: Colonial Knowledge, Alcohol, and Native Americans." *American Indian Culture and Research Journal* 25 (2001): 57–71.

Quiroz Márquez, Jorge. *Mezcal: Origin, Elaboration, and Recipes*. Oaxaca: Códice Ediciones, 1997.

Raminelli, Ronald. "Da etiqueta canibal: beber antes de comer." In *Álcool e drogas na história do Brasil*. Edited by Renato P. Venâncio and Henrique Carneiro, 29–46. São Paulo/Belo Horizonte: Alameda/Editora PUC Minas, 2005.

Ramírez, José C., Ricardo León, and Oscar Conde. "La estrategia económica de los Callistas." In *Historia general de Sonora*, vol. 5, *1929–1984*. Edited by Gerardo Cornejo Murrieta, 69–77. Hermosillo, Mexico: Gobierno del Estado de Sonora, 1985.

————. "Una época de crisis económica." In *Historia general de Sonora*, vol. 5, *1929–1984*. Edited by Gerardo Cornejo Murrieta, 53–66. Hermosillo, Mexico: Gobierno del Estado de Sonora, 1985.

Ramírez, Susan Elizabeth. *To Feed and Be Fed: The Cosmological Bases of Authority and Identity in the Andes*. Stanford, CA: Stanford University Press, 2005.

Ramírez Rancaño, Mario. *Ignacio Torres Adalid y la industria pulquera*. Mexico City: Instituto de Investigaciones Sociales, Universidad Nacional Autónoma de México, 2000.

Rao, Sujay. "Arbiters of Change: Provincial Elites and the Origins of Federalism in Argentina's Littoral, 1814–1820." *The Americas* 64, no. 4 (2008): 511–46.

Recio, Gabriela. "El nacimiento de la industria cervecera en México, 1880–1910." In *Cruda realidad. Producción, consumo y fiscalidad de las bebidas alcohólicas en México y América Latina, siglos XVII–XX*. Edited by Ernest Sánchez Santiró, 155–85. Mexico City: Instituto Mora, 2007.

Reeves, René. *Ladinos with Ladinos, Indians with Indians: Land, Labor, and Regional Ethnic Conflict in the Making of Guatemala*. Stanford, CA: Stanford University Press, 2006.

————. "From Household to Nation: The Economic and Political Impact of Women and Alcohol in Nineteenth-Century Guatemala." In *Distilling the Influence of Alcohol: Aguardiente in Guatemalan History*. Edited by David Carey Jr., 42–70. Gainesville: University Press of Florida, 2012.

Reiche C., Carlos Enrique. "Estudio sobre el patrón de embriaguez en la región rural Altaverapacense." *Guatemala Indígena* 5 (1970): 103–27.

Reina, Ruben. *The Law of the Saints: A Pokoman Pueblo and Its Community Culture*. New York: Bobbs-Merrill, 1966.

Rendón Garcini, Ricardo. *Dos haciendas pulqueras en Tlaxcala, 1857–1884*. Mexico City: Gobierno del Estado de Tlaxcala/Universidad Iberoamericana, 1990.

Richard-Jorba, Rodolfo. "Los empresarios y la construcción de la vitivinicultura capitalista en la provincia de Mendoza (Argentina), 1850–2006." *Scripta Nova. Revista Electrónica de Geografía y Ciencias Sociales* 12, no. 271 (2008), http://www.ub.edu/geocrit/sn/sn-271.htm.

Richmond, Douglas W. *Venustiano Carranza's Nationalist Struggle, 1893–1920.* Lincoln: University of Nebraska Press, 1983.

Rick, John W. "The Evolution of Authority and Power at Chavín de Huántar, Peru." In *Foundations of Power in the Prehispanic Andes.* Edited by Christina A. Conlee, Dennis Ogburn, and Kevin Vaughn, 71–89. Arlington, VA: American Anthropological Association, 2005.

Rocco, Paola P., et al. "Composición genética de la población chilena." *Revista médica de Chile* 130, no. 2 (2002): 125–31.

Rockwell, Elsie. "Schools of the Revolution: Enacting and Contesting State Forms in Tlaxcala, 1910–1930." In *Everyday Forms of State Formation: Revolution and the Negotiation of Rule in Modern Mexico.* Edited by Gilbert M. Joseph and Daniel Nugent, 170–208. Durham, NC: Duke University Press, 1994.

Rodrigues, Jaime. *De Costa a Costa: Escravos, marinheiros e intermediários do tráfico negreiro de Angola ao Rio de Janeiro (1780–1860).* São Paulo: Companhia das Letras, 2005.

Romanucci-Ross, Lola. *Conflict, Violence and Morality in a Mexican Village.* Palo Alto, CA: National Press Books, 1973.

Rosales, Diego de. *Historia general del reino de Chile, flandes indiano.* Santiago, Chile: Editorial Andrés Bello, 1989.

Ruiz, Ana María, and Hernán Vila. "Cambios en la demanda de vinos en el fin del milenio." *IDIA XXI, Revista de información sobre investigación y desarrollo agropecuario* 1 (November 2001): 41–46.

Ruy-Sánchez Lacy, Alberto. "In the Shadow of Tequila." In *Artes de México, El Tequila: Arte Tradicional de México.* Mexico City: Artes de México y del Mundo, 1994.

Saggers, Sherry, and Dennis Gray. *Dealing with Alcohol: Indigenous Usage in Australia, New Zealand and Canada.* Cambridge: Cambridge University Press, 1998.

Saignes, Thierry, ed. *Borrachera y memoria: La experiencia de lo sagrado en los Andes.* Lima: Instituto Francés de Estudios Andinos, 1993.

Salinger, Sharon V. *Taverns and Drinking in Early America.* Baltimore, MD: Johns Hopkins University Press, 2002.

Sánchez, George. *Becoming Mexican American: Ethnicity, Culture, and Identity in Chicano Los Angeles, 1900–1945.* Oxford: Oxford University Press, 1993.

Sánchez Santiró, Ernest, ed. *Cruda realidad. Producción, consumo y fiscalidad de las bebidas alcohólicas en México y América Latina, siglos XVII–XX.* Mexico City: Instituto Mora, 2007.

Sayre, Matthew, David Goldstein, William Whitehead, and Patrick Ryan Williams. "A Marked Preference: Chicha de Molle and Wari State Consumption Practice." *Ñawpa Pacha* 28 (2012): 231–58.

Scardaville, Michael C. "Alcohol Abuse and Tavern Reform in Late Colonial Mexico City." *Hispanic American Historical Review* 60, no. 4 (1980): 643–71.

Schell, Patience A. *Church and State Education in Revolutionary Mexico City.* Tucson: University of Arizona Press, 2003.

———. "Nationalizing Children Through Schools and Hygiene: Porfirian and Revolutionary Mexico City." *The Americas* 60, no. 4 (2004): 559–87.

Schivelbusch, Wolfgang. *Tastes of Paradise: A Social History of Spices, Stimulants, and Intoxicants.* Translated by David Jacobson. New York: Vintage Books, 1993.

Scholliers, Peter, ed. *Food, Drink, and Identity. Cooking, Eating, and Drinking in Europe Since the Middle Ages.* Oxford: Berg, 2001.

Schreiber, Katharina J. "The Wari Empire of Middle Horizon Peru: The Epistemological Challenge of Documenting an Empire Without Documentary Evidence." In *Empires: Perspectives from Archaeology and History.* Edited by Susan E. Alcock, Terence N. D'Altroy, Kathleen D. Morrison, and Carla M. Sinopoli, 70–92. New York: Cambridge University Press, 2001.

Schurman, Rachel. "Shuckers, Sorters, Headers, and Gutters: Labor in the Fisheries Sector." In *Victims of the Chilean Miracle.* Edited by Peter Winn, 298–336. Durham, NC: Duke University Press, 2004.

Schwartz, Norman B. "Drinking Patterns, Drunks and Maturity in a Petén Town (Guatemala)." *Sociologus* 28, no. 1 (1987): 35–53.

Schwartz, Stuart B. *Segredos Internos: Engenhos e escravos na sociedade colonial, 1550–1835.* São Paulo: Compahnia das Letras, 1988.

Schwartzkopf, Stacey. "Maya Power and State Culture: Indigenous Politics and State Formation in Nineteenth-Century Guatemala." PhD diss., Tulane University, 2008.

———. "Consumption, Custom, and Control: Aguardiente in Nineteenth-Century Guatemala." In *Distilling the Influence of Alcohol: Aguardiente in Guatemalan History.* Edited by David Carey Jr., 17–41. Gainesville: University Press of Florida, 2012.

Scott, James C. *Domination and Arts of Resistance: Hidden Transcripts.* New Haven, CT: Yale University Press, 1990.

Segura Llanos, Rafael. *Rito y economía en Cajamarquilla: Investigaciones arqueológicas en el conjunto arquitectónico Julio C. Tello.* Lima: Pontificia Universidad Católica del Perú, 2001.

Seminario de Historia Moderna de México. *Estadísticas económicas del Porfiriato. Fuerza de trabajo y actividad económica por sectores,* vol. 2. Mexico City: Colmex, 1960.

Serrano Álvarez, Pablo. *La batalla del espíritu: El movimiento sinarquista en el Bajío (1932–1951).* Colección Regiones 2. Mexico City: Conaculta, 1992.

Shimada, Izumi. *Pampa Grande and the Mochica Culture.* Austin: University of Texas Press, 1994.

Silverblatt, Irene. "Andean Women in the Inca Empire." *Feminist Studies* 4 (1978): 36–61.

———. *Moon, Sun and Witches. Gender Ideologies and Class in Inca and Colonial Peru.* Princeton, NJ: Princeton University Press, 1987.

Simonsen, Roberto C. *História Econômica do Brasil, 1500–1820.* Brasília: Senado Federal, 2005 [1937].

Smith, Frederick H. *Caribbean Rum: A Social and Economic History.* Gainesville: University Press of Florida, 2008.

Snodgrass, Michael. "'We Are All Mexicans Here': Workers, Patriotism, and Union Struggles in Monterrey." In *The Eagle and the Virgin: Nation and Cultural Revolu-*

tion in Mexico, 1920–1940. Edited by Mary Kay Vaughan and Stephen E. Lewis, 314–35. Durham, NC: Duke University Press, 2006.

Socolow, Susan Migden. *The Women of Colonial Latin America*. Cambridge: Cambridge University Press, 2000.

Souto Maior, Mário. *Dicionário Folclórico da Cachaça*. Recife: Fundação Joaquim Nabuco/Editora Massangana, 2004.

Staples, Anne. "*Policía y Buen Gobierno*: Municipal Efforts to Regulate Public Behavior, 1821–1857." In *Rituals of Rule, Rituals of Resistance: Public Celebrations and Popular Culture in Mexico*. Edited by William H. Beezley, Cheryl English Martin, and William E. French, 115–26. Wilmington, DE: SR Books, 1994.

Stein, Steve. "Grape Wars: Quality in the History of Argentine Wine." In *Wine, Society, and Globalization: Multidisciplinary Perspectives on the Wine Industry*. Edited by Gwyn Campbell and Nathalie Guibert, 99–117. New York: Palgrave Macmillan, 2007.

———. "New Markets and New Strategies in Argentina's Wine Revolution." *Economics, Management and Financial Markets* 5, no. 1 (2010): 64–98.

Stepan, Nancy Leys. "*The Hour of Eugenics*": Race, Gender, and Nation in Latin America*. Ithaca, NY: Cornell University Press, 1991.

Stern, Alexandra Minna. "Buildings, Boundaries, and Blood: Medicalization and Nation-Building on the US-Mexico Border, 1910–1930." *Hispanic American Historical Review* 79 (1999): 41–81.

———. "Secrets Under the Skin: New Historical Perspectives on Disease, Deviation, and Citizenship. A Review Article." *Society for Comparative Study of Society and History* 41, no. 3 (1999): 589–96.

Stern, Steve J. *The Secret History of Gender: Women, Men, and Power in Late Colonial Mexico*. Chapel Hill: University of North Carolina Press, 1995.

Stølen, Kristi Anne. "Gender, Sexuality and Violence in Ecuador." *Ethos* 56, nos. 1–2 (1992): 82–100.

Swarthout, Kelley R. "*Assimilating the Primitive*": Parallel Dialogues on Racial Miscegenation in Revolutionary Mexico*. New York: Peter Lang, 2004.

Takaki, Ronald. *Iron Cages: Race and Culture in 19th Century America*. Oxford: Oxford University Press, 2000.

Taylor, William B. *Drinking, Homicide, and Rebellion in Colonial Mexican Villages*. Stanford, CA: Stanford University Press, 1979.

Tax, Sol. "Changing Consumption in Indian Guatemala." *Economic Development and Cultural Change* 5, no. 2 (1957): 147–58.

———. *Penny Capitalism: A Guatemalan Indian Economy*. Chicago: University of Chicago Press, 1963.

Teixeira-Pinto, Márnio. *Ieipari: Sacrifício e Vida Social entre os índios Arara (Caribe)*. São Paulo: Hucitec/Associação Nacional de Pós-Graduação e Pesquisa em Ciências Sociais/Editora Universidade Federal do Paraná, 1997.

Tenorio-Trillo, Mauricio. *Mexico at the World's Fairs: Crafting a Modern Nation*. Berkeley: University of California Press, 1996.

Toner, Deborah. "Maize, Alcohol, and Cultural Identity in Colonial Mexico." MA thesis, University of Warwick, 2006.

———. "Everything in Its Right Place? Drinking Places and Social Spaces in Mexico City, c. 1780–1900." *Social History of Alcohol and Drugs* 25 (2011): 26–48.

————. "Drinking to Fraternity: Alcohol, Masculinity, and National Identity in the Novels of Manuel Payno and Heriberto Frías." *Bulletin of Hispanic Studies* 89, no. 4 (2012): 397–412.

Torgovnick, Mariana. *Gone Primitive: Savage Intellects, Modern Lives.* Chicago: Chicago University Press, 1990.

Toxqui, Áurea. "Taverns and Their Influence on the Suburban Culture of Late Nineteenth Century Mexico City." In *The Growth of Non-Western Cities: Primary and Secondary Urban Networking, c. 900–1900.* Edited by Kenneth R. Hall, 241–69. Lanham, MD: Lexington Books, 2011.

Toxqui Garay, María Áurea. "'El Recreo de los Amigos': Mexico City's Pulquerías During the Liberal Republic (1856–1911)." PhD diss., University of Arizona, 2008.

Urbina Burgos, Rodolfo. *Población indígena, encomienda, y tributo en Chiloé, 1567–1813.* Valparaíso, Chile: Universidad Católica de Valparaíso, 2004.

Valadares, Virginia. "O consumo de aguardente em Minas Gerais no final do século XVIII: uma visão entre os poderes metropolitano e colonial." In *Álcool e drogas na história do Brasil.* Edited by Renato P. Venâncio and Henrique Carneiro, 123–39. São Paulo/Belo Horizonte: Alameda/Editora PUC Minas, 2005.

Valdez, Lidio M. "Molle Beer Production in a Peruvian Highland Valley." *Journal of Anthropological Research* 68 (2012): 71–93.

Vaughan, Mary Kay. *Cultural Politics in Revolution: Teachers, Peasants, and Schools in Mexico, 1930–1940.* Tucson: University of Arizona Press, 1997.

Vaughan, Mary Kay, and Stephen E. Lewis, eds. *The Eagle and the Virgin: Nation and Cultural Revolution in Mexico, 1920–1940.* Durham, NC: Duke University Press, 2006.

Venâncio, Renato Pinto, and Henrique Carneiro, eds. *Álcool e drogas na história do Brasil.* São Paulo/Belo Horizonte: Alameda/Editora PUC Minas, 2005.

Verdi, Adriana Renata. "Dinâmicas e Perspectivas do Mercado de Cachaça." *Informações Econômicas* 36, no. 2 (2006): 93–98.

Verger, Pierre. *Fluxo e refluxo do tráfico de escravos entre o golfo do Benin e a Bahia de Todos os Santos do século XVII a XIX.* São Paulo: Corrupio, 1987.

Viegas, Susana de Matos. *Terra Calada: Os Tupinambá na Mata Atlântica do Sul da Bahia.* Rio de Janeiro/Lisbon: 7Letras/Almedina, 2007.

Villa-Flores, Javier. "'To Lose One's Soul': Blasphemy and Slavery in New Spain, 1596–1669." *Hispanic American Historical Review* 82, no. 3 (2002): 435–36.

Viqueira Albán, Juan Pedro. *Propriety and Permissiveness in Bourbon Mexico.* Wilmington, DE: SR Books, 1999.

Voekel, Pamela. "Peeing on the Palace: Bodily Resistance to Bourbon Reforms in Mexico City." *Journal of Historical Sociology* 5, no. 2 (1992): 183–208.

Wagley, Charles. *Economics of a Guatemalan Village Memoirs of the American Anthropological Association* 43, no. 3, pt. 3 (1941).

Walker, Charles F. *Smoldering Ashes: Cuzco and the Creation of Republican Peru.* Durham, NC: Duke University Press, 1999.

————. "Civilize or Control?: The Lingering Impact of the Bourbon Urban Reforms." In *Political Culture in the Andes, 1750–1950.* Edited by Nils Jacobsen and Cristóbal Aljovín de Losada, 74–95. Durham, NC: Duke University Press, 2005.

Wasserstrom, Robert. *Class and Society in Central Chiapas.* Berkeley: University of California Press, 1983.

Weber, David J. *Bárbaros: Spaniards and Their Savages in the Age of Enlightenment.* New Haven, CT: Yale University Press, 2005.

Weismantel, Mary. "Have a Drink: Chicha, Performance, and Politics." In *Drink, Power, and Society in the Andes.* Edited by Justin Jennings and Brenda Bowser, 257–77. Gainesville: University Press of Florida, 2009.

Williams, Derek. "The Making of Ecuador's *Pueblo Católico*." In *Political Culture in the Andes, 1750–1950.* Edited by Nils Jacobsen and Cristóbal Aljovín de Losada, 207–29. Durham, NC: Duke University Press, 2005.

Williams, Patrick Ryan. "The Role of Disaster in the Development of Agriculture and the Evolution of Social Complexity in the South-Central Andes." PhD diss., University of Florida, 1997.

———. "Cerro Baúl: A Wari Center on the Tiwanaku Frontier." *Latin American Antiquity* 12 (2001): 67–83.

———. "Rethinking Disaster-Induced Collapse in the Demise of the Andean Highland States: Wari and Tiwanaku." *World Archaeology* 33 (2002): 361–74.

Williams, Patrick Ryan, and Johny Isla. "Investigaciones arqueológicas en Cerro Baúl, un enclave Wari en el valle de Moquegua." *Gaceta Arqueológica Andina* 26 (2002): 87–120.

Winn, Peter, ed. *Victims of the Chilean Miracle: Workers and Neoliberalism in the Pinochet Era, 1973–2002.* Durham, NC: Duke University Press, 2004.

Wisdom, Charles. *Chorti Indians of Guatemala.* Chicago: University of Chicago Press, 1940.

Wolfe, Joel. *Working Women, Working Men. São Paulo and the Rise of Brazil's Industrial Working Class, 1900–1955.* Durham, NC: Duke University Press, 1993.

Wright, Melanie F., Christine A. Hastorf, and Heidi A. Lennstrom. "Pre-Hispanic Agriculture and Plant Use at Tiwanaku: Social and Political Implications." In *Tiwanaku and Its Hinterland: Archaeology and Paleoecology of an Andean Civilization*, vol. 2, *Urban and Rural Archaeology.* Edited by Alan Kolata, 384–403. Washington, DC: Smithsonian Institution Press, 2003.

Zúñiga Moreno, Germán. "Comentarios sobre la ley seca en Sonora de 1915." *Memorias del Simposio de Historia de Sonora (Hermosillo, Sonora)* 6 (1979): 264–73.

Websites

Carey, Elaine. "A Colombian's Queen Tale: The End and Beginning of Griselda Blanco." *Points: Blog of the Alcohol and Drugs History Society*, September 26, 2012, http://pointsadhsblog.wordpress.com/2012/09/26/a-colombian-queens-tale -the-end-and-beginning-of-griselda-blanco/.

Cleeland, Nancy. "A Bottle Full of Fire." *San Diego Reader*, February 12, 1987, http:// www.sandiegoreader.com/news/1987/feb/12/bottle-full-fire/.

Great Wine Capitals Global Network. "Mendoza." http://greatwinecapitals.com/capitals/ mendoza/introduction, accessed August 27, 2013

Instituto Nacional de Vitivinicultura. "Consumo mercado interno." http://www.inv.gov .ar/est_consumo.php, accessed July 8, 2010.

———. "V censo vitícola nacional." http://www.inv.gov.ar/PDF/Estadisticas/Registro Vinedos/registrovinedossuperficie2005, accessed June 11, 2010.

Morgan, Brian. "Cachaça from Brazil and Protected Geographic Indication." *TED Case Studies* 14, no. 2 (2004). http://www1.american.edu/TED/cachaca.htm.

Parker, Robert. "Argentina's Greatest Wines." *Businessweek*, May 29, 2008. http://www.businessweek.com/lifestyle/content/may2008/bw20080529_268512.htm.

———. "2007 mendel unus." *Wine Advocate*, December 31, 2008. http://www.mendel.com.ar/img/prensas/68.pdf.

———. "Argentina Is the Most Exciting New World Country." *Wines of Argentina*, July 1, 2009. http://www.winesofargentina.org/en/mercados/uk/ver/2009/07/01/e-robert-parker-argentina-is-the-most-exciting-new-world-country/.

———. "2006 mendel unus." *Wine Advocate*, August 31, 2009. http://www.mendel.com.ar/img/prensas/53.pdf.

Saieg, Laura. "Malbec Consumption Triples." *Winesur*, May 12, 2010. http://www.winesur.com/top-news/malbec-consumption-triples.

Schachner, Michael. "Malbec in the Spotlight." *Wine Enthusiast*, February 9, 2010. http://www.winemag.com/Wine-Enthusiast-Magazine/February-2010/Top-10-Argentine-Malbecs-of-the-Past-Year/.

Robinson, Jancis. "Argentina Gets More Polish." *Jancis Robinson.com*, October 11, 2008. http://www.jancisrobinson.com/articles/a200810073.html, accessed May 31, 2010.

Wines of Argentina. "Frequently Asked Questions." http://www.winesofargentina.org/en/faq/, accessed June 2, 2010.

———. "Export Stats." http://www.winesofargentina.org/en/estadistica/exportacion/, accessed June 2, 2010.

Contributors

Aaron P. Althouse is associate professor of history at the University of Tennessee–Chattanooga, where he teaches courses on Latin American and world history. He received his PhD from Stanford University, and his research investigates comparative urban and rural notions of individual and collective caste identity in the colonial Pátzcuaro (Mexico) region.

David Carey Jr. is professor of history and women's and gender studies and associate dean of the College of Arts, Humanities, and Social Sciences at the University of Southern Maine (Portland). His publications include the books *Our Elders Teach Us: Maya-Kaqchikel Historical Perspectives. Xkib'ij kan qate' qatata'* (2001) and *Engendering Mayan History: Kaqchikel Women as Agents and Conduits of the Past, 1875–1970* (2006), the edited collection *Distilling the Influence of Alcohol:* Aguardiente *in Guatemalan History* (2012), and *I Ask for Justice: Maya Women, Dictators, and Crime in Guatemala, 1898–1944* (2013).

Anton Daughters is assistant professor of anthropology at Truman State University. In addition to his research on rural communities in Chiloé, he is editing documentary histories of the Hopi and O'odham. He received his PhD from the University of Arizona in 2010.

João Azevedo Fernandes is professor in the Department of History at the Universidade Federal da Paraíba. He has published several articles and books on the history of natives and alcoholic beverages. Among them are

De Cunhã a Mameluca: a mulher tupinambá e o nascimento do Brasil (2003) and *Selvagens Bebedeiras: Álcool, embriaguez e contatos culturais no Brasil Colonial—Séculos XVI–XVII* (2011). He is currently preparing a book about the history of *cachaça* in Brazil between 1600 and 1850.

Nancy Scott Hanway teaches Latin American literature and culture at Gustavus Adolphus College in Minnesota. She is the author of *Embodying Argentina: Nation, Space and Body in 19th Century Literature* (2003). A graduate of the Iowa Writers' Workshop, her short fiction has been published in literary journals across the country, among them *PMS, Florida Review, Southern Indiana Review,* and *Southern Humanities Review.* She lives with her husband and son in Saint Paul, where she blogs about books and wine (mostly Malbecs) at wordvine.org.

Justin Jennings is curator of New World archaeology at the Royal Ontario Museum and assistant professor of anthropology at the University of Toronto. He has conducted archaeological fieldwork in southern Peru over the last fifteen years. His most recent books are *Globalizations and the Ancient World* (2011), *Beyond Wari Walls* (2010), and *Drink, Power, and Society in the Andes* (2009).

José Orozco is associate professor of history at Whittier College. He is currently writing a history of tequila and Mexican nationalism. His book, *Receive Our Memories: The Letters of Luz Moreno, 1950–1952,* is forthcoming from Oxford University Press in 2014.

Gretchen Pierce is assistant professor of history at Shippensburg University of Pennsylvania. She has published on temperance in Mexico in the journal *Social History of Alcohol and Drugs* and in the book *A Companion to Mexican History and Culture,* edited by William H. Beezley (2011). She is currently working on a manuscript with the working title, *Altered States: Mexico's Anti-Alcohol Campaigns and the State-Building Project, 1910–1940.*

Steve Stein is professor of history at the University of Miami. The author of six books on twentieth-century Peruvian history, he is presently engaged in an extensive, multifaceted project on the history of the Argentine wine industry. His volume *El vino y sus revoluciones: Una antología histórica sobre el desarrollo de la industria vitivinícola argentina* (2008), coedited with Ana María Mateu, is the first comprehensive treatment of the industry from its nineteenth-century origins to the present. Dr. Stein is also Director of Wine Education at the Societá Dante Alighieri of Miami, where over the past decade he has been regularly teaching wine classes.

Áurea Toxqui is assistant professor of Latin American history at Bradley University in Peoria, Illinois. She has published on pulque and alcohol consumption in Mexico in the books *Alcohol and Drugs in North America* (edited by David M. Fahey and Jon Miller, 2013) and *The Growth of Non-Western Cities: Primary and Secondary Urban Networking, c. 900–1900* (edited by Kenneth R. Hall, 2011). Currently, she works on the history of pulque in Mexico and whiskey distilleries in Peoria. She holds a PhD from the University of Arizona.

Index

advertising, 195–97, 200–201, 202–3, 211, 219, 222, 234, 237. *See also* Catena, Nicolás; Tequila Sauza

agave, 186, 187, 190, 191, 192, 193. *See also* maguey plant

aguamiel, 106, 116, 163, 195

aguardiente, 4, 12, 15, 52, 57–58, 108, 131, 133, 134, 135, 138, 147; contraband, 169; identification with slaves, 4, 23, 48–52

alcabala, 115–16. *See also* taxation

alcohol: and colonization, 24, 32–33, 46–47, 50, 52–53, 54–58; and communal ties, 9–10, 25, 38, 242–58; and ethnicity, 5, 7, 52, 148–49; and identity, 10–11, 58–59, 159, 185–207; commodification of, 23; origins, 26; profitability, 4, 5; regulation of, 114–15, 138–39; sales restrictions, 12, 13, 162; varieties of, 48, 194; women's employment, 170. *See also* women

alcohol consumption, 5, 26; and crime, 135; and ethnicity, 58–60; and festivities, 53, 134, 257; and poverty, 142; and rituals, 25, 36, 37, 39; and social status, 7, 46–49, 59–60, 131, 139–40; and violence, 6, 68–82, 132; and women, 142; origins of, 26–27, 38–39.

See also Andes; Brazil; feasting; gender; indigenous; Mexico; women

alcoholism, 94–95, 132, 135–37; among working class, 162; and disease, 163–64; impact on nation, 164; socioeconomic causes, 174

Alteño. See Los Altos de Jalisco

Amerindians. *See* indigenous people

Andes, 8, 91, 96, 101, 212, 230, 248; pre-Columbian, 9, 13, 21, 25–40

anti-alcohol campaign, 13, 161, 163; and class, 165; and women, 165, 168; economic resistance to, 166–68, 170–71. *See also* Mexico

apples, 244–45, 252, 256–58. See also *chicha de manzana*

Archipelago of Chiloé, 246; disconnect from mainland, 248; indigenous labor practices, 246–48

Argentina, 6, 8, 10, 13, 89–101, 210–41. *See also* wine

Atahualpa, 27–28

Atlantic world, 48, 132; commerce, 53

Aztecs, 22, 106, 188–89; iconography, 197

beer, 9, 25, 27, 28, 29, 31, 33, 35, 36, 38, 39, 49, 87, 88, 100, 160, 161, 174, 197,

302 • *Index*

beer *(continued)*
198, 219, 226, 228, 252; low alcohol
content of, 171, 195; refusal of, 27–29;
sacred, 29. See also *cerveceros; chicha;*
maize: beer
beer industry, 163, 166, 170, 195; anti-
pulque myths, 195; marketing of, 195,
206*n*42. See also *cerveceros*
bodegas, 90; Esmeralda, 226; La Rural,
215; López, 213–15; Suter, 236; y Viñedos Corces, 219; y Viñedos Gargantini, 220; y Viñedos Peñaflor, 222. *See
also* wineries
Bolivia, 6, 21, 33–35, 117
Brazil, 5, 7, 8, 22, 23, 24, 88, 99; colonial
period, 6, 10, 13, 46–60

cachaça, 10, 23, 46–51, 54–55, 60; and
class, 59; and national identity, 46, 59–
60; as *jeribita,* 52–53; origins, 54. See
also *aguardiente*
cannibalism, 6, 53–54
cantina, 87, 122, 134, 135, 143, 148, 149,
164–67, 175
Cárdenas, Lázaro, 162, 193, 195, 208*n*70
casillas, 106, 108, 112–15; food sales,
109–10, 118, 122; gendered sites, 108.
See also *pulquerías*
castas, 3, 11, 23, 106; in Brazil: *cabras,* 59
Catena, Nicolás, 218; and advertising,
220–22, 225–31, 237. *See also* wine industry: Argentinian
Catholic: Church, 23, 87, 189, 201; culture, 201; Mass, 90, 172; missionaries,
27, 54–56, 189, 217, 247; movement,
201, 202; nation, 10, 155*n*84
caudillismo, 92–93, 96
cauim, 6, 53, 55
cauinagens, 53–54. *See also* rituals
cerveceros, 161–62, 168, 171
charape, 15, 71
Chavín, 21, 39; de Huántar, 38–39
chicha, 9, 10, 11–12, 13, 15, 22, 23, 29,
33, 108, 135, 136, 159–60, 194; establishments selling, 23; post-conquest
term, 26; sellers, 117; varieties of, 242–
43. *See also* maize: beer

chicha de manzana, 10, 160; in Chile,
242–58
chicheras. See *chicha:* sellers
Chile, 5, 7, 10, 21, 90, 94, 96, 160, 242–
58. See also *mingas*
chilmoleras, 109–10, 111, 117, 118, 119–
24; and credit, 118; and press, 119. See
also *enchiladeras; casillas*
Chilotes. *See* Archipiélago of Chiloé
cholas, 6
citizenship, 87, 105, 122
civility, 68, 72; violations of, 69–74, 76–
77; and racial equality, 79–80
civilized: beverage, 188, 191, 196; effect,
195; man, 100; nation, 92, 95, 100,
149, 197
coca. See drugs
Cochabamba, 33–35
colonial order, 82; civilizing efforts, 57–
58, 70, 83, 189; rural perceptions of,
24, 70–82
Comité Nacional de Lucha contra el Alcoholismo (CNLCA), 164–65, 174;
gender ideology in, 173; paternalism
of, 173–74
Companhia Geral de Comércio do Brasil, 51
Compañía Expendedora de Pulques, 114,
117, 172, 175
containers, 25, 28, 29, 30, 34–36, 54,
213, 250
conquest, 23, 58; of Guatemala, 131; of
Mexico, 67, 69, 106, 108, 189; of Peru,
25, 26, 27–28
corn, 22, 26, 29, 34, 53, 106, 109, 116,
243; diet based on, 119, 189; Incan demand for, 29–30. *See also* maize
criollos, 4, 23, 132
Cuba, 4, 23, 159
Cuervo family, 186, 187, 198, 199

Díaz, Porfirio. *See* Porfiriato
distilled beverages, 10, 23, 46, 47, 48, 52,
53, 160, 162, 186, 191, 192; and colonization, 24; and slaves, 49; impact on natives, 52, 53–58; industrial production
of, 88, 192. *See also* mezcal; tequila